Prodigals and pilgrims

To my parents

PRODIGALS
AND
PILGRIMS

The American revolution against patriarchal authority, 1750–1800

JAY FLIEGELMAN
Department of English, Stanford University

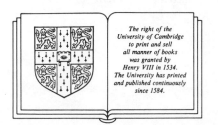

The right of the
University of Cambridge
to print and sell
all manner of books
was granted by
Henry VIII in 1534.
The University has printed
and published continuously
since 1584.

CAMBRIDGE UNIVERSITY PRESS

CAMBRIDGE
LONDON   NEW YORK   NEW ROCHELLE
MELBOURNE   SYDNEY

Published by the Press Syndicate of the University of Cambridge
The Pitt Building, Trumpington Street, Cambridge CB2 1RP
32 East 57th Street, New York, NY 10022, USA
296 Beaconsfield Parade, Middle Park, Melbourne 3206, Australia

First published 1982
First paperback edition 1984

Printed in the United States of America

Library of Congress Cataloging in Publication Data
Fliegelman, Jay.

Prodigals and pilgrims.

Includes bibliographical references and
index.

1. United States – Intellectual life – 18th
century.   2. Literature, Modern – 18th century –
History and criticism.   3. Literature and
history.   4. Parent and child in literature.
5. Family – United States – History – 18th century.
6. Patriarchy – Psychological aspects.
7. American literature – Revolutionary period,
1775 – 1783 – History and criticism.   8. American
literature – 1783 – 1850 – History and criticism.
9. Books and reading – United States – History –
18th century.   I. Title.
E163.F58   306.8'0973   81–10179
ISBN 0 521 23719 X hard covers   AACR2
ISBN 0 521 31726 6 paperback

CONTENTS

v

ACKNOWLEDGMENTS

I have incurred many debts in writing this book. Perhaps the greatest are to Albert Gelpi, who has encouraged and supported me in this work since its inception, and George Dekker, from whom I have learned so much, not the least of which is the fundamental importance of integrating intellectual and literary history. David Levin, Gordon Wood, Peter Shaw, Ronald Paulson, Thomas Moser, W. B. Carnochan, and Hugh Dawson all read the manuscript at its earliest stage of development and offered leads, comments, corrections, and invaluable encouragement. Professor Levin's painstaking criticisms, in particular, were all very much to the point. More recently, Jack Rakove, Max Byrd, and Mitchell Breitwieser helped me in several important matters. In addition, I have benefited from the counsel of five of my doctoral students: Jenny Franchot, Harold Hellenbrand, Wyn Kelley, Robert Levine, and Richard Silver. Finally, I have drawn so often on the expert knowledge and warm friendship of my fellow colonialists, Alasdair Macphail and Donald Weber, that no simple acknowledgment suffices.

Thanks of a different kind are owed to the expert staff of the Stanford Libraries, particularly Bill Allan and Jim Knox; Jean Marshall Simpson, who not only typed the first draft of the manuscript but deciphered and assembled it; Pauline Tooker, who prepared the final version with great expedition and accuracy; Susan F. Riggs, who prepared the index; and the staff of Cambridge University Press, who have been so supportive.

This book is dedicated to the two people who, by their example, showed me how to love. The enormous importance of such exemplary instruction is the subject of my book.

INTRODUCTION

In his study of the differing psycho-biographical profiles of Patriot and Tory leaders in the American Revolution, Kenneth Lynn concludes:

> The men who broke with Britain in 1776 had been prepared by their upbringings to make a successful separation from their parents and to face with equanimity the prospect of living independently. The psychologically painful enterprise of overthrowing the father figure of George III and of breaking the historic connection between the colonies and the imperial *parens patriae* was led by colonists who had not been tyrannized over by their own fathers, and who in fact were accustomed to thinking of paternal authority as the guarantor of filial freedom and self-realization.
>
> So satisfying, indeed, was their experience with their fathers that it has caused me to wonder whether father–son relations in the Revolutionary generation did not mark a special moment in the history of the American family; certainly in no other period of our past can we find the top leaders of American society speaking as gratefully as these patriots did about the fathering they had received.[1]

This book is a study of that "special moment in the history of the American family" and, more especially, of the ideology that underlies it. By the middle of the eighteenth century family relations had been fundamentally reconsidered in both England and America. An older patriarchal family authority was giving way to a new parental ideal characterized by a more affectionate and equalitarian relationship with children. This important development paralleled the emergence of a humane form of childrearing that accommodated the stages of a child's growth and recognized the distinctive character of childhood. Parents who embraced the new childrearing felt a deep moral commitment to prepare their children for a life of rational independence and moral self-sufficiency.[2]

1

The sources of this reconsideration of family relations are many. Prime among them, however, is Locke's sensationalist epistemology and new understanding of the mind as a tabula rasa. Locke argued that a child's character is not inherited at birth but rather is "created" by the sum total of sense impressions and experiences written on the blank slate of his mind. Thus no longer was the fundamental responsibility of parents to restrain their children and render their fallen natures obedient to external authority – an attitude symbolized by the widespread use of swaddling clothes. Instead, parents must by their example and instruction seek to control those earliest impressions and influences that form a child's mind and character and must develop in their children the rational faculties essential to a proper evaluation of experience. In short, the success of nurture rather than the prescriptions of nature would ultimately determine the moral and spiritual character of a young man. (The education of women, as we shall see, was a different matter.) As Alexander Pope, who had his doubts about the new position, declared in his first "Moral Essay": "'Tis education forms the common mind / Just as the twig is bent the tree's inclin'd."[3] The sacred responsibility of parents and teachers was to finish the work of creation begun by God.

In his popular poem *The Task* (1785), William Cowper, reflecting on that responsibility, asked a question that preoccupied his age:

> Now blame we most the nursling, or the nurse?
> The children crooked, and twisted, and deformed
> Through want of care; or whose winking eye
> And slumbering oscitancy mars the brood?

He answered without hesitation or qualification:

> The nurse, no doubt. Regardless of her charge,
> She needs herself correction; needs to learn
> That it is dangerous sporting with the world,
> With things so sacred as a nation's trust,
> The nurture of her youth, her dearest pledge.[4]

Those deformed in character and twisted in thought (for surely Cowper intends his language to suggest moral corruption as well as physical disability) must not be asked to bear the responsibility for their own deformities. The rod of correction should be applied more appropriately to those negligent teachers and self-absorbed parents who permitted their children's "fall." Implicitly denying original sin, Lockean sensationalism and the new emphasis on education and nurture it generated temptingly suggested that personal faults of individual character might better be charged to the behavior of one's parents, the character of one's education, or the premature exposure to a corrupting society, rather than to one's own moral failings. Though such a view was fast becoming the received wisdom of the age, it might seem odd that it was

Nurture over Nature

expressed by a Calvinist like Cowper, a man afflicted with a lifelong conviction of his own certain damnation. Yet even for those, or perhaps especially for those, who believed in man's sinful nature, the doctrine of the primacy of nurture, like that of a restorative divine grace, held, at some level, a deep and absorbing attraction.

No less important to the eighteenth-century reconsideration of family relations than the new understanding of the growth of the mind and the consequent emphasis on nurture was what Lawrence Stone has recently described as the "growth of affective individualism."[5] This ultimately political appreciation of the importance of personal autonomy and individual identity insisted upon the right and obligation of all children to become fully autonomous and self-reasoning adults. It also insisted upon the complementary responsibility of parents to encourage that transition from adolescence to adulthood.

Writing a year after the Peace of Paris, which ended the American Revolution, Immanuel Kant defined the term that would later be used to describe his age:

> Enlightenment is man's emergence from his self-imposed nonage. Nonage is the inability to use one's own understanding without another's guidance. . . . "Have the courage to use your own understanding," is therefore the motto of the enlightenment.
>
> Laziness and cowardice are the reasons why such a large part of mankind gladly remain minors all their lives, long after nature has freed them from external guidance. They are the reasons why it is so easy for others to set themselves up as guardians. It is so comfortable to be a minor.[6]

Though nonage or adolescence unnaturally protracted by moral cowardice was a shameful abdication of adult responsibility, the imposition of a protracted adolescence by one generation upon another was an even more pernicious violation of the laws of nature. Indeed, such an imposition of "perpetual guardianship" was, according to Kant, the ultimate tyranny, a blow to the very process of history: "An epoch cannot conclude a pact that will commit succeeding ages, prevent them from increasing their significant insights, purging themselves of errors, and generally progressing in enlightenment" (p. 378). Each generation must be allowed the full growth of its mind by being given an education that encourages an independence of mind; for as Kant concludes, "Man can only become man by education."[7]

Such a call for filial autonomy and the unimpeded emergence from nonage echoes throughout the rhetoric of the American Revolution. It is its quintessential motif. At every opportunity Revolutionary propagandists insisted that the new nation and its people had come of age, had achieved a collective maturity that necessitated them becoming in politi-

[handwritten annotation at top: Call for filial autonomy ... of Revolution]

[handwritten marginal note: Generational argument in Declaration]

cal fact an independent and self-governing nation. Jefferson's first draft of the preamble to the Declaration of Independence reads: "When in the course of human events it becomes necessary for a people to advance from that subordination . . . to assume the equal and independent station to which the laws of nature and of nature's God entitle them. . . . "[8] The language of the draft makes clear the generational or morphological argument that underlies the necessity identified in the final draft: "that political bands be dissolved." Like the revolution of the spheres or the changing of the seasons, "the course of human events" must also obey the laws of nature that required, in the language of Blackstone's *Commentaries on the Law,* that "the empire of the father . . . gives place to the empire of reason."[9] For Britain to deny her child colonies "that equal and independent station" was to confess itself, in the popular phrase of the period, "an unnatural and tyrannical parent."

[handwritten marginal note: Filmer]

Most scholars have associated the familial rhetoric of the War with the ongoing rejection of seventeenth-century patriarchalism. Although that political theory had been almost vestigial by the time of its best-known formulation, Robert Filmer's *Patriarcha* (which later provoked Locke's *First Treatise of Government*), it was kept alive in America by such Tories as Jonathan Boucher. The theory asserted that kingly authority derived from parental powers that kings received as a special inheritance from the first father, Adam, and that were understood to oblige subjects to a lifelong filial obedience. Contrary to the impressions given by most historians, however, the sources of the antipatriarchal rhetoric and ideology of the Revolution were far from exclusively political. Rather, numerous widely read works of fiction and pedagogy popularized the new understanding of parental responsibility and filial freedom set forth by Locke in *Some Thoughts concerning Education,* a work reprinted nineteen times before 1761.[10] On the eve of the American Revolution such a constellation of ideas and values had already become an essential part of Anglo-American culture and, most especially, of English literature.

[handwritten marginal note: New parental responsibility and filial freedom]

In *A Cultural History of the American Revolution* (1976) Kenneth Silverman coins the term "Whig Sentimentalism" to describe "a pervasive idiom" preoccupied with images of violent attacks on youthful innocence, which "fused political theory with popular moral sentiment and which reached the colonies through a literary as well as political tradition." "Colonists," he concludes, "quoted Addison, Thomson, Pope, Milton, and Shakespeare as political authorities hardly less than they quoted Locke or Montesquieu. Even in nakedly political pamphlets it is often impossible to tell which is the nearer source of ideology."[11] Silverman's remark needs to be taken up seriously. Our received notions as to who were the most important transmitters of Enlightenment ideas

[Handwritten margin notes: Locke's Education the most significant text of the Anglo-Amer. Enlightenment]

central to the American Revolution are in need of revising as much as our understanding of what constitutes a "political" text is in need of broadening. Only by so revising our frame of reference will we be able to appreciate the larger cultural context of the American Revolution.

That much remains to be done in this area is suggested by Henry May's major study, *The Enlightenment in America* (1976). Though based on a contents analysis of eighteenth-century American libraries, May's book neglects to address the ideology and values popularized by the most widely read literary and educational works of the period. And he is silent on the subject of Locke's *Education,* which not only exerted a controlling influence on the familial themes featured in those bestsellers but also served in its various popularized forms as perhaps the most significant text of the Anglo-American Enlightenment.[12] For education was, after all, the art of "government," as Locke made clear.[13] The problems of family government addressed in the fiction and pedagogy of the period – of balancing authority with liberty, of maintaining a social order while encouraging individual growth – were the larger political problems of the age translated into the terms of daily life.

This book is a study of the broader cultural revolution in eighteenth-century England and America of which the American Revolution, in its rhetorical and thematic dimensions, was the most important expression. My subject then is not the American Revolution as such, but what I have called the American revolution against patriarchal authority – a revolution in the understanding of the nature of authority that affected all aspects of eighteenth-century culture. Because that antipatriarchal revolution was not confined to America, my study is necessarily comparative as well as interdisciplinary. It examines a constellation of intimately related ideas about the nature of parental authority and filial rights, moral obligation and personal autonomy, the character of God and the morality of Scripture, and the growth of the mind and the nature of historical progress. The book traces these ideas from their most important English and continental expressions in a variety of literary and pedagogical texts to their transmission, reception, and application in Revolutionary America and on through their various modifications in the early national period of American culture.

[Handwritten margin notes: Method; Re Parental authority and filial rights]

Much emphasis is placed on relating eighteenth-century literary history to social, theological, and political events in America. My purpose is to explore further the crucial point made a generation ago by Leslie Fiedler that, because of their shared eighteenth-century origins, "Between the novel and America there are peculiar and intimate connections."[14] As the American colonies had chosen to escape tyranny and moral corruption, declared their independence, and fled to God's protective embrace; so, too, had a generation of sentimental heroes and

[Handwritten note at bottom: Fiedler on peculiar connections between the novel and America]

heroines, prodigals and pilgrims similarly fled. To understand properly the history of one set of rebels is to understand better the history of the other.

Though necessarily dealing with political and social history, it must be stressed that this work is fundamentally a study in intellectual and cultural history. It concerns itself with the primary language and paradigm with which Americans, in the last three decades of the eighteenth century, thought about the issues most central to their culture. It examines the history, logic, and limitations of that paradigm, the perception of reality assumed by it, and, finally, the ways such formulations, in part, determined and prescribed responses to certain situations.[15] My purpose is not, however, to demonstrate an immediate or direct causal relationship between a set of ideas and a sequence of political or social events. Such overly insistent arguments are invariably unsatisfying; for the relationship between idea and event is intractably complex. Mine is the more manageable and, I hope, more useful task: to clarify the crucial thematic connections between key historical events and the important literary, pedagogical, theological, and political texts of the period under consideration. Though often seemingly unrelated, these events and texts all reflect the same overarching preoccupations of their culture. Certainly one such preoccupation in England and America in the last half of the eighteenth century was the deeply problematic character and uncertain future of traditional family relations. This work seeks to place that decisive moment in the history of the American family in its broadest cultural context and, by so doing, to illuminate the first great epoch in what may properly be called the natural history of American affections.

Idea
+
event
)
event
+
Text

cite
Kuhn,
Foucault,
Wise,
Pocock

PART I

THE IDEOLOGICAL INHERITANCE

1

EDUCATIONAL THEORY AND MORAL INDEPENDENCE

[handwritten annotation: A preoccupation "to prescribe terms of a new ideal relationship between generations"]

English and American literature of the last half of the eighteenth century shared the same intense thematic preoccupation: familial relations. On both sides of the Atlantic, novelists, poets, playwrights, and anonymous authors of didactic periodical fiction joined together in an effort – an effort almost without historical precedent – to anatomize the family, to define "the familial, the parental and the social duties," and to prescribe the terms of a new ideal relationship between generations.[1] For those who preferred their didacticism undiluted by the palliative of fiction, the novels of Richardson, Sterne, and Fielding, along with Chesterfield's *Letters* and other related works, were "systemized and methodized" into popular volumes with such titles as *Sentimental Beauties, Moral and Instructional Sentiments,* and *Illuminations for Sentimentalists.* These collections – part anthology, concordance, and conduct book – arranged their entries under such characteristic subject heads as "parent's duty to children," "children's duty to parents," "gratitude," "friendship," and "power and independence"; for these, in short, were the great moral subjects of the age.[2]

The enormous demand for precepts and examples relating to these issues suggests that by midcentury a large segment of the Anglo-American reading public had become responsive to a shifting social reality. The values of that new social reality had to be formulated, and its challenges to long-established assumptions about the right relations between generations had to be answered and met. In recent years, demographic historians investigating American society in the second half of the eighteenth century have demonstrated convincingly that significant changes in traditional generational relations were indeed occurring at least on one side of the Atlantic.

The following findings have been shown to obtain in one or more American communities during the period immediately preceding the Revolution: (1) the growth of a newly emergent class of propertyless

9

[handwritten annotation: Creation of a new social reality now challenged long established assumptions re right relations between generations]

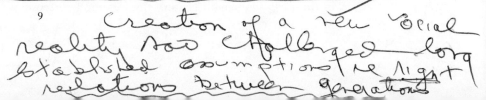

and mobile young men, many of whom were either drawn away from home by increased opportunities for nonagricultural work or forced away by the practice of partible inheritance, which divided paternal land into individual plots too small to be economically viable forms of patrimony; (2) the gradual replacement of land as the primary medium of value by more portable forms of capital, further permitting generations, once obliged to share the same land, to live now farther apart; (3) increased premarital sex and a sharp rise in premarital conceptions, and last (4) a declining emphasis – both social and legal – on the necessity of parental permission and approval in the question of a child's marriage.[3]

In his *The Evolution of American Society, 1700 – 1815,* James Henretta sees declining parental authority and the decreasing extent of generational cohabitation – inferences implicit in all the preceding – as an index of the evolution in the last half of the eighteenth century of a new understanding of paternity:

> Underlying all . . . was a new conception of parental duty and authority. Fathers had begun to consider their role not as that of patriarchs grandly presiding over an ancestral estate and minutely controlling the lives of their sons and heirs, but rather as that of benefactors responsible for the future well-being and prosperity of their offspring. . . . Once the farm had been an end in itself; now it was the means to another and a more important end. The tendency for parents to find the fulfillment and justification of their own lives in the success of their children marked the appearance of a new and different type of family life, one characterized by solicitude and sentimentality toward children and by more intimate, personal and equal relationships.[4]

This new equitable relationship, as David Hackett Fischer has shown, is iconographically represented in the changing composition of the eighteenth-century family portrait in America. Whereas before 1775 virtually all extant family portraits present the father standing above his seated family, after that date the vertical or hierarchal composition gives way to a horizontal or equalitarian composition in which all family members are shown on the same plane.[5]

The emergence of this "different type of family life" is reflected in the history of the word "family." Prior to the eighteenth century the word – consistent with its Latin root *familia,* itself a derivative of *familus,* or servant – most frequently denoted an entire household. The following sentence appearing in a volume published in 1631 is representative of seventeenth-century usage: "His family were himself and his wife and daughters, two mayds and a man." "Family," in the King James Bible, as Raymond Williams has pointed out, means an extended family – "a large kin-group ostensibly synonymous with tribe," or the kin-group of a common father extended over several generations. Only sometime in the early eighteenth century does its modern sense of "a small kin-group usually living in one house," what is now called a nuclear family, definitely emerge and begin to predominate. As late as the early part of the nineteenth century, however, James Mill still felt obliged to offer this definition: "The group which consists of a Father, Mother and Children is called a Family."[6]

In the most important modern treatment of a long-neglected subject, *Centuries of Childhood: A Social History of the Family,* French historian and archivist Philippe Ariès traces the rise of modern familial relations to what it has become fashionable to call "the discovery of childhood." In the medieval society of western Europe, Ariès argues, "children were mixed with adults as soon as they were considered capable of doing without their mothers or nannies, not long after a tardy weaning . . . about the age of seven."[7] Consequently, such a society had neither a conception of nor a vocabulary for late childhood or adolescence as we know it. The very idea of a morphology of emotional and intellectual growth was an alien one.

The emergence in the late sixteenth century of a new and insistent emphasis on the social function of education would eventually, Ariès argues, break down the generational fluidity of European society and change family relations radically. Those who were to introduce this new view of education, at least in France, were not the Renaissance humanists but the Renaissance moralists, who passionately opposed the Church's subordination of family obligation to the quest for personal salvation. The moralists, who emphasized family education and worship in their teaching and writing, saw the two as intimately related:

> They taught parents that they were the spiritual guardians, that they were responsible before God for the souls, indeed the bodies too, of their children.
> Henceforth it was recognized that the child was not ready for life, and that he had to be subjected to a special treatment, a sort of quarantine before he was allowed to join adults (p. 412).

Such a recognition, Ariès argued, "would gradually install itself in the heart of society and transform it from top to bottom":

> The family ceased to be simply an institution for the transmission of a name and an estate, it assumed a moral and spiritual function, it moulded bodies and souls. The care expended on children inspired new feelings, a new emotional attitude, to which the iconography of the seventeenth century gave brilliant expression. . . . .Parents were no longer content with setting up only a few of their children and neglecting the others. The ethics of the time ordered them to give all their children, and not just the eldest – and in the late eighteenth century, even the girls – a training for life (pp. 142–3).

This life as well as the next had to be properly prepared for.

The process Ariès describes was greatly intensified by the spread of certain Reformational doctrines. Sixteenth and seventeenth-century English and continental Protestants who denounced the idealization of virginity, and religious chastity for the priestcraft, insisted instead on the moral character of families and on the religious obligations of fatherhood. Paternity had in effect become a religious office, or as Christopher Hill says of the English household in the early seventeenth century: "A special caste of priests no longer mediated between God and man: the residual legatee was (or in the Puritan view should be) the father of the family."[8] Can you "be careful to teach your children and servants the way of your trades and callings, and neglect to instruct them in the way of life?" asked John Alleine in one of the numerous seventeenth-century English works promoting family religion.[9] The question admitted of only one answer.

THE LOCKEAN PARADIGM IN THE EIGHTEENTH CENTURY

The figure who most effectively and distinctively addressed the cause of family education in England and who made the greatest contribution to the contemporary rethinking of familial relations and parental authority was the philosopher John Locke. Though it was clearly influenced by the Puritan education he received at Oxford during the Interregnum, Locke's pedagogy, like his politics, did not derive from the new emphasis on family religion; instead, it derived logically and consistently from his psychology.[10]

In his *Essay concerning Human Understanding* (1690), Locke had rejected Descartes's doctrine of innate ideas "brought into the world with the soul" and, in particular, Descartes's presumption that such ideas provided paradigms for all subsequent thought.[11] Instead, Locke proposed a model of the mind as a tabula rasa, insisting that all reflection necessarily followed upon sensation. The receipt of sense information about the "primary qualities of things" – solidity, extension, figure, motion, and number – and the more subjectively perceived "secondary qualities" – color, texture, odor, and taste – produced generalizations, or "ideas." For example, the mind's idea of power, Locke argued, could be traced to an initial awareness of motion. All knowledge was a function of experience of the world.

The pedagogical implications of a sensationalist model of the mind were enormous, as Locke himself would be the first to demonstrate in *Some Thoughts concerning Education* (1693), a volume whose influence on eighteenth-century English culture and especially eighteenth-century English literature can hardly be overemphasized. The primary assumption of Locke's *Education* was that, because the mind is not formed at birth, "the little, and almost insensible Impressions on our tender Infancies have very important and lasting Consequences."[12] Such a view led Locke to conclude that education must rest not on the teaching of "precept," but on the force of "example," specifically parental example, for it registers the earliest impressions on the human mind.

> You must do nothing before him, which you would not have him imitate. . . . If you punish him for what he sees you practice yourself, he will not think that Severity to proceed from Kindness in you careful to amend a Fault in him; but will be apt to interpret it, as Peevishness and Arbitrary Imperiousness of a Father, who, without any Ground for it, would deny his Son the Liberty and Pleasures he takes for himself. . . . For you must remember Children affect to be men earlier than is thought (p. 172).

Locke's concern here is not with circumscribing parental authority, but with rendering it more effective by making it noncoercive. Parents who too rigorously or irrationally insist upon obedience undermine the cause of their own authority. For such authority to be effective – in the broadest sense of establishing normative values – it must be founded on filial "esteem," perhaps the most crucial word in the Lockean lexicon.

Locke's educational theory redefined the nature of parental authority in very much the way that the Revolution of 1688, which replaced an absolute monarchy with a constitutional one, redefined the rights and duties of the crown. The revolution Locke enthusiastically defended in his political writing declared there was "no king in being." The authority of William III was legislatively and not divinely created and thus was not sovereign in the manner of an agent of God on earth. Rather he was bound by the law of the land, constrained by his conscience, "his coronation oath and the laws of nature and Christianity" to preserve and protect the lives, possessions, and rights of his subjects.[13] Working through Parliament the king less reigned than governed. The word "governed," though a synonym for rule in the seventeenth century, took on in the eighteenth more of its root sense: "to steer," "guide," "direct," and "regulate." It carried with it, that is, all the force of its other sense: "to educate." For a "governor" in the seventeenth and eighteenth centuries referred to a tutor in charge of a young man's education as much as it did to an officer of the state.[14]

In his *Education* Locke declared that "the great Work of a Governour is to fashion the Carriage and inform the Mind" (p. 198). In a new political world in which government was to exist for the governed, the educational paradigm would provide a new model for the exercising of political authority. If, as the philosopher Helvetius declared, "the art of forming man is so closely linked to the form of government," then "it may not be possible to make any considerable change in public education without making changes in the very constitution of the state."[15] A revolution in one sphere either obliged or reflected one in the other.

The ultimate point of the new education and childrearing was not to secure a child's obedience, but to prepare a child for his eventual emergence into the world—in effect, to prepare him for the death of his parents. Thus, according to Locke, it is essential that parental instruction encourage the development of a child's reason, or "internal governor"; for it will be reason, along with a carefully ingrained set of habits, that ultimately will replace the external parent as that "power of restraint which permits an individual to *deny himself* his own Desires and cross his inclinations" (p. 139), to restrain his passions and act according to his own best interest. As a child grows older, parental authority must increasingly defer to filial reason to allow it the exercise necessary to its growth, for it to become, in effect, an introjected parent. In sum, Lockean pedagogy was essentially rational and sensationalistic—placing example over precept; morphological—emphasizing the gradual displacement of prerational childhood with rational adolescence; and equalitarian—subordinating the importance of "birth" to nurture. In addition, it was stoical—urging physical hardiness as well as rational self-sufficiency; tolerant and utilitarian—emphasizing the need to tailor expectations to the different capacities of children at different ages; and finally moral—insisting "'tis Vertue which is the hard and valuable part to be aimed at in education" (p. 170).

The following summary passage from Locke's *Education* contains the primary message of his pedagogy and anticipates a number of themes that will be developed in the course of this book:

> Would you have your Son obedient to you when past a Child, be sure then to establish the Authority of a Father *as soon* as he is capable of Submission, and can understand in whose Power he is. If you would have him stand in Awe of you, imprint it *in his Infancy;* and, as he approaches more to a Man, admit him nearer to your Familiarity: So shall you have him your obedient Subject (as is fit) whilst he is a Child and your affectionate Friend when he is a Man. . . . For, Liberty and Indulgence can do no good to *Children:* Their Want of Judgment makes them stand in need of Restraint and Discipline and, on the contrary, Imperiousness and Severity is an ill way of treating Men, who have Reason of their own to guide them unless you have a Mind to make your children, when grown up, weary of you, and secretly to say within themselves, 'When will you die, Father?' (p. 145).

The great challenge of eighteenth-century politics, familial and national, was to make authority and liberty compatible, to find a surer ground for obligation and obedience than "the fear of the rod." If imperiousness and severity create in men a slavish temper and a dissembled obedience that awaits but the right moment to throw off all restraint, force must be replaced with reasonableness, the imposition of an abso-

[handwritten margin note at top: Locke emphasizes dangers of a fallen world + importance of education to prevent corruption by experience]

lute will with the creation of shared values. The gradual granting of freedom and responsibility will keep children bound by the heart and that is the surest of all bonds:

> We must look upon our Children, when grown up, to be like ourselves; with the same Passions, the same desires. We would be thought Rational Creatures, and have our Freedom; we love not to be uneasie under constant rebukes and Browbeatings. . . . Whoever has such Treatment when he is a Man, will look out other Company, other Friends, other conversation; with whom he can be at Ease (pp. 145–6).

Locke's insistence on the equalitarian relations of grown generations is as much a moral injunction as an ideological one. Because it is impractical for a parent to follow his child constantly about and immoral to imprison him in the home, rational self-sufficiency and the habits of right conduct must be encouraged to protect a child's virtue in a corrupt world of flatterers and seducers. Only thus may innocence survive the embrace of experience. Locke's emphasis on the dangers of a fallen world of false appearances betrays the Puritan character of the education he himself had received. His stress on the probationary nature of childhood and adolescence suggests an almost theological anxiety about being corrupted by "worldliness."

Locke's insistence on the importance of education followed not only on the bright but on the dark implications of his epistemology. Because the mind will inevitably be formed by experience, it is essential that it be properly formed before it is corrupted by exposure to the wrong set of influences and impressions. For as easily as the mind might be formed and guided, so might it be misinformed and misguided. Because, finally, education alone made virtue possible, to educate the mind early was of the first importance. That obligation was even more urgent if, as Locke's theory of mind suggested, our ideas were "unreal representations of unknowable objects"[16] and we were adrift in a world of appearances. For in such a world the danger of mistaking or being manipulated into mistaking a false appearance or a projected wishfulness for a certain reality was ever present.

John Trenchard and Thomas Gordon concluded the third volume of *Cato's Letters* (1723), their influential and often reprinted series of essays on civil and religious liberty, with an essay entitled: "Of the Weakness of the human Mind and how easily it is misled." It was but one of many in the highly Lockean collection dedicated to exploring the anxious vulnerability to deception and corruption that the new sensationalism made such an emphatic concern in the eighteenth century. If our mind be dependent for all its knowledge on the information provided by the senses, we should pay much heed to how easily, for example, magicians and "jugglers do many Things by sleight of Hand, which to a gaping Beholder appear to be Witchcraft; and when he knows how they are done, he wonders at himself for wondering at them."[17] Similarly, Cato warned, a leader of a political party, by applying to his audience's "reigning Appetites, appearing Interests, and predominant foibles," can succeed "in influencing their Minds" to accomplish the worst evil. Indeed, a speaker's "lucky thought, a jest, a fortunate accident . . . shall bring about designs and Revolutions in human affairs, which twenty legions in the field could not bring about" (III, 334). The empire of influence is infinitely more powerful than the empire of force.

Compounding the dilemma of deception was the problematic relationship between language and reality, between words and the things for which they stand. Locke attacked scholastic education for stressing not only precept rather than example, but also "names" rather than "things."[18] Because language is artificial and words have no fixed and perfectly shared meanings, but rather only the infinitely various subjective meanings our personal experience gives to them, language removes man one step further from "reality" and deeper into a world of deceptive appearances. Thus, in another of Cato's letters, Trenchard and Gordon warn that the multitude of men is forever misled because "they are ever abused with Words, ever fond of the worst of Things recommended by Good names, and ever abhor the best Things, and the most virtuous actions, disfigured by ill Names." They urged that if the blessings of the Revolution of 1688, which had secured Englishmen their liberties, were to be maintained, "something must be done to rectify or regulate the Education of Youth"; for the historical failure to do so is the "source of all our other Evils" (I, 139). Without rational education there is no independence of mind and thus eventually no liberty.

Within twenty years after their publication, the doctrines to which Locke had given definitive expression were being popularized not only by *Cato's Letters* but by the *Spectator* and *Tatler* papers as well as by a host of didactic works on family government.[19] A brief history of these popularizations will clarify exactly which themes in the new pedagogy were perceived to be of vital and continuing significance to eighteenth-century English culture.

The most popular early didactic work on family government was by no less a personage than Daniel Defoe. Persecuted by the Whigs for treasonable publications in 1713 and convicted for libel in 1715, the dissenting journalist decided to turn his attention from political pamphleteering to the less controversial subjects of family relations and moral pedagogy. As had been the case with Locke, Defoe shifted ground only to reapply microcosmically his political themes: toleration and rational "government."

Considerably more pietistical than Locke's work, Defoe's *The Family Instructor* (Part 1, 1715; Part 2, 1718) followed the seventeenth-century conduct books in their insistence on family catechizing and family worship. Parents must provide their children not only with a moral education but with the spiritual training essential for their ultimate salvation. Even this theme is subordinated to the broader concern with "parental tyranny" and "the disastrous consequences of evil and incompetent family government."[20] The purpose of the volume, Defoe announces, is "to reprove those parents who neglect the instruction of their child and to direct young persons to their first reflection, guiding them to reflections about themselves and their progress in the world . . . the method is new but perhaps may be the more pleasing" (p. 8). "The method" is to present a series of dramatic dialogues between family members in which readers "may see their likeness and blush" (p. 7). As Locke had urged the use of shame in the education of children, Defoe employs it in the education of parents: "Those who call themselves Christians and Protestants and who will not instruct their children and servants, here will they find their children and servants instructing them and reproving them, too" (p. 6).

In the first dialogue, the younger of two daughters (none of the family members are given names) learns from a friend's parent that God has given her "an immortal soul for which she should thank him in prayers" (p. 11). When the daughter asks her own parents why they have not informed her of so important a fact, they are obliged to confess their shameful negligence. In the course of the next several dialogues they are further forced to acknowledge that not only is the ignorance of their younger children the fault of their own parental dereliction, but so is the dissoluteness of their eldest son and daughter. The parents conclude that they must commence a family "reformation" to save their children from ruin (p. 34).

Because she has spent some time at a pious aunt's home where she was instructed in the ways of the Lord, the second of the family's three daughters is least addicted to that "manner of looseness," which makes of her "father's family a kind of hell" (p. 92). She, more than her parents, realizes the urgency of the situation:

> *Mother:* How then would good instruction have wrought upon thee if I had begun it 10 or 12 years ago?
> *2nd Daughter:* Dear Mother, I hope it is not too late. (p. 92)

Though perhaps it is not too late for their daughter, it is for their eldest son. Unmoved by the impassioned solicitations of his newly reformed parents, the young man runs away from home, squanders all his money in the fashion of the prodigal son, and joins the army.

Some time later, having been wounded in the war, he asks to be readmitted to his parents' house. His father, however, will not readmit him until the youth confesses to the sin of "withstanding the reformation of his father's house" (p. 35). Angered that parental compassion should be so conditional, the son refuses. The daughter stretches the truth and brings word to her father that his son has asked his pardon. Yet the parent, with a pridefulness born of his own sense of guilt, insists once again on a specific confession of filial disobedience. The eldest daughter conveys the parent's message:

> *Sister:* He leaves you to your liberty.
> *Brother:* What does my father call liberty, sister? He leaves me to my liberty; that is, either to submit or starve, come on my knees to him or beg: is this leaving me to my liberty?
> *Sister:* My father is none of these tyrants, he says he hopes God may eventually open your eyes, that repentance is God's gift, it is not in his power (p. 312).

The daughter skillfully invokes a Christian apology for her father's severity. But her brother will have none of it. For him the issue is liberty versus tyranny.

Soon after, however, the soldier is found on his deathbed calling plaintively for "his father, his father . . . to beg his forgiveness" (p. 39). Before the parent, who is away in the country, can be summoned, the young man dies. Defoe leaves little room for the reader to infer anything but that the father is primarily responsible for the boy's death. Though children must be severely punished and held accountable for disobeying their parents, the original sin in this case is parental: the failure to provide a Christian education and example. No longer can that "first disobedience" be wholly ascribed to the fallen willfulness of children.

Defoe's *Instructor* may be said to popularize certain aspects of the new pedagogy, but nowhere, as Peter Earle has pointed out, is an affectionate word spoken.[21] Affections seem to play no part in Defoe's conception of the ideal family. Nor does Defoe seem to believe with Locke that a child's rational growth eventually limits parental authority. Rather, Defoe's attack is directed at parents who do not assert their legitimate authority or fulfill their moral responsibility. And such parents are far from the exception. The state of family government in England, Defoe declares, is such that "many fathers are removed from their family either by death or disaster, by the discretion of providence, that the children may fall into better hands" (p. 191). Such a Providence – that later will provide Robinson Crusoe with an explanation for his shipwreck – forestalls the need for open rebellion.

By the middle of the eighteenth century the principal popularizer and Christian interpreter of Lockean childrearing was the nonconformist

minister Isaac Watts, whose hymns and spiritual songs were unprecedented bestsellers throughout the century. Watts's principal contribution to pedagogical theory was his *Improvement of the Mind* (1747), a
volume whose emphasis on the Christian rather than the political implications of Locke exerted a major influence on colonial American
education.[22] Watts argued that the essentially conservative character of
the new pedagogy had been fatally lost sight of by his generation. The
Lockean doctrine of "a just and reasonable liberty" had become for
such as the prodigal son in Defoe's *Instructor* no more than a rallying call
to justify filial license and parental indulgence.

According to Watts, the new pedagogy emerging at the beginning of
the eighteenth century had effected a vast revolution in generational
relations and in the character of English youth. It was a necessary
revolution but one that had now gone too far:

> In the beginning of the last century and so onward to the middle of it,
> the children were usually obliged to believe what their parents and
> masters taught them . . . to almost every punctilio; as though it were
> necessary for salvation. . . . But in this century when the doctrine of a
> just and reasonable liberty is better known, too many of the present
> youth break all the bonds of nature and duty and run into the wildest
> degrees of looseness both in belief and practice (p. 4).[23]

For Watts the transcendent importance of the new pedagogy, rightly
understood, was that it retaught a Protestant nation the greatest article
of its own faith: the doctrine of rational voluntarism. Parents who
thwart the development of their children's reason by insisting that they
accept without examination or inquiry all doctrines taught them put
their children's salvation in jeopardy; for saving faith is, by definition,
that faith one freely and rationally chooses to embrace. But the child's
salvation is threatened, no less, by parents who fail to discourage older
children from wandering where their fancy leads them. Just as the
earlier pre-Lockean parent failed to distinguish between childhood and
adolescence, so the post-Lockean parent now fails to distinguish between adolescence and adulthood.

> The last age taught mankind to believe that they were mere children
> and treated them as such till they were near thirty years old, and the
> present give them leave to fancy themselves complete men and women
> at twelve or fifteen and they accordingly judge and manage for them-
> selves and too often disparage all advice of their elders (p. 378).

Believing the dangers of license as great as those of tyranny, Watts
sought to still the historical pendulum.

One of the primary misconceptions of a Christian society becoming more and more liberalized was this crucial confusion of adolescence with adulthood. Though, as Locke declared, the period of

one's rationality begins around the age of twelve or thirteen,[24] for Watts, it is not until one reaches one's twenties that real independence of mind, essential to the making of any moral decision, is achieved: "Only then upon the clearest judgment of his own mature reason, a thorough and impartial search into the subject, the inward dictates of his conscience and the full evidence of his parents's mistakes" can a son begin to call cautiously into question "the doctrines of his ancestors" (p. 317). Obliged by his Protestant faith to insist on the right of each adolescent to think for himself, Watts, like Defoe, is nonetheless deeply aware of the dangers of confusing that right with the license to become a freethinker or with the permission to exercise that right too fully, too early.

Consistent with Locke's insistence that example is more effective than precept, Watts reinforces his polemic with a case study of one Eugenio. Having been raised by a tutor who takes him through a sequence of carefully graded catechisms, each tailored to his level of competence, he is provided the "Public form, more universally taught" only when he is ready to understand it (p. 314). After the age of fifteen he "was suffered to admit nothing into his full assent till his mind saw the rational evidence" lest his convictions be but the products of a "wanton pride of free thinking" (p. 315). At no time during his youth does Eugenio rail against his parents' or tutors' authority. For he carries within him the conviction of "the great love and wisdom of his parents and tutors," who tempered the restraints of his younger years "by so much liberty" and tenderness and who loosened the bonds of discipline "only so fast as he grew wise enough to govern himself" (p. 320).

Because our knowledge is based on our sense perceptions and our senses are easily misled and deceived, a loving parent must, Watts contends, insist that reason be always on its guard. Such vigilance is essential to self-government. Reason must be taught "to see into things deeply" and through "the disguises and false colorings in which many things appear."[25] Thus, education must concern itself less with content, doctrinal or otherwise, than with perfecting the mind's ability to evaluate and judge. The ideal teacher trains his charges in the free use of their judgment such that they might eventually become independent not only of his authority, but of the authority of all others. Protected from corruption, an educated mind is free, whereas an ignorant and unprotected one is enslaved.

In 1725, Watts published *Logick or the Right Use of Reason* to provide such instruction, to show how one's reason can be developed to resist the appeal to emotions and to learn to judge "the inherent rationality or irrationality of an argument" (p. 4). Such skills, Watts argued, are not only vital to one's progress in this world, but may determine one's fate in the next. Only with them may one successfully thwart, as Eve had tragically failed to do, the "great deluder" in his multitude of disguises. Only thus may a Protestant nation thrive and triumph.

The two figures who, in addition to Watts, did the most to familiarize the reading public in England and America with a Christianized version of Locke's rationalist pedagogy were Phillip Doddridge and James Burgh. Doddridge, like Watts, was a dissenting minister and hymn writer whose *Rise and Progress of Religion in the Soul* (1745) stressed the relationship of the growth of reason and the growth of the soul. In more strident terms than Watts or Defoe, Doddridge insisted on the momentous character of parental responsibility:

> Give me leave to plead with you, as the instruments of introducing them into being. O remember it is, indeed, a debased and corrupted nature you have conveyed to them. Consider that the world into which you have been a means of bringing them is a place in which they are surrounded with many temptations . . . , it is on the whole much to be feared that they will perish in their ignorance and forgetfulness of God, if they do not learn from you to love and serve him. . . . He has made them thus dependent upon you that there might be a better opportunity to forming their minds and influencing them to a right temper and conduct.[26]

Parents are obliged to compensate for transmitting Adam's curse by applying themselves to the task of developing the fallen faculties of their children, the task of renaturing through nurture.

Better known today for his political pamphlets, James Burgh made explicit in the very popular *Thoughts on Education* (1747) what Doddridge left implicit: "The souls of youth are even more immediately committed to the care of parents and instruments of their education than even those of a people are to their pastor; for the latter having arrived at years of discretion, if properly educated may be supposed capable of conducting themselves."[27] Even a minister wielding the power of God's word is seldom able to undo the damage caused by parental neglect or authoritarianism. Because Christianity contains "no doctrine that is not intelligent and consistent with reason," to inhibit the growth of reason is, once again, to inhibit the acquisition of a real and saving faith. A child hellbound is a child improperly raised. The failure is in nurture rather than nature.

Even more than Watts or Doddridge, Burgh responded to the paranoid strain of Lockean sensationalism. In his chapter on child management in *The Dignity of Human Nature* (1754), Burgh advised that a husband take the utmost care that his pregnant wife be kept as much as possible from "the sight of uncouth objects lest she produce a monster."[28] The tabula rasa could be written upon before birth. In *The*

Art of Speaking (1762), perhaps his most popular work, Burgh addressed the same fear of corruption. Here he set forth the reasons why that particular art more than any other must be acquired by all men "who wish to do good in the world":

> Supposing a person to be ever so sincere and zealous a lover of virtue and of his country without a competent skill and address in speaking, he can only sit still and see them wronged without having in his power to prevent or redress the evil. An artful . . . statesman has the power to mislead the judgment of the house.[29]

Because the spectacle is addressed to the eye as well as the ear, oratory is a greater and more powerful art form than either painting or poetry. Its "influence," in the Lockean sense of the word, is thus twice as great. Consequently, Burgh's volume emphasizes at length the gestures, expressions, and movements that must be cultivated as part of the spectacle of oratory. Satan seduced Eve through his "insinuating address." Fire must be fought with fire. Only one with a skill in speaking can save one's nation or properly form a child's mind.

If parents neglect to teach their children how to defend themselves against evil influence, they will cheat a child of a virtuous life *and* a saving faith. If committed by enough parents, such lapses might ultimately remove "the divine blessing from the English nation." In *Britain's Remembrancer* (1746), written immediately after the Battle of Culloden, Burgh sees the Jacobite revolt as punishment for Britain's sins, chief among them the failure "in an age of wealth and prosperity to educate properly their [its] children."[30] By 1750, irresponsible parents had become the nation's scapegoat.

A decade after Burgh's work, the popular dictionary maker Thomas Sheridan published a treatise extending the argument even further. Its title contains its thesis: *British Education; or the Source of the Disorder of Great Britain, Being an Essay toward proving that the immorality, ignorance and false tasks which so generally prevail are the natural and necessary consequences of the present defective system of education* (1756). If all parents would attend diligently to the work of education not only would God refrain from punishing the nation, but such attendance, Sheridan concluded, would bring nearer to completion the great design of the Reformation: "Each generation of Christians properly raised insures there will be another." The influence of education "on a general reformation and on the propagation of the gospel to those who are yet unborn is beyond calculation."[31]

The more immediate goal of forming the child's mind, however, was the moral independence of the child and the development of his rational self-sufficiency. Fearing that even at twenty-one a child's reason might not be adequately developed to serve in place of parental guidance,

Burgh recommended the following ritual to be enacted on the day of a young man's independence from home. A letter should be written in the hand of the parent or tutor and "a promise desired of the student or young man, as a last and parting favor, that he would constantly, wherever he lived, continue to give it a fair reading." Such a letter should consist of "(1) an abridgement of the maxims and lessons of prudence and virtue (2) a brief view of the doctrines and precepts of Christianity (3) an abstract of the most forcible and convincing arguments for the truth of Christianity . . . (6) directions in case of a fatal defection from virtue and religion."[32] Not trusting parental diligence, Burgh published precisely such an anthology, one popular both in England and America: *Youth's Friendly Monitor or the Affectionate School Master containing his late pathetic farewell lecture to the young people on the entrance into a Busy World* (1754). Burgh's schoolmaster–narrator is to the student sent out into the wide world as Michael is to Adam in *Paradise Lost.* The latter's words echo throughout the *Monitor:* "Then wilt thou not be loath to leave this Paradise, but shalt possess / A Paradise within thee, happier far."[33] Self-sufficient independence made possible by the right education replaces the circumscribed paradise of a well-ordered family. Not surprisingly, Burgh, a friend of Franklin's, would publish in the last year of his life *Political Disquisitions* (1775), which contained a defense of colonial resistance to Parliament. The new pedagogical understanding of personal independence easily extended to an argument for colonial rights. Bernard Bailyn was more than just when he concluded twenty years ago: "What was recognized even before the Revolution as typical American individualism, optimism, and enterprise resulted also from the processes of education."[34]

Though begun as a reaction against the assumptions of Lockean psychology, a second major school of thought contributed to the eighteenth-century Anglo-American preoccupation with the concept of nurture: the Scottish Common Sense movement. Its belief in an innate moral sense and its related concern with the way man is rather than with the way man should be might suggest that such a philosophy placed little emphasis on nurture and education. The opposite is true, however. To realize how much in agreement the two most important schools of eighteenth-century English thought were on the primacy of nurture is to realize how much the new pedagogical ideology had become a part of English and Scottish culture. To understand the Common Sense attitude toward generational relations one must first understand its basic premises. The Scottish common or moral sense philosophers, notably Adam Ferguson, Francis Hutcheson, and Thomas Reid, rejected both the identification of virtue with self-interest implied by

Lockean rationalism and the identification of virtue with sensory pleasure implied by Lockean sensationalism. They found intolerable the
supposition that God had made the accomplishment of virtue in the
world dependent on the calculated deliberations of human reason. Good
deeds were surely intended to be more than the chance by-product of
private interest and an intellectual computation of obligation. Man was
designed by the Creator not only to be capable of disinterested benevolence but to take exquisite pleasure in it. Thus, Hutcheson declared in
1741: "As God has not left the propagation of the species and self-
preservation to chance, but imbued man with the sexual passion and
the instincts of hunger and thirst, so has he also assured the life of
virtue."[35]

Accepting Locke's sensationalist framework, however, Hutcheson
posited a sixth common sense, antecedent to rational judgment, called
the moral sense, or affection. When stimulated by the sight of a fellow
creature in great pain, for example, it is the moral sense that involuntarily inspires one to assist the sufferer even before the consequences
of such assistance can be rationally calculated. Man does not choose to
pursue happiness or goodness, but rather his choice presupposes, in
Francis Hutcheson's phrase, "an instinct toward happiness," a moral
sense and affection.[36] Behind the rational decision to be virtuous is
always the spontaneous motive of affection: self-love or love of
others.[37]

For the Scottish philosophers the moral sense is identified with the
latter of these, an innate principle of sociability that inspires man to
define himself in relationship to others, to recognize the fact of his
obligations to others, and to seek the pleasure of human companion-
ship. All the Scottish philosophers agreed with Montesquieu's assertion:
"Man is born in society and there he remains. All history proves man's
instinctive reluctance to be alone, his desire if imprisoned alone in a
dungeon to cultivate the friendship of the spiders."[38]

Qualifying Locke's notion of a tabula rasa by positing an innate instinct, the Scots refocused eighteenth-century thought on the question
of what man is, not what he can be. The lengthy treatise on moral
philosophy in the 1771 first edition of the *Encyclopaedia Britannica,* the
great corporate achievement of the Scottish Enlightenment, made clear
the emphasis of the new philosophy:

> Its object is to shew whence our obligations arise and where they
> terminate. Moral philosophy is concerned not with what he may be,
> by education, habit or foreign influence come to be or do, but what by
> his nature or original constituent principles he is formed to be and do,
> what conduct he is obliged to pursue.[39]

By providing man with a period of infancy longer than that of any other creature, God makes clear the nature of that obligation. Though man is "born a weak, helpless, delicate creature" he finds

> immediate and sure resources in the affection and care of his parents who refuse no labors and forego no dangers, to nurse and rear up the tender babe. By these powerful instincts, as by some mighty chain does nature link the parent to the child and form the strongest moral connection on his part before the child has the least apprehension of it (III, 271).

Because children, "unlike brute creation [are] not clothed and armed by their structure and their infancy and nonage is such that they advance slowly to strength of body and maturity of reason," the parental charge is "a mighty one" (III, 271). The child in his turn contracts a fondness for those who take care of him, "is uneasy when they his parents are gone and these feelings become the foundation of the moral attachment on his side" (III, 272). God has designed this reciprocal sympathy to serve as the ideal paradigm for all future social relations.

Though natural parental affection renders their charge agreeable, the *Britannica* essay concludes that "unless both parents concur in this rightful task and continue their joint labours, till they have reared up and planted out their young colony, it must become prey to every rude invader, and the purpose of nature in the original union of the human pair be defeated" (III, 289). Like a sovereign state, the individual is vulnerable to invasion, to having his mind misled and his heart enthralled. Whereas Locke's individualistic assumptions led him to assert the importance of nurture, the communitarian assumptions of the Scots led them, by another route, to the same conclusion. For in their view, human sociability, the essential component of human life, is finally no more than nature's divinely designed response to that initial parental nurture. Without such nurture society suffers no less than does the individual soul of the child. No longer is parental neglect simply sinful. In the Scottish formulation it is unnatural, a violation of one's God-granted nature: "A character who feels no love for his species . . . we reckon totally immoral and unnatural" (III, 275).

In his study of the influence of Common Sense philosophy on Jefferson's political philosophy, Garry Wills recently stressed the importance of recognizing a fundamental opposition in eighteenth-century thought between the Lockean insistence on the primacy of the individual, reason, and self-interest and, on the other hand, the Scottish insistence on the primacy of the social bond, affections, and disinterested benevolence. Certainly the caution is salutary.[40] Locke's rationalist pedagogy did indeed stand in radical opposition to the optimistic sentimentality, derived from Scottish Common Sense assumptions about the sociable character of man, which extolled "soul kinship," "affinity," "sympathetic attachments," and "the power of sympathy." For Locke, such subrational and noncontractual relationships endangered the sacred principle of moral independence.

In certain regards, however, the opposition is much less absolute than Wills suggests. Both the Lockean and Scottish traditions addressed the problem of man's relationship to society through a reconsideration of the obligation parents and children owed one another. Both insisted on a noncoercive rather than authoritarian model of the family. Both, perceiving man as corruptible rather than corrupt, posited the necessity of there being an internal guide, be it reason or the moral sense, to enable one to lead a virtuous life in a world of corrupters and seducers. Both philosophies combined, as we shall see at greater length, to force a revolutionary rethinking of the relationship of individual and family, and, by extension, of obligation and personal liberty, of the progress of the soul and the progress of society.

By the 1740s the issues raised by both traditions found dramatic expression and their definitive popularizations in the new literary form, the novel.[41] Because it assumed that the impressions made by fiction are as real to the mind as those made by other experience, sensationalist epistemology radically intensified the cultural anxiety over the influence of immoral fictional literature. Yet, the same assumption implied that the right kind of imaginative literature might be enormously useful. Literature could play the exemplary role parents were obliged, but often failed, to fill. It could educate as well as corrupt.

The Scottish assertion of a sixth moral sense that when exposed to virtuous behavior – on the page or in the world – instinctively sought moral pleasure by imitating it further encouraged the emergence and acceptance of moralistic works of fiction. In his popular *Elements of Criticism* (1762), Henry Home, Lord Kames, made clear the grounds of the acceptance: "A signal act of gratitude produceth in the spectator or reader not only love or esteem for the author but also a separate feeling . . . of gratitude without an object, a feeling which disposeth the spectator or reader to acts of gratitude."[42]

Whereas Laurence Sterne and Henry Mackenzie would popularize the new Scottish sentimentality a generation later, Samuel Richardson, the most influential of the first generation of English novelists, took up the familial dramas of Defoe's *Instructor* and Watts's works and, by a new attention to the underlying psychological issues, transformed them into works of great literary art. His novels addressed the dilemmas raised by the rationalist pedagogy: the achievement of rational self-sufficiency, the survival of innocence in the embrace of experience, the relationship between the autonomy of one generation and the authority of another. Richardson's version of these dilemmas would have a decisive impact on the imagination of his generation.

Pamela

In Part 1 of *Pamela or Virtue Rewarded* (1740), the first fully developed example of the genre of the novel in English and one of the most widely read books of the century, Richardson details the history of a serving girl who eventually marries her master. In Part 2 of the novel, Richardson recounts the trials of Pamela's domestic life as wife and mother, and devotes over a hundred pages of the volume to a discussion and endorsement of Lockean pedagogy. Addressing her husband in a characteristically long letter, Pamela anxiously observes that whereas poverty all too often forces the poor to seek out servile and demeaning relationships with wealthy friends, wealth all too often leads the rich to the equally destructive paths of extravagance and of lapsed "perseverance in virtue."[43] Restating the Lockean credo in the vocabulary of the sentimentalized Puritanism of the mid-eighteenth century, Pamela concludes that to preserve both the poor and the wealthy from "a servile state," self-sufficiency must be taught at the earliest age:

> And to this end, as I humbly conceive, the noble doctrine of *independence* should be early instilled into both their minds, and upon all occasions inculcated and inforced; which would be an inducement for the one to endeavour to *improve* his fortune by his honest industry, lest he should never be enabled to rise out of a state of dependence; and to the other, to *keep*, if not *improve*, his own, lest he should ever fall into such a servile state, and thereby lose the glorious power of conferring happiness on the deserving (p. 399).

Here Richardson sets forth a theme that will preoccupy eighteenth-century literature and politics: the corrupting effects of dependence and indolence. So concerned is Pamela, the dutiful mother, about the consequences attending the idleness and indulgence brought about by wealth that she suggests that her young son share his tutor with the child "of some honest neighbor of but middling circumstances . . . who should give apparent indication of his natural promptitude, ingenious temper, obliging behavior and good manners" (p. 398). Because self-sufficiency, a sound mind, and a sound body offer the only real "fence to virtue," even class lines must be crossed in pursuit of it.

The contemporary revulsion against dependence is nowhere better suggested than by the sending of debtors to prison in eighteenth-century England and America in punishment for their "idleness and ill-husbandry."[44] Such idleness if left unchecked would eventually lead to further moral corruption, and the dependence it obliges would violate the larger Protestant insistence that man be dependent on God alone, that he reject all "papist" mediators who seek to enslave him. If the wealthy must beware complacency, the poor must beware a laziness and indolence that would render them indebted and dependent and, as Poor Richard would declare, "tax" them more than any king.[45]

Some years later in a digression on "Toryism" in *The Vicar of Wakefield,* whose hero himself ends up in a debtor's prison, Oliver Goldsmith would make Richardson's point in another context. A monarchy, he argued, must be supported by all Englishmen for the compelling reason that the wealthy must at all cost be kept from making the poorer classes utterly dependent on them: "The possessor of accumulated wealth, when furnished with the necessities and pleasures of life," can employ the superfluity of his fortune only "in making dependents, in purchasing the liberty of the needy or venal, of men who are willing to bear the mortification of continuous tyranny for bread." Even if tyranny must be risked, Goldsmith concludes, better one tyrant who may later be deposed than "a number of tyrants."[46] This fear of a corrupting dependence and the complementary insistence on financial and moral independence would later serve as a pervasive theme in the rhetoric of the American Revolution. In this regard Edmund Morgan has concluded: "In the eyes of many Americans the Revolution was a defense of industry and frugality, whether in rulers or people, from the assaults of British vice."[47]

If *Pamela* began the novelistic popularization of Locke's doctrine of raising a child to a state of industrious independence, Richardson's next and even more influential work, *Clarissa or The History of a Young Lady* (1748), mounted an attack on the bourgeois patriarchal family to point out a complementary Lockean moral: the multiple evils that result from a parent placing family honor, wealth, and social standing above the moral responsibility to his children. Mr. Harlowe, Clarissa's patriarchal father, insists that "to raise a family" his daughter marry the wealthy Mr. Solmes, even though she finds him personally hateful.[48] The pointed phrase does not refer to childrearing, but to elevating the family position by consolidating its estate and – taking the Latin sense of "family" – adding to the number of its servants. In the patriarchal view, it is the *family* that must be delivered from the corrupting touch of the "middling classes" by becoming self-sufficient through wealth, rather than the *child* who must be liberated from a stunting dependence on the family by the proper education of her reason and the permission to choose freely a spouse who will protect her from the corruptions of the world. Clarissa, confused and prideful, flees with her suitor Lovelace from her father's home only to be later victimized by her deliverer. Abandoned by Lovelace and rejected by her parents, she dies before a reconciliation can be achieved with her parents. Through Richardson's influence, Locke's briefs against parental tyranny and filial pride (for Clarissa's ultimate disobedience no matter how provoked must be punished) would become controlling themes of the eighteenth-century fiction.[49]

The issue of personal autonomy within a structure of family obligations and role expectations was also implicitly reflected in the epistolary form of Richardson's novels. The contemporary fascination with that form can be traced, in part, to the establishment of the London penny post in the 1680s. As Robert Adams Day has pointed out, for the first time "the personal letter was no longer restricted to business matters or emergency messages and might become a vehicle for something approximating conversation."[50] Young women, children, and even servants began to write letters with some frequency. The passion to write and read letters suggests, as Patricia Spacks has recently argued about eighteenth-century autobiography, a desire "to discover, defend, assert and manufacture the self," to set down a personal interpretation of experience, to assert in the face of a view of the self as constantly being formed the "stability of identity."[51] The letter affirmed the importance of the individual voice.

The popularity of letter writing led to the appearance of letter manuals whose often fictional content and narrative continuity crudely set the stage for the novel. Indeed, Richardson's *Pamela* followed hard on the success of his own letter manual: *Familiar Letters Written to and for Particular Friends on the Most Important Occasions* (1740). The emergence of the genre of the familiar letter book suggests the degree to which the larger ideal of "familiarity," or rational friendship, had begun in the first half of the eighteenth century to challenge the more exclusive and authoritarian world of familial relations. To her correspondent Miss Howe, Clarissa confided thoughts she would never confide to her sister. The sympathetic and voluntaristic relations become more primary than the accidental and formal relations of birth. And as Locke had implied in *Education*, the former, ideally, should provide the model for the latter. In short, the letter allowed one to reflect on his or her experience, to learn from it, and to reach out beyond the prescriptive world of the household and its roles. It enhanced the development of the self, just as the novel built around the letter asserted the claims of that self.

ROUSSEAU AND THE NEW AUTHORITY

In 1762, Jean Jacques Rousseau in his seminovelistic pedagogical work *Emile* would advance Locke's understanding of the development of the child and his relationship to parents one step further than either Richardson or the Christian pedagogues. Early in *Emile*, a book much more widely advertised by eighteenth-century American booksellers than *The Social Contract*, Rousseau takes issue with his predecessor:

Locke's maxim was to educate children by reasoning with them; and it is that which is now most in vogue. Of all man's faculties, that of reason, which is in fact only a compound of all the rest, unfolds itself the last, and with the greatest difficulty, yet this is what we make use of to develop the first and easiest of them. The great end of a good education is to form a reasonable man; and we pretend to educate a child by the means of reason.[52]

Rather than educating a child by slowly forming and deferring to his reason, a child is best educated by giving him the free expression of his "natural inclinations" and then, as we shall see, manipulating the consequences of that freedom. Because Rousseau, unlike Locke, subscribes to a view of man's nature as inherently good, believing with the Scottish moralists that the first promptings of nature should be followed, he dismisses the criticism that such a free reign would habituate a child to the indulgence of passion. The discipline of natural consequence – a child free to play with fire would soon learn the virtue of restraint – would keep him from harming himself.

To be truly free and independent, Rousseau argues, is to learn by experience the limits of one's own nature. To adjust one's expectations and desires to the possible is to be freed from the ultimate slavery of excessive desire and unrealistic dreams: "that man is truly free who desires only what he is able to perform, and does what he desires," who is "dependent only on things not men" (I, 80, 96). Perceived as neither tyrannical nor galling, the "easy yoke" of necessary restraint is submitted to willingly and without bitterness. Defined in almost Calvinist terms Rousseau's freedom is made synonymous with the virtue of self-restraint, with a self-mastery that alone allows one an independence of all other masters and enables one eventually to live within society yet uncorrupted by the servile dependencies it encourages.

But for such a natural education to be successful, it must, paradoxically, be controlled by artifice. It must be directed by a tutor who is given total control over the child and who removes him from society, from all competing sources of authority and influence. Though appearing to raise the child in a state of natural freedom, independent of any will but the child's own inclinations, the hidden hand ("la main cachée") of the tutor is controlling all situations. As Lester Crocker puts it in his masterful biography of Rousseau: "Emile is 'free' because he is supposedly dependent only on things, but things are under the control of the 'guide,' who manipulates them secretly."[53] "Never command him to do any thing," Rousseau insists, "let him not even imagine you pretend to have any authority, let him only know that he is necessarily at your mercy" (I, 124). For "there is no subjection that is so compleat as that which preserves the appearance of freedom" (I, 204).

Such was the new pedagogical ideal of authority, an authority that transformed coercion into conditioning. The price of true authority being divested of obnoxious shows of force was that it, in effect, went underground. Playing on the distinction between appearance and reality and comfortable with deception justified by utopian goals, such authority ran the risk of becoming indistinguishable, in method if not in intention, from the corrupting forces with which it competed both for the kingdom of mind and heart and for the control of human motivation that, as the faith in a designing Providence declined, was presumed to control history.[54] Yet that deception was essential if noncoercive power were to be effective.

Though man is naturally good, his goodness, unless successfully guided and tended, is no defense against the corrupting influences of the society in which he will eventually live. Thus he must be socialized, and his first inclinations replaced by a new set of habits, a new nature, "natural" to society. As "plants are formed by culture" – protected thus not only from corruption but wild growth – so, too, men are formed "by education" (I, 4). Nurture must direct the course of nature; for without cultivation there is no culture, no possibility of a harmonious society. Rousseau's analogy between gardening and education, ubiquitous in eighteenth-century prose, reflected the period's faith in the transforming power of nurture which, when properly applied, created a new set of naturalized social relations. It could turn (as had been successfully done with the education of Peter the Wild Boy at the court of George I) primitive nature into social nature.[55] The enormous contemporary interest in gardening, and the equally vast literature concerned with it, addressed, as one critic has commented, "a rage for order in a world of perceived chaos."[56] The enclosed grotto, a popular feature of English country estates and the subject of poems by Pope and others, was a type of the individual fenced off from corruption as the perfect garden was an image of an unfallen natural order lost and now recovered, an Eden where man's art perfected God's creation rather than competed with it.

The analogy between gardening and education was given its most influential early formulation by Locke's admirer Richard Steele in the 455th number of the *Spectator Papers,* one devoted to "education or modern culture." With an urgency reflecting the sensationalist understanding of the mind's vulnerability, Steele exclaims:

> How many good Qualities in the Mind are lost, for want of the like due Care in nursing and skillfully managing them, how many Virtues are choked, by the Multitude of Weeds which are suffered to grow among them; how excellent Parts are often starved and useless, by being planted in a wrong Soil and how very seldom do these moral

> Seeds produce the novel Fruits which must be expected from them, by . . . an artful management of our tender Inclinations and first Spring of Life.[57]

The faith that the "vegetable principle" in man might be acted upon for the good by controlling the influences brought to bear on it was developed by Rousseau's contemporary Franz Anton Mesmer into the most popular pseudoscience of the eighteenth century: Mesmerism. In experiments conducted just as America was declaring its independence, Mesmer claimed to have discovered an invisible fluid, an agent of nature that enveloped and penetrated the universe and all the bodies in it, and was the source of all health. Robert Darnton has succinctly summarized the theory: "Individuals could control and reinforce the fluid's action by 'mesmerizing' or massaging the body's 'poles' and thereby overcoming the obstacle, inducing a crisis, often in the form of convulsions, and restore health or the harmony of man with nature."[58] Children in particular would be brought to the mesmerist to be, as Darnton puts it, "educated" by the fluid, to ensure that they grow up "natural men" (p. 6).

In a 1789 letter, the Revolutionary Jacques-Pierre Brissot made clear the fundamental connection between mesmerism and the new understanding of parental responsibility: "I love mesmerism because it identifies me with my children. How sweet it is to me . . . when I see them obey my inner voice, bend over, fall into my arms and enjoy sleep, the state of a nursing mother is a state of perpetual mesmerism. . . . By mesmerism we become fathers once again. Hence a new benefit for society, and it has such a need of one."[59] Brissot's letter combines a solicitous desire to express love with an anxious desire to exert authority. Though one might cynically ask which informs which, the point is that Mesmerism suggested not only that the two were compatible but, as Locke and Rousseau had argued in their different ways, that the two were intimately related. The mediating term was, as Mesmer used the word, "rapport." Perhaps the supreme contemporary expression of the power of influence and education most broadly construed, Mesmerism, like gardening, carried with it the unspoken warning that parents not neglect the vital task of forming their children, inoculating them against corruption. It gave pseudoscientific validation to Rousseau's belief that "there is no scoundrel whose natural inclinations, had they been better directed, could not have produced great virtues."[60]

Defoe, Watts, and Richardson held parents who neglected their children's education ultimately responsible for the future disobedience of those children, but all dwelt at length on the sin of filial pride. Adam and Eve were guilty whether or not Jehovah had adequately prepared them for their confrontation with their corrupting tempter. Rousseau's belief in the natural goodness of the presocial state, however, obliged him to convict parents of disobedient children of the more serious crime of corrupting the pristine infant mind, rather than merely of the Lockean crime of having failed to form it. In his novel *Julie ou la Nouvelle Héloïse* (1760), Rousseau offered indictments more unqualified than anything a generation before: "Public manners can only be reformed by beginning with private vices, which naturally arise from parents," and "The vices and misfortunes of children are owing chiefly to the father's unnatural despotism."[61]

By the middle of the eighteenth century the family had become, in Ronald Paulson's words, "a context of explanation . . . a mitigation for the child's sins."[62] This was the final consequence of the loss of faith in an original nature, in original sin, implicit in Locke's theory of mind and the pedagogy it generated. By the period of the first organized colonial disobedience of English law, the Edenic drama had been naturalized: no longer a lazy sexton outside the garden of childhood innocence, an unnatural or neglectful parent or master was the serpent within.

For Rousseau, as much as for Locke, the end of education was the granting of a final "safe" independence. Parents who pit their own will against the little strength a child has to exercise condemn him to a fatal impotence and fail in their sacred responsibility of preparing their child for emergence into the world. "Children must then remain," Rousseau declared in the *Social Contract,* "bound to their father only as long as they have need of him for their own preservation. As soon as this need ceases the natural bond is dissolved."[63] Neither Locke nor Rousseau conceived of the granting of independence to grown children to be synonymous with, or necessarily antecedent to, the dissolution of the family. The point was not so much to create autonomous individuals, as individuals who could and would participate in society. They are made independent so they may become social and ultimately more truly filial. The granting of filial independence permitted the family to reorganize on a voluntaristic, equalitarian, affectional, and, consequently, more permanent basis. Indeed, the point most reiterated in Locke's *Education* is that the parent who provides his child with the proper education and access to experience will be revered long into his child's adulthood, as, similarly, the child who is dutiful and gratefully obedient to his parents will remain loved long after he has left home.

In summary, the new model of government argued by the new education insisted that force and imperiousness be surrendered in favor of guidance, a guidance more overt in Locke, more covert in Rousseau, a manipulated providence. It imagined as its ideal product a man made independent of all authority but that of the introjected voice of his educated reason, moral sense, or guided inclination. What the seventeenth and eighteenth centuries anxiously called "a masterless man" need not be feared if he had become his own master. "If you were a Servant," asked Franklin in 1758 in "The Way to Wealth," reminding his readers of the great lesson of the new education, "would you not be ashamed that a good Master should catch you idle. Are you then your own master, be ashamed to catch yourself idle."[64] The child properly educated stands "ashamed" rather than guilty, because he has violated not a code imposed upon him but his own expectations of himself.

That the new education could be successful even in its most extreme form is nowhere more amply demonstrated than by the case of what was arguably the most talented family raised in Revolutionary America, the family of Charles Willson Peale. The great painter, key figure in radical Philadelphia politics, and founder of the first museum of natural history in America was an ardent follower of Rousseau and raised his family in the 1770s and 1780s according to the prescriptions of Emile. Indeed, Peale went so far as to hang over the family hearth an allegorical Swiss engraving showing Rousseau as "liberator of childhood."[65] Repeatedly refusing to discipline his children and thus exercise a tyrannical authority, Peale rather encouraged their interests and constantly exposed them to the glorious experience of the natural world. Three of his sons (Rembrandt, Raphael, and Titian) were to become among the period's most important painters and naturalists.

But Peale's pedagogical enthusiasm went further than his family. He wanted to educate the new nation itself. Just after the war in 1784, he began to assemble his great museum that he dreamed would eventually contain taxidermically preserved examples of every animal species known to natural scientists, and all arranged according to Linnaeus's categories. It would be "a world in miniature," a "school of education" in which one could experience in a single building the awesome totality and grand design of nature.[66] Here would be the ultimate tended garden, not pictorial representation but real example, the world brought indoors and made available for the safe experiencing of all (the rattlesnakes only looked alive), the ultimate Rousseauistic "manipulation of things" in the service of education. Here would be the wonder of the American Enlightenment.

The hidden hand of education, the nurture that directs and guides nature rather than subdues it, offered not only a model for a new relationship between parents and children but, in its own way, a resolution of the larger question of the relationship of free will to determinism. In *The Freedom of the Will*, written four years before *Emile*, the great theologian Jonathan Edwards set forth a new understanding of the relation of formal to efficient cause, of man's will to God's. For half a century Edwards effectively closed debate on the issue by arguing brilliantly the doctrine that reduces (only somewhat uncomfortably) to the formula: Man has the freedom to do as he pleases, although he has no control over those influences that determine what it is he finds pleasurable. He may do as he will, but he does not determine his will. Volition follows the prevailing motive.[67] Rousseau's insistence that Emile "will do only what he wants to do, but the master's job is to see that he wants to do only what he should" domesticates Edwards's argument.[68] Edwards's accommodation and that of the new pedagogy are related expressions of that ultimate reconciliation sought by the mid-eighteenth century – in theology as well as in politics – between a just authority and a circumscribed but real liberty, between the psychological necessities of submission and assertion. Rousseau's hidden hand, Locke's exemplary influence, and the Scots' enlightened inclination functioned like Adam Smith's "invisible hand" to suggest that self-interest and the greater good could be served simultaneously. Indeed, the new pedagogy offered an even greater accommodation. It made compatible the two great competing intellectual systems of the age: idealism that viewed the universe as other-directed and materialism that saw matter as self-moving.

2

THE TRANSMISSION OF IDEOLOGY AND THE BESTSELLERS OF 1775

More than simply exerting a considerable influence on the eighteenth-century English novel, the new rationalist pedagogy (and its moral sense and Rousseauistic variations) may be said to have contributed immeasurably to the form of the novel's development. It is no accident that the rise of the English novel coincided with a new social emphasis on the moral and cultural significance of education; for it was only as a form of pedagogy that much of eighteenth-century fiction was considered acceptable and useful by a large portion of the English reading public.[1]

In consequence, an inordinate number of post-Richardsonian eighteenth-century novels are explicitly dedicated to preaching the new Lockean gospel either by positive or negative example. Their insistence upon the double necessity of filial obedience and parental restraint is part of a larger implicit glorification of the nuclear family and of the essential part the family was believed to play in returning purity and virtue to society. The major theme of such fiction is familial estrangement occasioned by one or another violation of the familial contract. The most common infractions of that contract by children are disobedient rebellion, prodigality, and too early departure from the parental roof – all of which result in the loss of honor, virginity, parental approval, or inheritance. The common infractions by parents all fall under what may be called parental tyranny: the unwillingness to acknowledge a child's reason and the rights it confers, the unwillingness to distinguish between childhood and adolescence or young adulthood. Parental tyranny thus parallels two other major concerns of eighteenth-century fiction and political rhetoric: flattery and seduction, both of which are attempts to subvert reason. Such tyranny usually takes one of several forms: denying a child a proper education, arranging a marriage for "familial aggrandizement," unjustly denying a child an inheritance, or irrationally preferring one child to another; in short, infringements of filial liberty or independence.

36

A short list of some of the more strident titles of late eighteenth-century fiction may suggest the spectrum of concern and the implicit terms of the Lockean contract. The first sixteen are novellas or fictional serials appearing in British magazines, and the last four are early American novels: *Filial Affection* (1798), *Benevolence and Gratitude* (1775), *Female Gratitude* (1788), *The Lost Daughter Recovered* (1783), *The Fatal Effects of Indulging the Passions* (1785), *The Lost Son* (1790), *The Fair Apostate* (1774), *The Indiscretions of Youth* (1786), *The School for Fathers* (1764), *Parental Tyranny* (1783), *The School for Parents* (1798), *Good Mother* (1764), *Bad Mother* (1768), *The Rigid Father or Paternal Authority* (1802), *Maternal Advice or The Good Effects of a Virtuous Education* (1808), *The Dangerous Effects of a Wrong Education* (1774), *Filial Affection or The Clergyman's Daughter* (1810), *Infidelity or The Victims of Sentiment* (1797), *The Fatal Effects of Parental Tyranny* (1798), *The Hapless Orphan* (1793).[2]

Though dozens of earlier English examples might serve as illustrations, two passages drawn from early American novels may suffice to represent the multitude of didactic accounts of the "fatal effects" of either filial disobedience or parental tyranny. The first is taken from Enos Hitchcock's *The Memoirs of the Bloomsgrove Family* (1790), which following hard on William Hill Brown's *The Power of Sympathy* (1789), the first American novel, cautions against the dangers of that power. Having served as a chaplain in the Revolutionary army, Hitchcock turned from the pulpit to pedagogical fiction.

The Bloomsgrove children are taught repeatedly that no happiness may be discovered outside the sway of parental sovereignty. The lesson is given force by way of illustrative examples, of which the following description of an unrepentant prodigal is characteristic:

> He never stopped in his fatal career, till he had reduced himself to beggary and broken the hearts of his parents. His vices at length undermined his constitution. . . . Emaciated by sickness and worn out with pain, he gave up the ghost, amidst the horrors of an awakened conscience, and the tremendous apprehensions of his future condition; and what rendered the scene most distressing was, that reflecting upon the neglect and indulgence of his parents, as the cause of all his miseries, he curses them with his dying breath.[3]

On second reading it is not clear if what is most "distressing" is the prodigal's blaming his broken-hearted parents for his own sinfulness or perhaps, as he claims, that *their* neglect is ultimately responsible for his fatal career. The passage suggests once again how complex questions of moral accountability become in a world preoccupied with distinguishing the one who acts from the one who influences.

Pointing up a complementary moral in her 1797 novel, *Parental Cru-*

elty, a "Mrs. Patterson" of Boston summarized generational relations as she observed them in late eighteenth-century New England:

> Parents are either the dupes or the tyrants of their children. Some parents keep their children at such an awful distance that home becomes a prison and they will flee to their neighbor's fireside for refuge, to secure themselves from the frowns of a turbulent parent. Several by misfortune, by their parents not granting them their wishes, are driven into a state of melancholy, languish, and die. . . . Others will indulge their children from their infancy until they are at a state of maturity, then check them for the same familiarity which they always indulged them in, and will not allow them to love for themselves, but they must love for them, which is many times the cause of conflict, banishment and death. . . . [4]

Both writers implicitly call for a new kind of familial relationship that would accommodate the new valuation of personal liberty rather than be sacrificed to it. Those volumes that most effectively answered that call, some famous and some now forgotten, became in almost every instance the bestsellers of their age and gave dramatic and rhetorical form to an ideology whose political implications were soon to become clear. Therein lies, as we shall see, their larger historical importance.

THE NEW PATERNITY AND THE BESTSELLERS OF 1775

In their monograph-length article "Ideology and the Psychology of National Liberation," one of the more influential studies of the American Revolution in recent years, Edwin Burrows and Michael Wallace make a convincing case that the rhetoric of familial discord was "the lingua franca of the Revolution." Nevertheless, they do not attempt in their article to trace that rhetoric to sources more immediate or specific than "the gradual displacement of patriarchalism by contractualism" and the generalized political influence of Locke's *Two Treatises of Civil Government* or to relate it to larger cultural issues.[5] Though they briefly deal with Locke's *Education,* they err in overemphasizing the influence of the *Treatises.* In fact, there is little evidence to indicate that any more than a small group of political figures and polemicists had an acquaintance with either Locke's *Treatises* or English political tracts directly influenced by them. A great deal of evidence does indicate, however, that a significantly large portion of the literate colonial population on the eve of the Revolution was acquainted with the basic arguments of Locke's *Education.* The arguments of *Education* and of the Scottish moral sense treatises were reproduced and championed by almost every bestselling pedagogical and literary work of the age. Such arguments prepared the colonial reading public to be responsive to a particular kind of political persuasion.[6]

Following Bernard Bailyn and others who have investigated the ideological and rhetorical origins of the American Revolution, Burrows and

Wallace implicitly presume that such origins must be searched out primarily in earlier political ideology and rhetoric. They make little effort
to examine texts other than those that are explicitly political or to
grapple with the problem of identifying implicit political or ideological
content in works of fiction, pedagogy, or in other "nonpolitical"
genres.[7] In consequence, they have chosen – as did Bailyn and Gordon
Wood before them – to ignore the important work done by Frank
Luther Mott, James Hart, Howard Mumford Jones, and to a lesser
degree Bernard Fay, which identifies through analyses of booksellers'
importation records, newspaper advertisements, and sales records the
titles of those books most widely purchased and read in Revolutionary
America.[8]

Only three of some five hundred extant titles published in the colonies in the critical year of Lexington and Concord would, eventually,
sell in excess of 20,000 copies, a figure representing one percent of the
population at the time of initial publication and Mott's definition of a
"bestseller." The three "bestsellers" of 1775 were *Lord Chesterfield's
Letters to His Son* (New York: Rivington and Gaine), John Gregory's *A
Father's Legacy to His Daughters* (Philadelphia: Dunlop), and Daniel Defoe's *Robinson Crusoe* (New York: Gaine).[9] The first two – intended to be
read by both adolescents and adults – were popular expositions of Lockean pedagogy. Whereas Chesterfield described the ideal education of a
son, Gregory set forth the ideal education of a daughter. So complementary were they that later in the century they would be bound together under a single imprint.[10] Unlike its companion bestsellers, the
heavily abridged Gaine edition of *Robinson Crusoe* was explicitly a "juvenile" intended, by the admission of its title page, for "young
readers." That *Crusoe*, first published in 1719, should receive its first
American edition in 1774 (reissued in 1775) during the period when the
American colonies were most vociferously declaring that they themselves had come of age is highly significant. That significance becomes
clear in light of Rousseau's declaration a dozen years earlier in *Emile,*
that as it "affords a compleat primer of natural education" (II, 60),
Robinson Crusoe is the "sole" volume a child entering the first stage of
self-sufficient manhood need own.

In 1772, to step back chronologically, the single bestselling volume in
America, according to Mott's list, was the first Philadelphia edition of
Oliver Goldsmith's *The Vicar of Wakefield* (1766), whose title character
represents one of the most successful attempts in eighteenth-century
fiction to set forth the ideal Lockean parent. In 1774 (there is no bestselling title in 1773), Mott's honor goes to the first American edition of
Laurence Sterne's *The Life and Adventures of Tristram Shandy* (1760), a
novel primarily and profoundly preoccupied with the great question of
how best to form a child's mind. Indeed, throughout the novel, Tris-

tram's father is engaged in composing a Lockean treatise on education entitled the *Tristapaedia*.[11]

The three most consistently popular French titles for the critical period 1770–4, according to Bernard Fay in *The Revolutionary Spirit in France and America,* were François Fénelon's *Telemachus,* Jean François Marmontel's *Moral Tales,* and Charles Rollin's *Ancient History.*[12] The first two of these are didactic fictions intended to set forth the proper relationship between parents and children, and the third, written by an educator, advances a theory of history ideologically consistent with the values set forth in his earlier pedagogical work.

As we shall presently see, the volumes Americans chose to read on the eve of Revolution constituted virtually a crash course on rational pedagogy, in general, and the ideal redefinition of parenthood and generational relations, in particular. When examined as a group, these volumes present a remarkably consistent ideology, one the Revolutionary reading public found particularly attractive. It provided those readers with a new paradigm or framework for perceiving the larger meaning of their political situation.

THE PEDAGOGUES

The more than 300 letters Lord Chesterfield addressed to his son Philip during the latter's extended tour of Europe were designed to "form and enlighten" his "young and giddy mind." At the heart of the epistolary relationship between father and son is a contract: "I think I offer you a very good bargain, when I promise you upon my word that, if you do everything that I would have you do till you are eighteen, I will do everything that you would have me do ever afterwards."[13] A true parent, Chesterfield suggests, does not fear his child leaving home upon coming of age, for by then such a parent would have discharged properly his responsibility for morally educating his child. In contrast, the parent who persists in imposing the parental yoke on grown children unwittingly confesses to his failure to prepare his charges for the temptations of a life of dutiful independence. In a later letter Chesterfield develops the theme:

> After that I promise that you shall be your own master, and that I will pretend to no other title than that of your best and truest friend. You shall receive advice, but no orders from me; and in truth you shall want no other advice but such as youth and inexperience must necessarily require (p. 116).

Recognizing that the purest bond between father and son is affection rather than consanguinity, Chesterfield humbly relinquishes the aristocratic name of "father" for the sentimental name of "friend." Immediately after Philip's eighteenth birthday, Chesterfield conscientiously changes the salutations of his letters from "Dear Boy" to "Dear Friend." Throughout the letters, he scrupulously refuses to call upon parental authority in his precepting. The following passage is representative:

> These are not the dictates of a peevish, sour old fellow who affects to give good rules, when he cannot longer give bad examples, but the advice of an indulgent, tender friend, I had almost said, parent (p. 92).

As rational equalitarian friendship was neither habitual, like the instinctive and dutiful affection of an infant child for his parent, nor dangerously passionate, it was hailed in numerous eighteenth-century volumes as the ideal relationship. In *Amelia* (1751), Fielding identifies it with sensibility, defining it as "that tender disposition which feels the misery of others," calling it elsewhere "the balm of life."[14] John Adams uses "Dear Friend" as the salutation of choice in his letters to Abigail.[15] Edward Young declares it "flow'r of heav'nly seed": "Poor is the friendless master of a world / A world in purchase of a friend is gain."[16] And Julie, the heroine of Rousseau's *La Nouvelle Héloïse,* invoking the cyclical view of history, goes so far as to declare: "The empire of love is at an end, that of friendship has begun."[17] In the age of enlightenment, the acquisitive tyranny of love and the servility of duty will give way to the rational, protective, and mutually satisfying "contracts" of friendship, which Chesterfield defines as the voluntary appreciation of "reciprocal merit."[18]

Chesterfield's politics, though far from republican, are noticeably consistent with his pedagogy. In the last known letter to his son, dated December 27, 1765, he makes this connection explicit. Parliament has just learned of the colonial resistance to the Stamp Act:

> The Administration are for some indulgence and forbearance to those forward children of their mother country; the Opposition are for taking vigorous, as they call them, but I call them violent measures; not less than *les dragonades.* . . . For my part, I never saw a forward child mended by whipping; and I would not have the mother country become a step-mother (p. 284).

Though tainted with an element of politic affectation, Chesterfield's reluctance to call himself "father" before his grown son and his implicit belief in the equality of all adult generations are both natural corollaries of a larger historical assumption, one much debated in the eighteenth century: the equality of the ancients and moderns. In one letter to his son he declares, "I can no more suppose that men were braver, wiser, fifteen hundred or three thousand years ago, than I can suppose that the animals or vegetables were better than they are now" (p. 92). In another letter he adds, "Speak of the Moderns without contempt and the Ancients without Idolatry" (p. 46). For "Ancients" and "Moderns," one might read

"Fathers" and "Sons." As parents must learn to respect their children, so children must respect their parents for their merits rather than blindly and irrationally idolize them.

In keeping with most of the Enlightenment theorists, Chesterfield holds, instead of the older degenerative view, a cyclical (and thus leveling) view of history, one that, in effect, presupposed natural and periodic "revolutions" in the root sense of that word.[19] He is adamant in urging Philip "to know perfectly the decline of ancient and modern empires and to trace out and to reflect upon the cause of both" (p. 41). Such advice, common to pedagogical works of the period, implicitly suggests that the study of the sins and errors of earlier generations and civilizations may lead eventually to a breakthrough: a passage from cyclical to progressive history. As we shall see later, the American Revolution was one attempt to realize that hope: to bring cyclical history to a glorious standstill by an accommodation of liberty and authority, thereby permitting the final empire to "rise" indefinitely.

The course of empire theme that Chesterfield insists his son search out "perfectly" was given its most popular nonpolitical restatement in James Thomson's *The Seasons* (1726–30), one of the most quoted volumes of poetry in Revolutionary America. The round of seasons was the natural model for all other true revolutions (as opposed to "rebellions," which violated the processes of nature), not the least of which was the succession of generations. Thomson describes the coming of spring in the same terms Chesterfield describes his epistolary enterprise:

> infant reason grows apace, and calls
> For the kind hand of an assiduous care
> Delightful task! to rear the tender thought,
> To teach the young idea how to shoot
> To pour the fresh instruction o'er the mind.

It is far from surprising that both Paine and Franklin would cite *The Seasons* prominently in their great antipatriarchal works.[20] The volume Chesterfield recommends for such an important exercise as the study of the cyclical course of history, however, is a long work by the Jansenist educational theorist Charles Rollin. Popular in England and imported to the colonies in multivolume sex-decimos, Rollin's bestselling *Ancient History of the Egyptians, Carthaginians, Assyrians, Babylonians, Medes and Persians, Macedonians, and Grecians* (1730–1738) outsold such ancient and contemporary classics as Josephus's *History of the Jews* and Daniel Neals's *History of the Puritans*.[21] It saw in the rise and fall of all these empires the same revolutionary alternation of national virtue and corrupting luxury.

Rollin traces the origin of this fatal cycle of empires to the earliest institutionalizing of primogeniture:

In these early ages, every father was the supreme head of his family . . . the defender and protector of those, who, by their birth, education, and weakness, were under his protection and safeguard. But although these masters enjoyed an independent authority, they made a mild and paternal use of it. . . . They dealt as equals . . . with such children as were come to years of maturity. . . . But different motives gave rise to different laws. One man overjoyed at the birth of a first-born son, resolved to distinguish him from his future children, by bestowing on him a more considerable share of his possession, and by giving him a greater authority in his family (p. 202).

The irrational preference by a parent for one son over another is the original sin that inaugurates modern history. Thus is established the conflict between first and second sons that will bring down empires.

The alienation of sons is not, however, the only cause of the historical dynamic. The cycle of rise and decline also carries with it a divine message. In his Preface, Rollin feels compelled to justify the study of profane history by arguing its ultimate "usefulness with regards to religion." Put simply, his argument is that a history of the "glory and felicity" and "declension and fall" of empires properly presented is elevated to the level of sacred history by the moral to which it necessarily points:

> that God disposes all events as supreme Lord and Sovereign; that He alone determines the fate of kings, and the duration of empires and that He transfers the government of kingdoms from one nation to another because of unrighteous dealings and wickedness committed therein (p. 3).

Despite its orthodox ring, Rollin's justification contains a seed of heterodoxy. For insofar as it suggests that God maintains an identical relationship with all nations, it calls into question the essential premise of the Old Testament: Jehovah's special relationship to the Israelites. Rollin does all he can to have it both ways. He hastily invokes a distinction between father and master in order to insist that though God has embraced the Israelites as his chosen people, he is innocent of the charge of parental favoritism Rollin was to level against "the latter races."

> It must be confessed, that if we compare the attentive, beneficial and evident manner in which the Almighty presided anciently over his people, with that which appeared in his governing all other nations of the earth, one would be apt to conclude that the latter were foreign and indifferent to him. . . . God looked upon the holy nation as his own domain and inheritance; he resided in the midst of it, as a father in his family. Israel was his son, his first born, he had made it his delight to form him from his infancy and to instruct him in person. . . . Though it would be an error highly injurious to the Al-

mighty to suppose him the master only of one family, and not of all
the nations of the world; he is father to only one (p. 16).
If sacred history, that period in which God still deigned to reveal himself to his disciples, may be described as an account of a parent's relationship to his child, profane or modern history may be described as a
period of guardianship during which God withholds his presence and
delegates to others the specific responsibility of forming infant minds.
Though he has created all men, he is father only to those whose minds
he has educated. The parent who does not form his child's character is
only that child's master, but not, in the new republican sense of the
word, his father. In modern history parents, by becoming educators,
must assume the role God had assumed for his chosen people.

John Gregory's *A Father's Legacy to His Daughters,* the next volume in
this constellation of bestsellers, was the most popular contemporary
account of how to discharge that divinely delegated responsibility with
regard to daughters rather than sons.[22] That Gregory's work is completely without literary merit suggests the transcendent fascination its
theme held for the American reader. The "legacy" in question is neither
cash nor property – meanings that word would almost automatically
have carried a generation before – but wisdom, in the form of extended
epistolary advice from a dying father to his two daughters. Like Chesterfield's *Letters,* Gregory's *Legacy* was popular precisely because it was
believed not to have been written for publication. Having made this
point, one American editor concludes that in Gregory's *Legacy,* readers
may hear "paternal love and paternal care speak their genuine sentiments undisguised and unrestrained" (p. vi).

Gregory is convinced that an even more pressing threat to a young
woman than the corrupting influences of others is the temptation to
abuse her own power over men: "The power of a fine woman over the
hearts of men, of men of the finest parts, is even beyond what she
conceives. They are sensible of the pleasing illusion but they cannot,
nor do they wish to dissolve it" (p. 54). A good daughter, like a good
king, will not abuse her power or tyrannize over the hearts of men.
Rather, she will "dispell the charm and may soon reduce the angel to a
very ordinary girl" (p. 55), understanding that to be an object of idolatry dangerously tempts one to believe one is an idol worthy of such
esteem. Like Chesterfield, Gregory strikes the rationalist note: power
must be demystified and equated with merit. And the anxious note:
charm and the illusion it creates must not be confused with reality.

In an age that extolled the marriage bond, Gregory's sentiments on
that much-discussed subject are highly unorthodox. Acknowledging
"the forlorn and unprotected situation of an old maid" and conceding
"that you may attain a superior degree of happiness in a married state to

what you can possibly find in any other," Gregory still insists: "I know nothing that renders a woman more despicable, than her thinking it essential to happiness to be married. Besides the gross indelicacy of the sentiment, it is a false one" (p. 116). Gravely he cautions his daughters: "miserable will be your fate, if you allow an attachment to steal on you before you are sure of a return, or what is infinitely worse, where there are wanting those qualities which can alone insure happiness in a married state" (p. 116). Such warnings that only the fully reciprocated "return" of affections justifies the surrender of independence contributed to an argument that would soon be invoked to justify colonial separation from England.[23]

Gregory draws at one point an implicit analogy between a daughter exercising her feminine charm and a king controlling the hearts of others. Because flattery may contribute as much to a woman's downfall as to a king's, Gregory urges his daughters to pay special heed to their father, for he alone among men "has no interest in flattering or deceiving you" (p. 143). The parental role is made analogous to that of a trusted court adviser. Bernard Bailyn has convincingly demonstrated the degree to which eighteenth-century Anglo-American political science was preoccupied with the corrupting powers of flattering and conspiratorial ministers.[24] The king's ministers were feared to represent, in the anxious words of one observer whom Bailyn cites, "a kind of fourth power that the constitution knows nothing of, or has not provided against," whose arbitrary power "absolutely controls King, Lords and Commons" (p. 124). Yet like the related anxieties over the "enchanting sound" of Whitefield's Awakening sermons[25] and the insinuating address of Lovelace, the concern over ministerial conspiracy and "misrepresentation" was far from being, as Bailyn describes it, solely a political anxiety. Rather, it followed inevitably on the emphases of Lockean sensationalism: the impressionistic nature of the human mind, the power of positive and negative examples, and the inherent predilection of man to surrender to subrational appeals. Here were the philosophical origins of Country party politics. Flattery was the dark reverse side of rational education. It sought to inform the mind in order to control it rather than to free it. It was the "poysonous and pernicious weed" that would destroy the carefully tended garden.[26] And as such it was to be abjured even in places it had long been appropriate. The dedication to Paul Rapin's History of England (1724–31), an extremely popular book in the colonies because of its sympathetic account of Cromwell and the Commonwealth period, reads in part: "Here then from a faithful servant, uninfluenced by hopes and fears, Your Royal Highness will agree that to Princes nothing is so pernicious as flattery." A half century later, Jefferson defended the "freedom" of his language in *A Summary View of the Rights of British America* by concluding "Let those flatter, who fear: It is not an American art."[27]

Whereas lying and deceitful ministers were condemned by the Whig press on both sides of the Atlantic for misinforming George III as to the real state of affairs in America and for providing him with, in Jefferson's phrase, a "Tory education,"[28] the beneficent effects of honest ministers on aging kings or those of virtuous tutors on young princes were applauded. Works of fiction or history that recounted such relationships, although popular since the Renaissance, found especially ready audiences in both eighteenth-century England and America. In colonial America the two most widely read volumes dealing with this theme were Maximilien Sully's *Memoirs*,[29] an account of his years as "incorruptible minister" to Henry IV, and François Fénelon's *Telemachus*, a narrative written by the tutor to the Dauphin's son expressly for the latter's use, which popularized the modern sense of the word "mentor."

From 1689 to 1697, François Fénelon was engaged as tutor to the Duke of Burgundy, eldest son of the Dauphin and eventual heir to the French crown. That his pedagogical novel, *Telemachus* (1699), detailing the hero's search for his father, Ulysses, should continue to enjoy a popularity seventy-five years after its initial publication must command our attention. That one of the most popular British journals, *The Universal Magazine of Knowledge and Pleasure*, should choose to run a redaction of the novel in twelve installments over the three-year period 1778–80 suggests that at least one editor resolutely believed it relevant for the times. More than Gregory or Chesterfield, Fénelon spoke directly to the most pressing psychological issues of Revolutionary Americans and their relation to Britain. Fénelon's epic of the son was designed to be for the Moderns what Homer's epic of the father had been for the Ancients: the distillation of an age's values and wisdom into a narrative of one man's adventures.

Telemachus has two themes: the moral education of a prince and a son's search for his lost father. These themes are deliberately interwoven so as to suggest that they are ultimately identical. For the more than ten years since the fall of Troy, Ulysses has been prevented from returning home to his wife and son by the malevolent winds and waves under the command of Neptune. Before he left for war, however, fearing that in his absence his son might be cheated of an education or seduced from virtue, Ulysses instructed his friends, "I leave with you this son, whom I so tenderly love: watch over his infancy; if you have any love for me, keep flattery far from him; teach him to vanquish his passions."[30] Later, Telemachus would recall "at that time they treated me not as a child but as a man, whose reason might assist them" (I, 119).

Fearing for his mother, Penelope, who had for so long been besieged by suitors, Telemachus, now nearly grown, chooses to trace his father's sea route to locate his lost parent. The lessons he will learn in the course of his travels will complete the education begun at home. He is assisted throughout his quest by Minerva, the goddess of wisdom, who has disguised herself in the male form of Mentor, presumed by Telemachus to be one of his father's friends.

Early in their first voyage their vessel is saved from shipwreck when Mentor takes over the wheel from the pilot. Having earlier failed to heed his advice, Telemachus turns to his guide:

> My dear Mentor . . . why did I reject your counsel? Am I not most wretched in having presumed to trust my own opinion, at an age which can form no judgement of the future, has gained no experience from the past. . . . If we should survive this tempest, I will distrust myself as my most dangerous enemy, in you alone, Mentor, will I ever confide (I, 56).

Having learned to look to the proper authority outside of himself, Telemachus begins an education that, when secured, will ultimately allow him to trust himself.

In the course of his travels Telemachus embraces a series of surrogate fathers, from each of whom he learns a particular moral lesson. First, he encounters Termosiris, who Telemachus says, "called me his son and I afterward addressed him as a father" (I, 78). Termosiris instructs him in the human passions he should avoid. Next, he encounters Hazael, who is typical of the adoptive parents who try to quiet Telemachus's anxious mind: "Follow me, son of Ulysses! I will be your father till you find him from whom you have derived your being. The earth like a good parent multiplies her gifts in proportion to the number of her children who merit her bounty!" (I, 138). Telemachus at last discovers the aged Nestor, Ulysses's own preceptor and the "father" of Ulysses's mind. Telemachus is overjoyed:

> O my father! I fear not to claim you by the dearest tie. The loss of him from whom I derived my birth, and the parental kindness which I have experienced in you, give me a right to call you by that tender name. You are a father whom I again am permitted to embrace. O might I once more be permitted to embrace you! If anything can atone for his loss, it is the finding his wisdom, his virtue, and his tenderness, in you (I, 302).

As in the Psalms, "father" is used here at once as a term of praise and as denoting the ideal parent of one's disposition, in opposition to the parent of one's being.

Early in the second volume of the novel, Mentor, Nestor, and Telemachus discuss familial relations in the ideal republic:

> As to the children, Mentor said that they belonged less to their parents than to the state. "They are the children of the community," said he and "They are at once its hope and its strength. . . . Let him enforce, with inflexible constancy, the laws of Minos, which ordain . . . that children from their tenderest youth, shall be taught to commemorate the achievements of heroes . . . who have sacrificed private interest to their country" (II, 52).

Nestor's account is meant to encourage Telemachus to take consolation in *patria* for the loss of *pater*. But by now Telemachus is preoccupied with a second loss that he has been forced to endure, one even more painful than the first: a loss of esteem for the man who gave him birth. Having learned from both friends and enemies of his father that Ulysses, although a great hero, was less than a "perfect" man, Telemachus reluctantly surrenders the idealized image of his father to which he had long naively clung. When later he learns that Idomeneus, the surrogate father to whom he is most attached, had once many years before sacrificed his son to the gods in a moment of passion, Telemachus despairs that there is not a man alive who is a perfect model of virtue. Minerva confirms his dark speculation, but cautions her charge not to be blinded to a man's virtues because of his vices: "You ought not only to love, respect and imitate your father, notwithstanding his imperfections, but you ought very highly to esteem Idomeneus, notwithstanding such parts of his character and conduct which I have shown deserve censure" (II, 336).

Minerva's advice reflects the essentially neo-Platonic character of Fénelon's own Quietistic faith. An uneasy marriage of Platonic idealism and Catholicism, seventeenth-century Quietism abjured the "idolatrous" worship of the Catholic saints in favor of a purer worship of the divine Christ. Just as Fénelon, under the guidance of Madame Guyon, had surrendered his idolatrous faith in the existence of ideal beings, so Telemachus must surrender his faith in his perfect father.[31] A parent must tailor what he expects from his child to the latter's youthful capacities, but no less must a child recognize and accept his parent's limitations. The point Fénelon makes through Minerva again and again is that all men, no matter how virtuous they may seem, are fallen versions of a transcendent virtue and that no one among them should be expected to be more worthy of imitation than any other. The example of one's parent, like that of any other man or woman, should not be allowed to be any more prescriptive than its merits demand, and thus it must also be supplemented both by other equally partial examples of virtue and by the tutorial character of experience. Minerva, Telemachus's "male" guardian, functions as the Platonic ideal in the novel, the transcendent paternal exemplar who, though she does not condemn, exposes the imperfections of all men. Thus, the persistent irony of the novel is that Telemachus has been traveling with his true father or, in his words, "greater father," Mentor – alternately as divine wisdom, reason, and virtue incarnate – from the very first.[32]

In this eighteenth-century retelling, Ulysses's absence is finally less a curse to his son than it is a blessing; for it permits Telemachus to see beyond the illusion of human perfection to the tutorial parenthood of all men and to the divine perfection of the deity. It permits him finally to realize that in the course of his quest for his parent he has attained the very wisdom he once believed he might only receive from that parent. It is to these lessons that Minerva refers when she declares: "The best precepts of the wise Ulysses would instruct you less than his absence, and the suffering which, while you sought him, you have endured" (II, 304). Minerva is ultimately more than a divine guide. She is finally Telemachus's own informed reason; when she disappears (or is internalized), he has become an adult. The child has become its own father.

Joseph Nancrède, instructor of French at Harvard, dedicated his 1794 translation of *Telemachus* to "the youth of America."[33] He believed they stood to profit as much as the novel's hero by the counsels of Minerva. One significant index of the pervasive influence of Fénelon's book in America is the extent to which the Minerva/Mentor figure appears in late eighteenth-century iconography. In a cartoon print entitled "The Deplorable State of America," advertised in Boston in 1765, Britannia, the British parent, is shown handing her daughter, America, a gift labeled "Pandora's Box." Minerva in full Roman garb hovers over America counseling her not to take the "gift." Significantly, the cartoon opposes Minerva to Britannia as true parent to false. There is some small irony in the fact that Thomas Hutchinson, the exiled Loyalist governor of Massachusetts, should be obliged to sail home on the *Minerva*.[34] As Minerva was also the national symbol of France, her presence in cartoons that appeared after France had allied itself to America in 1778 takes on a more explicitly political significance and suggests symbolically the degree to which the friendship of France served to fill the void left by the loss of British parenting.[35] Eventually, Minerva would give way to a more naturalized icon, "the genius of America," most often represented as an older woman sorrowing for young America.

The point that Gregory, Chesterfield, Sully, and Fénelon all make is that the true parent of a child, be that child prince or pauper, is he or she who has exercised the most influence on that child's mind and character and who encourages and helps develop a self-trust. Francis Hutcheson put it succinctly in his *System of Moral Philosophy* (1755): "Whoever voluntarily undertakes the necessary office of rearing and educating, obtains the parental power without generation." Thus, tutors and court ministers are as emphatically "true parents" as natural parents who forfeit their pedagogical responsibility to their children may be designated "false parents." From this perspective, it is not surprising to find then the heroines of several of the most popular novels in eighteenth-century America rebelling against parents "who [her] education cruelly neglected" or withholding affection from parents "who never took a part in forming [her] mind and from whom [she] never received the caresses or the counsels of a father."[36]

With the appearance of Rousseau's *Julie ou la Nouvelle Héloïse,* the theme of a young girl falling in love with her tutor, whose influence over her had eclipsed that of her father, would become a commonplace of romantic fiction. By delegating the parental responsibility for his daughter's education to a private tutor, Julie's father unwittingly had surrendered part of his parental authority.[37] The debate over the pros and cons of private tutors – which Locke had taken up at some length – logically extended to a debate at midcentury over the merits and demerits of fiction itself. Were novels a beneficial supplement to parental authority or did they undermine the primacy of that authority?

Though few could hope to have their own tutors, those of the Anglo-American literate class who scrupled to read the "new" fiction most probably had a favorite novelist on whose didactic counsel they relied. In the preface to the third edition of Richardson's *Pamela,* an enthusiastic admirer of the novel is quoted as commending Richardson on the tremendous moral influence he has exerted in England, an influence that has made the novelist "Parent to millions of minds."[38] It is very much in this sense that the "virtuous Washington" would displace George III and become designated "Father of his Country." That displacement would come to symbolize, as we shall see, the greater triumph of the moral preceptor over the "consanguineous" parent. Whereas one must remain a son or daughter until the death of one's parent, one's tenure under a preceptor is necessarily more circumscribed. Indeed, the refrain of the ideal parent *is* the refrain of the moral preceptor. Gregory's *Legacy* concludes:

> If I live till you arrive at that age when you shall be capable to judge for yourself and do not strangely alter my sentiments, I shall act towards you in a very different manner from which most parents do. My opinion has always been that when that period arrives, the parental authority ceases (p. 123).

Gregory's works had no less than eight American editions between the years 1775 and 1782. Few other titles, if any, achieved equivalent wartime success. The tender solicitude of a dying parent for the future welfare of his children and his commitment to preparing them *for* the world rather than keeping them *from* it, undoubtedly moved those

American readers who were, at that moment, anxiously embracing their independence without the benefit of such a legacy as Gregory's. Chesterfield, Gregory, and Fénelon were but three of the most-read authors who contributed to popularizing values whose political implications in the pressurized American context would be put to revolutionary purposes. We now turn from bestselling works of pedagogy to bestselling works of fiction. In the eighteenth century the distinction is far from absolute, as the figure of François Marmontel testifies.

THE MORALISTS

The eldest of five orphaned children, Jean François Marmontel served in his adolescence as "father"[39] (the word is his) to his siblings. The trauma of being orphaned, combined with the satisfaction of successfully managing his fraternal family, no doubt predisposed him to embrace and champion the Lockean ideal of a "created" family, united by choice and not merely by the accident of birth. Again and again, Marmontel would extol the family bound by mutual affection and respect rather than by the accidental and habitual ties of blood and duty.

In his tale "The Errors of a Good Father" (1764), the heroine expresses what for the author was one of the most important truths when she declares of her adopted parent: "Natural affection between him and me is become so habitual that it has acquired the force of natural attachment, and the ties of adoption have connected us with the same strength as if they were the bonds of consanguinity."[40] Marmontel makes the bond of affection as much a relationship of nature – through habituation it has become second nature – as the bond of consanguinity. The "blind fondness" of natural children for their parents is the *habit* of nature; felt and reasoned affection, whether ultimately given to blood relations or nonconsanguineous loved ones, is the *will* of nature, its only will.

Perhaps no single book in the eighteenth century was more responsible for popularizing the rationalist criteria by which good and evil parents might be distinguished than Marmontel's three volumes of *Les Contes Moraux (Moral Tales)* (1766). Having remarked on the unprecedented frequency with which the *Contes Moraux* were individually reprinted in eighteenth-century British periodicals during the period 1765–1800, Robert Mayo, the foremost bibliographer of those periodicals, concludes:

> The rage for Marmontel . . . seemed to transcend the transient conditions of the literary climate, and govern the taste of a whole age. It was supported by . . . magazines, including the *Gentleman's* and even won the grudging approval of the monthly reviewers. It is altogether the single most extraordinary phenomenon in the realm of magazine

fiction in translation, although the *Contes Moraux* have received only slight attention from modern historians of the novel.[41]

It is characteristic of the directness with which Marmontel approached contemporary issues that two of the most popular of the tales are entitled "The Good Mother" and "The Bad Mother."

If neglecting a child's education and preparation for moral and physical independence were, by Lockean lights, the greatest of parental sins, a close second was a parent's irrational preference of one child, usually the eldest, over another. Rational pedagogy took up with a vengeance the cause of "second sons" against the institution of primogeniture, the original sin in Rollin's history, which not only inequitably distributed the parental estate, but all too often inequitably divided parental affection and thus forced the second son into the prodigality for which he is blamed in Christ's parable. Merit, not the accident of age, must establish social status and earn a parent's love. Echoing the contemporary attack on court "favorites," Marmontel's "The Bad Mother" opens with a definition of the human species to be examined:

> Among the monstrous productions of nature, we may reckon the heart of a mother who loves one of her children to the exclusion of the rest. I do not mean an enlightened tenderness, which distinguishes among the young plants it cultivates, that which yields the best returns to its early care; I speak of a blind fondness.[42]

Having argued with her dying husband that "in order to retain children under the dependence of a mother, it was necessary to render her the dispenser of the effects intended for them," Madame de Carandon succeeds in extorting from him the right "to regulate the partition of his effects" (p. 216). She has gone to such lengths to secure that privilege in order to disinherit her youngest son Jemmy, whom she irrationally despises and chooses to deprive of all education. Thus, she is in a position to bestow the entire parental estate upon her adored firstborn, Corée, whom she intends to provide with a private education. Convinced that Jemmy is a bad moral influence on his elder brother, Madame not only arranges to disinherit him but orders him to leave home at once. Obedient to his parent's wish, Jemmy goes to sea and eventually arrives in America. There he marries a kind and compassionate American girl, Lucella, and settles down to a successful and contented life.

Three years later, however, the disturbing news arrives that his mother has been reduced to poverty through the excessive indulgence of her eldest son. After she is no longer a reliable source of funds, Corée viciously snubs her and leaves her to struggle alone. Moved to tears by this news and supported by his new wife, Jemmy decides to sell his small estate and to take the capital with him to France to pay his mother's debts. When pirates attack the ship on which he is sailing, Jemmy slays a half-dozen of them single-handedly, all the while crying out, "Oh! my poor mother!" Inspired by his sacred mission, he acts like "a god who fights for us" (p. 229).

At last arriving in France, he redeems his mother's accounts and is reunited with Madame de Carandon, whom he finds deathly ill. "The revolution created by joy, and the calm which succeeds it insensibly re-animated in her the organs of life" (p. 231). Fully recovered, Madame repents of her severity and confesses her belief that "heaven has punished me for having loved too much an unnatural son" (p. 230). It is indicative of the new values for which Marmontel is a spokesman that "natural" and "unnatural" as applied to children in his tales are always judgments of conduct rather than designations of legitimacy or illegitimacy. Madame de Carandon's decision to embark with her son for America "restored her a new life" and the story ends with Jemmy joyfully anticipating embracing at once his mother and his wife. Lucella, as expected, receives "the mother of her lover as she would have received her own mother" (p. 232).

Thus do son, wife, and mother-in-law become the nucleus of a new family whose members have essentially chosen to live with one another. Significantly, the home of this rehabilitated family is America. There one may marry for love; there the son who is denied a fortune may earn it by the sweat of his brow; and there the prodigal parent must come and repent. Marmontel has consciously reversed the roles of the gospel parable of the prodigal son. In "Bad Mother," it is the parent who, once separated from the wise counsels of her son, riots in indulgence and destroys her reputation. And it is the child to whom the parent must return penitently to live.

As was true of its complementary *histoire*, "The Good Mother" also opens with a pronouncement once again making clear that only parental care can make safe the passage to a world of a "thousand seducing forms":

> The care of a mother for her children is, of all the duties, the most religiously observed in nature. This universal sentiment governs all the passions; it prevails even over the love of life. It renders the fiercest of animals sensible and gentle, the most sluggish indefatigable. . . .
>
> In the midst of a world, where vice, ingenious to disguise itself, takes a thousand seducing forms; the more selves there are . . . the more need has the frail bark of innocence and happiness of a prudent pilot (p. 233).

This tale also concerns a widow, but one who on her husband's deathbed vows to dedicate her life to the education and befriending of her only daughter, Emilia: "I have lost my husband. . . . I have nothing but my daughter and myself: shall I live for myself? or shall I live for her? The world smiles upon me, and pleases me still; but if I give myself up to it, I abandon my daughter, and hazard her happiness and my own" (p. 234).

The primary action of the story revolves around Emilia's inability to choose one of two suitors as her future husband. Though her mother knows full well that one of these two is a rogue, Madame de Tröene is reluctant to oblige her daughter to marry a man who may not be the choice of her own affections. For, as this enlightened parent declares: "There is no loving out of duty." Though good parents must not be indifferent to the cause of their children's happiness and thus "present to the world odious examples of too early desertion, neither ought they interfere in matters in which personal volition is essential." The good mother resolves her dilemma by arranging a colloquy between the two suitors that serves to reveal to Emilia their true characters. Madame de Tröene defends her position on parental interference in terms that echo Rousseau's domestication of Jonathan Edwards's argument on the will: " . . . let her inclination decide it [the question of which spouse]; but I may direct her inclination by enlightening it, and that is the only lawful use of authority given me" (p. 242).

"The Good Mother" concludes, as had its companion, with a polemical reminder that the child allowed to love freely will love his or her parents more, not less. It is not the heart inclined to another that will tempt a child to abandon his or her parent, but only the severity of an unloving parent. Unlike so many other sentimental fictions, Marmontel's tales do not revolve around the conflict of romantic love and filial duty; for his point is invariably that a marriage freely undertaken will necessarily strengthen rather than weaken the nuclear family: "Belzor's affection was divided between Emilia and her mother and it was a moot point among the world which one of them he loved best" (p. 258). In the family truly founded on affection, there is no distinction made between the love of a wife and the love of a parent. In such a family there is but one kind of love: Christian love and friendship.

As with virtually all eighteenth-century novelists who chose to take up the familial theme, Marmontel is primarily concerned with preserving and strengthening the institution of the family. His commitment renders him – as it did Richardson – a conservative in politics, though a conservative of a special sort. Marmontel's only explicitly political work is a fictionized treatment of the last years of the Roman general, Belisarius (*Bélisaire,* 1765).[43] For twenty-five years Belisarius had distinguished himself as counselor to his sovereign, Justinian, and as a benefactor to the Roman people. When Justinian is overthrown, however, by a republican faction, Belisarius is tried and convicted of treason for his unwillingness to participate in the rebellion. Though blind and bent over in age, he is exiled to the countryside. There, after much wandering, he meets Justinian, who, disguised as a beggar, has himself escaped the same tribunal. Unaware that he is speaking with the king for whose cause he has become a martyr, Belisarius launches into a defense of his political views. Although acknowledging the injustices of Justinian's reign, he declares: "laws perverted" were better than ineffectual laws that would "suffer open violation" (p. 17). He pleads that compassion be shown the deposed king, arguing the tremendous difficulty of the kingly office: "For if the father of a family, who has the charge of five or six children to educate, and to establish in the world, feels an incessant anxiety—what must be the care of the chief of a family which is counted in the millions?" (p. 37). Though Belisarius vigorously argues the virtue of passive obedience, his reasoning is neither Filmerian nor monarchical; rather, it is consistent with the values of sensibility. As parents must not make unrealistic and severe exactions in their demands on their children, so must not—to reverse the terms—the governed of the governors. Belisarius's argument follows precisely the Lockean/Rousseauistic argument summarized by Mrs. Brant in her popular *Sketches in Intellectual Education* addressed to midcentury mothers: "By demanding too much we shall disgust or discourage him [one's son] from performing what he might find able to perform under more cheering influence."[44] In different contexts, and in the service of different morals, the figure of Belisarius would be conjured by both Whigs and Tories during the long course of unrest between England and her colonies.

    ⊁ Among the significant events of the year 1766 were the repeal of the Stamp Act—the first and most important Parliamentary concession to organized colonial opposition—the appearance of the first full-length English translation of the *Contes Moraux,* and, finally, the publication of the next bestseller in our sequence: Oliver Goldsmith's slim but enormously important novel, *The Vicar of Wakefield.* Though delicately wrought and gently moral in its tone, the *Vicar* is a story of survival, the story of how one family—the Primrose family—survives intact its "Odyssey of Undeserved Disasters."[45] Their saga, however, is emblematic of a larger dilemma, one central to most of what are the great works of eighteenth-century fiction: the problem of how the innocent and the good may be allowed to survive and triumph in a world that is at once corrupt and amoral. Presuming the world to be as constitutionally good as himself, Dr. Primrose trusts in all the men he meets only to be betrayed by all but one.

Yet, the Vicar is not so naive as to be unaware of the need to clothe

Vicar of Wakefield

ideal embodiment of Lockean Paternity

innocence in armor. Thus he is deeply committed to providing his children with the kind of education that will protect them from the world's insensitivity, with "such an education as could render them callous to contempt" (p. 167) when neighbors scorn them for the poverty into which they are forced, an education that will imbue them with an instinct for survival to balance the selflessness that good Christians too often take to excess. Early in the novel, the Vicar, whose children have never "had the least constraint put upon their affections," speaks of his family in terms that identify him as the ideal embodiment of Lockean paternity:

> My children, the offspring of temperance, as they were educated without softness, so they were at once well formed and healthy . . . When I stood in the midst of the little circle which promised to be the supports of my declining age, I could not avoid repeating the famous story of Count Abensberg, who in Henry II's progress through Germany, when other courtiers came with their treasures, brought his thirty-two children and presented them to his sovereign as the most valuable offering he had to bestow. In this manner, though I had but six I considered them as a very valuable present made to my country, and consequently looked upon it as my debtor (pp. 19–20).

Consistent with his crucial awareness that his children belong finally not to him but to society at large, the Vicar conceives of himself not as a patriarch to whom absolute obedience is owed but, rather, as one who presides over a republic:

> The little republic to which I gave laws, was regulated in the following manner: by sun-rise we all assembled in our common apartment, the fire being previously kindled by the servant. After we had saluted each other in proper ceremony, for I always thought fit to keep up some mechanical forms of good breeding, without which freedom ever destroys friendship, we all bent in gratitude to that Being who gave us another day (p. 33).

The Vicar best evidences his parental compassion, however, in his reaction to the news that his daughter has eloped with a notorious libertine. Though Mrs. Primrose, who could "scarce speak for weeping," reviles her disobedient daughter as "an ungrateful creature" and swears never "to call her daughter more," the good Vicar pleads with her not "to speak thus harshly." He declares " . . . my detestation of her guilt is as great as yours but ever shall this house and this heart be open to a poor returning repentant sinner":

> The sooner she returns from her transgression, the more welcome shall she be to me. For the first time the very best may err; art may persuade, and novelty spread out its charm. The first fault is the child of simplicity; but every other the offspring of guilt. Yes, the wretched

creature shall be welcome to this heart and this house, tho' stained with ten thousand vices. I will again hearken to the music of her voice, again will I hang fondly on her bosom, if I find but repentance there (p. 93).

And, indeed, when his daughter does return, the Vicar assures her that she "should never perceive any change in my affections and that during my life, which yet might be long, she might depend upon a guardian and an instructor. I armed her against the censures of the world" (p. 119). In this version of the prodigal's return that stresses the steadfastness of parental compassion rather than the horrible consequences of a too early withdrawal from the family, the doctrine of original sin is silently called into question. The first fault is "simplicity" that, as a failing of natural rather than moral ability, exculpates rather than damns.

Urging time and again the necessity for stoical fortitude, the Vicar, however, is far from a perfect practitioner of his preaching. Before the conversation with his wife cited previously, the Vicar, in the presence of his son, had first received the news of his daughter's elopement. At that moment his own emotions had not yet been checked:

> "Now then," cried I, " . . . may heaven's everlasting fury light upon him and his! Thus to rob me of my child! And sure it will, for taking back my sweet innocent that I was leading up to heaven. Such sincerity as my child was possest of. But all our earthly happiness is now over! Go, my children, go and be miserable and infamous; for my heart is broken within me!" . . . "Father," cried my son, "is this your fortitude?" . . . "Fortitude, child! Yes, he shall see I have fortitude. – Bring me my pistols" (p. 91).

The Vicar's reaction, his initial sense of irrevocable loss, points to a tension between stoicism and sentimentality not only in the novel, but in eighteenth-century society in general and, even more specifically, within Lockean ideology. On the one hand, Lockean pedagogy warned parents against indulging their children and thus rendering them "fondlings" ill-prepared for independence; on the other hand, it encouraged a parental solicitude that made it all the more difficult for parents to allow their children to leave the parental roof even into the arms of loving spouses. Though not always explicit, one of the most powerful as well as important themes in eighteenth-century fiction is the struggle between stoicism and solicitude in the parental heart. Three additional brief examples taken together make clear the dilemma.

In his early play *The Fathers or the Good-Hearted Man* , Fielding has his ideal sentimental parent deliver this soliloquy:

> How wretched is that animal whose whole happiness centers in himself, who cannot feel any satisfaction but in the indulgence of his own appetite. I feel my children still a part of me. They are, as it were,

additional senses which let in daily a thousand pleasures to me. My
enjoyments are not confined to them which nature hath adapted to my
years, but I can in my son's fruition taste those of another age. Nor
am I charitable, but luxuriant when I bestow on them the instruments
of their pleasure.[46]

The children of Fielding's good father are not part of his property, but
part of his "propriety" – extensions of himself. They are "additional
senses" that in Lockean terms allow him access to new dimensions of
experience. The strengthened and more affectional nuclear family
bound children closer to parents and made it harder for them to emerge
into the world at precisely the time that the controlling rationalist pedagogy insisted on parents facilitating just such an emergence. The paradox that the more one loved a child, the more one relinquished one's
hold over that child was a lesson hard-learned. Fielding's speaker is
confessing to more than the self-interestedness of a benefactor who
finds joy in his own beneficence. In his love there is a degree of luxury,
of self-indulgence.

In Fielding's earlier work, *Joseph Andrews* (1742), Parson Adams concludes his lecture to Joseph on the sinfulness of grieving over the divine
dispensations of providence with a rhetorical flourish: "Had Abraham
so loved his son Isaac as to refuse the sacrifice required, is there any of
us who would not condemn him?" At that very moment the Parson
receives a false report of his son's death and succumbs to loud weeping.
Fielding's point, for all the broad humor, is serious: the will of God is
one thing, but the loss of a son, whether to the harlots of London or the
angels of Heaven, is another.[47]

In a popular pre-Revolutionary American children's book, *The
Happy Child,* a widowed mother is unable to bear the imminent loss of
her dying daughter and is comforted by the "Happy Child" herself:

> Dear mother for me do not weep,
> Come kiss your child and don't complain
> We only separate to meet again.
> I'm coming Lord, the child did say.
> Don't weep, don't weep dear mother mine.
>
> In learning she took great delight.
> Above all the rest her mind was given
> To find the nearest way to heaven.[48]

Here the parent must accept the bitter fruits of the very education she
herself has administered to her child, one that taught the child to recognize God as her first and greatest parent. Sentimental parents were
reluctant to surrender their children not only to death, however, but to
the world at large.[49] In an age that sanctified the parent–child relation-

ship, it was all too easy for a parent, in the name of protecting a child's virtue (as colonists reminded apologists for English policy), to justify denying that child his rightful and necessary access to a larger world.

Locke himself encouraged parents to educate their children at home, rather than sending them to schools where they might be corrupted by the evil examples of their peers. Yet the inevitable question arose: How does a parent prepare a child for his emergence into a world of which he has been allowed no previous knowledge or experience? Locke records one popular objection to home education: "In my house he [my son] will perhaps be more innocent, but more ignorant too of the World: Wanting there change of Company, and being used constantly to the same Faces, he will, when he comes abroad, be a sheepish and conceited Creature."[50]

To those who pressed the advantages of boarding schools, Locke answered:

> Vertue is harder to be got, than a knowledge of the World; and if lost in a young man, is seldom recovered. Sheepishness and ignorance of the World, the faults imputed to a private Education, are neither the necessary Consequents of being bred at home, nor if they were, are they incurable Evils. Vice is the more stubborn, as well as the more dangerous Evil of the two; and therefore, in the first place, to be fenced against. If that sheepish softness . . . be carefully to be avoided, it is principally so for Vertue's sake.
>
> It is preposterous therefore to sacrifice his Innocency to the attaining of confidence, and some little Skill of bustling for himself among others, by his conversation with ill bred and vitious Boys (p. 166–7).

Locke was sufficiently practical, however, to concede "that it is not possible now (as perhaps it once was) to keep a young gentleman from vice by a total ignorance of it, unless you will all his life lock him up in a closet and never let him go into company" (p. 180). Thus, while he strenuously maintained his objections to boarding schools, Locke was obliged, finally, to conclude:

> The only Fence against the World, is a thorough Knowledge of it; into which a young Gentleman should be enter'd by degrees, as he can bear it; and the earlier the better, so he be in safe and skillful hands to guide him (p. 195).

The knowledge of good and evil was sufficiently necessary to require a properly managed fall from innocence; for only the knowledge of evil (which ultimately distinguished virtue from natural goodness) could protect from evil. The eighteenth-century debate over the dangers and virtues of inoculation recapitulated the basic issue: Could a small exposure to corruption protect one from a fatal exposure or was that small exposure itself potentially fatal?[51]

Even if an introduction to the world "by degrees" was safe, as Locke suggested, what did that mean in practice? If the home could not provide a child with an adequate education, must that child at some point take leave of his home to complete his moral and social education? The introduction in the 1750s of the first geographical or travel games with board and dice, sometimes even advertised "with cuts upon the plan of Mr. Locke," like Peale's museum, begged rather than resolved this crucial question.[52] In eighteenth-century England the debate as to whether a saving education required leaving home usually resolved into another: Was the "European tour" the making or the unmaking of a Christian gentleman? In part, the debate was between the views of a younger and those of an older generation. In 1711 Juba, the spokesman in Addison's *Cato* for the virtues of Christian stoicism, declared: "If knowledge of the world must make men perfidious, May Juba ever live in ignorance." At midcentury the socially conscious Chesterfield, equating such knowledge with "common sense," proclaimed on the contrary: "A knowledge of the world, by our own experience and observation, is so necessary, that without it, we shall act very absurdly."[53]

The larger issues once again were these: Were tutors – as Julie's father in *La Nouvelle Héloïse* feared – seducers; or were they – kin to Fénelon's Minerva – deliverers? Was knowledge of the world – like the Edenic knowledge of good and evil – fatal? Or, like the knowledge of the classics, was it unchristian wisdom, but wisdom nonetheless? And if another world were to be visited, which world would it be? Was it the tutelage of a sublime and uncivilized nature that was necessary to supplement the instruction of parents? Or, was it, as Sterne suggested, a sentimental journey through Italy and France, during which a heart might be engaged by affecting scenes of misery and ruins and the divine spark of sensibility allowed to burn brighter? Or, was it, as Fielding – whose "cheerful Pelagianism insisted on charity over Christ and goodness over grace" – was to suggest in *Joseph Andrews,* a pilgrimage into the English countryside such as Parson Adams would take in order to teach and learn the lessons of benevolence to and from his own countrymen?[54] For Fénelon, Sterne, and Fielding, and in a more secular way for Chesterfield, there was something "saving" about the knowledge of a world apart from home. Indeed if, as Bishop Berkeley argued, drawing upon Locke, "the world as we see it is a construct slowly built up by every one of us in years of experimentation during which the mind weaves sensations into impressions constantly corrected by other impressions," to be cheated of new experiences and perceptions was to be cheated of the raw matter out of which we actually "make" the world, the only world we will ever have.[55]

Perhaps the most succinct presentation of the issues of the Grand

Tour debate is contained in Sterne's *The Sermons of Mr. Yorick,* which made up volumes three and four of the *Complete Works* issued in Philadelphia in 1774. The best of those extremely popular sermons concerns the prodigal son and takes as its verse Luke 15:28: "Many days after, the younger son gathered all his things and took a journey into a far country and there wasted his sustenance in violent luxury." After opening the theological significance of the text – that sinful man remembers his God but in affliction – Yorick applies it to the question of the European tour. The father of the prodigal pleads with his son:

> Poor inconsiderate youth, from whose arms art thou flying, from what shelter art thou going forth into the storm? Art thou weary of a father's affections, of a father's care, or hopest thou to find a warmer interest, a truer counselor or a kinder friend in a land of strangers where thou may be prey to so many jades? He would dissuade his son from the folly of so rash an enterprise by shewing him the dangers of the journey, – the inexperience of his age, the hazards of his life, the temptations which virtue would run, without a guide, without a friend . . . the little knowledge he would gain except of evil.[56]

The father's primary concern is to address the fallacy of the tutorial definition of paternity espoused by both Locke and Fénelon; that is, that a truer friend, counselor, or "parent" may be found outside the family. Only secondarily does he declare the uselessness of foreign knowledge; for the knowledge that he fears his son may acquire *is* the knowledge that such a truer friend may, indeed, be found.

Sterne first agrees with the prodigal's father, declaring: "We should all of us rest at ease with such objects as present themselves in the parish or province in which we first took breath" (p. 240). But in the course of the sermon, the archsentimentalist – convinced of the fundamental goodness of the world – shifts allegiance to the prodigal, gently disagreeing with his father:

> The spur which is ever in our sides, this desire for traveling – the passion is in no way bad – order it rightly, the advantages are worth the pursuit, the chief of which is to learn the languages, laws and customs and understand the government of other nations and to take us out of the land of our aunts and grandmothers, from the track of nursery mistakes, and by shewing us new objects or old ones in new light to reform our judgement and by tasting perpetually the varieties of nature to know what is good by feeling the difference of so many various humours, to make us look into ourselves and form our own (p. 238).

The prodigal's desire to leave home is acknowledged to be neither a problem nor a sin. Indeed, leaving "the land of our aunts and grandmothers" will allow him to rectify "nursery mistakes" by permitting him to form his own nature and humor. The real issue is a son's inability "to turn this venture to such account" without "cart and without company." For without these, "he will be cast back as naked as he first left." One solution is to let the child go, but send parental sovereignty along with him. The sermon abruptly climaxes in midsentence. "But if you will send an able pilot with your son, a scholar . . . " (p. 242). Sterne's characteristically abrupt ending suggests his unwillingness to follow through with such a resolution; for to forbid a child from travel according to the inclinations of his heart is as objectionable as denying a daughter the choice of a husband by prescribing her one.

In *A Sentimental Journey* (1768), Sterne says as much by including among "peregrine martyrs" in his anatomy of travelers "young gentlemen transported by the cruelty of parent and guardians and traveling under the directions of governors recommended by Oxford, Aberdeen and Glasgow."[57] Cheated of a purer access to the world, the plight of the overguarded traveler is caught up in the refrain of Yorick's caged starling: "I can't get out."[58] Sterne called *A Sentimental Journey* his "work of redemption."[59] As the education of the heart was a form of salvation, travel was, Luke notwithstanding, a justifiable disobedience. In the same year that Sterne's *Complete Works* were published in America, John Woolman, the American Quaker itinerant, published his famous journal, which is in some sense an American equivalent to Sterne's *Sentimental Journey*. Woolman's book, a homage to the God-given "principle in the human mind which incites to exercise goodness to every living creature," glorifies ministerial itinerancy as a personal spiritual pilgrimage, an education of the moral sense.[60]

Though *A Sentimental Journey* and *The Sermons of Mr. Yorick* are, in different ways, concerned with the formation of the mind, the volume in which Sterne most directly addresses the larger issue of education is *The Life and Adventures of Tristram Shandy*, which Garry Wills has recently reminded us was among Jefferson's favorite books.[61] To understand that novel it is important to distinguish between two very different eighteenth-century attitudes toward Lockean thought. To environmentalists like Crèvecoeur, Peale, and Jefferson, the revolutionary displacement of the theory of innate ideas by Lockean sensationalism suggested the dawning of a new and glorious order. For if those influences that "wrote the character" upon the tabula rasa of a child could be controlled, screened, and modulated, certainly it was in man's power, like the ideal gardener, to use the right set of influences to "form" a generation of near perfect men whose presence in the world would in turn hasten the coming of a glorious civil millennium.[62] One finds the period's most extreme statements of such optimism in republican treatises arguing the necessity of universal common school education. Noah Webster was not alone in calling the education of youth "an

*Noah Webster
on education*

employment of more consequence than making laws or preaching the gospel, because it lays the foundation of both." Nor was he alone in his ecstatic preoccupation with the implications of the doctrine, in his words, that "the minds of children are like blank paper, upon which you may write any characters you please."[63] Crèvecoeur's famous argument for the appearance of a "new man" in America draws on a broader environmentalist argument based on natural history theories of transplantation.[64]

More skeptical men, however, recognized that education, climate, diet, the form of government under which one lives, and the nature of one's work were but five influences on an individual's character. There were, in addition, an infinity of accidental influences and sensations constantly presented to the mind over which the mind had no control. And on a human mind whose thought processes were in all probability subjective and associational rather than logical and predictable, such an influence might make an impression enormously disproportionate to its original significance. To those who dwelt on the darker implications of sensationalism, the disappearance of the innate idea marked the arrival of a new epoch in which the human mind had become, to a degree it never had before, terrifyingly conscious of its position of vulnerability before the formative influences of uncontrollable impressions, distractions, and random events. The fatalistic perspective that Sterne would embrace, part in jest and part in all seriousness, had as one of its most outspoken exponents the Marquis de Sade: "It is in the mother's womb that are fashioned the organs which must render us susceptible of this or that fantasy; the first object which we encounter, the first conversations we overhear, determine the pattern; do what it will, education is incapable of altering the pattern."[65] In its emphatic insistence on the need to separate from a fatal European corruption, to seal the garden, the rhetoric of the American revolution would wishfully describe America as the world's last refuge from precisely such terrifying vulnerability.

Seeking to hold up a mirror to this new consciousness, Sterne seems to have set out in 1759 to write a novel that would, among other things, as literally as possible reflect the sensationalist view of the life of the mind in all its anarchic vulnerability. Sterne constructed a novel that backtracked on itself, included some chapters nonsequentially ordered and others one sentence long, and had as its appropriate subject the accidental formation of a child's mind and character. The three most important influences on Tristram's character, Sterne informs us with seeming seriousness, are the choice of his name, the size of his nose, and the date and place of his birth.

Its structural uniqueness must not obscure the fact of the thematic similarities between Sterne's novel and the majority of literary works contemporary with it. Though it mercilessly parodies the conventions of Lockean fiction, it still very much espouses the ideology of that fiction. The conceit on which much of the novel is built is that a "homunculus" or fetus is "A BEING guarded around and circumscribed with rights. . . . He may be benefited, he may be injured – he may obtain redress; – in a word, he has all the claims and rights of humanity."[66] By insisting on securing for the fetus what others saw fit to claim only for grown children, Sterne is going his contemporaries one step further. The novel opens with the traditional filial complaint against parental severity, but now extended to its logical extremity:

> I wish either my father or my mother, or indeed both of them, as they were in duty both equally bound to it, had minded what they were about when they begot me; had they duly considered how much depend'd upon what they were then doing; – that not only the production of a rational Being was concern'd in it, but that possibly the happy formation and temperature of his body, perhaps his genius and the very cast of his mind (p. 4).

If the earliest influences, as Locke claimed, are the most critical, even more important than forming a child's mind after the fact of birth is the future parent's responsibility to enter with absolute concentration and solemnity the sex act in which a child may be conceived. Unsettling her husband at the very moment of ejaculation by asking whether or not he had wound their clock, Tristram's mother had committed what amounts to the primordial parental sin. Thus, Sterne, echoing Burgh, tells us that their son's lifelong miseries "began nine months before ever he came into the world" (p. 11).

The irony of this tragedy is that Mr. Shandy is far from being an irresponsible parent. He is deeply, even obsessively, aware of the power of accidental influences over the mind. Indeed, much of the novel deals with a debate he has with his wife as to the relative significance of a child's having been brought into life by a male instead of a female midwife, and of having been born in the city instead of the country. Yet, so caught up is he with the knotty problems of protecting his son from harmful influences that Mr. Shandy absentmindedly neglects putting his theories into practice. Tristram says of the *Tristrapaedia*, the Lockean volume of pedagogy that Mr. Shandy sets out to write:

> This is the best account I am determined to give of the slow progress my father made in his *Tristrapaedia*; at which (as I said) he was three years and something more, indefatigably at work, and at last, had scarce completed, by his own reckoning, one half of his undertaking:

> the misfortune was that I was all that time totally neglected and aban-
> doned to my mother; and what was almost as bad, by the very delay,
> the most of his pains was rendered entirely useless, every day a page
> or two becomes of no consequence (p. 375).

As if this were not enough Sterne sharpens the irony: "In order to
render the *Tristrapaedia* complete – I wrote the chapter myself," Tristram concludes (p. 384).

Far from being motivated by larger republican or benevolent principles, Mr. Shandy's commitment to the welfare of his son is rooted in
the political assumptions of none other than Locke's old antagonist,
Robert Filmer, to whose *Patriarcha* Locke had responded with his *Second
Treatise*:

> Another political reason which prompted my father so strongly to
> guard against the least evil accident in my mother's lying in [at] the
> country – was, that any such instance would infallibly throw a balance
> of power, too great already, into the weaker vessels of the gentry, in
> his own or higher stations; – which, with the many other usurped
> rights which that part of the constitution was hourly establishing, –
> would in the end prove fatal to the monarchial system of domestic
> government established in the first creation of things by God (p. 47).

Had an accident occurred in the country, the gentry would, by implication, have fathered the character of the infant as much as Mr. Shandy,
and the balance of power would have been thrown off with this dimi-
nution of unmixed paternal power.

> In this point he was entirely of Sir Robert Filmer's opinion, that the
> plans and institutions of the greatest monarchies in the eastern parts of
> the world were, originally, all stolen from that admirable pattern and
> prototype of this household and paternal power; – which, for a cen-
> tury, he said, and more, had gradually been degenerating away into a
> mixed government (p. 47).

At a climactic moment later in the novel, Yorick, the gentle spokesman
for Sterne's own position, contests the primary assumption of Mr.
Shandy's Filmerianism – that the "accidental" fact of a man's fathering a
child necessarily imposes upon that child a lifelong obligation to obey
that man regardless of his subsequent behavior.

> – I enter upon this speculation, said my father carelessly . . . merely to
> show the foundation of the natural relation between a father and his
> child; the right and jurisdiction over whom he acquires these several
> ways –
> 1st, by marriage.
> 2nd, by adoption.
> 3rd, by legitimation.
> And 4th, by procreation; all which I consider in their order.
> I lay a slight stress upon one of them, replied Yorick – the act,

especially where it ends there, in my opinion lays as little obligation upon the child as it conveys power to the father (p. 391).

Identifying Lockean sensationalism as a main subject of Sterne's volume renders explicable what at first reading may seem inexplicable: the endless conversations between Sir Toby (Tristram's uncle) and his friend Trim on the subject of the history of military "fortifications." The pair not only discuss virtually all the devices ever impressed in the service of defending a castle or fortress, but enact on their lawns famous stormings of military strongholds. The serious philosophical question behind their wild disquisitions is no more and no less than the great Lockean question of the age: To what degree can a parent isolate his child from the corruption and destructive influences of the world, to prevent the invasion of the sovereign country of self?

If Sterne gives any answer at all to this question, it is not to be found in *Tristram Shandy* but in *The Sermons of Mr. Yorick*. And there the answer is more or less the one Locke had given a half century before: "the only fence against the world is a thorough knowledge of it." As Sterne's thematic intentions in *Tristram Shandy* ultimately prevail, in spite of his decision to surrender to the impulse to digress; so, too, may reason, informed by experience, prevail against the random influences of the world – if not as an impregnable fortification against them, then as a filter through which those influences may be purified.

In their own way Chesterfield, Gregory, Fénelon, Marmontel, Richardson, Sterne, and others each popularized the rational ideal of the new family and family relations. All emphasized the importance of properly preparing a child for a moral life of rational independence. All condemned the forms of parental tyranny that stood in the way of that ideal. It is not surprising that in his 1771 letter to Robert Skipwith advising him on what reading is essential to the education of a young man, Thomas Jefferson should include all of the titles dealt with in this section but Gregory.[67] Taken together they articulate an ideology and paradigm that by 1776 had become, in effect, a new cultural orthodoxy, one that provided the terms in which men and women thought about political, moral, and social issues. That ideology had to be accommodated to the larger value system of orthodox Protestantism before it could achieve its ultimate impact. Our two final bestsellers, *Robinson Crusoe* and *Clarissa*, make clear how that radical accommodation was achieved.

3

THE FAMILIAL POLITICS
OF THE FORTUNATE FALL

None of the pedagogues of the eighteenth century believed more deeply
in the importance of a knowledge of the world than Rousseau. But for.
Rousseau the only world whose laws and arrangements were essential
to understand was nature and natural ability, not the artificial world of
European society. Even more than Locke, he believed that reason must
be primarily educated by experience rather than by instruction: "To
make him a master, be you in everything an apprentice; and reflect that
he will learn more by one hour of manual work than he will retain
from a whole day's verbal instruction."[1] Having declared in *Emile*, "I
hate books," Rousseau yet asks: "Is there no expedient . . . to collect
the various instructions which are scattered up and down so many
voluminous tomes. . . . If one could only conceive a situation in which
all the natural wants of man would be displayed in a manner adapted to
the understanding of a child wherein the means of satisfying these
wants are gradually discarded with the same ease." And he answers his
own query: "Give yourself no trouble; such a situation has already been
discovered. . . . What is this wonderful book? Is it Aristotle? Is it Pliny?
Is it Buffon? NO: it is *Robinson Crusoe*" (II, 60).

THE PRODIGAL AS PILGRIM: ROBINSON CRUSOE IN AMERICA
First published in London in 1719, *Crusoe* appeared long before the
other books it would join among the American bestsellers of 1774–
1775. Yet it, more than any of the others, clarifies the moral, political,
and spiritual significance the drama of filial disobedience held for the
American reader on the eve of the Revolution. Indeed, Defoe's novel
offered nothing less than a theologically and hence politically acceptable
model for precisely such disobedience. Unlike the optimistic sentimental fiction of Sterne, Fielding, and Goldsmith, Defoe's novel belonged
to an earlier literary tradition – that of the Puritan spiritual relation, or
conversion narrative – a tradition that receded back through Milton and

Bunyan to St. Augustine and the Book of Job. The primary concern of the spiritual relation was with the protagonist's realization – one usually hastened by divine affliction – of his own personal sinfulness and the consequent necessity of choosing God over the world and over all the things in it, including one's family. Bunyan's Christian, Crusoe's immediate literary ancestor, closes his ears to the cries of wife and child and chooses to leave them behind in order "to flee the wrath to come." In the arch-individualistic tradition of the Puritan picaresque, personal salvation must be placed even before the cause of familial unity. Christian is not only justified in leaving his family behind, he is obligated to do so by the most urgent and primary of Christian considerations: the state of his soul. His sanction is the gospel. Indeed, on no point is Christ himself more insistent than on the necessity of subordinating natural affections to divine ones:

> Think not that I am come to send peace on earth: I came not to send peace, but a sword / For I am come to set a man at variance against his father, and the daughter against her mother, and the daughter-in-law against her mother-in-law / And a man's foes shall be they of his own household / He that loveth father or mother more than me is not worthy of me: and he that loveth son or daughter more than me is not worthy of me (Matt. 10:34–7).

Thus it is that a child who is told that all he need do to discharge his responsibility to God is to obey his parents in all things is not told enough to ensure his salvation. Yet it was precisely this pedagogically expedient partial truth that identifies parent with God, filial disobedience with death, and parental approval with redemption that was the staple sentiment of eighteenth-century children's literature: "Children your parents love and obey / And the Lord will bless you here on earth /And give you the crown of glory after death."[2] Though such sentiments served the cause of familial and social order, no eighteenth-century Protestant minister would have denied the Arminian unorthodoxy of a verse that boldly suggested that grace was constrainable by filial obedience and that earthly blessings foretold heavenly ones.

From the beginning, Christianity had preached the necessity of submission both to earthly authority and to God; both to the Fifth Commandment, "Honor thy father and mother," and the First, "Thou shalt have no other gods before me." In most respects the two injunctions were compatible; in one fundamental way, however, they were not. Luke's parable of the prodigal son had traditionally been preached as a moral tale, encouraging obedience to the Fifth Commandment. The fact remained, however, that it was a parable and, as such, its primary meaning was not literal but spiritual. Indeed, the gospel point of the parable was not that a sinful child must return to the protective embrace of his parent, but that he must embrace and return to God. Thus whoever used the parable for moral purposes to show that it taught the Fifth Commandment and not the First had to assume the burden of proof that the address to the prodigal, "For then my Son was dead, and he is alive / He is lost and he is found," referred to filial penitence and not primarily to conversion and the death of the Old Adam.

At the heart of Defoe's great novel is a radical objection to the blurring of the distinctions between the spiritual and the moral significances of the Gospel parable, to the subordination of the former to the latter, and to the moralization of religion, which such subordination implied. With the daring of which only orthodoxy is capable, Defoe calls attention to the incompatibility of these two explications of the parable in a novel whose commitment to separating piety from moralism as well as heavenly parent from earthly parent justifies separating a son from his living parent. Whereas Mr. Harlowe some years later in Richardson's *Clarissa* would declare: "The merit of obedience consists in giving up an inclination,"[3] Robinson defends his decision to leave his parents by announcing that not to follow his "inclination" would be "resisting providence."[4] The same "inclination" that in 1697 Locke had identified with passion and insisted must be suppressed is identified with providence in Defoe's novel. In this most Puritan of novels, providence and not reason will be Robinson's guide and "mentor."

Crusoe was the laboratory fiction dedicated to demonstrating the viability of that very self-government under God in preparation for which, a half century later, Lord Chesterfield's *Letters to His Son* and Gregory's *A Father's Legacy to His Daughters* would urge parents to provide their children with a sound moral education. For this reason it is significant that the first American editions of *The Adventures of Robinson Crusoe*, issued from the New York press of Hugh Gaine in 1774 and 1775, should make their appearance in the years of emerging Anglo-American crisis that also witnessed the first American publication of Chesterfield's and Gregory's work. Because the Gaine edition radically abridged the original English version and included several interpolated passages, the first American edition differs in significant respects from the original novel. The implications of these differences are important to our discussion of ideology and genre, in general, and of Revolutionary American sensibility, in particular. But those implications may be appreciated properly only after an initial consideration of the unabridged novel, which, it may be added, was popular under an English imprint in its own right throughout the Revolutionary period.

The full-length novel begins with what would become familiar in eighteenth-century fiction as the scenario of the prodigal son:

> Being the third son of the family and not bred to any trade, my head began to be filled early with rambling thoughts. My father, who was very ancient, had given me a competent share of learning . . . but I

would be satisfied with nothing but going to sea; and my inclination to this led me so strong against the will, nay the commands of my father (p. 8).

Reluctant to enter into "the state of life" prepared for him, Robinson sets to sea, fully aware that he must be "overtaken by the judgment of Heaven for my wicked leaving my father's house and abandoning my duty" (p. 12). Indeed, in short order a storm dismasts the ship on which he is sailing, terrifies the crew, and lands Robinson back in Yarmouth. Yet Crusoe will not act the prodigal son and return home:

> Had I now had the sense to have gone back to Hull, and have gone home, I had been happy, and my father, an emblem of our blessed Saviour's parable, had even killed the fatted calf for me.
>
> Yet my ill fate pushed me on with an obstinancy that nothing could resist; and though I had several times loud calls from my reason and my more composed judgment to go home, yet I had no power to do it. I know not what to call this, nor will I urge that it is a secret overruling decree that hurries us on to be the instruments of our own destruction, even though it be before us, and that we push upon it with eyes open (p. 13).

Crusoe sees no inconsistency in declaring that both the instruction of the storm and his wayward "inclination" are decrees of the same providential will; for the message of the storm is not that Robinson must return home, but that he will necessarily suffer. As he is irresistibly led, Crusoe's leave-taking becomes less a wickedness than an accession to a greater will.

The second ship he boards is attacked by pirates and Robinson is sold into slavery. He escapes his Moorish captivity and reaches Brazil, where he buys a "plantation" that becomes successful in a short time. Wishing to improve his profits by acquiring cheap labor, he joins a group of planters on a ship destined to pick up a slave cargo. Sailing into a reef, the ship is destroyed, and all the crew lost except Crusoe, who discovers himself on an uninhabited island. He mournfully reflects: "I refused their help and assistance, who would have lifted me into the world, and would have made everything easy to me; and now I have difficulties to struggle with . . . too great for even nature itself to support, and no assistance, no help, no advice" (p. 107). Chastened by these reflections, Crusoe turns to his Bible for the first time in years. He is particularly struck by one scriptural passage that converts him to a new understanding of God's providence and of the true nature of his island captivity:

> Now I began to construe the words mentioned above, "Call on Me, and I will deliver you," in a different sense from what I had ever done before; for then I had no notion of anything being called deliverance,

> but my being delivered from the captivity I was in; for though I was indeed at large in the place, yet the island was certainly a prison to me, and that in the worst sense of the word. But now I learned to take it in another sense. Now I looked back upon my past life with such horror, and my sins appeared so dreadful, that my soul sought nothing from God but deliverance from the load of guilt that bore down all my comfort. . . . And I added this part here, to hint to whoever shall read it that whenever they come to a true sense of things, they will find deliverance from sin a much greater blessing than deliverance from affliction (p. 108).

Now realizing that, though man is born to be "his own destroyer," he who has faith in divine providence will be delivered from sin and, thus, be made an instrument of his own deliverance, Crusoe is freed from both his guilt and dejection. Whereas his Adamic fall from parental care to island isolation obliges him to a greater dependence on God, it correlatively obliges him to a greater self-sufficiency. Unlike the prodigal son, who is destroyed by his independence and must return to his parents for guidance and instruction, Crusoe becomes "master of every mechanical art" (p. 75), a society unto himself. His isolation from family and world makes possible independence *and* conversion. Though the solitary life of the island is replete with affliction, it is also equally free of the temptations and vain company that were the ruin of the biblical prodigal:

> I gave humble and hearty thanks that God had been pleased to discover to me even that it was possible I might be more happy in this solitary condition, than I could have been in a liberty of society and in all the pleasures of the world. That He could fully make up to me the deficiencies of my solitary state, and the want of human society, by His presence, and the communications of His grace to my soul, supporting, comforting and encouraging me to depend upon His Providence here and hope for His eternal presence hereafter.
>
> It was now that I began sensibly to feel how much more happy this life I now led was, with all its miserable circumstances, than the wicked, cursed, abominable life I led all the past part of my days (p. 125).

The passage reads as might the ultimate utterance of a returning prodigal in a sentimental novel, with the exception that it is addressed to God and not to Robinson's father in the stead of his God. But in that exception there is a world of difference. Crusoe's conversion does not inspire him with the wish to return home penitently but, rather, encourages him to covet his solitariness with God. Since it is his sinful nature for which he has learned to repent and not the circumscribed sin of filial disobedience, it is to God's graciousness and not to his father's that he must turn. By turning to God, Crusoe is released from the obligation to turn back to his parent.

Defoe has Crusoe live fifteen of his twenty-eight years – the greater half – alone on the island in order to demonstrate the absolute sufficiency of God's providence, to prove that, though deprived of parent and society, he who has God as company and providence as preceptor may nonetheless lead a Christian life. To declare the full truth of this, his glorious theme, Defoe incautiously allows himself to suggest in the previously quoted passage – a suggestion that is inseparable from the structure of the novel – that society and parents are not only unnecessary when God and providence are present, but somehow stand in opposition to them – just as luxury and indolence do to saving virtue.

Defoe denies that the purpose of divine deliverance is to return Crusoe from affliction back to society, declaring, rather, that its purpose is to deliver him from sin to redemption by sustaining him triumphantly *in* affliction. As Crusoe's conversion attends on his island isolation, Defoe is obliged orthodoxly, if perversely, to redefine "all the past part" of Robinson's life, that is, the part during most of which he remained dutifully at home, as "wicked and abominable," and to declare (echoing Adam's "felix culpa") his present life in captivity "more happy." Parent and prescriptive Christian society are not only denied an identification with God and their functions separated from the divine function, but both, in consequence, are implicitly identified with the "evil company" of the moralistic prodigal scenario. By literalizing Calvinist or Puritan doctrine, Defoe has both wittingly and unwittingly succeeded in turning what began as a story of a prodigal into a radical fable of the fortunate fall. The circle of the prodigal's return has snapped; it has become again the straight line of the pilgrim's progress.

Clearly, the salvational scheme enunciated at this point in Defoe's novel had heretical implications: implications that Defoe was later forced to confront. In his second sequel to *Crusoe, The Serious Reflections of Robinson Crusoe* (1723), Defoe in the persona of Crusoe defensively denies the unorthodoxy of the conversion passage quoted previously. In particular, he addresses himself to those readers who have misconstrued him as advocating papist monasticism. After roundly condemning those Catholic orders that would renounce their responsibility for perfecting Christian society to pursue a specious personal purity, Crusoe insists that the "virtue" of his isolation was "not as a confinement from the enjoyment of the world, and restraint from human society," but as an inducement to "the contemplation of sublime things" (III, 5). Having recognized that it is "unlawful . . . to forsake the assemblies" and "public worship of God" and having conceded that "a frame of mind that is above the world" may as well be maintained "in the midst of infinite multitudes" (III, 12), as on an island, Crusoe is reduced to declaring that his solitude is fortunate only in that it further hastens and obliges such an other-worldly frame of mind.

Yet for all his concessions to the necessity of embracing Christian society, the fact remains that Crusoe, both when he has no choice and later when he does, prefers to satisfy the Christian injunction to embrace society and to participate in its perfection in his own way. He does so not by returning to English society – he returns once temporarily and a second time, at age 74, to live his life out in *solitary retirement* – but, rather, primarily by creating his own society, by his own lights, in the wilderness. Still, as had been the ironic case with New England, the society he designs is no less intolerant of the inclinations of the heart than the one he had disobediently left behind.

Referring to Poll and his other animals, Robinson remarks:

> It would have made a Stoic smile to have seen me and my little family sit down to dinner; there was the majesty, the prince and lord of the whole island: I had the lives of all my subjects at my absolute command. I could hang, draw, give liberty and take it away, and no rebels amongst my subjects (p. 167).

Himself initially a rebel, Crusoe has become a model king. With the arrival of Friday and the recovered Spanish prisoners, Crusoe becomes "rich in subjects." With the arrival of three English sailors set ashore by their mutinous crew, he becomes no less than a version of Jehovah, supplying "bread in the wilderness" (p. 278).

Having repossessed the English ship from the mutineers, Crusoe as "Governor" of the Island decrees that the chief mutineers and the Spanish prisoners shall be forced to remain on the island with plots of land assigned to each. As God had chosen to sustain Crusoe on his island for twenty-eight years rather than returning him to parental justice in England, so too does Crusoe choose to leave the new prodigals behind. His design is that they shall become the nucleus of a new society, one he will supply with Brazilian women for wives and sundry provisions. (In the second volume he will once again give in to his impulse to travel and return to the island to find to his delight that the population of his "colony" has tripled.)

Crusoe returns alone to England – Friday having been slain by pirates – to discover that his life "of Providence's chequerwork" (p. 344), although beginning "foolishly," has "closed much more happily than any part of it ever gave me leave so much as to hope for" (p. 297). His thriving plantation in Brazil, the other base of his New World society, had reaped him, in his absence, a fortune of five thousand pounds sterling, "an estate . . . as I might call it . . . as sure as an estate of lands in England" (p. 322). As the ripened fruit of his own labors has replaced the inheritance he might have received from his father, Robinson, in the great particular of the eighteenth-century fiction – inheritance—has assumed the role of his own parent. When he discovers upon visiting Hull that both his parents are dead, he baldly reports the fact to his readers, expressing neither surprise nor the self-recrimination one might expect of a prodigal. The "Robinson" who left the Old World had his name contracted to "Robin" by Poll, the parrot, the first creature of the New World with whom he exchanged words. In the New World the filial suffix had to be suppressed.

In the *Further Adventures of Robinson Crusoe,* the fortunate fall structure is repeated once again with but the smallest modifications. Having settled down to marriage, Crusoe remarks:

> Now I thought indeed that I enjoyed the middle state of life that my father so earnestly recommended to me, and lived a kind of heavenly life, something like what is described by the poem on the subject of a country life:
>> Free from vices, free from care,
>> Age has no pain, and youth no snare (II, 6).

But once again a glorious "prelapsarian" home life is exposed as an impossible dream:

> But in the middle of all this felicity, one blow from unforeseen Providence unhinged me at once; and not only made a breach upon me, inevitable and incurable, but drove me, by its consequences, into a deep relapse into the wandering disposition; which, as I may say, being born in my blood, soon recovered its hold of me, and, like the return of a violent distemper, came on with an irresistible force upon me, so that nothing could make any more impression upon me. This blow was the loss of my wife.
>
> She was in a few words, the stay of all my affairs . . . the engine that, by her prudence, reduced me to that happy compass I was in, from the most extravagant and ruinous project that fluttered in my head, as above, and did more to guide my rambling genius than a mother's tears, a father's instructions, a friend's counsel, or my own reasoning powers (II, 6–7).

Because his wife had, as the description indicates, served him as a surrogate parent, her death is a heavenly affliction designed once again to oblige Crusoe like Telemachus to set out to become his own parent. So that the element of conscious prodigality – the choice of fate over family – is not lost in the paradigm of the fortunate fall, Crusoe is left with three children. In this volume it is the children whom he prodigally abandons.

Defoe is deeply committed to stating his theme – that man under God does not need the mediation of a parent for his salvation – in as unqualified a manner as possible. He is, nonetheless, extremely anxious to do everything he can, short of direct qualification, to remove the impression of morally equivocating over the necessity of filial obedience. The novel's subplot, which deals with Friday's relationship to his father, seems consciously designed to offset the more extreme terms of Crusoe's relationship to his own father. Having escaped his besieged village, Friday becomes guiltily preoccupied with thoughts of the father he has been obliged to leave behind. When father and son are finally and remarkably reunited, Friday is ecstatic. The scene momentarily reawakens in Robinson an appreciation of the bonds of nature:

> But when Friday came to hear him speak, and look in his face, it would have moved anyone to tears to have seen how Friday kissed him, embraced him, hugged him, cried, laughed, halloed. . . . It is not easy for me to express how it moved me to see what ecstacy and filial affection had worked in this poor savage at the sight of his father (II, 268).

In the course of his description of the scene, however, Crusoe refers to "the extravagancies of his affection after this" and to Friday as "a distracted creature" (II, 269). Even in praising filial affection, Defoe cannot resist the impulse to smuggle in the antithetical values of his brand of Protestant stoicism—a stoicism even more stern than what Locke had preached.

In *The Further Adventures of Robinson Crusoe,* Defoe moderates the subversive implications of his theme in two ways. First, he has Crusoe experience a number of vicissitudes in financial fortune. By reasserting the transitoriness of all earthly fortune, he undercuts what in the first volume he had implied: that a self-made fortune on earth is a type of the fortune given the fallen who are returned to Heaven. Second, he features prominently in one of the more important scenes of the volume an exposition on the virtues of filial obedience worthy of Richardson or *The New England Primer.* Crusoe engages Will Atkins, a fellow adventurer, in discussion of the education Atkins's clergyman father had given him:

> *W.A.* He would have taught me well, sir; but I despised all education, instruction, or correction, like a beast as I was.
> *R.C.* It's true, Solomon says, "He that despises reproof is brutish."
> *W.A.* Ay, sir, I was brutish indeed; I murdered my father; for God's sake, sir, talk no more about that, sir; I murdered my poor father.
> *Pr.* Ha! a murderer!
> (Here the priest started, for I interpreted every word as he spoke it, and looked pale. It seems he believed that Will had really killed his own father.)
> *R.C.* No, no, sir; I do not understand him so. Will Atkins, explain yourself. You did not kill your father, did you, with your own hand?

> *W.A.* No, sir, I did not cut his throat; but I cut the thread of his comforts, and shortened his days; I broke his heart by the most un-grateful, unnatural return for the most tender, affectionate treatment that ever father gave, or child could receive.
>
> . . . .
>
> *R.C.* You talk too feelingly and sensibly for me, Atkins; I cannot bear it.
>
> . . . .
>
> *R.C.* Yes, Atkins, every shore, every hill, nay, I may say every tree in this island, is witness to the anguish of my soul for my ingratitude and base usage of a good tender father – a father much like mine by your description; and I murdered my father as well as you, Will Atkins; but I think for all that my repentance is short of yours too, by a great deal (II, 150–1).

But once again, Defoe cannot leave well enough alone, parricide apart; the *fortunateness* of the fall into filial disobedience must be reasserted. Robinson recounts Atkin's confession to a young clergyman, who de-clares:

> Did I not say, sir, that when this man was converted he would preach to us all? I tell you, sir, if this one man be made a true penitent there will be no need of me; he will make Christians of all on the island (II, 166).

If a reformed rake makes the best husband, a reformed sinner is the best minister, a prodigal the best son. In a fallen world, grace has but one currency – not innocence, but repentance, repentance to which sin is prerequisite.

In the second sequel to his novel, *The Serious Reflections of Robinson Crusoe,* Defoe forsakes ambiguous narrative for moralistic exposition. He clarifies his "separatism" in an "Essay on Solitude," from which we have quoted previously. In "A Vision of the Angelic World," he dis-misses the problem of "the locality of bliss and misery" as "no part of my search" (III, 247–8), permitting him to escape a discussion of the typological nightmares of Canaan's relationship to Heaven, and earthly to Heavenly geography – hard theological questions that had so radi-cally underpinned his original novel.

Structured as a Calvinist spiritual autobiography, the original edition of Defoe's novel (we shall discuss the Gaine edition later) offered the American reading public a theologically and hence politically acceptable model for successful filial disobedience, a justifiable assertion of inde-pendence. Indeed, Defoe's contrapuntal emphasis on the virtue of filial obedience made the model even "safer" and more compelling. If Fénelon had suggested that the anxiety about parental loss may be relieved by embracing the truths of a neo-Platonism that declared a child's moral salvation need not be dependent on any one man but that all men might serve as preceptors, the suggestion of Defoe's novel was that the guilt attendant on abandoning parents may be relieved by embracing a works-oriented capitalist Protestantism emphasizing a self-sufficient and self-justifying individualism (under God), pitted eternally against the challenge of affliction.

In Crusoe's exclamation, "Deliverance from sinfulness is a much greater deliverance than from affliction" (p. 108), one hears the theological verity that, as we shall see in a later chapter, would inform nearly all the American ministerial justifications for rebellion. As Crusoe had taken the lesson of his affliction to be that he must return to his divine father in penitence for his disobedience, so had the Continental Congress immediately after the first shots fired at Lexington declared "a day of publick humiliation, fasting and prayer":

> that we may with united hearts and voices unfeignedly confess and deplore our many sins, and offer up our joint supplications to the all-wise, omnipotent, and merciful Disposer of all events; humbly beseeching Him to forgive our iniquities, to remove our present calamities, to avert those desolating judgments with which we are threatened.[5]

As Perry Miller has observed, the first obligation the colonists felt "was to cleanse themselves, not to shoot Redcoats,"[6] that is, to accept their punishment as just and their afflictions, like Crusoe's shipwreck, as an opportunity to surrender themselves wholly to the sovereignty of God.

Because it was not for being an evil earthly son, but for being a backsliding son of God, that the Lord had punished America with taxation, tyranny, and war, so it was not England but the Lord who must be reconciled. And since that reconciliation might be achieved only by separation from England, America, like Crusoe, had to pass beyond a reconciliation with the nostalgic "heavenly life" of the English countryside, to restore to itself God's enclosing presence.

By locating Crusoe's island "off the coast of America," Defoe's novel encouraged colonial readers to perceive an analogy between the fate and significance of Crusoe's island and their own Atlantic nation. Indeed, one wonders if there is not some irony in Defoe's pinpointing Crusoe's wreck "at the mouth of the Orinoco River" (p. 242), the river up which Raleigh, having failed to plant Eden in Virginia, sought Eldorado, the City of Gold. If in the drama of the fortunate fall Crusoe's island might become the site of glorious repentance and the cell of a new world, might not the Atlantic nation become, through its hilltop conversation with God, if not a Canaan, then a Mount Pisgah?

The widespread cultural acceptance in the eighteenth century of the novel, of fictions like Crusoe, suggests the larger acceptance of a faith in the ability to realize the imagined; to make what was once fiction fact; a faith in the possibility of a new reality, nature reformed through nurture, education, and experience. Henry Steele Commager sets forth the thesis of his recent book *The Empire of Reason* in these terms: "The old world imagined, invented and formulated the enlightenment. The New World, certainly the Anglo-American part of it, realized and fulfilled it."[7] America could be made the utopia Europe could only imagine. This is surely to overstate the case, but through its revolution, America did in a real sense make a fact of the fiction of Crusoe's island.

⊁ Defoe's long poem *The True-Born Englishman,* which had its first American appearance in 1778, was intended as a "satyr" addressed to the misconception that there was such a thing as a racially pure Englishman and against the claims of those who would believe themselves "gentle" because of such purity. The argument appealed to the new "Americans" of 1778.

> Thus from a Mixture of all Kinds began,
> That Het'rogeneous Thing, An Englishman:
> In eager Rapes, and furious Lust begot,
> Betwixt a Painted Britton and a Scot. . . .
> A True-Born Englishman's a Contradiction,
> In Speech an Irony, in Fact a Fiction . . .
> A Metaphor invented to express
> A man a-kin to all the Universe. . . .
> For Fame of Families is all a Cheat
> The Personal Virtue only makes us great.[8]

The only pure race are the sons of virtue. Robinson, who will, by his own efforts, win his place on earth and in Heaven, would become a glorious example of what Defoe describes as a new breed of self-created gentlemen whose fame is theirs and not their family's. For virtue and purity are personal qualities and cannot be inherited.

In 1776, a broadside with the title "The Happy Man or True Gentleman," intended to recall Defoe's well-known poem, was issued from a Salem press.[9] In what amounts to an unwitting parody of the formulaic opening paragraph of so much eighteenth-century familial fiction, the broadside combined the messages of both Defoe's poem and novel and announced to the world the nature and lineage of the new American gentleman, the new American family:

> The Happy Man was born in the City of Regeneration in the Parish of Repentance unto Life, he was educated at the school of Obedience and lives now in Perseverance; he works at the Trade of Diligence, notwithstanding he has a large Estate in the Country of Christ's Continent, and many Times does Jobs of Self-Denial . . . often walks in the

valley of self-abasement. . . . Happy is he who has Gospel submission
in his will.

The True Gentleman is God's servant. The world's Master and his
own Man: Virtue is his Business, Study his Recreation, Continence his
Rest and Happiness his Power; God is his father and the Church his
mother, and Saints are his Brethren, all that need him his friends,
Heaven is his Inheritance, Religion his mistress. . . . Thus the Whole
Family are made upon virtues. He is master of that family.

⋊ Though the 1774 first American edition of *Crusoe* issued by
Hugh Gaine (and reissued each of the next three years) abridges the
original 364 pages to 138, it adheres with some faithfulness to the
overall structure of the novel and includes in one form or another all the
passages from the first volume cited earlier with the significant exception of the final conversion soliloquy. Though the scriptural verse is
mentioned, Defoe's most radical statement of divine sufficiency is suppressed. Consistent with the character of this suppression, the Gaine
edition cavalierly interpolates into the end of its narrative Will Atkins's
confession of parricide, lifted from *The Further Adventures.* And as if
this were not enough, in the scene in which Friday and his father are
reunited, Crusoe is made to speak this polemical reflection that does not
appear in the original: "If there was the same affection in our part of the
world there would be no need of a fifth commandment."[10]

The Gaine edition redacts the novel in such a way as to balance—and
to some degree suppress—what we have called the theme of the Puritan
picaresque with interpolations of sentimentality. With the theological
passages, which serve to explain the paradox of the heroic prodigal
drastically cut, and with Atkins's confession to parricide juxtaposed
with Crusoe's inheriting his Brazilian fortune, the result is very much
one of mixed ideological messages. For all its additional emphasis on
filial obedience, the title of the Gaine edition, to add further to all the
confusion, is decidedly more picaresque than had been the title of the
first English edition. "*The Life and Surprising Adventures of Robinson
Crusoe of York, Mariner*" is replaced by "*The Wonderful Life, and Surpriz-
ing Adventures of the Renowned Hero, Robinson Crusoe who lived twenty-
eight years on an uninhabited island, which he afterwards colonised.*" Crusoe
becomes the first "renowned hero"of fiction to challenge seriously the
reign of scriptural and historical exempla on the American bookstall.

In the first chapbook edition of *Crusoe,* published in 1779 by R.
Coverly of Boston, the picaresque title is retained but the sentimental
impulse of the Gaine edition is given its head. Crusoe is transformed
into a full-fledged prodigal. The wholly interpolated ending of the
volume has Crusoe return to York to discover his "rambling disposi-

tion . . . had bro't my dear father and mother to their graves. They died shortly after I left Hull." The volume concludes with these lines:

> I can not express the anguish now caused in me. I count myself entirely the author of their death; and though sufficient is left to me to live life as a gentleman, I can't have peace to enjoy it, and at this moment I really believe myself the most miserable object living and heartily I repent giving way to the restless disposition which resulted in losing my parents, as from that hour I date all my subsequent misfortunes.[11]

The radical discrepancies in didactic emphasis among the original novel, the Gaine edition, and the Coverly chapbook, in which even Crusoe's fortune is transformed into a parental inheritance, may be explained with reference to the basic tenets of rationalistic pedagogy. As the chapbook edition of *Crusoe* is clearly geared to a preadolescent and, thus, prerational readership, its primary stress is on filial obedience and the absolute necessity for children to remain under the parental roof. In contrast, the mixed message of the Gaine edition may be attributed to the fact that it is, by its own admission, "designed for youth" (title page), "youth" almost certainly meaning an audience over the age of twelve – those adolescents who have begun to enter the age of reason but have yet to become fully adult. Such readers are trusted to be exposed to the original themes of the novel, but are given didactic antidotes to their more radical implications. The confused character of the Gaine edition mirrors with uncanny precision the political and psychological ambivalence that lay behind the debate in the American colonies over the extent of their filial obligation to England and its parental obligation to them.

The critical differences in both form and content between the full-length novel, Gaine's edition for adolescents, and the chapbook edition for children make clear the enormous influence Locke's understanding of the morphology of rational growth and independence had on eighteenth-century publishing. This crucial fact has received virtually no attention. Indeed, not just *Crusoe* but most of the important novels of the period appeared simultaneously in three formats.[12]

The first postwar edition of *Crusoe* is also a chapbook, this one appearing from the press of Isaiah Thomas in 1787. The Thomas edition takes the Coverly text one step further. In an epilogue Crusoe moralizes to the reader:

> Now as many of my readers from a wild inclination of their own or from the advice of bad children may wish to ramble from one country to another, they may rest assured by me that it will only bring them into affliction, for every word of my father's advice I found it strictly to be true.[13]

At the bottom of the last page of text appears a woodcut of a sailing ship, to which is appended these lines:

> Twas in that ship which sail'd from Hull
> That Crusoe did embark
> Which did him vex and much perplex
> And broke his parents' heart (p. 31).

Yet in one important respect the Thomas edition differs from its predecessor. It acknowledges that under certain circumstances leaving home may not be a sin. Having denounced the desire of young men to go to sea, Crusoe's father qualifies himself: "was you the son of a poor man and had got into bad company wherein your character had suffered, in that instance the resolution to go to a strange country in the interest of retrieving your character and fortune, would be commendable" (p. 6). By acknowledging that the heroic embrace of fate may be socially redemptive for those who have already lost parental grace through sinning, Crusoe's father opens the door to the argument that since all men are already sinners, such a heroic embrace is not only appropriate but required of all men.

From 1774 through 1825, an unprecedented 125 American editions of *Crusoe* appeared, virtually none reprinting the full text of the original— though that, too, in imported editions was advertised consistently throughout the period.[14] Detailed textual comparisons of these editions might provide a scale – whimsical, as it necessarily would be – by which to chart the ever-present battle in American literary history between the romance and the didactic parable, between metaphysics and moralism, between obedience to God and service to man.

In 1808, Swiss author Johann Wyss published what was to become the most famous of the dozens of adaptations of the *Crusoe* story: *The Family Robinson Crusoe,* or later, *Swiss Family Robinson.* By having an entire family leave home and become shipwrecked, Wyss resolved the great picaresque dilemma. In his version of the story no individual is obliged to choose between obedience and salvation, purity and experience, a parental inheritance that shields one from the world, and Adam's curse that permits one, eventually, to master it. Indeed, whereas Crusoe loses a parental inheritance by leaving home, the very reason the Robinson family set sail for America is that, according to the terms of a relative's will, they will inherit a large fortune if they are "settled in America."[15] Once again, as in Marmontel's "The Bad Mother," America is identified with a form of parental inheritance.

The Wyss family consists of a father, mother, and four sons; a young girl, also shipwrecked, joins them in the novel's second half and is adopted into the family – the "community of misfortune supplied the place of the ties of blood" (p. 666). When a rescue ship appears ten years after their "wracke," the two youngest sons choose to return to England. The rest of the family chooses to stay. Mr. Robinson comments: "My wife did not wish to return to Europe, I myself was too strongly attached to my patriarchal life, besides we were fast growing old and approaching the age at which peril and chance give place to a yearning after repose and tranquility" (p. 687). The Old World is left behind, yet patriarchy and the heavenly life of the English countryside have been successfully relocated in the New World. As Rousseau would have liked it, the natural and the civil states have been united. The cake is had and eaten, too.

It is altogether fitting that the first English translator of Wyss's book should have been the radical polemicist and novelist William Godwin, who maintained, as one critic summarizes it, that "natural relationship had no claim on man, nor was gratitude to parents or benefactors any part of justice or virtue." From the spiritual radicalism of Defoe to the political radicalism of Godwin, a line may be drawn that, if not straight, is most certainly distinct.[16] It is perhaps to Defoe that one South Carolinian, defending the opposition to the Stamp Act, refers when he claims Americans first learned the virtue of resistance "through the honest impressions of education, and notions derived from old storybooks."[17]

      ➤ Ronald Paulson has forcefully characterized the central structure of much eighteenth-century English fiction as that of a spiritual pilgrimage:

> His [the hero's] journey then becomes an attempt to re-create with Crusoe, literally to reconstruct—out of available materials—that lost Eden; and as it turns out this was a fortunate fall in that it gives him an opportunity to make choices of his own, become a moral agent, prove and educate himself, and win for himself a 'heaven' that would have been out of the question if he had remained in Eden.[18]

The fallen Puritan hero of Bunyan, Milton, and Defoe, like his later female counterpart in the Richardsonian novel, is, as Christopher Hill describes him, cut free by his disobedient departure or expulsion from "the inherited traditions, customs, and laws of society" and thus "set alone to work out his personal salvation in the sight of God only in a state of 'freedom.' It is of a piece with that individualism which the new bourgeois society created in reaction against the corporate loyalties and customs of subordination which had united feudal society."[19] After the falsely accused Tom Jones is expelled from Squire Allworthy's Paradise Hall, Fielding concludes: "The world, as Milton phrases it, lay all before him; and Jones, no more than Adam, had any man to whom he might resort for comfort and assistance."[20]

Fortunate Fall

Lockean pedagogy of the eighteenth century was in large measure an adaptation and secularization of the Puritan narrative of the fortunate fall. God had "allowed" Adam and Eve to fall to permit them eventually to return to an even more intimate relationship with their Father than that they had originally lost; so, too, according to Locke, must parents allow their children, at an appropriate moment, to leave the parental roof. For only by granting such liberty (or sanctioning such disobedience) might that new and greater family be made possible, which can only be founded by the free and affectional choice of children to return to the parental roof to embrace a new life.

TWO VIEWS OF THE FALL: CLARISSA IN AMERICA

The novel that even more than *Crusoe* domesticated the Puritan spiritual relation and translated it into the vocabulary of Lockean independence was Richardson's *Clarissa*. It succeeded in linking the rational and scriptural traditions in precisely the manner that the rhetoric of the American Revolution would link them a generation later. The archetypal story of a young woman's tortured escape from parental tyranny and the designs of an evil seducer offers more than a conveniently invoked literary parallel to America's flight from its parental tyrant, England, and later its "treacherous ally," France. It also demonstrates the profound degree to which eighteenth-century English literature and the educational and scriptural paradigms on which it rested gave a shaping form and a deeper meaning to the conflict between the claims of independence and authority, the conflict that would find its greatest expression in the debates over American independence. In this regard, the novel is the quintessential presentation of the inner drama that would inform the rhetoric and ideology of the American revolution against patriarchal authority. *Clarissa*'s considerable popularity in the colonies in the period under consideration has been so amply documented as to oblige us to add it as the last of our closely attended bestsellers on the eve of war.[21]

Clarissa's greatness has to do, in large measure, with its attempt to telescope the Lockean and Puritan "narratives." Given this ideological debt, Richardson's novel – even more fundamentally than Defoe's – is built upon ambivalent motives. One obligation Richardson feels is to set forth the hope that the ideal Lockean family, made possible by filial obedience and parental compassion, may serve as a type and emblem of the heavenly family on earth. Another equally strong obligation placed upon him by his Puritan orthodoxy is to declare that such a family ideal is illusory on earth and may be discovered *only* in heaven.

Part of the paradox of the Fortunate Fall is that from one perspective Adam and Eve are sinful prodigals who are deserving of their punishment and, yet, from another, they are victims more sinned against than sinning, who, by courageously accepting their fate, are transformed ultimately into hero and heroine. From one perspective, Jehovah is the most gracious of parents; for he has allowed Adam and Eve to fall only so that he might sacrifice his son to permit their progeny the opportunity to choose to return to his embrace. From another perspective, however, Jehovah may be seen as a parental tyrant enforcing a covenant of works that, as it demands perfect obedience, extorts an excessive payment from those who are guilty of nothing but natural inability. Richardson at once condemns parental tyranny and justifies it as a divine instrument of a greater good. He exacts from Clarissa the penalty of death for her disobedience but renders her a martyr. The tension between these two views of the fall would eventually become reformulated in political terms in the Revolutionary debate over the justness of British policy and the justifiableness of American "disobedience."

Spurred on by his scheming son, who seeks to purchase himself a peerage, the elder Mr. Harlowe resolves that his daughter Clarissa must marry the wealthy Mr. Solmes, even though she cannot tolerate his company. Upon learning of her baleful situation, Robert Lovelace, suitor to Clarissa's younger sister, chooses to turn his attention to Clarissa in the hope of turning her misfortune to his own lustful advantage. And, indeed, in little time he is able by his ardent address to engage, if not Clarissa's affections, her respect and gratitude. Hearing of Lovelace's interference, Mr. Harlowe orders him never again to communicate with his daughter. In defiance of that order, however, Lovelace sends Clarissa a missive urging her to meet him secretly in her father's garden two days before the date of her proposed marriage. Clarissa reluctantly agrees to the meeting but only because she desires an opportunity to reiterate to Lovelace her belief that her father's authority is "unimpeached by any greater" (II, 314). She will do everything to forestall her imminent marriage, but she will not actively disobey her parent by running away. Yet, like Satan addressing Eve or the flatterers condemned in *Cato's Letters*, Lovelace presses his "insinuating address":

> Speed away, my charmer, – this is the moment of your deliverance – if you neglect this opportunity, you never can have such another. . . . Remember only that I come at your appointment, to redeem you, at the risk of my life, from your gaolers and persecutors, with a resolution, God is my witness . . . to be a father, uncle, brother, and as I humbly hope, in your own good time, a husband to you all in one (II, 312, 316).

Though even this promise of freedom and a new family does not sway Clarissa's Lockean resolution "to follow my own judgment," Lovelace has yet another trump card. He has hired accomplices to pose as Clarissa's angered father and brother and to "give the appearance" by their shouting of being about to descend on the pair. In the frightening confusion that follows their arrival, Clarissa flees the garden with Lovelace. The serpent, manipulating appearances, succeeds in seducing an Eve who has not yet sufficiently learned to distrust language (for words are not things) and the evidence of her senses (for appearances are not reality). Once outside the garden wall, Clarissa will never be permitted to return.

When Mr. Harlowe discovers Clarissa's elopement, he places a curse upon her that she be forever ruined for her sin of filial disobedience, a curse Clarissa profoundly fears will extend "to both worlds" (I, 261). In marked contrast to what would later be the resolution of Dr. Primrose, the Vicar of Wakefield, Clarissa's father vows that under no circumstances will he readmit her to the parental roof. Separated from parental support, Clarissa is made utterly dependent on a man who she soon realizes has no intention of marrying her. Having placed her in a drugged stupor he rapes her and deprives her of that virginity her father had sought to exchange for a fortune.

In desperation, Clarissa writes to her parents, hoping to effect a reconciliation. Repeatedly she insists that she never had any pride in being "independent" at all and that her only wish is to return to the bosom of her family. Her early letters, however, are ignored and her later ones are intercepted by Lovelace's accomplice. Eventually, Mrs. Norton, Clarissa's friend, discovers these more desperate letters and brings them to the attention of Mr. Harlowe, urging him to moderate his severe judgment. Learning that Clarissa has become seriously ill, he finally and penitently agrees to embrace at last a "reconcilement." But the news of his change of heart comes too late. Weakened by her miseries, Clarissa is on her deathbed, condemned to die without that for which she had most fervently hoped – a final parental blessing:

> To be so much exposed to temptation, and to be so liable to fail in the trial, who would not rejoice that all her dangers are over? – All I wished was pardon and blessing from my dear parents. Easy as my departure seems to promise to be, it would have been still easier, had I had that pleasure. BUT GOD ALMIGHTY WOULD NOT LET ME DEPEND FOR COMFORT UPON ANY BUT HIMSELF (VIII, 94).

As Christopher Hill has pointed out, this last sentence is perhaps the most important of the novel; for it is precisely the converting truth, which Clarissa's miseries have been divinely designed to teach her. Like Adam, she is ultimately made glorious by recognition of an eternal life in which she shall find a *second* and greater paternal blessing. On the verge of death, Clarissa declares: "It was good for me that I was afflicted" (VIII, 102).

In an appendix to the novel, Richardson defends his decision to have Clarissa die at the end of the novel. He ridicules those who would see "poetical justice" done (VIII, 342) and Clarissa married to a reformed Lovelace. Earthly life, he insists, is not comedy but tragedy. He quotes Addison to the effect that on earth the doctrine of "equal distribution of rewards and punishments" (VIII, 346) is an ideal; only in Heaven is it a reality. The sinner who has repented must surely be rewarded – but only after death. Unlike Defoe, Richardson insists the spirit is witnessed only in the divinely tranquil moment of a Christian's death and not in the enthusiastic moment of conversion. Clarissa must die for her disobedience to her father's will. But since her disobedience was finally more unwitting than willful, Clarissa will be rewarded for her afflictions in Heaven. Richardson succeeds in making both his evangelical and his moral points. But to ensure that his evangelical ending does not obscure his belief that men must fervently strive to achieve a perfectly happy family and, by extension, a perfect society on earth, Richardson, like Defoe, introduces a subplot whose theme serves as a counterpoint to that of his main plot.

Having reckoned that all his children were sufficiently well-off financially, Clarissa's grandfather had chosen on his deathbed to will his estate to his granddaughter. As proof of her desire never to seek an "independence" of her father, Clarissa had placed her inheritance in trust with her father. As that sum remains legally hers throughout the novel, though she loses the favor of her own parents, she is, in fact, possessed of another "parental" inheritance. Not wanting to enter shamefully into litigation with her parents whom she so dearly loves, even when reduced to absolute poverty, Clarissa decides she must not seek to collect on it. Yet, in her own last will and testament she asks her father if he could "pardon the errors of his unworthy child so far as to suffer her corpse to be deposited at the feet of her grandfather." Her last wish is to reside "till eternity" at the feet of her grandfather in acknowledgment of "his goodness and favour which knew no bounds" (VIII, 186). Thus, at the moment of her death, Clarissa is united both with her heavenly father and with the spirit of her ideal earthly parent. Thus is the dream of heaven on earth, the discovery of a true parent who expresses his love by facilitating one's independence, conjured the very moment it is denied.

⊁ Whereas the earliest American editions of *Crusoe* adapt the novel so as to urge more explicitly the necessity of filial obedience, the first American editions of *Clarissa* perform the opposite operation. They virtually "rewrite" the novel in such a way as to render it an unadulterated polemic against parental severity. Though the novel was extremely popular from the moment of its publication, its first American imprint did not occur until 1772. Unfortunately no examples survive of either that chapbook edition or a 1786 abridgment. Both fragile editions were probably read to pieces. Only newspaper advertisements attest to their existence. The earliest surviving copy is of a 1791 Philadelphia abridgment entitled *The Paths of Virtue Delineated or A History in Miniature of Clarissa*. As had been true of *Crusoe* (and very much in contrast with the English printing history of both novels), *every* surviving eighteenth-century American edition of *Clarissa* is likewise abridged. The four other printings published in the last years of the century all seem to base their text, in one form or another, on that 135-page Philadelphia edition. Yet the shared title of those four nonepistolary editions departs significantly from both that of the earlier Philadelphia edition and that of the first English edition. The full title of Richardson's original work reads *Clarissa or the History of a Young Lady, Comprehending the Most Important Concerns for Private Life and Particularly shewing, The Distresses that may attend the Misconduct Both of Parents and Children in Relation to Marriage*. The title of these American editions follows up to "Private Life" but then continues *wherein the Arts of a Designing Villain and the Rigours of Parental Authority, conspired to Complete the Ruin of a Virtuous Daughter*. In the latter, "the misconduct of children" disappears. Clarissa is purely a victim caught between two tyrannies.[22] Her rebellious spirit is not censured in these volumes.

The same interpolated first paragraph – in one or another state—opens all the eighteenth-century American editions. It limits the moral of the novel in a way Richardson certainly had not intended:

> Miss Clarissa Harlowe, the subject of the following and the youngest daughter of James Harlowe, Esq. was adorned with great personal charms, and such perfections as rendered her the subject of a general admiration. Her father was a gentleman of a rigorous and inflexible temper and extremely tenacious of his authority as a husband and a parent. Her mother was a lady of a mild and gentle disposition; but too much ruled by her demanding husband and imperious son, who left her little power of exerting the fine qualities she possessed.[23]

The Christian paradox of the original novel, the blessing of affliction, which had provided a spiritual context "justifying" Mr. Harlowe's severity, is wholly dismissed. Clarissa becomes less a prideful martyr to the glorious cause of filial obedience than a simple victim of unjustifiable parental severity.

The title page of the earliest American edition also carries the announcement that the volume "has been familiarised and adapted to the capacities of youth." As Mr. Harlowe's sin is that he unreasonably demands perfection from his daughter and is unwilling to make any allowances for her "youthful capacities," the moral of the novel is reinforced in its American edition by the form in which that novel appears. The very word "familiarised" carries with it the rejection of a too narrowly consanguineous understanding of family.

Two years before the Philadelphia edition of *Clarissa* appeared, the first novel by an American to be published, William Hill Brown's *The Power of Sympathy,* issued from Isaiah Thomas's press. Brown's novel follows closely the model of *Clarissa* and features a heroine who is "caught between the ingratitude of her seducer and the severity of her father's vengeance." Like Clarissa, she entreats her father

> to believe her misfortunes proceeded from credulity and not from an abandoned principle – that they arose more from situation than a depraved heart; in asking to be restored to the favor and protection of a parent, she protested she was not influenced by any other motive, than a wish to demonstrate the sincerity of her repentance and to establish the peace and harmony of the family.[24]

What Brown's heroine asks of her father is that he abandon a Calvinistic understanding of moral accountability for a Lockean one that demands nothing "beyond nature," that acknowledges that children are not small adults but individuals whose reason is not fully formed. That the misfortunes of children proceed "from credulity and not an abandoned principle" is the great filial insistence of the familial fiction of the period. Whereas the ideal parent must recognize the right of all children to independence through educated rationality, he must also recognize that such rationality, even when properly educated, develops very slowly.

To an age that was radically calling into question the doctrine of Original Sin and the orthodox understanding of total accountability, the novel of seduction offered a refashioned account of the myth of the Fall and of the culpability of Eden's children. Because her reason is not yet fully formed nor her education complete, the fallen woman in this new myth is far less accountable than she is victimized. The daughter of Eden becomes an innocent martyr. Milton himself had opened the way for such a reformulation by describing Eve as "our credulous mother."[25]

In the first volume of his *Decline and Fall of the Roman Empire,* published in the great year of 1776, Gibbon argued that Christianity with its superstitious rituals and supernatural mythos destroyed the critical philosophical spirit of classical and pagan thought and thus "secured the victory of infantile credulity over ancient philosophers."[26] This superstitious spirit brought in by Christianity weakened the empire and was, finally, the remote cause of its fall. Like the fall of Clarissa, so may the fall of nations and empires be attributed to a failure to form the rational faculty, a failure to make the credulous skeptical. The true governor or parent seeks to educate his children. The tyrant, however, as Paine also writing in 1776 was to say of George III, manipulates language, particularly by his use of an expression such as "parent or mother country" as part of a "low papistical design of gaining an unfair bias on the credulous weakness of our minds."[27] Paine, himself no mean manipulator of language, is trying to tar George with the brush of popery. The Catholic faith builds on credulity, Protestantism on rationality. Thus tyranny by its very nature seeks to return the world to a time before the glorious emancipation of human judgment brought about by the Protestant Reformation.

➤ Writing in 1800 for his own journal, the *Monthly Magazine,* Charles Brockden Brown, the preeminent American novelist of the period and one deeply influenced by the radical doctrines of William Godwin, made the following comment about the novels of the man who most popularized the genre:

> The virtue on which much stress is laid in the portraits of Clarissa and Grandison is filial piety. . . . Duty to parents is not the sole or the chief duty of man, and is to give way when it clashes with other and higher duties; our treatment of parents must be regulated by their characters. When vicious, our duties lie in rejecting their demands.[28]

Though *Clarissa* did not preach such a radical gospel, it prepared the way for it. In March of 1779, there appeared in the *United States Magazine* published in Philadelphia a short piece entitled "A Vision of the Paradise of Female Patriotism." In it an angel appears to a daydreaming woman named Clarissa. As Raphael had done for Adam, the angel takes Clarissa to the top of a mountain and vouchsafes her a vision. In the vision, Clarissa is permitted to see Deborah, Miriam, Portia, Zenobia, and "The Maid of Orleans" as well as a surprisingly large number of American women in conversation in Heaven.[29] The angel encourages the young woman to follow their heroic models and serve the national cause. It is not by chance that the woman's name is Clarissa. For Clarissa was to the eighteenth century what The Maid of Orleans had been to the fifteenth: a martyred heroine who had led a revolutionary cause. "The people," declared John Adams, a generation after the war, "are Clarissa."[30]

PART II

FORMS OF FILIAL FREEDOM

4

THE DEBT OF NATURE RECONSIDERED

Once upon a time . . . there lived a certain Nobleman who had long possessed a very valuable Farm, and had a great number of Children and Grandchildren.

. . . .

He never exercised any undue Authority over his Children . . . neither indeed could he oppress them if he was disposed; for it was particularly covenanted in his Marriage Articles that he should not at any Time impose any . . . Hardships whatever upon his Children without the free consent of his Wife Parliament.

. . . .

In Process of Time, however, some of his Children . . . requested Leave of their Father to go and Settle on this distant Tract of Land. . . . The old gentleman, on his part, engaged to protect and defend the Adventurers. . . . assuring them that although they should be removed far from his Presence they should nevertheless be considered as the Children of his Family.

. . . .

[Yet soon] the old Gentleman fell into great Wrath declaring that his absent Children meant to throw off all Dependence upon him, and to become altogether disobedient.

. . . .

These harsh and unconstitutional Proceedings irritated Jack and the other inhabitants of the New Farm to such a Degree that★★★★★ *Coetera defunt* [1]

THE LIMITS OF GRATITUDE: THE ARGUMENT APPLIED

The relationship of the American colonies to England had long been accepted by both the British government and its subjects in America as analogous to that of a child's relationship to its parent. The analogy reflected not only the reality of colonial dependence on Britain for its protection and prosperity but the additional historical fact that over the years the majority of those who had been hearty enough to make the transatlantic crossing had been of a generation sufficiently young to have left parents behind. Far from carrying the presumption that the child colonies would one day attain to independent manhood, however, the analogy was ultimately more judgmental than descriptive. A child colony *should* be no less dependent on its parent country than, in a slightly different context, a subject should be submissive to his government and sovereign. The status was a fixed one rather than a temporary stage in a larger development. Childhood for the colonies was not, as Franklin would later describe childhood in the *Autobiography,* an apprenticeship or a period of growth, education, and preparation for adulthood. It indicated a permanent relationship to external authority.

Though colonists found the analogy congenial insofar as it reassured them of Britain's continuing nurture and diminished their sense of cultural and social isolation, it concomitantly served to strengthen the terms of Britain's authority over her distant charges. By implying that the obedience due Britain was synonymous with the debt of nature owed by a child to his or her progenitor, the analogy, in effect, bound the colonies more securely to their parent than could either the rule of force or civil law. In addition, filial obedience had the time-honored sanction of Scripture as well as of nature. The volume from which generations of colonial children were taught their catechism, *The New England Primer,* included a section of scriptural texts entitled "The Duty of Children to Parents."

> God hath commanded saying, Honour thy Father and Mother and whosoever curseth Father or Mother, let him die the Death. Matt. 15:4.
> . . . .
> Father I have sinned against Heaven, and before thee. Luke 15:10.
> [15:]19. I am no more worthy to be called thy Son.
> . . . .
> My Son help thy Father in his Age, and grieve him not as long as he liveth.
> . . . .
> And if his Understanding fail, have patience with him, and despise him not when thou art in thy full Strength.

In section after section, the *Primer* taught that to sin against the earthly father was to sin against God. What is owed the natural father cannot, as Crusoe had succeeded in doing, be separated from what is owed the heavenly father. Even when "grown to full Strength," as the colonies themselves had grown, children may not revile their parents. Rather, they must expect and accept the fact that as senility approaches their parents' understanding of and attendance on them will decline and fail.[2]

Indeed, English law as Blackstone made clear in 1765 declared that even those whose father had not provided them with "any way of gaining a livelihood" were not exempted from "having to provide for their father when fallen into poverty." Contrary to Athenian law, and despite Blackstone's own formulation that "the empire of the father" must give place to "the empire of reason," English law insisted that "the tie of nature is not dissolved by any misbehavior of the parent." A child is obliged to maintain and provide "for a wicked and unnatural progenitor as for one who has shewn the greatest tenderness and parental piety."[3] The debt is owed nature, not nurture. The message was reinforced in America by the warnings contained in chapbooks with such titles as *The Undutiful Daughter who . . . took to all manner of evil course . . . and continually scoffing her aged mother* (1765) and, even more dramatic, *The Prodigal Daughter . . . who because her parents would not support her in all her extravagance bargained with the Devil to poison them* (1771).[4] The revolutionary insistence on redefining and limiting the debt of nature according to parental character would not only cut against the grain of the older didacticism but was, in effect, an attack on a basic principle of the common law.

By the middle of the eighteenth century, the widely accepted Scottish formulation of natural affections and the Protestant "rediscovery" of familial responsibilities intensified rather than limited the scriptural and legal sanctions by elevating filial obedience to the level of a natural as well as sacred duty. One late eighteenth-century American children's book emblematized filial duty and affection with the following verse:

> See the young stork his duteous wing prepare
> His aged sire to feed with constant care;
> O'er hills and dales his precious load conveys
> And the great debt of filial duty pays.
> Careful return! By nature's self design'd.
> A fair example set to human kind.
> Shouldst thou refuse thy parent's needful aid,
> The very stork might the foul crime upbraid:
> Be mindful how they rear'd thy tender youth,
> Bear with their frailties, serve them still with truth[5]

The values of eighteenth-century sentimentality expressed in this poem and numerous others combine a classical notion of filial honor with both a moral sense reminder of the heart's natural response to parental kindness and a rationalist insistence on the debt of nature. For although the new sentimentalized family was "new" in contrast to a medieval understanding of family, it was not "new" when contrasted to the family as

understood – and prized – by Roman society. That the rise of sentimentality should follow hard on an age of neoclassicism is far from coincidental. In part, the point may be made by reference to Polybius's *General
History of the Wars of the Romans,* one of the most important classical
influences on eighteenth-century English political theory. Polybius
argues that the origin and justness of political obligation lie in the self-
evidence of children's natural obligations to their parents for nurture. A
great deal of revolutionary rhetoric would be indebted, at some remove,
to passages such as the following. The language of the eighteenth-
century translation reflects the contemporary mix of natural-obligation
theory, moral-sense epistemology, and Lockean contractualism.

> When any of these, therefore, being arrived at perfect age, instead of
> yielding suitable returns of gratitude and assistance to them by whom
> they have been bred, on the contrary attempt to injure them, either by
> words or actions, it is manifest that those who behold the wrong after
> having also seen the sufferings and the anxious care that were sus-
> tained by the parents in the nourishment and education of these chil-
> dren *must be greatly affected. . . . And from hence arises, in the mind of
> every man, a certain sense of the nature and force of duty,* in which consists
> both the beginning and end of justice.[6] [emphasis added]

It is not surprising that when colonists began to disobey what they
called the "Intolerable Acts," those loyal to the British crown should
ascribe that disobedience to unnatural ingratitude. In his Tory history
of the Revolution, Peter Oliver, the Chief Justice of the Massachusetts
Superior Court, voiced his moral outrage in language nearly identical to
that of Polybius:

> But for a Colony, which had been nursed, in its Infancy with the
> most tender Care & Affection, which had been indulged with every
> Gratification that the most forward child could wish for, which had
> been repeatedly saved from impending Destruction . . . for such
> Colonies to plunge into an unnatural Rebellion . . . this surely, to
> an attentive Mind, must strike with some degree of Astonishment.[7]

Perhaps the most articulate of the Tory spokesmen, The Reverend
Jonathan Boucher, extended the complaint, insisting the issue to be an
obligatory gratitude rather than a voluntary gift of love.

> The moment that our parent ceases to foster and fondle us, or that we
> imagine she ceases, our affections are withdrawn and instead of loving
> and reverencing the mother that bore us, we vilify and insult her. If
> love be a voluntary offering, gratitude is a debt, and surely it is not a
> little that the parent State is entitled to claim from us on the score of
> past benefits.[8]

Taking the part of Richardson's Mr. Harlowe, Francis Hopkinson
likened the colonists to an all-too-seducible daughter, blithely and in-

cautiously making her way in a world of demagogical Lovelaces the
likes of Paine and Samuel Adams:

> Should the colonies with base ingratitude, attempt to throw off all
> dependence on the mother country, they would put themselves in a
> situation of a silly girl, who leaves the guidance and protection of a
> wise and affectionate parent and wandering away exposes herself to
> ruin by the artful insinuations of every wicked and designing
> stranger.[9]

Once they had come to recognize the error of their ways, Hopkinson
suggested, the rebellious colonists like the prodigal son or daughter
would learn at last that only an ancient family name can repair a tattered
respectability and would penitently return to the graciously welcoming
arms of their parent. Defoe notwithstanding, the child who leaves
home to find a better life is not heroic but foolish; for England, in
William Eddis's reassuring words, would "be found till the end of time
a fostering parent."[10] William Whitehead, England's poet laureate, made
clear the threat beneath that reassurance in his "Ode for the New Year:
January 1, 1776":

> Nor let your parent, o'er the flood
> Send forth her voice in vain!
> She courts you to be free,
> Submissive hear her soft command,
> Nor force unwilling vengeance from a parent's hand.[11]

The underlying assumption of all the previous selections is that an
ideal parent is one who is and will always remain possessively protective of his children. The debt of gratitude one owes one's parents is
lifelong and should take the form of continued deference and dependence on that protection. Indeed, the more extreme Tory spokesmen
such as Jonathan Boucher agreed with Filmer that "Where subjection of
children to parents is natural, there can be no natural freedom . . . in
nature there is no nonage; if a man be not born free, she doth not assign
him any other time when he shall attain his freedom."[12] It was, of
course, this very point Locke was to deny. The natural subjection of
children to parents and the doctrine of natural freedom were compatible – if perceived as sequential. One was in the service of the other.
The point of education was to prepare a child for independence, to arm
him against, rather than hide him from, the corruptions of the world.
Whether patriarchal or sentimental, parental protectiveness that prolonged filial dependence served only to render children "helpless found-
lings" deprived of an essential moral self-sufficiency.

Whereas Tories accused rebels of falsely believing that the filial obligation ended with the period of infancy, rebels accused Britain of
failing to release them into adulthood, of confusing separation and

abandonment, of failing to recognize the compatibility of liberty and loyalty, of manhood and sonship; in short, of seeing the least attempt to assert autonomy an attempt to "throw off all dependency." As Burrows and Wallace have fully documented, Whig rhetoric and ideology in the decade between 1765 and 1775 drew extensively on the language and arguments of the familial contractualism that Locke had popularized.

In a 1775 sermon the Philadelphia minister Jacob Duché affirmed:

> We venerate the parent land from whence our progenitors come. We wish to look up to her as the guardian, not the invader of her children's rights. We glory in the name of children. But then we wish to be treated as children. And children, too, that have arrived at years of discretion. But, if we are to judge from the late ungenerous and ill-digested plans of policy. . . . We cannot but think that they began to be jealous of our rising glory, and from an ill-grounded apprehension of our aiming at independency, were desirous of checking our growth.[13]

For Reverend Duché, to be a "child" does not refer to a particular circumscribed period of life but rather to the fact of having a living parent. Consequently, what Duché objects to is not the colonies being "treated as children," but Britain's jealous attempt to inhibit the growth of its offspring. Though one may never outgrow the fact of being a parent's "child," one must outgrow childhood. Adolescence must be distinguished from childhood. To this point a letter printed in the *New York Packet* for February 2, 1776, asked:

> If in a private family the children, instead of being so educated as to take upon them the function of good citizens, should be brought to years of maturity under the apparel, food, and discipline of infancy, what laws, natural or civil, would acquit the parent of the child of infamy and criminality? A set of great lounging infants tied to mama's apron at two and twenty, with long bibs and pap spoons would put a Sybarite to blush.[14]

To be denied a proper education not only makes it impossible for one to function as a good citizen, but it also makes one vulnerable to a "sybarite" indolence that breeds moral corruption.

To prevent grown children from having contact with the corrupt world—far from protecting them—cheats them of learning how to deal with those corruptions. The point was made in a related context by John Morgan, doctor for the Continental Army, in a 1775 pamphlet arguing the necessity of universal smallpox vaccination. Those who oppose the use of the inoculation fail to grasp, he argues in a Lockean manner, that glorious paradox that a little exposure prevents a future fatal encounter: "Those who esteem themselves responsible to their children and yet forbid it . . . are guilty of a great violation of the natural rights of mankind to make use of the means of self-preservation."[15]

In yet another of their famous *Cato's Letters,* Trenchard and Gordon develop an image of that unnatural parent that would be quoted by the colonial press during the Stamp Act crisis:

> All nature points out that course. No creature sucks the teats of their dam longer than they can draw milk from thence or can provide themselves with better food. Nor will any country continue their subjection to another only because their Great Grandmothers were acquainted.[16]

Whereas "Cato" suggests that the breast has been outgrown, John Adams suppresses any such claims for American adulthood to make tenable his accusation that Britain has unnaturally rejected its infant. He ferociously elaborates on Trenchard's image:

> But admitting we are children, have not children a right to complain when their parents are attempting to break their limbs, to administer poison, or sell them to the enemies for slaves? Let me entreat you to consider, will the mother be pleased when you represent her as deaf to the cries of her children . . . when you resemble her to Lady Macbeth in Shakespeare (I can not think of it without horror) who
> "Had given suck, and knew
> How tender 'twas to love the babe that milked her,"
> but yet, who could
> "Even while 'twas smiling in her face
> Have pluck'd her nipple from the boneless gums
> And dashed the brains out."[17]

Lady Macbeth with this boast is upbraiding Macbeth for not having yet killed Duncan. Beneath Adams's analogy of England and Lady Macbeth may be a projection of the unacknowledgeable regicidal dimension of colonial American anger. Such sentiments as Adams's reflected the position held both by rationalists and moralists, which was fast becoming the received wisdom of the age, and which the 1771 *Encyclopaedia Britannica* succinctly summarized:

> Whatever power or authority then, it may be necessary or lawful for parents to exercise during the nonage of their child, to assume or suppose the same when they have attained the maturity or full exercise of their strength and reason, would be tyrannical and unjust. From this it is evident that parents have no right to punish the person of their children more severely than the nature of that wardship requires; much less to invade their lives, to encroach upon their liberties.[18]

In brief, the rhetorical position of the Whigs held that because Britain had unnaturally failed to release its child colonies from nonage – or to recognize the necessity of such an eventual release – it had in effect abrogated the implicit contract of nature and freed the colonies from any future payment of the debt of gratitude. Though Whigs and Tories disagreed on the compatibility of gratitude and independence, both subscribed initially to the idea of an implicit contract and the rationalist assumption that though love was unconstrainable by its nature, gratitude was a debt that could both be computed and constrained. The extent of that debt became an object of heated debate.

As early as 1765, the year of the first active colonial disobedience, Benjamin Franklin received a letter accusing America of being ungrateful for the services its parent country rendered during the Seven Years' War with France for control of the continent. Writing to another correspondent, Franklin quotes from the letter and responds to it:

> 'Tis evident, beyond a Doubt, to the intelligent and impartial that after the very extraordinary efforts, which were effectually made by Great Britain in the late War to save the Colonists from Destruction, . . . that the same colonists, now firmly secured from foreign Enemies, should be somehow induced to contribute some proportion toward the Exigencies of state in future.' This looks as if he conceiv'd the war had been carried out at the sole expense of Great Britain, and the colonies only reaped the benefit, without hitherto sharing the burden and are therefore now indebted to Britain on that account. And this is the same kind of argument that is used by those, who would fix on the Colonies the heavy charge of unreasonableness and Ingratitude.[19]

In Franklin's view, by misrepresenting her benevolence as disinterested, Britain was, in effect, extorting a specious debt of gratitude, fraudulently invoking the laws of nature.

While lobbying for the repeal of the Stamp Act in 1766, Franklin designed a cartoon that threatened real ingratitude. Printed on a card and dispensed to members of Parliament, the cartoon depicts "Britannia" missing both her arms and legs, and lying on the ground beside a toppled globe of the world. Each of her limbs is labeled with the name of an American colony, and across her torso a banner reads "Date Oblorum Belisaria." The moral is clear. The young Britannia without the love and literal support of its children would degenerate into a pathetic icon of the last Tory, the lame and exiled Belisarius – the Roman general made popular that same year (1766) by the first appearance of Marmontel's volume. In the name of their own preservation, the American colonies would not be above joining the Romans in committing the great act of ingratitude: the banishing of their once beloved guardian.[20]

Some twenty years before the Stamp Act, Franklin had issued from his Philadelphia press the first novel published in America, Richardson's

Pamela, of which, unfortunately, no copy survives. In an analogous con-text *Pamela* had dealt with precisely the same issue addressed in Frank-lin's letter and cartoon: the abuse of the debt of gratitude, a theme that Richardson would make a staple concern of English fiction. When Pam-ela refuses the overtures of her master and fails to be blackmailed into reciprocating with sexual favors his "repeated acts of kindness," Mr. B threatens that she will soon have occasion to complain of "real as well as imaginary" injuries for her refusal to act the "true servant" (pp. 119–20). Pamela fires back: "Well might I forget that I am your servant, when you forget what belongs to a master" (p. 12). She has remembered her father's caution that she must beware not only her master's "authority to command" but also his "power to oblige" (p. 9). Even an "angel of a master" may fall from the "merit of that title" as England had done, Franklin was to suggest, in pressing its financial demands.

Rather than denying with Franklin the legitimacy of the debt, the Reverend John Zubly of Savannah, who would later be a delegate to the Continental Congress, in his important review of the Stamp Act crisis, *An Enquiry into the Nature of Dependence,* took another position. Granted that gratitude is a debt, unlike love, which is a voluntary offering, is it not also, from another perspective, Zubly asked, still an expression of love? As such, is not its character then radically altered if constrained? The relationship between colony and mother country, the minister insisted, was affectional as well as contractual. What the colon-ists wanted, as Zubly pointed out, was "their affections conciliated," affections British policy had alienated.[21] If they could not be ruled by affection, the colonies would not be ruled by force. Zubly cited a passage from Clarendon's history of the English Civil War that he believed to describe aptly the American reaction to the Stamp Act:

> When people heard ship money demanded as a right, and found it by sworn judges of the law adjudged so . . . so had [they] then lost the pleasure and delight of being kind and dutiful to the King and instead of GIVING were required to PAY . . . THAT logicke left no man anything that he might call his own (p. 6).

The most praised of eighteenth-century virtues, benevolence, had as its original meaning in fifteenth-century English law the payment of a peasant tax required by the king to be in the form of a "gift of good will." The term was intended to cloud the distinction between an unso-licited expression of goodwill and obliged obedience.[22] In this regard it was an instance of the Rousseauistic hidden-hand theory of government that made the required gesture appear free. For Zubly, the Stamp Act, like the hated naval impressment, made power obvious and thus ob-noxious again. It cheated man of the illusion of being "kind" as well as the opportunity to be "dutiful."

As the colonists' desire for "actual" rather than "virtual" representation in Parliament gave silent expression to the larger cultural anxieties about the merely virtual representation of things by language, of intentions by professions, of reality by appearances, so the question of excessive taxation resonated with larger cultural concerns: the question of moral accountability so central to contemporary theological debates, the character of the debt of nature and the justness of expectation that exceeds natural ability. On a symbolic level the stamped paper Britain sought to oblige colonists to buy stood in silent opposition to Locke's image of the tabula rasa, that "blank sheet" Paine declared America could write its new government upon.[23] If the latter optimistically suggested freedom from original sin and the power to create a new nation, the former symbolically reflected a world of fixed values and fixed characters, one in which men are born already marked and indebted. In the best of all possible worlds, taxation and debt (and ultimately debtor's prisons in a liberalized society and the concept of hell in a liberalized Protestantism) would be abolished in favor of "benevolences" freely proffered by men and women who choose to do what is expected but unasked of them.

Zubly's insistence that filial obedience must, ideally, be voluntaristic (or in Marmontel's more pointed phrase "no loving out of duty") drew on the distinction in contemporary political theory between "internal obligation . . . which is produced only by our own reason" and "external obligation . . . which arises from the will of a being on whom we allow ourselves dependent."[24] The distinction is nowhere more forcefully implied than in Jefferson's remark to his young friend Robert Skipwith in 1771: "Thus a lively and lasting sense of filial duty is more effectively impressed on the mind of a son or daughter by reading *King Lear,* than by all the dry volumes of ethics and divinity that were ever written."[25] The example of filial obedience in *King Lear* is, of course, Cordelia, whose refusal to reduce her love to the empty forms of flattery demanded by her father obliges her to an act of apparent disobedience. Unable to heave her heart into her mouth, she declares in a most Lockean way, "I love your majesty according to my bond: no more, nor less."[26] Lear can see love only in the forms he seeks it. Like mercy, the quality of filial love and gratitude cannot be constrained.

Jefferson's invoking of *Lear* implicitly raised a question Thomas Paine would take up explicitly and with a vengeance. What if a debt of gratitude or of filial obedience was neither a rationally calculable debt nor a voluntary gift but, as the Scottish moralists had argued, an involuntary response? Perhaps the issue was not whether colonial obedience should be constrained by force if not fully embraced as a rational obligation, but whether it *could* be so constrained, *could* be so embraced.

By arguing from the assumptions of moral sense theory rather than from rationalist assumptions, Paine's *Common Sense* in one stroke radically redefined the issue, took it outside the realm of rational argumentation, and, in effect, ended the decade-long wrangling about the debt of nature. Let us attend closely to exactly what he is saying at perhaps the most revealing moment of the text:

> Everyday wears out the little remains of kindred between us and them; and can there be any reason to hope that as the relationship expires the affection will increase . . . ?
>
> . . . .
>
> Ye that tell us of harmony and reconciliation, can ye restore to us the time that is past? Can ye give to prostitution its former innocence? Neither can ye reconcile Britain and America. That last cord now is broken, the people of England are presenting addresses against us. There are injuries which nature cannot forgive; she would cease to be nature if she did. The Almighty hath implanted in us these inextinguishable feelings for good and wise purposes. They are the guardians of his image in our hearts. They distinguish us from the herd of common animals. The social compact would dissolve, and justice be extirpated from the earth . . . were we callous to the touches of affection.[27]

The common sense of Paine's title, which distinguishes us from the "herd of common animals," is not the power of reason to judge self-interest or what is self-evidently just or obliged. It is rather "the inextinguishable feelings for good and wise purposes," the moral sense or affections. The familial compact, Paine implies, is not entered into out of rational self-interest, but is the involuntary reciprocation of affections that, by definition, cannot be constrained. It is nature, not reason, that cannot forgive England, not because its crime is so egregious, though it is that; but because nature "would cease to be nature if she did." Nature's response is involuntary and unitary and so conveniently beyond debate. It cannot change its mind. Love that can be bought, sold, or constrained is, by definition, not affection, but a form of "prostitution." Thus any future connection with a Britain whom one can "neither love nor honor" (p. 22) will be forced and unnatural. In short, for Britain to ask for love she does not inspire is like the Deity demanding perfect obedience without first making available an enabling grace. It is in violation of the great principle of the age that man cannot be held responsible for what he cannot control.

Paine's pamphlet gave powerful political expression to the basic principles of the new moral philosophy and made clear that "sensibility," understood earlier in Lockean terms as a rational faculty, was in truth, as the great Scottish *Britannica* described it, a quality of heart:

> The idea of moral obligation is not a creature of the mind, but arises on certain occasions or when certain other ideas are presented to the mind, as necessary, instantaneously and unavoidably as pain does upon too near an approach to the fire or pleasure from the fruition of any good. It does not, for instance, depend on whether we shall feel the obligation to succour a distressed parent.[28]

When Paine calls George III that "wretch with the pretended name of *Father Of His People* who can unfeelingly hear of their slaughter" (p. 25), he is invoking the corollary to that basic principle set forth in the 1771 *Britannica*: "a character who is divested of these public affections, which feels no love for species, but instead of it, entertains malice, rancour and ill will, we reckon totally immoral and unnatural."[29] At the heart of the affectional philosophy Paine is popularizing lies the concept of disinterested benevolence. According to Adam Ferguson, the pleasure of serving a child in need or a parent in distress is its own reward. "It is unthinkable that a mother in presenting the breast to her child has in view some future returns."[30] Benevolence as its own reward invalidates any concept of the *debt* of nature.

The revolutionary message of *Common Sense* (like that of Edwards's *A Treatise concerning Religious Affections* a generation earlier) was that there literally can be no union where no affections are excited. One gives the other life. If Edwards had displaced duty from the center of American Protestant thought and put in its stead love defined as disinterested benevolence, so had Paine in *Common Sense* effected a similar reversal in politics. The American colonies need not choose to sever the political bond (and suffer the guilt of that self-interested choice); for as the disinterested natural affections of love and gratitude have disappeared, so has all connection. It was not a political bond or contract but the magnetic chain of feeling, the "rapport" that the *Pennsylvania Gazette* in 1776 described Mesmer as trying to account for scientifically, the "positive charge" or attraction that Franklin had discovered in his electrical experiments, that had bound them together.[31]

Paine's insistence that a parent without a true spirit of love is no parent and thus may be left behind by his children extended an argument made a generation earlier by Gilbert Tennent, a minister of the Great Awakening who argued that "to bind men to a particular Minister against their Judgement and Inclinations" was tyranny.[32] No matter his learning, status, or tenure, if parishioners judge their minister, their church father, to be without a converted spirit, they must be free to choose another whose spirit is regenerate, whose ministry is not dead but alive with gracious influences.

In the year of the Peace of Paris, Ezra Stiles reflected on

the tender distress we felt at the first thoughts of the dissolution of the ancient friendship. We once thought Britain our friend, and glorified in her protection. But . . . Britain forced upon America the tremendous alternative of the loss of liberty or the last appeal, either of which instantly alienated and dissolved our affections, never more to be recovered.

Stiles urged his auditors to glory "in the name of a Columbian or American" as once "we gloried in being a part of the British empire . . . when our attachment grew to unexampled vigor and strength"[33] England lost the revolution not only on the battlefields but, to take John Adams's phrase more literally than is usually done, "in the minds and hearts" of her children whose alienated affections were never to be recovered.[34]

    ⊁ A hundred and forty-five years before the Revolution, an accusation of unnatural abandonment had been leveled by their countrymen against those colonists about to set sail for New England on the *Arbella*. The accusation was not very different from ones that would appear more than a century later in numerous Tory pamphlets. John Winthrop responded to the accusation in a 1630 pamphlet entitled *The Humble Request of his Majesties / loyall Subjects . . . / To the rest of their Bretheren, in and out the Church of England / For the obtaining of their Prayers, and the removall of suspitions, and misconstructions of their Intentions:*

> For wee are not those that dreame of perfection in this world; yet we desire you be pleased to take notice of the principals and body of our company, as those who esteem it our honor, to call the Church of Eng [sic] whence we Rise, our dear Mother, and can not part from our native Country where she specially resideth, without much sadness of heart, and many tears in our eyes ever acknowledging her bosom. Wee leave it not, therefore, as loathing that milk wherewith we were nourished then, but blessing God for the parentage and education.

Winthrop asks his English readers not "to despise us, nor to desert us,"

> but to consider rather that they are so much the more bound to express the bowels of their compassion towards us, remembering always that both nature and grace doeth ever binde us to relieve and rescue . . . such as are dear unto us, when we conceive them to be running uncomfortable hazards.[35]

The theory of a "nonseparating" congregationalism espoused by the Puritans and rejected previously by the Pilgrim "separatists" maintained that Winthrop's followers were separating only from the corruption of the church, not from the church, itself. When the Church of England had fully cleansed itself of its Romish trappings, they would return to it.[36] The paradox of a nonseparating separation satisfied the need to assert independence and to insist upon an absolute purity while at the same time maintaining an unbroken relationship with one's parent nation.

By 1776, that delicate balance so long sustained had at last become untenable. Yet, ironically, in English politics non-separation had recently been rediscovered. The English party system that had grown up in the middle of the eighteenth century had obliged the coining of the oxymoron "the loyal opposition" to suggest that opposition to the party in power need not necessarily mean opposition to either the Crown or to national interests. Rather such opposition might simply suggest a different understanding of those interests. Indeed, by 1776 the word "party," once a synonym for the abhorred and divisive term "faction," had achieved in England a merely neutral meaning.[37] But the political lesson Britain had learned internally – that opposition need not mean rejection, that the call for liberty need not mean disloyalty – she was unable or unwilling to apply abroad to the case of her colonial children.

FRANKLIN AND THE NEW ORDER OF THE AGES

Paine's attack on England as lacking the true character of parents and thus only pretending to the "violated name" of parent rested on a primary assumption of the new antipatriarchal ideology: The character of a man and not his title or office must command one's respect and response. The character and office must at last be separated so that the world may no longer, as Gibbon had described Rome, "be governed by names." This idea received an early formulation in *Eikonoklastes*, Milton's attempt to demystify Charles I. It took fuller form a century later when in the first salvo of the pre-Revolutionary pamphlet war, Jonathan Mayhew declared that far from being a "blessed saint and royal martyr," Charles, when judged as a man, was no more than a "mock saint" and "royal sinner."[38]

The new empiricism, made more insistent in response to Berkeleian skepticism, required that men and situations be seen as they really are and not as titles and offices and names suggest them to be. The work of Gilbert Stuart, Paine's contemporary and the greatest of eighteenth-century American portrait painters, made the point most forcefully. As his father had changed the spelling of his name from Stewart to Stuart to reflect his support of the thwarted cause of Bonny Prince Charlie, Stuart expressed his own rebelliousness by refusing to flatter his socially prominent sitters. He insisted on the truth of character over convention, judgmental naturalism over deferential formulas and the traditional demand that portraits have a "distinguished air." "I will not follow any master," he wrote. "I wish to find out what nature is for myself."[39]

If Stuart's naturalism called into question the iconographic world of names, the emergence of the new rococo style in the fine and domestic arts questioned traditional values and the fixed order in its own particular way. Its unbalanced forms and asymmetry, its broken scrolls and inverted pear shapes that put the weight precariously on the top rather than below – the latter illustrated in some of Paul Revere's best teapots – all expressed a desire to be free from the fixed and hierarchical orders of neoclassicism.[40]

Perhaps, however, the most revealing contemporary attack on the fixed orders of society and the government of names was Franklin's *Autobiography*, the first and most important section of which was completed in 1771 and then set aside until after the war. Far from being a parable of American independence – in 1771 independence was not yet a serious consideration – the first part of the *Autobiography*, with its account of the fortunate fall of yet another prodigal son, represents the literary Americanization of the themes and structures of the sentimental and Puritan picaresque traditions we have examined at length. When placed in that broader antipatriarchal tradition that informs both those literary modes, young Ben's successful thwarting of the obstacles and objections to his rise in the world becomes less an archetypal narrative and more obviously a richly historical one. By providing what Franklin's friend Benjamin Vaughan called "a table of the internal circumstances of your country," the *Autobiography* illuminates the cultural context of the Revolutionary debates with which we began this chapter.[41]

As a young boy, Franklin tells his son to whom the narrative is addressed, he had "risen gradually from the Middle of the Class of that Year to be head of it, and farther was remov'd into the next class above it" (p. 53). Thus Ben's earliest experience of school taught him to expect that learning would be rewarded, that application and talent would allow him a degree of mobility not only through the fixed classroom structure, but perhaps through the fixed ranks of society. Education suggested a model of progress.

Having learned of his son's reading skills, Ben's father's first response is to want to offer him up as the "tithe of his sons for the church" (p. 52). But his inability to pay for Ben's continued education undermines such plans and Ben is taken out of school and put to work assisting his father in the tallowmaker's trade. This, however, hardly suits him and Ben quickly, like Crusoe before him, develops an intense inclination to go to sea rather than have his future decided for him, an inclination calculated to force his father's hand: "My father was under apprehensions that if he did not soon find one [a trade more agreeable] I should break away and get to sea, as his son Josiah had done to his great Vexation" (p. 57). So to prevent the "apprehended Effect of such an

Inclination" (p. 58) and ensure that the prodigal remain at home, Josiah senior (his sea-faring son had been named after him) is obliged to consult his son's interests. After being allowed to inspect various trades, Ben is finally bound to his eldest brother James who has recently returned from England with a printing press and letters. Soon, however, the work of setting and printing the manuscripts of others feeds Ben's desire to print and publish his own efforts. But the broadside ballads Ben composes and prints are ridiculed by his father and the essays he submits to his brother's paper are refused because he is "still a Boy" (p. 67).

To demonstrate that its merit rather than its author's identity or previous experience must be the final criterion for judging a work, Ben contrives "to disguise my Hand" (p. 67) and anonymously submits a new round of short pieces that quickly win approval. Franklin would later extend his insistence that knowledge of the author should not prejudice the response to his works to the case of the supreme author. Having declared, "Revelation indeed had no weight with me," the young man who had discovered deistical literature concludes: "Actions might not be bad because they were forbidden by it" but "forbidden because they were bad for us" (pp. 114–15). God's supposed authorship does not make his laws good, He makes such laws because they are good. Good and evil exist in the nature of things not in the identity of their author. The young must not be prejudged because they are young, so too the biblical laws of God must not be assumed to be all just because they are believed to issue from our supreme Father.

The painful anomaly of still being legally a boy and treated as such while, in effect, functioning as an adult was aggravated by the fixed-term apprenticeship that bound Ben to his brother until he was twenty-one. Though he dreamed of "shortening it" (p. 69), apprenticeship was intended to ensure that society would not be flooded with "masterless men." Though supposedly an educational experience that was to prepare an individual for an economically self-sufficient adulthood, it was more often merely a form of continual servitude. As such it stood in radical opposition to Locke's morphological model of education with its flexibility, its gradual relaxation of restraint, and its insistence that "the sooner you treat him as a man, the sooner he will begin to be one" (p. 202). Not surprisingly, Franklin insists that his brother's "harsh and tyrannical Treatment of me might be a means of impressing me with that Aversion to arbitrary Power that has stuck to me thro' my whole life" (p. 69).[42] What made that treatment particularly galling was that though his master was his own brother he did not receive "more indulgence." The hierarchical patriarchal relationship had not yet given way to the affectional one.

Franklin's attack on apprenticeship, fueled by his discovery of an apprenticed "Oxford scholar," anticipates the colonial insistence that England recognize youth as a time of education and not of servitude and simple probation. But an even more contemporary parallel can be found in the angry demands being made by rioting Harvard and Yale students throughout the early 1770s. After complaining for six years of being treated as children and subjected to corporal punishment and arbitrary authority, the students at Yale finally succeeded in forcing the austere President Clap to resign. His damning offense had been to introduce a statute into the college regulations that gave him absolute power by fiat over his charges. In 1774, the year of his resignation, the statute was rewritten to read that the president and tutors were to be given only "discretionary or parental authority according to the plain and general rules of the moral law."[43] Paternal authority must be subordinated to a higher law.

Franklin, too, was to have his reprieve. To allow his press to continue printing after he had been censured for libel, James was obliged to assert publicly (though privately to insist otherwise) that his brother had been set free from his apprenticeship. Such a ruse would keep the press running and still in the family. Playing on the discrepancy between the appearance and reality of the situation, Franklin, however, takes the opportunity to make the public fiction fact and moves once again, as it were, to the head of the class and out: "I took upon me to assert my Freedom, presuming that he would not venture to produce the new Indentures. But the Unfairness of it weigh'd little with me" (p. 70).

Though assured of his friends' and relatives' goodwill and that "every thing would be accommodated to my mind if I would return" (p. 76), the prodigal leaves Boston for Philadelphia. Once out on his own, Franklin fortuitously engages the support of Governor William Keith of Pennsylvania. Shown a long letter of Franklin's, Keith is surprised by how young the author is. When "told my age," he requests to see "the young Man of promising Parts" who he believes "should be encouraged" (p. 80). In a reversal of earlier incidents, Ben's age now makes his prose seem *more* impressive, not less. His youth has, to a more sympathetic audience, become his virtue. The governor assures Ben that were he to set up shop on his own he would receive some of the public printing of the colony and suggests that his father support the project financially. On Ben's "doubting whether my father would assist me in it," Sir William writes out the advantages and, in a significant reversal of roles, gives Ben "a letter of recommendation to my Father" (pp. 80–81). Though impressed by Ben's industriousness, Josiah rehearses the prejudice against youth and its claims to the privileges of age and concludes that the governor was of "small Discretion, to think of setting a Boy upon Business who wanted yet 3 years of being at man's estate" (p. 82).

Much of the rest of the first part of the *Autobiography,* and it is like *Crusoe* in this regard, will be in the service of disproving his father's judgment about the premature character of his entry into the world and, in the process, relieving his own anxiety about being "removed from the Eye and Advice of my Father" (p. 115). When Franklin commits his first "errata" and loses money left with him for safekeeping, he fears "his father was not much out of his judgment when he supposed me too young to manage business of importance" (p. 86). But William Burnet, the second governor with whom the young Franklin deals, soon eases his self-doubt. Having read Keith's letter, he declares Josiah overprudent and, speaking in the voice of the true Lockean parent, reminds Ben of the great antipatriarc¹ l truth: "There was a great Difference in Persons and Discretion did not always accompany Years, nor was Youth always without it" (p. 86).

When events make clear that Franklin had been duped by Governor Keith, a bankrupt sentimentalist like Goldsmith's Mr. Thornhill who, wishing to give what he didn't have, offered promises instead, Franklin is obliged to confront the fact that in relying so much on Keith's letter of introduction and credit ("so advantageous a Character" Josiah calls it [p. 83]), he had once again compromised his independence. He learns that he must rely on his own valuation of his character and not on anybody else's, whether higher or lower. Thus he resolves: "I had therefore a tolerable character to begin the World with. I valued it properly and determined to preserve it" (p. 115). Franklin's deistical rejection of the Calvinist theory of imputation that declared that man is made sinful by the imputation of Adam's sin and made righteous by the imputation of Christ's merit, would later build on this point. When in the last part of the *Autobiography* George Whitefield accepts a dinner invitation from Franklin for "Christ's sake," Franklin reminds him the offer had been made for "your sake" (p. 178).

That Ben's tolerable character is, indeed, good enough to allow him to make his successful way in the world will be attested to not only by his subsequent career but by the careers of others. Having become partners with his former employer, Samuel Keimer, Franklin remarks of the apprentices who are now bound to him and his office: "They respected me the more they found Keimer incapable of instruction, and that from me they learned something daily" (p. 109). Now in a position of power, Franklin would act the Lockean parent and prepare his charges for the world.

The first part of the *Autobiography* ends abruptly with Franklin's plan for the first subscription library. But no more fitting moment could be found. As his own library had allowed Franklin to "repair . . . the loss of the learned education my father had intended for me" (p. 143), the subscription library would allow men to become their own masters, to educate themselves without sacrificing their freedom to parents, tutors, or masters. Indeed, his own memoirs would provide the rising generation, in Benjamin Vaughan's words, with that "pattern for all youth," with that "influence on the private character" (p. 136) that the British parent would or could no longer provide them. It would teach the example of self-education to "young persons . . . left destitute of other just means of estimating and becoming prepared for a reasonable course in life" (p. 136). And if, as Vaughan concluded, "the nearest thing to having experience of one's own, is to have other people's affairs brought before us in a shape that is interesting" (p. 137), it along with the rest of the great eighteenth-century literature of the prodigal pilgrim would go a long way toward resolving the fundamental Lockean dilemma: how to acquire an inoculating knowledge of the world in advance of one's eventual emergence into it. And getting out into the world early was even more important in America than in Europe. Locke, himself the supreme apologist for home education, had made the point in his posthumously published *Conduct of the Understanding*. In Europe, where birth matters more than talent, one may stay at home like the Prodigal's brother and still rise in the world. However, in "a poor man's nation the lucky chance of education and getting into the world gives one infinitely the superiority in parts over the rest who, continuing at home, had continued also just of the same size as his brothers."[44]

The ultimate importance of Franklin's *Autobiography* lies in the fact that it is the optimistic report of a prodigal son, who by his own confession had carefully read in Locke's "On Human Understanding" (p. 64), that the world is not as dangerous a place as advertised, that its deceit and corruption could not only be withstood but, in fact, turned to advantage. No lightning rod is needed to protect oneself. The terrifying implication of Lockean epistemology that things are not as they seem turns out to provide opportunities for the successful manipulation of appearances, and the related problematic distinction between words and things allows Franklin, who has learned the distinction between manner and matter, to argue so effectively as to consider starting his own religion. As easily as we may be victims of language so may we be its masters when we have succeeded in learning – here Franklin quotes Pope with Rousseauistic approval – that "Men should be taught as if you taught them not" (p. 66). And even if, as Hume suggested, reason were not an investigative faculty capable of discerning truth but rather merely an instrument serving to rationalize our passions, Franklin concludes: "So convenient a thing it is to be a reasonable Creature, since it enables one to find or make a Reason for every thing one has a mind to do" (p. 88).

In a world that warns that Charles Cotton's parodic translation of the Bible should not be published because "it might have hurt weak minds" (p. 74), in which defenses of orthodoxy make converts to Deism, and the entire relationship between cause and effect has become problematic, Franklin no less than Lovelace thrives. For it is in that limitless and inconstant world where change and, to use the morally ambiguous word of the period, "design" are possible; where roles may be reversed and boys prove themselves capable of behaving as men, and moderns that they have the wisdom of ancients; where the verbal manipulation of "daylight savings" can reorder nature's balance of light and dark; that literally a new order of the ages, a *novus ordo seclorum,* may be conceived. Franklin's account of his championing of paper money over a fixed silver and gold currency reflects his insistence on a new more flexible scheme of valuation and his absolutely unanxious acceptance of a world of mobility and transformation (p. 124).[45] Here, in short, was the great rebuttal to all those narratives of the prodigal's "fatal progress."

Rather than have his character formed in a world in which he is passive and vulnerable before the least impression, rather than be a victim of "the Circumstances of my life" (p. 43) (Franklin's announced subject), man may, by making the most of those circumstances, become self-made. Even though undercut by irony, the scheme for moral perfection detailed in the second part of the *Autobiography* makes clear Franklin's faith that one can form one's own character as easily as the printer can "impress" his own "characters" – the two great Lockean terms – and correct his own "errata." If Paine had decisively argued the necessity of separation, Franklin would offer his services as Minerva to the American Telemachus, as tutor to the unparadised Adam.

He would also be the supreme apologist for the prodigal son. In his multivolume *Histoire Naturelle* (1749–89), the greatest eighteenth-century work of natural history, the Comte de Buffon argued that in the new world not yet fully drained from the biblical flood and thus not yet having achieved its final form, the human as well as plant and animal species had visibly degenerated. Rather than improving a species by moving it to fresh soil, transplantation "corrupted it by mixture" and endangered it by taking it from its divinely designated environment.[46] Here was the great scientific defense of the ancien régime, the kind of argument that gave substance to the patriarchal claim that children who dare leave home will end up as had the prodigal son, that the emergence into the world was, in fact, unsafe. In the 1770s, many years after the first edition of Buffon's history, Franklin sent the great scientist examples of American flora and fauna and reports of the current projects to drain swamps and fell forests as evidence in refutation of his theory. Buffon recanted and, in his 1778 supplement published at the height of the American war, revised his theory. In his illustrious career Franklin achieved no greater triumph.[47]

ICONOGRAPHY: PRODIGALS AND PARENTAL TYRANTS

Given the crucial relevance of the parable of the prodigal son to the concerns of later eighteenth-century Anglo-American culture, it is far from surprising to discover that perhaps no subject was more often depicted in contemporary popular engravings than the progress of the prodigal. Sold individually or often in sets of six illustrating the key moments of the parable – "receiving his patrimony," "taking leave," "reveling with harlots," "in misery," "returns reclaimed," "feasted on his return" – such prints were as eagerly purchased in America as in England. Indeed, after 1755, the successful English printer Robert Sayer, following the model of his German-born contemporary Le Clerk, presented the parable not in biblical clothing but in modern dress. Most engravers of the parable shortly followed the practice; for the story was as modern as it was ancient.[48]

The image of the reclaimed prodigal on his knees was a less heroic version of Clarissa's great gesture of submission to her father implied in her forsaking her grandfather's legacy. It satisfied the public's desire to contemplate what J. M. Tompkins insists in her discussion of late eighteenth-century fiction was "not the collapse of the weak . . . but the abnegation of the strong." This "at once suggests why the surrender of the son was the most moving form that situation could take. Such submission was not a degradation, but a spiritual grace. The harsh groundwork of dependence, where this exists, is overlain with a pattern of fantastic . . . beauty."[49] The "spiritual" beauty or grace of such self-denial rested on the assumption that one's earthly father represented one's heavenly father, that the absolute surrender of personal will to one was a type of the converting surrender of self to the other. The literature of the puritan picaresque, as we have seen, however, called into question precisely that assumption by its orthodox declaration that God alone must be served. If "rebellion against tyrants was obedience to God," as the Revolutionary motto had it, then obedience to tyrannical parents might in fact constitute disobedience to God and run counter to the will of Providence.

The last plate of the prodigal son etchings offered by Robert Sayer and of the more baroque 1760 mezzotints based on them showed the

Plate 1. Though based on the first modern-dress English engraving of the parable, Robert Purcell's 1760 mezzotint *The Prodigal Son Returns Reclaim'd* betrays by its baroque character its earlier Teutonic ancestry. The kneeling son observes the deferential formulas of early eighteenth-century aristocratic family life. (Courtesy of The Library Company of Philadelphia.)

young man, coiffed and groomed for the gracious ceremony of submission, kneeling before his father. Here the prodigal declares that as he is "no more worthy to be called thy son make me as one of thy hired servants" (Luke 15:17) (Plate 1). In 1775, the year of the American edition of Yorick's sermon on the prodigal and the battles of Lexington and Concord, Carington Bowles, "the printseller most attuned to the taste of the times" and one as popular in the colonies as in England, offered a competing series of mezzotints. In his sequence the prodigal is no longer on his knees but is, instead, as the parable in fact demands, shown embraced by his father, who is undisturbed by his son's tatters (Plate 2).[50] Freed from a posture of deference, he is allowed to stand, as it were, on his own. Only the promise of parental love and forgiveness, not the gracious resignation to a disciplining authority, will ensure that one's prodigal child will return. Sons and servants must forever be distinguished. It is now the servant who kneels before the son.

The point was made eloquently the following year in a long extract

Plate 2. In this middle-class and Anglicized version of *The Prodigal Son Returns Reclaim'd* (an enlargement of the last scene of the six-in-one sheet of the entire parable issued by Carington Bowles in 1776), the father affectionately welcomes his son with an embrace. (Courtesy of the Lewis Walpole Library.)

from a recently translated Italian work on education that appeared in no less a place than the semiofficial English *Annual Register or a View of the History, Politics and Literature for the Year 1776.* The author advises parents to "leave their children a liberal freedom, so that their father's house may not be their last choice; it is necessary that they should be happier there than elsewhere, and find those pleasures which may reasonably be expected from a parent who, though a friend to order, is indulgent from affection."[51] Like the captive bird released from its gilded cage, a motif common in eighteenth-century literature and illustration, the child must be taught to prefer the parental house made golden by affection rather than be made captive to it.

The lesson was a hard one to learn. Even Landon Carter, the venerable Virginian patriarch who supported the Revolution and believed himself "a tender and humane parent," could not understand his middle-aged son's resentful insistence that a "40 year old man . . . was not a child to be controlled." Tortured by such "filial disrespect" and ingratitude throughout the last years of his life, Carter darkly concluded his diary entry for March 16, 1776: "Every body then must be a selfish monster with himself. Surely it is happy our laws Prevent Parricide or the devil that moves to this treatment, would move him to put his father out of the way. Good God that such a monster had descended from my loins." Robert Wormeley Carter was indeed somewhat of an indolent spendthrift, but the elder Carter would go to his grave in 1778 failing to understand that his stern discipline and obsessive insistence on self-control encouraged his son's secret fondness for "torturing his father." Like so many of his generation, Carter could not appreciate that the fallen world around him that he so abominated in which "Everybody is for themselves" and the virtuous world of moral independence he so idealized in which every man is "master of himself" were but two ways of looking at the same phenomenon: the new age of independence Franklin's *Autobiography* would hail.[52]

If the political rhetoric of the Revolution and the popular prints provide one perspective on the larger American revolution against patriarchal authority, the political satire of the period provides another. Emphasizing the irrevocable ties of blood and interest that so complicated the Revolutionary conflict, the Reverend James Duane insisted in 1778: "Let this war be considered a family quarrel, disgraceful, shameful, into which we are innocently plunged by intolerable oppression." The quarreling family so often referred to was a particular family, that of John Bull, Esq. The iconography was known to everybody who read the popular press. In 1712, Dr. Arbuthnot published a series of pamphlets collectively known as *The History of John Bull,* in which John's mother is identified as the Church of England and his sister as Scotland, whose admission to the family in 1707 is reported to have caused considerable commotion. With his wife (the British Parliament) John had three daughters: Polemia, Discordia, and Usuria.[53]

A half-century later in the wake of the Stamp Act, the *Newport Mercury* for August 4, 1766, printed an anonymous political satire entitled "The History of John Bull's Children." John's three daughters – symbolic in Arbuthnot's work of the three great sins of government – are replaced by the thirteen American colonies. Internal deficiencies become external threats. All thirteen are bastards conceived by John Bull's maid, Doll. The satire tells of how "the old Lady [Parliament] would suffer no Bastards in her family" and "how the poor infants were turned adrift on the Fish Ponds as soon as born, how they landed on the Western shore, and were there nursed by a wild Bear under the green-wood tree." But, as soon as they "cut their Eye Teeth and were able to talk," Bull demands his children's return – thus convicting himself of both great parental sins: "too early abandonment" and parental severity.[54]

Such charges of parental abuse were common in popular cartoons as well as in newspaper satire. In one cartoon of the period Bull is shown sending a rope across the Atlantic Ocean to "reclaim his wicked children." In a complementary British cartoon Bull justifies his reclamation by accusing America of being "a slut" who must be saved from surrendering her virtue. From a Whig perspective, however, American virtue – its sexual significance always understood to resonate with its larger moral significance – could only be protected by leaving home rather than returning to it. The family could corrupt a child as easily as could the world. In a 1778 cartoon a bare-breasted American "daughter" is shown bound while Tory hands lustfully lift her skirt.[55] A verse satire published in Boston in 1775 even more closely identifies British possessiveness with sexual exploitation. Though its heroine is an orphan rather than a young girl sent out in service, the satire follows the broad outline of the first episode of *Pamela,* in which a kindly Mrs. B. dies, leaving her servant vulnerable to the advances of her lustful son:

> An orphan child fell to my care
> Fair as the morn was she
> To large possessions she was heir
> And friendly still to me.

> But George, my son, beheld the maid
> With fierce lascivious eye;
> To ravish her a plea he made
> And forced she was to fly.

> She's young and will no more depend
> On Cruel George or me
> No longer now my boasted friend
> Nor of my family.

> Britannia now in rags you see
> I beg from door to door.[56]

Britain is cheated by the lust of her unnatural son, George, of her virtuous and wealthy adopted daughter and "friend." Thus she is, like the villain of Marmontel's *Bad Mother,* reduced to poverty and forced to become like Belisarius, a beggar.

Significantly, neither *John Bull's Children* nor the verse satire just quoted describes America as the natural child of Britain. Defending the American resistance to the recently passed Townsend Acts, William Pitt addressed Parliament early in 1767: "It is my opinion that this Kingdom has no right to lay a tax upon the colonists. The Americans are the sons not the Bastards of England." Pitt's phrase struck a deep and responsive chord in many Americans. John Dickinson isolated them in his extremely popular *Letters from a Farmer in Pennsylvania* and Benjamin Rush, the Philadelphia physician, felt moved to declaim them as he approached the floor of Parliament when on a visit to England.[57] Whig satires represented America as England's bastard not only to suggest the prejudicial treatment colonists believed they had received from their parent, but to convict England of failing the sentimental test of a good parent – repenting parental licentiousness (as does Mr. B. in Richardson's *Pamela*) by adopting the child (and consequences) of one's sinfulness, and thus placing parental responsibility over family honor. In the chapbook version of *Tom Jones,* the format in which it was most often published in America in the last quarter of the eighteenth century, the entire plot is virtually reduced to the censuring of Tom's mother for abandoning him and the praising of Squire Allworthy's willingness to treat him as if he were his own child, to be "a father to him if he turns out to be a good boy." The true parent must treat bastard, orphan, and heir identically.[58]

The various depictions of English parental cruelty and severity in the satires, cartoons, and familial rhetoric of the American Revolution are more than the rhetorical inventions of Revolutionary polemics. Rather, they follow closely the formulaic depictions of unnatural parents in the popular English fiction of the last third of the century. The popularity of Marmontel's *Bad Mother,* in particular, generated numerous literary treatments of evil mothers. Two of the more extreme treatments of this figure, almost nightmare visions of her, appeared in popular British periodicals within months of the conclusion of the war. Paradoxically, images and themes that in a political context had explosive implications had already become in a popular-culture context favored and familiar fare of the British middle class. Thus at one level the mere appearance of these stories retrospectively suggests the futility of Britain's opposition to the antipatriarchal model of family relations that had so firmly taken hold of Anglo-American culture.

In July of 1783, the *Universal Magazine of Knowledge* published a 5,000-word "novel" entitled "Parental Tyranny or The History of Louisa and Narcissa." A "brutal" father and "unfeeling" mother are irrationally fond of their eldest, even though she is the least attractive and least well mannered of their three children. The "blind" fondness of "unfeeling" parents once again suggests, in the Lockean sense of those words, their denial of "sensible" knowledge. Seeing in the attention paid their beloved daughter by a visiting count an opportunity to rid themselves of their despised younger children, the couple deceitfully confide in them that their eldest sister's suitor will propose marriage only if he is assured that his betrothed will be sole heir to her father's estate. Although the mother already has given the count such assurance, she urges her other daughters to give credence to the arrangement by entering a convent. Louisa and Narcissa consent to this method "of rendering the family happy,"[59] but once within the convent walls, the younger sisters realize that they have been made prisoners. After a thwarted escape attempt and brutality at the hands of the abbess, Louisa, more frail than Narcissa, consents under duress to take her vows, becoming thus a "dreadful sacrifice" to the barbarous "policy of family aggrandizement." The story ends with the eldest daughter punished for her complicity in condemning her sisters to chastity by being "condemned" to a harsh marriage and no children.

The December 1783 number of the popular Dublin literary journal *The Hibernian* featured two articles with a particularly suggestive juxtaposition. The first of these was the inaugural installment of a reprinted serial entitled "The History of Leonara Cleland or the Jealous Mother," a tale of "unnatural parents who idolize themselves and pursue their pleasure inhumanely sacrificing the fruits of an hymeneal vow."[60] Jealous of the youth and beauty of her daughter and, more particularly, the attention paid her by a certain Mr. Williams, Mrs. Cleland, "a monster in human shape" (p. 621), imprisons her daughter's suitor, chains him to a wall, and allows him only bread and water. Leonara herself is sent to an abbey where she is tormented until she agrees to give up all thought of marriage, "to take the veil," and to accede to the doctrine that "parents are the images of God on earth" – this in the year colonial victory denies that very doctrine.

In the dramatic finale in a later installment, Leonara boldly declares her undying love for her suitor at the public vow-taking service, thereby revealing her mother's treachery. The novella ends with Leonara, obedient to the last, feeling guilt for having exposed her parent, thus overstating the truth of Richardson's understatement: "Most unhappy is the situation of that worthy child who is obliged in his own defence to expose a parent's failing."[61] The anonymous author prefaces his tale with the cynical and embittered moral: "A woman will never forgive her daughter for being more beautiful than herself" (p. 621). Age will always be jealous of youth, will always be reluctant to surrender to the course of nature and human events.

Appearing in the same number of *The Hibernian* was a lengthy account of the commission given a French medallist by the American Congress to strike a commemorative medallion in "Recognition of the independence of the United States of America "(p. 617). The medallion is pictured in an accompanying engraving. On the recto, strangling a serpent with one hand, is the infant Hercules with an assaulting lion, representing British tyranny, bearing down upon him. Minerva, the Genius of France, is shown protecting the child. The Latin motto affixed, "*Non sine Deus animosus infans,*" is translated "Not without God is the Infant Inspired" (p. 616). On the verso appears the head of an adolescent woman with long flowing hair intended to represent Liberty. The engravings on the medallion might serve equally well as illustrations for the *History of Mrs. Cleland,* so consistent are the values and imagery of the "novel" and the news article. Mrs. Cleland, who is likened to a "ferocious beast," finds a striking iconographic parallel in the British lion. The Latin motto seems almost a defiant reply to the baleful truth that jealous mothers will always seek to destroy their children's happiness, and the infant Hercules stands as a symbol of the claims and demands of the new generation. Those demands, as these stories make clear, are not only for independence, but for that higher state made possible by independence: a new unconstrained union.

The ubiquitous scene in late eighteenth-century familial fiction wherein a parental tyrant is shown condemning his or her child to a life of enforced chastity in an abbey or monastery – the scene at the heart of the two tales above – reflects what may be called the prevailing Protestant bias of the sentimental novel. From a Protestant perspective such parents were guilty of the Romish heresy of placing personal virtue – speciously identified with chastity – over the greater good of society. Marriage, like the eventual union of colonies in the political sphere, was an estate that all children reaching adulthood must be allowed to inherit.

But beyond the question of individual rights, to marry and "increase and multiply" were the sacred responsibilities of all Christian citizens. Those parents who would deny their children a happy marriage were dealing a blow to the future of society. One eighteenth-century commentator put it this way: "How frequently do they put an end to the existence of many of their offspring in their refusing to allow their children the most perfect happiness on earth?"[62] The great Milton himself had declared: "Our Maker bids increase, who bids abstain / But our destroyer, foe to God and Man."[63]

Perhaps nowhere is this bias more revealingly explicit than in the popular French novel *The Siege of Rochelle* by Stephanie de Genlis (whose reputation in America Howard Mumford Jones contends to have eclipsed that of Marmontel in the decade of the 1780s). Because it shows us another important aspect of the attack on parental tyranny, it is worth dwelling on briefly in concluding this section. As its title suggests, the novel is set in seventeenth-century France during the religious wars between Huguenots supported by their English allies and French Catholic Royalists. The fate of Clara, the novel's heroine, is identified specifically with the fate of the Protestant church in Europe. Her cause is its cause.[64]

Having confessed to the murder of her own child in order to protect her Catholic father, whom she believes to have committed the murder to ensure an inheritance, Clara escapes a prison sentence and takes refuge in a convent. Ironically, however, the Protestant forces have just won the first major battle and declared the convents opened.

> About two months after Clara's arrival, the Calvinists, no longer keeping any measures, suddenly declared the Catholic worship abolished, religious vows to be no longer permitted, and that all persons cloistered might leave their monasteries and resume their liberty. . . . The cloisters were thrown open, but the nuns never stirred from them. They were left free to choose between marriage and celibacy, between the world and solitude. It was not doubted but that such offers would depopulate all the monasteries in one day. . . . The nuns replied, that they preferred their solitude to the world. They had been invited, in the name of nature and humanity to return to society, but on their refusal a cry of fanaticism was raised, and it was determined that they should be forced from their cloister. (III, 82–83)

Convinced like the prodigal colonists that only in society is there liberty, Madame de Genlis suggests that the Calvinist opening of the convents represented a turning point in the history of European Christianity – just as it represented a turning point in Clara's life. It offered the great choice between "the world and solitude," between fearful retreat from and courageous emergence into the world. Once released, Clara learns that the criminal "parent" whom she has long been protecting is not her real father; her natural parent she discovers is not even Catholic, but Protestant.

Shortly after the revelation, Clara marries. Earlier she had vowed that she would never injure her future children "so far as to hide them from intercourse with the world." Though she fears the "dangerous world, she will urge them to go and shame it into virtue" (III, 68). Their success in that cause would be one with the triumph of the Protestant Reformation. The prodigal who goes into the world becomes a pilgrim. The fortune of the fall will be the success of the Protestant search for a new society.

As has already been pointed out, by discrediting virginity the Reformation elevated the moral status of the family. Implying a progressive view of history, it denied that there was a fundamental distinction between one's spiritual responsibilities and one's responsibilities to society. Husbands and wives were obliged to have Christian children to serve the ongoing cause of the Protestant church: the creation of a kingdom on earth. The American daughter fleeing parental severity in the sentimental tradition was but a later incarnation of the pregnant girl in the Book of Revelation, whose flight into the wilderness was "improved" by numerous colonial ministers to typify the course of the Protestant church.[65] In his sermon of 1775, "The Church's Flight into the Wilderness," Samuel Sherwood developed the analogy with reference to the Revolutionary situation:

> Hence when she appeared pregnant, ready to bring forth children, when the gospel began to have success, and new converts were borne, and added to the church, this dragon stood ready to seize and devour them, like a hungry lion, eagerly waiting for its prey.[66]

The woman on the verge of bringing about a new and virtuous generation was at once America and the Protestant Church. The dragon ready to devour that family was at once Britain and, as Paine had made clear in *Common Sense* by calling monarchy the "Popery of government" (p. 13), the reign of the Romish Antichrist on earth. Those prodigal pilgrims fleeing parental tyranny, popery, and the extorted debt of nature turned to their hearts for guidance and sought the promise of a new kind of relationship. Filial freedom was but the prelude to the dream of great voluntaristic union and the reordering of society it suggested when writ large.

5

AFFECTIONATE UNIONS AND THE NEW VOLUNTARISM

Central to the rationalist ideology of the American Revolution was the belief that in an ideal world all relationships would be contractual. In such a relationship all obligations and expectations are made explicit before the voluntary consent of the relevant parties. The failure of any one party to fulfill his or her obligations renders the contract no longer binding on the others involved. Simply defined, then, a contract may be said to be an agreement for which there exist fully defined grounds for its possible dissolution. Yet in eighteenth-century England, marriage, perhaps the most important of all social contracts, had no such fully delineated or accepted grounds for dissolution. In America, however, as Nancy Cott has shown, divorce laws were considerably more liberal. Irremediable cruelty and long absence were often sufficient grounds for divorce. But what of alienated affection, incompatibility, and unreciprocated love?[1] If marriage was essentially an economic agreement between the couple's parents in which the hand of a daughter was part of a larger economic transaction, then default was a relatively clear-cut issue. If, however, it was a reciprocated promise to treat one's spouse with love and affection and consider his or her best interests, might not the failure of one party to act the loving spouse be sufficient grounds for divorce? Whether separation was a justifiable response to such domestic tyranny was a question with great political ramifications.

WEDDED LOVE AND REVOLUTIONARY IDEOLOGY

In 1774, several months after arriving in Philadelphia from England where, because of irreconcilable differences with his wife, he had left behind an unhappy and childless marriage, Thomas Paine assumed the editorship of a journal entitled *The Pennsylvania Magazine*. To it he contributed articles not only about politics, but also about the true character of marriage. One of these, "Reflections on Unhappy Marriages," appearing in June of 1775, concluded with a critique of the

123

institution of marriage as offered by "an American savage." In anticipation of the argument in *Common Sense* a half-year later, Paine's noble savage declares that in a relationship between a man and a woman, only the laws of affection should be considered binding. The savage clearly is meant to speak for Paine.

> Hence, continued he, as soon as ever you meet you long to part; and not having this relief in your power, by way of revenge, double each other's misery: whereas in ours, which have no other ceremony than mutual affection, and last no longer than they bestow mutual pleasures, we make it our business to oblige the heart we are afraid to lose; and being at liberty to separate, seldom or never feel the inclination. But if any should be found so wretched among us as to hate where the only commerce ought to be to love, we instantly dissolve the bond: God made us all in pairs: each has his mate somewhere or other; and tis our duty to find each other out since no creature was ever intended to be miserable.[2]

Paine devoted a large percentage of his journal's pages to articles that, though glorifying the institution of marriage, warned readers that they must marry for the right reasons—love and compatibility. The journal's featured contributor, "The Old Bachelor," believed all reasonable men would agree with him when he declared, "I had rather be a solitary bachelor than a miserable married man."[3] Paine favored articles about marriage not only in justification of his own separation, but because domestic politics addressed the same ideological issues as international politics. One of Paine's most prominent contributors, John Witherspoon, signing himself Epaminondas, contributed several essays on marriage and then responded to readers' letters in the manner of an advice-to-the-lovelorn columnist. After the war, Witherspoon, then president of Princeton, campaigned for the liberalization of divorce laws in New Jersey. The campaign, like Milton's earlier one, applied and extended the principles of its author's own revolutionary politics.[4] Such a view is supported by Nancy Cott's conclusion that "the rise in divorce related . . . to the War . . . in the sense that a certain personal outlook—one that implied self-assertion and regard for the future . . . may have led a person to seek divorce and also to support independence" (p. 119). This seems certainly to have been the case with Paine.

In December of 1775, *The Pennsylvania Magazine* published an article entitled "One Cause of Uneasiness in the Married State." Perhaps written by Witherspoon, the article details the abuses a supposed correspondent of the journal has been receiving from his wife:

> After she had established her empire over me, by the means of that fondness which she too plainly perceived, she did not stick so close to that becoming modesty of fearful duty but began by thwarting me in

little trifles, which I did not at first take notice of, till by a repetition, not the least guarded, and I found, though a thing was known to be disagreeable to me, it was nonetheless put in practice, without any concern that it was so.[5]

As she escalates her demands, the unfeeling spouse becomes more and more "obnoxious," but her dutiful husband continues to protest that "he loved her in spite of discontent." At first, however, he is driven to making an ultimatum to which every colonist in December of 1775 would have subscribed: "I must have peace at home: It is in my interest to have everything easy where I fix the seat of my happiness" (p. 602). Unwilling to be a "weak husband ridiculed," the author implies that he will leave his wife who has "returned nothing for kind usage but momentous abuse. . . . Bad wives flatter fools and tyrannize over men of sense" (p. 602). The author invokes the twin Lockean evils so constantly invoked in the political rhetoric: flattery – the address to subrational faculties – and tyranny – the unwillingness either to act reasonably or to consult another's reason. The article seems to call out for an allegorical reading, but most probably it was intended only secondarily as a political allegory. Rather, its real importance lies in its testimony of the extent to which the theme of domestic tyranny of all sorts preoccupied the American mind on the eve of Revolution. In the same year that this article was published, an American edition of Gregory's *A Father's Legacy to his Daughters* would argue, in violation of the convention of its own genre, the necessity of placing personal happiness over the "obligation" to be married.

It was not, however, until five years after the war that *An Essay on Marriage or the Lawfulness of Divorce* appeared in Philadelphia, announcing itself as the first such pamphlet published in America. The occasion of the essay, the anonymous author tells us, was the suicide of a woman "who destroyed herself on account of some infelicity in marriage." Reflecting on the presumably large number of others "equally wretched but too fearful to plunge themselves in another world," the author has chosen to take up his pen to describe the "misery of marriage in those who are unsuitably united."[6] He plays not only on his readers' sympathetic feelings for the distressed but also on their republicanism. In America, a nation "famous for her love of liberty," should not "that same spirit of indulgence" extend to "those united together in the worst bondage"? (p. 3) If "God does not seek or rejoiceth in our infelicity," should man? (p. 20) Marriage is a sacred and solemn bond that must not be weakened. Nor, however, should it be coercively strengthened by denying the "reasonable liberty" of parting. The higher incidence of and interest in divorce reflected not only an emerging ideology of individual happiness and personal freedom: It reflected the new idealization of a loving marriage as the basic expression of the social character of man. In addition, a felicitous marriage served for a woman the function that education did for a man. It protected her from corruption and ensured personal happiness. Thus it was of vital concern to the pedagogical revolution.

Neither Locke nor Rousseau believed that daughters should be encouraged to the same spirit of independence as their male counterparts. Sons must be allowed to develop their rational faculties as early as possible to ensure their self-sufficiency in the world. But a daughter whose "fate through life," according to Rousseau, depended on her marriage was to be granted a different though complementary right of self-determination: the right to choose her own spouse or, at the very least, the right to veto the parental choice of the man who would, in effect, serve as her "reason" and guardian.[7] Whereas sons were freed from parental dependence by the development of autonomous reason, daughters, whose virtue must always have a protector, were to find a similar "liberation" through marriage.

As the British government sought to prevent the American colonies not only from becoming independent but also from entering into a voluntary and inviolate union among themselves, British tyranny was, in its own way, nothing less than interference "in the great article of marriage." "Join or Die," declared Benjamin Franklin.[8] "Only in union is there happiness," elaborated the Boston minister Jonathan Mayhew.[9] Reacting to the Declaration of Independence, Ezra Stiles wrote in his diary: "The colonies tied the Gordian knot Parliament can not undo."[10] The American cause was, in the broadest sense of the term, the cause of "union," of liberty not as a final autonomy but as the freedom to choose one's bond. Psychologically it was vital to the colonists to believe that they were fighting not the cause of a licentious freedom but that of a glorious voluntarism. Paine's denial in *Common Sense* of the English assertion that the colonies have no "relation to each other but through the parent country," (p. 19) and his complementary insistence that "Independence is the only Bond that can tye and keep us together" (p. 46) made the point succinctly. Indeed, over the next century, no word in the American political lexicon would be more consistently and more universally acknowledged to be sacred than "union."

So it is not surprising that one theme treated repeatedly in the pre-Revolutionary American press was the sacred character of the matrimonial estate. Paine's *The Pennsylvania Magazine* and Isaiah Thomas's equally partisan *The Royal American,* the only two American magazines published in the years 1774 and 1775, extolled the joys of a good marriage even more than they magnified the horrors of a bad one.

An article in the April 1775 number of *The Pennsylvania Magazine* declared matrimony to be "the highest state of human felicity," resembling that of "the beneficent beings above."[11] Edited by Isaiah Thomas, who was later to divorce his wife for her adulterous failure to observe the marriage vows, *The Royal American* declared in January 1774:

> Marriage collects a man's views to a proper center, calls in his wandering affections, animates him to new exertions for the welfare of the little circle with which he is more intimately connected. In this happy state, man feels a growing attachment to human nature and love to his country.[12]

Two months later an article in the same magazine suggested the deeper significance marriage held for Americans on the brink of war:

> It has been observed, that the more cities increase in wealth and the luxuries of life, the less the inhabitants are disposed to obey the laws of Reason, Nature and Heaven, by entering into that *social union* which the beneficent Creator instituted for the Happiness of Man, and which is at once the greatest ornament and blessing to human society . . . in proportion to the increase in learning, politeness and virtue, in every nation the importance of matrimony to the public welfare has appeared; and without this virtuous union, there cannot be prosperity and happiness in a community, or among individuals.[13]

The passage suggests the degree to which Americans were already preoccupied with laying the groundwork for the raising of their empire. The point of the Revolution would not be simply to dissolve an intolerable union but to establish a more glorious one founded on the most primary of social unions – the voluntary marriage contract, the ultimate Lockean relationship: "friendship made perfect."[14]

"Hail honour'd wedlock! Sacred Right / The Crown of life is thine," commenced one anonymous poet in the March 1776 number of *The Pennsylvanian Magazine,* seeking to improve upon the opening lines of Milton's "Hymn to Wedded Love" by changing "rite" to "right." The magazine verse was but one of many such paraphrases during the Revolutionary period.[15] According to George Sensabaugh's analysis, no passage in Milton's epic – first issued in an American edition at the height of the Revolution in 1777 – so captured American imagination as these lines from the Fourth Book of *Paradise Lost:*

> Hail wedded Love, mysterious Law, true source
> Of human offspring, sole propriety
> In Paradise of all things common else.
> By thee adulterous lust was driv'n from men
> Among the bestial herds to range, by thee
> Founded in Reason, Loyal, Just and Pure
> Relations dear, and all the Charities
> Of Father, Son and Brother first were known.
> Far be it, that I should write thee sin or blame,

> Or think thee unbefitting holiest place,
> Perpetual Fountain of Domestic sweets,
> . . . .
> Reigns here and revels, not in the bought smile
> Of Harlots, loveless, joyless, unindear'd
> Casual fruition, nor in Court Amours (IV, 750–67)

Milton makes two significant and related points. First, what separates man from beast is that the society of the former originates not in "casual fruition" but in wedded and lawful love; and second that "the charities of Father, Son and Brother," the virtues of fraternity and filial obedience, proceed and *issue from* the first social contract, the rational wedded love of kindred souls. Thus, contrary to Polybius (and Rousseau), the fundamental relationship of all societies is not that of parent and child but that of man and wife, whose affections for one another are no less sacred than the affections held by blood to blood. Each marriage begins a new history. Here were doctrines whose political implications were enormous. By identifying prelapsarian existence as a species of marital bliss, Milton pictured a paradise in which perfect virtue was fully compatible with sexual pleasure and natural and un-cursed procreation, in which love of the creature enhanced rather than diminished adoration of the creator:

> But thou hast promis'd from us two a Race
> To fill the Earth, who shall with us extol
> Thy goodness infinite, both when we wake,
> And when we seek, as now, thy gift of sleep.
>   This said unanimous, and other Rites
> Observing none, but adoration pure
> Which God likes best, into thir inmost bower
> Handed they went; and eas'd the putting off
> These troublesome disguises which wee wear,
> Straight side by side were laid, nor turn'd I ween
> *Adam* from his fair Spouse, nor *Eve* the Rites
> Mysterious of connubial Love refus'd:
> Whatever Hypocrites austerely talk
> Of purity and place and innocence,
> Defaming as impure what God declares
> Pure, and commands to some, leaves free to all (IV, 734–47).

The description of Adam's and Eve's sexuality contained in this passage and in the "Hymn to Wedded Love" reflects a historical shift in the theological perception of Paradise that occurred contemporaneously with the revaluation of parental responsibility in the course of the late sixteenth and early seventeenth centuries.

The patristic conception of paradise viewed Adam and Eve less as a conjugal couple made "glorious" by that love Milton would later specify as "wedded" than as essentially siblings, children of the same parent united by filial love for their progenitor. The Protestant view, however, embraced both these idealizations, believing that as long as the will is obedient to God there is "no filthiness in the actions of nature."[16] In *A Treatise of Paradise* (1617), a source for Milton, John Salkend argued that there would be multiple generations in heaven, that in heaven as well as on earth children might have natural parents as well as share a single divine one, for parenthood was part of the perfected estate of man. Had God not intended generation, Salkend concluded, he would have created two men "rather than one man and one less perfect woman" (p. 180).

Here was at once an early and ultimate expression of the revaluation of familial relations: the translation of the human family to heaven. Whereas Milton's "Hymn" had conferred a sacred character on conjugal relations, the Protestant view of Paradise made of Eden an earthly version of human society, thus permitting the eventual development of the view that at some future point through the perfecting process of parental example and Christian education paradise might be regained on earth. Christian society would become God's kingdom on earth.

The struggle for American independence and for subsequent federal union was intimately related to, and ideologically reflected in, a national affirmation of the sacred character of affectional and voluntaristic marriage. In his minor epic *The Happiness of America* (1786), David Humphreys invoked Milton's "Hymn" in order to extol a nation in which lovers listen to their hearts:

> Hail hallow'd wedlock! purest, happiest state,
> Thy untry'd rapture let my song relate. . . .
> Here uncontroul'd foll'wing nature's voice,
> The happy lovers make the unchanging choice,
> While mutual passions in their bosoms glow,
> While soft confessions in their kisses flow,
> While their free hands in plighted faith are given,
> Their vows accordant, reach approving heaven.[17]

The eighteenth-century popularity of "The Wedding Hymn" and its prelapsarian depiction of Adam and Eve – in contrast to the postlapsarian view of the scriptural parents epitomized in *The New England Primer* verse, "In Adam's Fall, we sinn'd all" – reflects perhaps the most important historical phenomenon in the eighteenth century: the ongoing rejection of the theory of innate and transmitted depravity. It is altogether fitting that the ultimate expression of the cultural revolution that would alter the political, theological, and pedagogical understanding of paternity should be the rediscovery and celebration of the prelapsarian nature of the "first form'd pair." The optimistic strain of Christianity, so much a part of late eighteenth-century American intellectual history,

Conversation

took up in a way the poet had not foreseen Milton's avowal in *Of Education* that the ultimate end of both Christian history and man's moral education was "to repair the ruins of our first parents."[18]

Sensabaugh cites over a dozen American references in the last quarter of the century to Milton's prelapsarian Eve as "an ancient 'model' of dignity and grace, indeed an 'original' which could like the sun 'impart' some of its 'rays' to the 'amiable sisters of America for the purpose of correcting their modern manners' " (p. 199). The fallen parent had been made exemplary. In his *Legacy,* even Dr. Gregory had turned to Milton's description of Eve in an effort to set before his daughters an ideal model of virtuous femininity, citing these lines: "Grace was in all her steps, Heaven in her eye / In every gesture dignity and love" (p. 58). Milton's description of Eve was among several texts that would play an important part in the secularization and feminization of "grace." By the end of the eighteenth century the secondary aesthetic sense of the word, innate and personal dignity, had become more and more indistinguishable from the theological sense, the received glory of Christ. Grace was not something for which one was beholden ("by his grace," "in his good graces"); it was, as Thomas Reid in one of the many new works on aesthetics to appear in the 1770s and 1780s proclaimed, "the last and noblest part of beauty."[19]

When Adam learns of Eve's having eaten the forbidden apple, rather than reproaching her for her disobedience, he laments her credulity and chooses to join the woman he loves in exile and in death:

> O fairest of Creation, last and best
> ·
> How art thou lost, how on a sudden lost,
> Defac't deflow'r'd, and now to Death devote?
> Rather how hast thou yielded to transgress
> The strict forbiddance, how to violate
> The sacred Fruit forbidd'n! some cursed fraud
> Of Enemy hath beguil'd thee, yet unknown.
> And mee with thee hath ruin'd, for with thee
> Certain my resolution is to Die;
> How can I live without thee, how forgo
> The sweet Converse and Love so dearly join'd
> To live again in these wild Woods forlorn? (IX, 896–910)

Here in the primordial act of filial disobedience, Adam chooses to honor his obligation to the creature over his obligation to the Creator: to die with his wife rather than live with his parent. Milton's sympathetic depiction of Adam's fall would open the way for other writers in other times – as would later Richardson's sympathetic depiction of Clarissa's "fall" – to transform Adam's fatal act of disobedience into a heroic rebellion, to set the claims of Romantic love against the claims of patriarchal authority, and to extend the issue of individualism in the marriage choice to a justification for familial revolution. The figure who most radicalized that issue and made clear its revolutionary implications was Rousseau, who did so not in his political writings, but in his fiction.

⊁ By making Clarissa's suitor a libertine, Richardson – a good Calvinist and an arch "anti-Romantic" – successfully avoided dealing with the most problematic issue relating to his declared theme of marriage: the conflicting demands of love and duty. Rousseau, however, did not avoid the issue. Though he paid Richardson the compliment of modeling *Julie ou La Nouvelle Héloïse* on *Clarissa*, Christopher Hill speculates:

> Richardson, who was disgusted by the *Nouvelle Héloïse*, would have appreciated it as little as Luther did the German peasants' appeal to his authority. For under a new revolutionary impulse in the later eighteenth century, the same inner voice to which Clarissa listened led more flamboyant spirits onto a deliberate flouting of the conventions which the old-maidish Richardson could not have conceived without horror.[20]

The second half of Rousseau's novel follows the conventions of the novel of filial obedience, with Julie marrying the suitor of her father's choice and reconciling herself to her father's and her husband's will. The first half of the 1200-page novel is, however, in Leslie Fiedler's phrase, "an anti-bourgeois" brief in defense of the claims of Romantic love.[21]

Indeed, taken together, two early pronouncements by St. Preux, Julie's thwarted lover, virtually constitute an eighteenth-century manifesto of the rights of the rational heart:

> Why should the vanity of a cruel father . . . wound those tender and benevolent hearts which were formed to soothe the pangs of others? Are not the ties of marriage the most free, as well as the most sacred of all engagements? Yes, every law to lay a constraint on them is unjust. Every father, who presumes to form or break them is a tyrant. This chaste and holy tie of nature is neither subjected to sovereign power nor parental authority; but to the authority only of that common parent who hath the power over our hearts, and by commanding their union, can at the same time make them love each other (I, 255).

In Volume II, St. Preux addresses Julie's father directly:

> If your daughter had deigned to consult me concerning the limit of your authority, doubt not but I would have taught her to disregard your unjust pretension. How despotic soever may be the empire you assume my rights are infinitely more sacred. The chain by which we are united marks the extent of paternal dominion, even in the estima-

tion of human law, and whilst you appeal to the law of nature, you yourself are trampling upon its institutions. . . .

Go inhuman father, and meditate the destruction of your only child, whilst she, full of duty and affection, stands ready to yield her happiness a victim to prejudice and opinion; but be assured your own remorse will one day severely revenge my injuries, and you will then perceive, when it is too late, that your blind and unnatural hatred was no more fatal to me than to yourself. (II, 171–2)

St. Preux's statements are at once the most compelling, the most extreme, and the most influential condemnations of parental tyranny to be found in the sentimental literature of the third quarter of the eighteenth century. Whereas Richardson condemned parental severity, urging parents to temper their natural authority with consideration for the best interests of their children, he at no time called into question that natural authority – even in the "article of marriage." Rousseau, however, finds sanctions both in heaven and in nature to make such a condemnation.

It would be a vast disservice to Rousseau to charge him, as some have, with glorifying adulterous passion; for the cause he champions in his only novel is none other than that Milton had championed earlier – wedded love. What differentiates La Nouvelle Héloïse from Clarissa, however, is that its didactic point is not simply to condemn parental tyranny over the filial heart, but to urge young men and women to listen to the promptings of their hearts, to consult their own affections. They should not succumb to blind and irrational passion, but neither should they confuse heart-felt affection and reciprocated interest with irresponsible passion. For to deny stoically the legitimacy of one's own sentiments is to do violence to the cause of one's own happiness.

Precisely this point is effectively made by a moral fable appearing in the August 1774 number of The Royal American. Though stricken with love, the tale's heroine feels obligated not to admit her affection for the young man. Glorifying in her own self-denial, she proclaims: "Shall I become a slave to the passions over which I have so often triumphed?" When the news arrives, however, that her loved one has been killed (presumably in the Boston massacre), she is brokenhearted and overcome with regret for not having "confessed her love."[22] Since everything in the pro-patriot magazines had a propagandistic dimension, it is not stretching a point to infer a political moral here. America must forsake her posture of passive obedience to a parent who, in one rebel's words, "has no compassion for the sons of her womb," and renounce an outworn moral code in order to express boldly her love for her own.[23] Lockean stoicism moves toward romanticism.

The expression of emotion was the new interest of the age. In 1775, John Behrent placed an advertisement in the Philadelphia papers announcing that he had made "an extraordinary instrument, by the name of the piano-forte," the first American-made example of the new instrument that in the past decade had become the rage of Europe. Unique because of its stroke-responsive action, the piano-forte was capable of expressing a spectrum of play from pianissimo to forte. As such it was fast replacing the harpsichord, whose tinny sound and weak hammers could not accommodate the range of spontaneous human emotion. In 1771, having been "charmed" by it, Jefferson changed an order for a clavichord to this new romantic instrument that stressed feeling over logic. Behrent's notice, no less than the popularity of Rousseau, suggests in the years immediately preceding the Revolution a new validation of human feelings and the necessity of their expression.[24]

There is more than a little evidence to suggest that Rousseau's novel as well as his opinions found a large and sympathetic reading public in colonial America. Within ten months of *La Nouvelle Héloïse*'s publication in France, John Livingston, a Philadelphia bookseller, advertised a translation for sale in *The Pennsylvania Gazette* for January 28, 1762:

> The New Eloisa, written by the ingenious Rousseau; this is the favorite novel; every one who hears of it, reads and admires it. Elocution, Sensibility, Refinement and Humour, constitute its principal Ornaments, and it is the only Novel that has been equally well received with the celebrated Clarissa Harlowe, to which it bears some Resemblance, only the New Eloisa is allowed to be a more masterly and instructive performance.[25]

Washington is known to have had a 1773 edition of *Eloisa* in his library and Jefferson is on record as recommending the novel for general edification to Robert Skipwith in 1771. But, perhaps, most significant of all is a piece of marginalia that survives in John Adams's copy of the novel.

In the second of its four volumes Adams underscored a passage describing the intervention of Julie's cruel parent in the affairs of her heart: "Let rank be determined by merit and the union of hearts by their own choice, this is the proper social order. . . . Those who regulate it [the union of hearts] by birth or wealth are the real disturbers of the system." Though suspicious of Rousseau's antinomian emphasis on the heart, Adams adds in agreement: "Peoples, nations, not individuals are guilty of this."[26] M. d'Etange's behavior, Adams's comment suggests, reflects less his personal values than it does those of his nation. In a nation ruled by an aristocracy that identifies rank with wealth, marriages will be arranged to perpetuate that order. But in an American republic such as envisioned by Adams, the choice of marriage partners would not only be free but, as it would reward virtue and merit, so it would serve as the foundation of a new order.

Adams practiced as well as professed his "matrimonial republican-

choice of spouse to be free

ism,"[27] at least with regard to his daughter's involvement with Royall Tyler. Though Tyler would go on to become a playwright and Supreme Court judge of Vermont, he was widely known in his youth for his womanizing, and in the spring of 1783 his fancy turned to Nabby Adams. In England, having drafted the peace treaty that would conclude the great war, Adams was apprised by his wife of their daughter's courtship. Apparently sympathetic to the romance, Abigail assured him that Tyler was no longer the libertine of whom he once had heard. Though John objected that he would not have his "model" daughter given to "every reformed rake," he conceded, "I can scarcely think it possible for me to disapprove of her final judgment formed with deliberation upon it which so deeply can concern her own happiness."[28] To Nabby he wrote: "You have my consent to arrange your plans according to your own judgments." Having said this, however, reverting to the hidden-hand model of authority, he slyly urged his daughter to join him in England. Once there, Nabby broke off her engagement, in large measure due to the epistolary slanders of Mary Branch, one of Royall's spurned companions.[29]

Some four years later the still unmarried Tyler wrote *The Contrast,* one of the most popular American plays of the eighteenth century. The contrast alluded to in the title is, among other things, between the characters of Maria's – the heroine's – two suitors, one of whom Maria loves and another whom she despises but her father insists she marry. From such plays as Sheridan's *School for Scandal* and Steele's *Conscious Lovers,* Tyler borrowed the stock "contrasts": affection and plainness, city and country, hypocrisy and sincerity. But what distinguishes Tyler's play and gives it its historical importance is the skill with which he develops these conventional dichotomies into a broader contrast between a corrupt and luxurious England and a virtuous and hearty America. By making one suitor the product of an American education and the other of a British education, Tyler succeeded in unobtrusively having the conventions of the eighteenth-century stage serve a patriotic and antipatriarchal theme.[30] Maria's American-bred suitor, Colonel Manly, proudly informs her that "In our country the affections are not sacrificed to riches or family aggrandizement."[31]

But as her bold dialogue with her acquisitive parent demonstrates, Maria is far from unfamiliar with such principles.

> *Van Rough:* Pray, what right has a girl of your age to be in the dumps? Haven't you everything your heart can wish; an't you going to be married to a young man of great fortune; an't you going to have the quit-rent of twenty miles square?
> *Maria:* One-hundredth part of the land, and a lease for life of the heart of a man I could love would satisfy me.

Van Rough; Pho, pho, pho! child; nonsense. . . . This comes of your reading your story books; your Charles Grandisons, your Sentimental Journals, and your Robinson Crusoes. No, no, no! child; it is money makes the mare go.

Maria: Marriage, Sir, is, indeed, a very serious affair.

Van Rough: You are right, child; you are right. I am sure I found it so, to my cost.

Maria: I mean, Sir, that as marriage is a portion for life, and so intimately involves our happiness, we cannot be too considerate in the choice of our companion (pp. 54–5).

These last are the words of John Adams to Nabby almost exactly. Van Rough is not inaccurate in tracing such sentiments to Richardson, Sterne, and Defoe. Maria soliloquizes at the end:

> How deplorable is my situation! How distressing for a daughter to find her heart militating with her filial duty. . . . Heaven knows with what reluctance I should oppose the will of a parent, or set an example of filial disobedience. . . . At my father's command . . . I could almost submit to what every female heart knows to be the most mortifying, to marry a weak man. . . . But to marry a depraved wretch, whose only virtue is a polished exterior . . . whose heart, insensible to the emotion of patriotism, dilates at the plaudits of every unthinking girl . . . I find my heart must ever despise (p. 55).

The debate as to whether marriage was essentially a property transfer between father-in-law and suitor or a sacred contract between lovers was a very real one in eighteenth-century America – one that reflected a larger debate as to whether property or personal rights were more sacred, as to whether the possession of the former or the exercise of the latter conferred upon men a more real independence. Inevitably, the debate over the proper balance of those rights was to divide rebels and Tories.

The following is a passage from a letter sent by Jonathan Boucher in 1760 to his prospective father-in-law asking for the hand of his daughter. Fifteen years later Boucher was to become the leading spokesman for the Tory cause in America.

> Dear Sir,
>
> Ashamed and weary of this unproductive and unprofitable course of life, I resolve to commence planting. There is in your neighbourhood a charming little plantation, unoccupied by anybody, which I think would exactly suit my purpose. As to buying it, that is out of the question; it is not venal, nor to be disposed of to the highest bidder: nor, if it were have I wealth enough to buy it. If it were to be sold for what it is worth, the wealth of the Indies could not purchase it. I should indeed like to have it seiz'd in-tail, which as I am sure I should never be disposed to part with it, might answer my purposes as well

as a fee-simple. However, I shall think myself quite happy to get it on a lease for life.

Scorning the little dirty finesses of common chapmen, who have an idle way of depreciating the commodities they want to purchase, I will frankly own to you I think this tenement inestimable: and I know that I greatly under-rate it when I offer not only all my worldly goods, but consent to bind myself to its fair proprietor till death us do part, or longer, if you can make the Deeds of Conveyance to be longer binding.[32]

Unabashedly, Boucher extends the analogy between his future wife and a "plantation" to a full six pages. Conceding that his correspondent, in effect, owns his daughter as property, Boucher wishes only to rent her, "to have it seiz'd in-tail." Here is contractualism of a far different kind than that espoused by "matrimonial republicans." Anxious to impress his future father-in-law with his legal knowledge, Boucher is concerned with a binding very different from that of the heart.

No greater contrast to Boucher's letter may be found than the one Joel Barlow, the Connecticut Wit, sent to his father-in-law in 1782. While a chaplain in the Revolutionary army, Barlow was given to fiery sermons. Later as Minister to France under Jefferson, he would champion the more extreme and dubious cause of the French Revolution. His attitude toward marriage not only anticipates his liberal political views but suggests, in contrast to Boucher's affiliation, the lower class and later generation to which he belongs.

Having graduated from Yale with considerably more interest in poetry than business, Barlow was certain that he would be denied the parental consent necessary to marry his sweetheart Ruth Baldwin. Because it remained a misdemeanor in Connecticut to court a woman without parental consent, Barlow chose to persuade Ruth to marry him secretly. Ten months later, however, the secret was out and Barlow chose wisely to confront his father-in-law in writing rather than in person. "To crowd himself into a family is what no Gentleman of my feelings ever will do," he wrote in his defense, "but to take a daughter from any family upon the principle of mutual affection is a right given by the God of nature wherever he has given that affection."[33]

Barlow's declaration recalls that of Rousseau's St. Preux and suggests that Barlow, along with Maria Van Rough, had drunk deep from the fountain of sentimental fiction. Yet more than simply rehearsing a relatively new ideological position, Barlow's convictions about marriage reflect what in effect was becoming a new social reality – one in which parental control of a child's future was almost more limited than it ever historically had been, a social reality that would make arguments for American independence seem, to most Americans in 1776, both just and plausible.

In his recent reconstitution analysis of two centuries of families of Hingham, Massachusetts, Daniel Scott Smith provides extensive demographic documentation of a significant decline "in the relation of parental power to the marriage pattern" over the last half of the eighteenth century in at least one, presumably representative, American community.[34] Smith concludes "that property considerations were less critical to marriage choice after the Revolution than before" and that by the end of the eighteenth century the perception of spouse as property had become antiquated (p. 426).

In a related study all surviving issues of eighteenth-century American magazines were examined (546 in all, 98 published between 1741 and 1775, and 447 published between 1776 and 1794) for references to romantic love. The concern of this survey was to disprove the "commonly held" sociological opinion that the romantic love complex developed early in the nineteenth century along with industrialization.[35]

Its statistics do indeed confirm Herman Lantz's hypothesis about the early appearance of the "romantic love complex." But, more important, its findings suggest the degree to which the American Revolution and the acceptance of romantic love were – if not directly related phenomena – historically contemporaneous ones. In the thirty-year period before the war there is on the average one reference to romantic love per four issues; in the twenty-year period immediately following the war the number more than triples.

The same study tabulates under three rubrics all references to marriage motives appearing in the "universe" of 546 magazine issues. Though wealth is given as a motive for marriage a third of the time, between 1776 and 1794 happiness is given twice as often. Parental interference in the marriage choice appears to remain an important theme in late eighteenth-century American fiction, but the "ego happiness" statistic suggests that daughters were standing up for their rights.

➤ No Revolutionary incident better reflects how strongly the cause of a voluntaristic marriage was tied in America to the ideology of revolution than the response to the death of Jane McCrea, the new nation's first folk heroine. In the spring of 1777, the British launched a two-pronged attack that was to converge on Albany and whose purpose was to isolate New England. If all went well, additional British forces were to meet a triumphant Burgoyne in an occupied Albany. Yet some in the upper Hudson Valley were not fleeing General Burgoyne but awaiting him. The twenty-three-year-old British partisan Jane McCrea, recently engaged to one of the General's lieutenants, David Jones, was among them. She and her mother looked forward to welcoming Jones to discuss with him their plans for the imminent wedding.

A troop of Wyandot Indians, however, traveling in advance of their British allies, came upon the McCrea household and, presuming its occupants were rebels, dragged mother and daughter out-of-doors and shot them. Because the British paid Wyandots for each rebel scalp brought back to the camp – indeed, even issuing them knives initialed G. R. (Georgius Rex) for that purpose – the Indians lost no time in scalping the corpses. The leader of the Indian troop, known as Panther, received the honor of strapping Jane's luxuriant chestnut locks to his belt. When Panther returned with his prize, the scalp was immediately recognized and the tragic error thus discovered, but fearing the desertion of his valuable Indian allies General Burgoyne chose to take no punitive action against Panther or his troop.[36]

The rebel press immediately picked up on the atrocity, holding it up as the most iniquitous example of the barbarous character of the British thus far in the war. The sanctioning of such brutal slaughter of youth and innocence was proof that they were in league with the devil. *The Boston Gazette* published this account even before such relevant information as Jane's name had been received:

> We have received an account of an extraordinary instance of cruelty at Fort Edwards . . . a band of Indians traveling with 400 British Regulars . . . draged [sic] an old woman and girl out of the house, killed and scalped the old woman, fired two braces of balls through the body of the girl, and then scalped her. The girl was a sweet-heart to an officer in the enemy's service, and a very great Tory. – Hear, Oh Heavens! and give ear, Oh America, and be aroused as a strong lion, at the infernal ferocity of our enemies who, devillike delight in the most barbarous acts of cruelty, . . . without discrimination of friend or foe. Tremble at, and flee from, and avoid Burgoyne's specious proclamation, as you would a snake, impregnated with every mischief to us, our country and posterity, that the first seducer of our race is capable of.[37]

The "specious" Burgoyne proclamation referred to was, indeed, a notorious one. In it Burgoyne had described his Indian allies as "the messengers of justice and of wrath . . . that a reluctant but indispensable persecution of military duty must occasion" and had defended his policy of encouraging scalping by declaring that he sanctioned it only when performed on the bodies of the dead.[38] Because such a qualification only encouraged the Indians to murder their victims first, Burgoyne's absurd defense and his implicit self-glorifying identification with Jehovah (who also dispatched "ministers of wrath") was parodied mercilessly in the rebel press. Even the great Burke was moved to declare with sarcastic vehemence before the assembled Parliament:

> Suppose there was a riot on Tower Hill. What would the keeper of his Majesty's lions do? Would he not fling open the dens of the wild

beasts and then address them thus: (My gentle lions – my humane bears – my tender-hearted hyenas, go forth! But I exhort you, as you are Christians and members of civil society, to take care not to harm any man, woman or child.)[39]

The death of Jane McCrea was more than just another British-sanctioned scalping. A savage bearing the banner of Georgius Rex had split the skull of a young woman who, as General Gates mentions in a letter, was dressed to receive her promised husband.[40] Here was the great scene of sentimental fiction horribly come alive: the tyrannical parent sending his ferocious minister to deny his child, his loyal Tory child, the sacred nuptial rites.

The psychological effect of the image was enormous. Fairfax Downey comments in his history of the Indian Wars:

> But the scalp of Jane McCrea, who was to have been the bride of a Tory officer with Burgoyne, exacted an incomparably greater price than was paid for it. Its image in the minds of men was one of the most compelling stimulants to recruiting the American army had ever known. Nothing except the hiring of Hessian mercenaries by the British matched it in fanning the flames of the Revolution.[41]

Ballads and broadsides, one after another, issued from the press:

> A lady richly dress'd, her name M'Crea;
> Stretch'd on the ground, and struggling there with death.
> She cannot live, she must resign her breath.
> The cursed Indian knife, the cruel blade,
> Had cut her scalp, they'd tore it from her head;
> . . . .
>
> Is this that blooming fair? Is this M'Crea?
> This was appointed for her nuptial day.
> Instead of smiles and a most brilliant bride,
> Her face besmear'd with blood, her raiment dyed;
> Instead of pleasure and transporting joys,
> There's naught but dying groans and bitter sighs.[42]

A popular ballad written several years later concludes with these verses:

> But a maiden fair lay weeping in her cottage day by day
> Tired was she, worn with watching for her true love far away.
> He was bearing noble arms and crest, in service to the King,
> While she waited sad and tearful near the pine tree, near the spring.
> . . . .
>
> Now a little fountain wells out cool and clear beneath the shade,
> Cool and clear as when beside it knelt that young and lovely maid.
> These bear witness for the story how upon that cruel day,
> Beauty, innocence and youth there died in hapless Jane M'Crea.[43]

This passage bears a close resemblance to the conclusion of *La Nouvelle Héloïse*. Julie has drowned while attempting to save her young child. Clara, Julie's dearest friend, bemoans her death:

> I see her in every object. . . . It was here she lived, here died; and here repose her ashes—As I go, twice a week, to the church, I cast my eye on the sad, revered spot—O beauty! is such thy last asylum! sincerity! friendship! virtue! pleasure! innocence! all lie buried in her grave (IV, 82).

With the death of Julie, as with the death of Jane, some degree of the world's innocence has fled. Once again the serpent has triumphed.

Jane's death inspired the first novel ever published on an American theme, *Miss McCrea* (1785), written in French by a young diplomat, Hilliard D'Auberteuil.[44] More revealing of the American perception of the Revolution than this novel, however, are some of the other postwar narratives that in one way or another dealt with the McCrea theme. One such brief narrative was first advertised in a Connecticut journal, *The Middlesex Gazetteer* for May 13, 1787. "To be had at this office," the announcement read, is "An account of a Beautiful Young Lady, who was taken by the Indians and then lived in the woods and then was Providentially returned to her parent, etc." Though the narrative included a strenuous protest of its truthfulness, it was, to all but the most credulous, quite obviously fictitious. More important than its being one of the earliest separately printed pieces of American fiction, however, this "Account of a Beautiful Young Lady" was, to judge by its eighteen editions from fifteen presses in twenty-one years, the most popular piece of short fiction in the early national period.[45]

The tremendous appeal of this strange "account" must be attributed to the power with which it combines the "severe parent" theme of sentimental fiction with elements of the popular Indian captivity narrative and then boldly sets the whole within a historical setting that not only seems to identify its heroine with Jane McCrea but in the process transforms the narrative into a naive allegory of the Revolution. Like so much subsequent American literature whose crude beginnings it represents, this incunabulum is a tale of independence within a tale of independence. The tale is pseudonymously signed "Abraham Panther," a name that links the first great patriarchal parent with the name and totem of Jane McCrea's murderer. The Panther narrative elevates the theme of parental severity to the level of myth.

"Excessively eager in pursuit of riches," the father of the narrative's nameless heroine refuses to accept as his son-in-law a young clerk "destitute of fortune" with whom his daughter has "acknowledged a mutual attachment." Convinced by her lover that she must join him before she is confined, the young woman agrees to "Quit my father's house and retire into the country to see whether my absence would not soften his heart and induce him to consent to my happiness" (p. 170). On May 10, 1777, the pair elope and leave the young woman's home in Albany, exactly the month and year the rebel population of Albany left Jane McCrea behind and began their evacuation in fear of a different kind of parental tyranny. The date, however, has yet another antecedent: May 10 had been made famous two years earlier in 1775 as the day Ticonderoga fell and the Second Continental Congress had convened to mobilize the nation and to acknowledge that a war had begun. Thus, the elopement announces the beginning of two sorts of familial conflicts. The young woman's disobedience, however, hardens rather than softens her father's heart, and he reviles the man whom he accuses of "treacherously engaging his daughter's affections" (p. 170). He threatens vengeance on both, declaring that he "would be the death of the man who carried off his daughter." Having received a report of her father's anger, the heroine, like Clarissa, regretfully accepts the fact that "a reconciliation" with her father would no longer be possible and agrees to move farther into the country.

Shortly after their departure, the couple is attacked by a band of Indians who enact the will of the heroine's father by capturing and mutilating the young suitor "in a most inhuman way." The maiden escapes, but only to be discovered by a mysterious "man of gigantic figure" while she is desperately seeking a "place of shelter and security" (p. 171). This personage confines her in a cave whose four apartments, containing weapons and dead bodies, give it the appearance of a charnel house. There with deceptive solicitude the giant (in one edition an Indian, in another a black man) attends to her needs for food and warmth, only later to turn on her, tie her up, and deliver a brutal version of her father's earlier ultimatum: "to accept his bed or expect death for [her] obstinacy" (p. 171). The metaphorical incestuousness of her father's possessiveness is made literal by the sexual demands of the giant, who serves as a symbolic embodiment of the violent aspect of the father, the Panther-half of Abraham Panther. The choice between suitor and father, between a reciprocated and voluntary union and a prolonged, unnatural attachment modulates into a choice between virginity and death.

Acknowledging that "to run . . . would be in vain and no less . . . to hide" (p. 171), the young woman vows what she could not vow in her father's house: to answer violence with violence. Retaliating in kind to the brutality she had earlier witnessed, in the middle of the night she mutilates and quarters her captor in a manner identical to that inflicted on her fiancé. But rather than flee the ghastly cave, whose arsenal and corpses suggest the war to which the narrative never explicitly refers, the young woman chooses to remain in the cave, transforming it into that "place of shelter and security" she earlier had sought. For nine years she remains there, living the life of a hermit.[46] In the spring of the ninth year – the detail suggests the Dis and Persephone myth – the heroine meets the first human beings she has encountered since the giant's death.[47] They are two travelers, whose names, Abraham and Isaac, serve not only to invoke the scriptural story of a father's willingness to sacrifice his child but also to identify the travelers as Old Testament types of the new Founding Father – for it will be they who at last deliver the young woman from her cave.

Abraham and Isaac had set out two weeks earlier to penetrate the western wilderness and "view the country," to explore and discover its distinctive flora and fauna. During their first thirteen days of travel they had failed to encounter "anything uncommon or worthy of description," except "a great variety of birds and wild beasts" (p. 169). On the fourteenth day, however, they encounter the young woman, whose appearance they proclaim to be "extraordinary." She is that rare creature, that new species worthy of description for which they have sought: "At first we were uncertain whether the voice was a human one or that of some bird, as many extraordinary ones inhabited these wilds" (p. 169). The confusion of her voice with a wild bird's note suggests the degree to which the young woman had made herself at home in the wilderness "of storms by day and wild beasts by night," a wilderness that nine years earlier she had feared and that now she has discovered to be "rich and fertile" and "affording a very comfortable living." Indeed, a spring of "excellent water" is noticed by the travelers to issue from beneath the ghastly apartments of the cave. It is as unpolluted by its source as is, we are made to feel, the young woman's innocence – and by extension the nation's – by the horrors she has experienced and suffered.

The presence of the strangers startles the heroine. Like Rip van Winkle awakening from a dream to discover the war over, she exclaims with a wild look: "Heavens! Where am I? And who, and from whence are you?" (p. 169). The young woman "starts" before the hunters in a fashion similar to that ascribed to the birds and beasts who, earlier in the narrative, had been "startled" by the hunters who approached them in order to kill them "for sport and amusement." The parallel between the passages reflects not only a fundamental theme of the narrative but one shared by the novel of parental severity and the Indian captivity: the difficulty of distinguishing the exploiter from the deliverer or, more simply put, the problem of trust. As America would react to England's alienation of her affection and betrayal of her trust by embarking upon a foreign policy of noninvolvement and neutrality, so, having been scorned by a parent who once loved her and having been betrayed by one who seemed at first to be her protector, the Panther heroine had chosen to become a hermit. Yet her traumas and betrayals have not lost the heroine the most glorious of her virtues and weaknesses: her trust. She consents to allow the travelers to take her back to her father: "I trust myself to your protection. I have no reason to question your good intentions and willingly believe, from my small acquaintance with you, that you will not seek to heap affliction upon a weak woman, already borne down with misery and sorrow" (p. 172).

Once at home she discovers her father is dying. She relates to him her tale of woe and on his deathbed extracts from him both an acknowledgment of his past cruelty and a plea for forgiveness:

> He seemed much affected and, when she had finished, he took her by the hand and affectionately squeezed it, acknowledging he had been unjustly cruel to her and asked her forgiveness and attempted to say something more, but immediately fainted. All our endeavours to recover him were in vain. He lay about seven hours and then expired (p. 172).

This is once again the conventional closing scene of the novel of familial discord, except here the parent does not ask for forgiveness at his daughter's deathbed, but on his own. Here it is not the child who must die denied the final parental embrace but the parent who dies "before he could fold her in his arms again." The daughter's presence and the guilt it inspires hasten the old man's death. The Panther heroine has slain her parent once in his grotesque form and now again, in the very act of familial reconciliation, Clarissa's death has been avenged: "He left a handsome fortune to his daughter who, notwithstanding his cruelty, was deeply affected at his sudden death" (p. 172). Though denied a husband, the young lady has at least received the benefit of her just inheritance.

A year before the Panther narrative, David Humphreys's *On the Happiness of America* offered this proud boast about the character of the new nation:

> No Eastern manner here consign the charms
> Of beauteous slaves to serve loath'd masters' arms
> No lovely maid in wedlock e'er was sold
> By parents base for mercenary gold
> Nor forced the hard alternative
> To live dishonored or with hunger to destroy.[48]

In America women will be spared Clarissa's "hard alternative."

The full significance of the Panther narrative can only be appreciated in light of its peculiar mixed genre: part Indian-captivity narrative and part sentimental tale of filial disobedience. Both Jane McCrea and the Panther heroine are Clarissa's daughters, but in her tragic and heroic incarnations, respectively. That the martyred Jane is succeeded by the triumphant Panther heroine reflects a crucial cultural event: the emergence of a new active understanding of Christian heroism. The story of that new understanding makes clear once again the deep thematic links between eighteenth-century literary and political history, between the two great novelties of the age: fiction and the American nation. The related development of these two genres and of their themes and structure further clarifies the broad cultural context of the American Revolution and its ideology and advances us to our next major topic of discussion: theological forms of filial freedom.

FROM PASSIVE TO ACTIVE DISOBEDIENCE

Though by the end of the eighteenth century they were to degenerate into simple adventure stories only loosely based on fact, the Indian-captivity narratives of the late seventeenth and early eighteenth centuries were in large measure factual accounts of the spiritual trials of white men and women captured by the Indians. The narratives, thematically and structurally modeled on the Book of Job and the scriptural account of the Babylonian captivity of the Israelites, were offered to the public as spiritually edifying supplements to the sermonic literature on Providence. In the earliest captivities the Indian is identified as an agent of God, sent by Jehovah as he might send a storm or plague, to chasten his sinful creatures through affliction to a converting realization of the literal truth of man's absolute dependence on the Divine Will and of the necessity of surrendering to that Will. Though evil by nature, the Indian captors in these narratives are thus ultimately instruments of good; they are part of God's scheme of merciful affliction.

The first and most consistently popular American captivity narrative was published in 1682 and carried the title *The Sovereignty and Goodness of God, together with the Faithfulness of His Promises Displayed: being a narrative of the Captivity and Restauration of Mrs. Mary Rowlandson, written by her hand.* Prefixed to the narrative is a verse from Deuteronomy announcing the moral of Mary's narrative: "See now that I even I am he, and there is no God with me. I kill and I make alive, I wound and I heal, neither is there any can deliver out of my hand." Few seventeenth-century readers would have been unaware of the verse that immediately follows in Scripture, a verse on which the entire genre depended for its logic: "I will make my arrows drunk with blood and my sword shall devour flesh with the blood of the slain and the captives from the long-haired heads of the enemies."[49] Scripture left no doubt that behind the mask of the red man was the face of Jehovah. All Indian captives were in truth captives of the divine will. Before her eventual ransom Mary herself learns the lesson Providence had intended for her. Her narrative closes:

> Before I knew what affliction meant, I was ready sometimes to wish for it. When I lived in prosperity, having the comforts of the World about me, my relations by me, My Heart cheerfull, and taking little care for any thing; and yet seeing many, whom I preferred before myself, under many trials and afflictions, in sickness, weakness, poverty, losses, crosses, and cares of the World, I should be sometimes jealous lest I should have my portion in this life, and that Scripture would come to my mind, Heb. 12.6 "For whom the Lord loveth he chasteneth, and scourgeth every Son whom he receiveth." But now I see the Lord had his time to scourge and chastise me. . . . And I hope I can say in some measure, as David did, "It is good for me that I have been afflicted" (pp. 166–67).

The year of Mary's captivity is also that of the first publication of Bunyan's *Pilgrim's Progress*. The former narrative stands in relation to the major tradition of American Protestant fiction as the latter does to the comparable British tradition.

As the Puritan God slowly disappeared from the captivity narrative, however, permitting by the end of the eighteenth century a new focus on individual heroism rather than on God's graciousness, the meaning of the narrative altered radically. Because it separated the captive from all sources of external strength, from family, and from the society of his or her own race, the experience of captivity taught the heroine of this later narrative not the lesson of obligatory dependence *on* God but, as in *Crusoe,* of self-reliance *under* God. As Indian captivity and other wilderness afflictions became harder to rationalize as providential expressions of a divine concern for human salvation – seeming, rather, to express if anything God's abandonment of his pilgrims or indifference to them – the captivity narrative secretly taught a still pious public how to live self-sufficiently alone, how to make a virtue out of the theological vice of self-dependence.[50]

As early as 1697, Cotton Mather's account of the captivity of Hannah Dustin raised a critical question, which, in effect, announced a shift in the character of the genre. Surely, it generally was the will of God that a captive endure passively his afflictions and patiently await the deliverance, or ransom, that a just God may or may not choose to send. But might not it also be the will of God, in some instances, for a captive to take his fate into his own hands and attempt to escape? In the context of a narrative traditionally designed to teach the saving virtue of passive obedience and, by extension, to affirm the supreme Christian heroism of a passive Christ on the cross, such a question was a radical one. It is for this reason that the following passage – so careful to identify one woman's choice to pursue her own survival as the will of God rather than as violation of that will – is so significant. In its small way it symbolically reflects a turning point in American intellectual history:

> These Two poor Women were now in the Hands of those, whose Tender Mercies are Cruelties; but the Good God, who hath all Hearts in His own Hands, heard the Sighs of those Prisoners, and gave them to find unexpected Favour from the Master, who laid claim unto them. . . . Now, they could not observe it without some wonder, that their Indian Master, sometimes, when he saw them Dejected, would say unto them, "what need you Trouble your self? If your God will have you delivered, you shall be so!" . . . and it seems our God would have it so to be . . . a little before Break of Day, when the whole Crew was in a Dead Sleep; (reader, see if it prove not So!) one of these Women took up a Resolution, to imitate the Action of Jael upon Sisera; and being where she had not her own Life secured by any Law unto her, she thought she was not forbidden by any Law to take away the Life of the Murderers, by whom her Child had been butchered. She heartened the Nurse, and the Youth, to assist her in this Enterprize; and all furnishing themselves with Hatchets for the purpose, they struck such Home Blows, upon the Heads of their Sleeping Oppressors, that e'er they could any of them Struggle into any Effectual Resistance, at the Feet of these poor Prisoners, they bow'd, they fell, they lay down dead.[51]

What is most telling here is not Hannah's decision to save her own life by slaying her captors but Mather's decision to hold up that action as heroic. Unlike Mary Rowlandson's updating of Job, Mather's narrative is not an account of conversion or resignation to God's will; nor is its primary emphasis the glorification of God's sovereignty. By using her wits and seizing "the main chance," Hannah takes her life into her own hands. Like the compulsively active Mather, she does not "stand still" and wait for the Lord.[52] Her justification "that she had not her life secured by any law" neglects to see that this is the divine truth captivity was to teach. The Dustin narrative with its romanticized Arminianism was to show the way eventually for the "captivity" to step out entirely from its theological frame and into the realm of "heroic exploits."

This brief account of the genre permits one to recognize a more complex structure in the Abraham Panther narrative than perhaps the historian might at first be willing to concede. The narrative superimposes the sentimental convention of the tyrannical parent interfering in the marriage choice onto the captivity convention in which Jehovah sends forth his Indians to enact his will. By using elements of the Jane McCrea story, it simultaneously invokes the memory of American objections to Britain's use of Indians, in general, and, in particular, to

Burgoyne's dispatching of his "ministers of wrath." The effect of identifying the severe parent not only with Britain but with Jehovah is to question the scheme of providential justice and the just character of Jehovah. Though the heroine, consistent with that scheme of justice, must lose her husband in recompense for her elopement – her initial filial disobedience – the treatment of the fortunate fall theme in the Panther narrative (as in *Robinson Crusoe*) allows its heroine to reap an inheritance after paying for her disobedience. But as there is no conversion scene explicitly setting parent against God – rather, an identification of God and parent by means of the captivity convention – the heroine's rebellion, manifested first in her Dustin-like murder of the giant and second in her fatal presence at her father's sickbed, is implicitly as much directed against a wrathful Jehovah as it is against her tyrannical parent.

Like the Indian-captivity narrative, the neo-Richardsonian novel also represented a subgenre of the Puritan spiritual relation, or conversion, narrative. Not only is its theme also that of the fortunate fall into converting wisdom, but its historical antecedents, *Crusoe, Paradise Lost,* and *Pilgrim's Progress,* link it to the same scriptural passages that underlie the captivity. Pamela will have the good fortune to receive as a reward for her afflictions an earthly husband rather than a heavenly father. Yet while confined to Birham Hall by the still unrepentant Mr. B. and his accomplice Mrs. Jervis, Pamela feels it appropriate to analogize her captivity to that of the Israelites: "I, remembering the psalm to be a little touching, turned to it, and took the liberty to alter it, somewhat nearer to my case" (p. 122). The 137th Psalm, the captive's lament, is the same psalm to which Mary Rowlandson had turned in her misery in an earlier era. Here are the first and eighth verses of the Psalm followed by Pamela's adaptations:

By the waters of Babylon,   When sad I sat in B – – –n Hall,
There we sat down and   All guarded round about,
Wept,   And thought of ev'ry absent friend
When we remembered Zion.   The tears for grief burst out.

O daughter of Babylon, you   Ev'n so shalt thou, O wicked one!
Devastator,   At length to shame be brought,
Happy shall he be who requites   And happy shall all those be call'd
You   That my deliv'rance wrought.
With what you have done to us.   (p. 122)

The wooed and captive Pamela does indeed learn successfully the theological lesson of captivity. With reference to her captor-turned-fiancé, she anticipates wishfully the paradox of Providence: "My happiness may be brought about by the very means that I thought my greatest grievance" (p. 120). In a similar vein Clarissa on her deathbed repeats with Mary Rowlandson the words of David: "It was good for me that I was afflicted" (VIII, 102). Though in Richardson's novel a stern parent and a libertine seducer replace the savage Indians divinely commissioned in the captivity to test God's faithful, the moral – the justification of the ways of God to man – remains the same. Tyranny must not be revolted against but be spiritually transcended. Hannah Dustin and the Panther heroine are challengers to the great tradition.

Having examined some one hundred post-Richardsonian novels in his *The Popular Novel in England 1770–1800*, J. M. S. Tompkins concludes:

> The tension, between love and filial obedience, a favorite theme time out of mind, especially occupied the eighteenth-century novelists. Nearly all of them came down heavily on the side of parental authority. By an overwhelming majority it was resolved, that while a parent ought not to force a child into a marriage repugnant to her, while a child is justified in passively resisting such tyranny, nothing justifies her in carrying resistance to the point of marrying against her parent's will.[53]

Even Rousseau's Julie, as we have mentioned before, endures her father's will and marries the husband of his choice. Following the Puritan convention that affliction chastens one to a converting acceptance of a higher sovereignty and a consequent self-purification, her marriage to Wolmar – her divine affliction – issues in a literal conversion. Rousseau makes the marriage ceremony itself into the converting text:

> The purity, the dignity, the sanctity of marriage, so forcibly expressed in the words of Scripture, the chaste, the sublime duties it inculcates, and which are so important to the happiness, the order, the peace, the being of human nature . . . all conspired to make such an impression upon me, that I felt a thorough revolution within me. An indivisible power seemed suddenly to rectify the disorder of my affections, and to settle them according to the laws of duty and nature. The eternal and omnipresent Power, said I to myself, now reads the bottom of my soul (II, 216).

Julie is at last convinced that "heaven directs the good intentions of parents and eases the duty of children." Ironically, however, the grace that attends her conversion – the reward Julie receives for submitting to her affliction – is, in her view, the freedom to declare her love for St. Preux. Having discharged her duty to her father who "controls my fate but not my affections" (II, 89) and having protected herself from her own rashness by her marital vow, Julie may now safely and in good conscience indulge her love. She has learned the paradoxical lesson that submission permits assertion and momentarily has achieved the great balance between those terms sought by the age. To St. Preux she describes the real substance of her conversion:

> I was sensible that I still loved you as much, if not more than ever; but I felt my affection for you without a blush. I found that I could venture to think of you without forgetting that I was the wife of another. My senses were composed; and from that moment I perceived that my mind was changed in reality. What a torrent of pure joy then rushed into my soul, what strange sensation, so long effaced to diffuse an unusual serenity through my whole frame. It seems as if I had been new born and fancied that I was entering into another life. O gentle and balmy virtue I am regenerated for thee (II, 246).

Julie's conversion is rewarded neither by the receipt of heavenly grace nor an earthly inheritance, but, in the words she would pen on her deathbed, by "the privilege of loving you without a crime, and of telling you once more: That virtue, which separated us on earth, will unite us forever in the mansion of the blessed. I die in that peaceful hope" (IV, 212). She is born into "another life" where one attachment does not cancel out another. But she must be born into yet *another* life before desire and virtue can be fully reconciled.

Shortly after her conversion, fearing Julie might be backsliding, her friend Clara "who has delivered [her] from the snares my affections had laid for [her]" (III, 73), upbraids her, invoking the great analogy of the genre: "All thy misfortunes come from thyself, O Israel" (III, 163). If with regard to her father's affliction Julie is a type of Israel, in the eyes of St. Preux, whom now she will never be able to marry, Julie herself has become a Jehovah. Her beleaguered lover describes her as "like the Divinity . . . [making] herself equally adored for the dispensation of good and evil" (II, 8). As Julie has resigned herself to afflicting Providence, so must St. Preux: "She has undone me. Yet cruel as she is, I love and admire her but the more. The more unhappy she makes me, the more perfect she appears" (II, 79). Though Julie's death eventually prevents the arrangement, St. Preux agrees to join her and her husband to serve as her child's tutor in a glorious spiritual ménage à trois.

Because Rousseau agrees that her misfortunes come from herself, Julie's triumph is finally more over herself in the manner of Mary Rowlandson than over her situation in the manner of Hannah Dustin. The passive model of Christian heroism, the subordination of the pursuit of happiness to the converting acceptance of affliction (a subordination Rousseau seemed to attack through the early characterization of St. Preux), is finally embraced by all. Passive heroism had to wait another decade before it would receive its greatest challenge. Two years before America chose to respond to English tyranny with a declaration of independence rather than a declaration of public fasting and humiliation, a new kind of hero emerged in eighteenth-century fiction who actively and violently sought to free himself from a tyrannical fate.

➤ In 1774, Johann Wolfgang von Goethe revolutionized the Puritan/sentimental tradition of the post-Richardsonian novel by publishing *The Sorrows of Young Werther,* in which his hero, like Rousseau's, is hopelessly in love with a married woman. But, unlike St. Preux, Goethe's Werther refuses to accept passively the afflictions of Providence, rejects as "intolerable" his beloved's professions of mere friendship, and denounces those who urge upon him an evangelical stoicism as staggering "under a benign delusion." He insistently declares that "human nature has certain limits . . . and beyond that degree it is annihilated."[54] One of Goethe's eighteenth-century American editors charged that Werther "calls into question the disposition of Providence, repines at what he cannot avoid and incessantly sees what is placed beyond his reach,"[55] the very opposite of Rousseau's Emile or Julie who are elaborately taught to accept the easy yoke of necessity. Though indebted to both Richardson and Rousseau, *The Sorrows of Young Werther* was to *Eloisa* what the latter had been to *Clarissa:* a radical extension of its implicit revolutionary principle.

Whereas St. Preux threatens suicide, only later to be dissuaded from it by the argument that such an act would represent at once a heinous ingratitude to God and an abdication of the Christian responsibility "to do good," Werther not only threatens suicide, but after enormous disputation and protracted dramatic announcements, commits it. Believing that "all the favors, all the attentions in the world cannot for a moment make amends for the loss of that happiness which a cruel tyranny [that of Lotte, the woman with whom he is vainly in love] destroys" (I, 48), Werther sees "no reason to prolong a miserable existence" (I, 50). (He thus anticipates the example of the woman whose suicide occasioned the first American pamphlet on divorce discussed earlier in this chapter.) Unable to live in a world with "those who abuse their power over the hearts of others" – a sentimental version of Hannah Dustin's justification – Werther determines to return "to my Father and thy Father." He will await his lover in a heaven which, as it makes of all men and women brothers and sisters, annuls all exclusive marriages and permits the claims of a greater love.

> Albert is your husband; but what of that? It is for this life only. – And in this life only it is a crime to love you, to wish to tear you from him. This is a crime and I punish myself for it: I have enjoyed it . . . from

> this moment you are wholly mine: I go to my Father, to thy Father, I
> shall carry my sorrows to the feet of his throne and he will give me com-
> fort until you arrive. Then will I fly to meet you, I will embrace you,
> and remain with you forever in the presence of the Almighty. (II, 85)

Werther redefines the heavenly reward along the lines of his own
fantasy. But what is most radical about Werther's convictions is his
view of the deity, a view essential to the justification of his suicide. Far
from being an afflicting tyrant who obliges man passively to accept the
intolerable, Werther perceives God to be a benevolent father who, mer-
cifully aware of the limits of human endurance, would embrace a son
"returned before the appointed time" (II, 55). Repudiating the paradox
of merciful afflictions on which the genre of the eighteenth-century
novel essentially had been built, Werther, in a book first published in
Germany the year before Lexington and Concord, defends his right to
personal revolution by recourse to an analogy with social revolution.
Defiantly, he answers Lotte and her husband Albert who have accused
him of spiritual cowardice: "Suppose a people groaning under the yoke
of a tyrant, do you call them weak, if they at length throw off and
break their chain?" (I, 72). Before 1774, the deaths of sentimental heroes and heroines were, on the model of *Clarissa,* cautiously semi-
voluntaristic; after 1774, the suicide becomes a common figure in the
sentimental novel; passive resistance gives way to active resistance.[56]
Indeed, the hero of the first American novel, *The Power of Sympathy*
(1789), having taken his own life, is discovered in bed with an open
copy of *Werther* beside his corpse. He, too, had chosen to escape tyranny and flee to another world, and in the act becoming not a prodigal
son but a heroic pilgrim.

Tompkins identifies the 1760s as the decade in which the significant
shift away from patriarchal didacticism in popular English fiction may
first be indentified:

> By 1770 these strenuous days lay in the past, and the outer forms of
> filial duty were falling out of use . . . moreover, there was a liberal,
> questioning spirit abroad soon to demolish all extreme tenets and to
> find its way into fiction in the works of Holcroft and Bage. Under the
> cold breath of this spirit the conservatives close their ranks (p. 85).

Just as the American Revolution was commencing, a turning point had
been reached in the history of sentimental fiction: Passive resistance –
and its view of God as dispenser of afflictive mercy – had given way to
active resistance and a vision of an indulgent Deity. A new generation
of sentimental heroes and heroines would declare with the American
Clarissa of Bage's *Mount Henneth:* "I demand my liberty. Deny it me
at your peril."[57] *Werther,* however, would not exert a major influence

in America until after the Revolution. Even then, its American editors, recognizing its explosive contents, took great care to remind their readers that "those who have called Mr. Goethe an apologist for suicide have failed to distinguish the author from his works."[58] Werther's suicide was condemned as self-indulgent, heretical, and antisocial by virtually all its critics.

On the other hand, the suicide of the protagonist of Joseph Addison's *Cato* (1712) was not only conceded to be acceptable because occurring before the Christian era, but in pre-Revolutionary America was judged to be heroic. Addison's play was widely read in the colonies at least as early as its first American performance in 1739 and had made the historical figure of Cato synonymous with the principles of antimonarchialism and the virtues of stoicism.[59] One Whig pamphleteer after another in both England and America would pseudonymously sign his works with the name of Caesar's great rival.

Whereas Werther takes his life to escape his pain, Cato "knows not how to wink at human frailty / or pardon weakness that he never felt" (p. 48). Captive to Caesar, he takes his life not out of moral or constitutional weakness but to transcend the curse of weakness. Because his suicide was explicitly intended to deliver him from political enslavement rather than love's enthrallment, its analogy to revolution was, unlike Werther's, literal rather than metaphorical. Hearing that Caesar will spare his life but not give him his freedom, Cato declares that death is infinitely preferable to slavery:

> My life is grafted on the fate of Rome.
> Would he save Cato, bid him spare his country
> Tell your dictator this and tell him, Cato
> Disdains a life which he has the power to offer (p. 21).

After Rome had surrendered to Caesar's "tyranny," Marius, Cato's son, asks, "What can Cato do against a world, a base, degenerate world that courts the yoke, and bows the neck to Caesar?" (p. 8). If Rome will not effect its own revolution, Cato will enact his private revolution by taking his own life and thus will again become, in words he uses in a slightly different context, "master of myself" (p. 46).

In the last issue of 1765, *The Boston Gazette* printed as part of its year-long campaign for the repeal of the Stamp Act a poem entitled "Cato's Soliloquy Imitated." In the original soliloquy, Cato, having been convinced of an afterlife by Plato's discussion of the immortality of the soul, asks the following and then takes his life.

> Why shrinks the soul
> Back on herself, and startles at destruction?
> 'Tis the divinity that stirs within us;

> 'Tis Heaven itself that points out an hereafter,
> And intimates eternity to man.

The soul's natural desire for an immortality, assured by heaven, justifies Cato in delivering himself from slavery through self-murder. In "Cato's Soliloquy Imitated," Addison's lines are altered to read:

> Tis the Divinity that stirs within him,
> Tis Heav'n itself points out his Birthright to him
> And intimates fair Liberty to Man.[60]

Here the soul's birthright is declared liberty rather than immortality, and what had been a justification for the sin of suicide becomes, in effect, a justification for the sin of revolution.

Of the five American editions of *Cato* published between 1779 and 1800, four have appended to them an anonymous poem, intended to serve as "A New Epilogue" to the play:

> Did Caesar, drunk with power, and madly brave,
> Insatiably burn, his country to enslave.
> The British Caesar too had done the same
> And damn'd this age to everlasting fame.
>
> Did Rome's senate nobly strive to oppose . . .
> Our Senate, too, the same bold deed has done
> And for a Cato, armed a Washington.
> Rise then my country men! For fight prepare.[61]

As Cato would free his soul from slavery, so Washington would free his nation from slavery. But revolution, no less than suicide, was a violation of the sacred principle of Christianity: passive obedience to Providence. That problem could not be ignored.

In his popular eighteenth-century school text, *Flowers of Ancient History,* John Adams of Philadelphia considered the circumstances of Cato's suicide.

> Whether the manner in which this great republican put a period to his life, was justifiable or not, has ever since been a matter of much dispute. It must be owned, that he did not on this occasion, act conformably to his own system of philosophy; and if we try him by the laws of Christianity, he will appear still more culpable. . . . We ought, however, to allow Cato some favorable circumstances . . . the age in which he lived . . . the barbarity of those times. . . . Shall Cato become the sport and mock of those people to whom he once gave laws? Shall he live to see his country, once the seat of sweet liberty and freedom, become the home of tyranny and oppression?[62]

Adams sympathizes with Cato's desire to escape the sight of his nation enslaved. Even given the Christian injunction, life without liberty can hardly be endured. Yet unlike Cato, the American Revolutionaries did not have "the favorable circumstance" of living in a pre-Christian era. Before the Christian people of the British colonies could allow themselves to embrace the idea of revolution, the Old Testament insistence that all earthly affliction must passively be endured as God's will had to be properly subordinated to a new understanding of the doctrine of Christian liberty.

Such subordination would in the course of time ultimately involve the dethroning of Jehovah and the rejection of the entire system of Old Testament morality. The Lockean ideology that would permit Americans to declare Britain "no true parent" would also permit the redefinition of divine paternity, the redefinition of God himself. If the American Revolution reflected in political terms the themes and issues of the broader cultural revolution articulated in eighteenth-century fiction, it also paralleled a revolutionary reconsideration of the basic elements of Protestant orthodoxy. The new understanding of personal independence and the attendant ideal of a free and perfect union both hastened and responded to a new understanding of the character of God and man's relationship to him.

6

FILIAL FREEDOM AND AMERICAN PROTESTANTISM

By the rationalist lights of Lockean ideology it was not only George III who might be convicted of parental tyranny, but Jehovah. For did not the God of the Old Testament send stillborn infants to hell and keep his living children bound in the enslaving determinism of original sin, perversely demanding of them, nonetheless, a blind and perfect obedience? Drawing on Locke's *The Reasonableness of Christianity,* Lord Shaftesbury in his *Characteristicks* (1711), one of the most popular works of the first half of the century, argued that Locke's model of the ideal parent must surely also describe the character of him whom mankind calls the True God. Because they were inconsistent with the true nature of virtue, all other conceptions of the Deity were to be condemned as false and idolatrous:

> If (as in the first case) there be a belief or conception of a Deity who is considered only as powerful over his creature, and enforcing obedience to his absolute will by particular rewards and punishments: and if on this account, through hope merely of reward or fear of punishment, the creature be incited to do the good he hates, or restrained from doing the ill to which he is not otherwise in the least degree adverse, there is in this case . . . no virtue whatsoever. . . . There is no more of rectitude, piety or sanctity in a creature thus reformed, than there is meekness or gentleness in a tiger strongly chained.[1]

Rather than serving the cause of virtue in the world, a tyrannical conception of the Deity compromised its very existence. The tiger must be tamed by love, not chained by fear. A benevolent conception of the Deity, however, encouraged virtue.

> If there be a belief or conception of a Deity who is considered . . . to have, besides mere power and knowledge, the highest excellence of nature, such as renders him justly amiable to all . . . a high and eminent regard to what is good and excellent, a concern for the good of all, and affection of benevolence and love towards the whole, such an example must undoubtedly serve . . . to raise and increase the affec-

tion towards virtue and help to submit and subdue all other affections to that alone (pp. 314–15).

A true God subdued the affections, not the will, and ruled by the force of his example.

THE ASSAULT ON JEHOVAH

Having declared that "loving fatherhood" was what distinguished his God from the Deity of the Old Testament, Thomas Paine was but one of many who boldly drew the ultimate inference from Shaftesbury's argument. If, by definition, a loving father would never sacrifice his only son, Christ could not be the child of the true God.[2] Though unwilling to take the logic to so Unitarian an extreme, liberal divines such as Jonathan Mayhew and Charles Chauncy later would use the argument of God's benevolence to call into question the doctrines, respectively, of arbitrary grace and limited grace. In the year of the Stamp Act, Mayhew insisted that God is "a compassionate Parent" and, since He is "father to all, so His government is parental, free from all unnecessary rigor."[3] The fact remained, however, that such a God bore little resemblance to the God of the Old Testament or of Calvin's *Institutes*, and Deists would not let it be forgotten.

Jefferson, whose disgust with Calvin's version of Jehovah was unbridled, wrote to John Adams, a New England scion sympathetic to some of the principles of Calvinism:

> I can never join Calvin in addressing his God. He was indeed an atheist, which I can never be; or rather his religion was daemonism. If ever man worshipped a false God he did. . . . It would be more pardonable, to believe in no God at all than to blaspheme Him by the atrocious attributes of Calvin.[4]

Agreeing with Jefferson that the Old Testament must be regarded as a historical document, Benjamin Franklin felt it incumbent upon him to excise the dangerously anachronistic and irrelevant elements from the scriptural presentation of the Deity. He cavalierly revised "Lead us not into temptation" to read "Keep us out of Temptation" and justified his change in almost Manichaean terms:

> The Jews had a Notion, that God sometimes tempted, or directed or permitted the Tempting of People. Thus it was said he tempted Pharaoh . . . etc. Under this Persuasion it was natural for them to pray that he would not put them to such severe Trials. We now suppose that Temptation, so far as it is supernatural, comes from the Devil only, and this Petition continued conveys a Suspicion, which in our present Conception seems unworthy of God, therefore might be altered.[5]

In the opinions of both Franklin and Jefferson the questionable morality of the Old Testament and its echoes in the New stood in opposition to the eternal and natural truths of Christ's Sermon on the Mount.

It is not surprising, then, that the most powerful Revolutionary polemic, although arguing the necessity for separation from a paternal England, implicitly identified England with an unreasonable Jehovah and the old Covenant of Works. At a climactic moment in *Common Sense,* Tom Paine declares: "Reconciliation is *now* a fallacious dream. Nature has deserted the connection and art cannot replace it. For as Milton wisely expresses, 'Never can true reconcilement grow where the wounds of deadly hate have pierced so deep'" (p. 23). The moment of reconciliation with their parents for which Clarissa and her sister heroines had so ardently wished has passed. What Paine does not mention is that Milton's words are spoken by Satan in justification of his rebellion against heaven. The front was forked: Puritanism, that other hierarchy of paternalistic authority, was, wittingly or unwittingly, to be fought along with England; Jehovah along with George. "We will never knock under, O George, we do not fear, the rattling of your thunder, the lightning of your spear," boasted Peter St. John of Norwalk, Connecticut, drawing on phrases descriptive of Jehovah.[6] Of the British officials sent to administer the colonies, Freneau wrote: "When first Britannia sent her hostile crew / To these far shores to ravage and subdue / We thought them gods, and almost seemed to say / No ball could pierce them and no dagger slay."[7] Like Cortez and Pizarro on the one hand and Jefferson's and Shaftesbury's Jehovah on the other, the English sovereign and his minions reveal themselves to the new "natives" of the Americas to be false idols rather than true gods. On July 17, 1776, the New York Sons of Liberty laid prostrate in the dust an equestrian statue of George III. "A gentleman who was present at this ominous fall of leaden majesty, looking back to the original hopeful beginning, pertinently exclaimed in the language of the Angel to Lucifer: 'If you b'st he. But ah, how fallen! how changed!' "[8] Implying that they had all fallen, another commentator declared, "there is not one Tory among the Seraphim."[9] As Paine's attack on George in *Common Sense* prepared the way for his attack on Jehovah in the *Age of Reason,* so Satan's fall from heaven and from his angelic status becomes silently prophetic of Jehovah's dethronement as well as George's.

In Tory rhetoric, Satan was the arch rebel, the prototype of the American revolutionary. Among Tories it was widely believed that the colonists were being manipulated by a group of "serpentine demagogues," most notably Paine and Samuel Adams, who "ingratiated themselves" in the same manner that Satan is represented seducing Eve "by a constant whispering."[10] Whig rhetoric, in contrast, by emphasizing the fallen angel rather than the serpent in the garden, made of Satan an appropriate analogy to England – the golden god whose majesty is leaden, whose true nature has at last been exposed to the eye of the moral empiricist. A correspondent for *The Boston Gazette* declared: "We swore allegiance to him . . . as a *Protector*, not as a *Destroyer* – as a *Father*, not as a *Murderer*."[11]

Though George might be dethroned symbolically by the pulling down of statues, no such idols of Jehovah existed. The *deus absconditus* would have to be reached another way. Andrew Fuller of New York, one of the most articulate Calvinist respondents to Paine's *Age of Reason*, unwittingly suggested how. Agreeing that God's government "is the government of a just and lawful prince," Fuller made the additional point that though God cannot be affected by man's feelings about him, yet like a human king he can appreciate or resent them:

> We do not think it lawful . . . to consider the Great Supreme as incapable of being offended with sin and sinners . . . or as unconcerned about his own glory. . . . What would he [the Deist] think of . . . a king of Great Britain who should suffer, with perfect indifference, his just authority to be treated with contempt? . . . But we are limited beings and are therefore in danger of having our rights invaded. True, and though God be unlimited and so in no danger of being deprived of His essential glory, yet He may lose His just authority *in the esteem* of creatures.[12]

By accepting Paine's analogy between human and divine authority throughout his rebuttal and thus conceding Locke's point that the authority of a true governor is ultimately only reflected in the esteem he inspires in those he governs, Fuller is manipulated into surrendering the vital distinction between the relations of man to a king and those of man to God. The analogy between political and divine relations has become an identification. Once the concession is made that God may be cheated of some of his glory and authority – even if only in the esteem of his creatures – the heavenly throne has been made vulnerable.

Whereas for the Deists the revolt against Geroge was part and parcel of a revolt against the principle of absolute sovereignty historically and symbolically embodied in the figure of Jehovah, for the Calvinist ministry, the war was a national attempt to free America from the very accusation that it had rebelled against that self-same Divinity. By strenuously avoiding the simplistic clarity of Manichaeanism, American Puritanism sought to explain the miseries of the world by insisting that all earthly afflictions were an expression of divine concern. Such a theology necessarily complicated America's understanding both of tyranny and of what constituted an "unnatural" parent. The Gordian knot of Puritanism's central paradox had to be undone before the categories of good and bad parents or of a good or evil Deity could be confidently distinguished.

All colonial Protestantism, following Augustine, posited that there was no independent agency of evil in the world. Either mediately or immediately, God himself allowed, and perhaps even authored, evil for the purposes of good. In the Puritan view of things there was but one vertical line of authority, and God was at its pinnacle. "Is there evil in the city and the Lord is not there?" asked Jehovah to this point.[13] Though the chain of command might appear so tangled as to make it seem as if the devil were an antagonist of God's will rather than his instrument, the fact remained that Satan was securely chained to God. When in 1653 Michael Wigglesworth was a much-troubled Harvard student, he concluded a diary entry with this seemingly ambiguous address: "Hear thou therefore the groanings of *thy poor prisoner* that is captivated and *oppressed by thine adversaries*"[14] (emphasis added). But, in fact, there is no ambiguity as to who is Wigglesworth's master God or God's enemies; for all God's adversaries are also his allies. The pain and affliction in the world express simultaneously the anger of God at his sinful creation and his abiding concern for man. Knowing that human pride and worldliness cannot survive the experience of helplessness, Jehovah sends plagues, war, and Indians to chasten man to a saving understanding of his dependence on the Almighty. But even those who have experienced conversion and accepted their utter dependence on God could not help being tempted on occasion to lay earthly anguish at the feet of the Almighty. The great diarist and magistrate Samuel Sewall confided to his diary on February 15, 1677:

> Having often been apt to break out against God himself as if he had made me a person that might be a fit subject of calamity, and that he led me into difficulties and perplexing miseries, I had my spirit calmed by considering what an absurd thing it was to say to God – 'Why hast thou made me thus?', and startled at the daring height of such wickedness.[15]

The ubiquitous Puritan protestation that God's afflictions were "tender mercies" echoed ominously the proverbial verse that declared "the tender mercies of the wicked are cruel."[16] What is wicked in man, though, must not be deemed so in God.

Philip Greven has recently called attention to a neglected dimension of the Evangelical personality: the enormous anger and hostility generated by the doctrines of God's sovereignty and by the correlative insistence that the human will be broken and made submissive to his will. Because these inadmissible feelings had to be denied, they were redirected either against the "hateful self" or against real or imagined enemies. Greven sees much historical truth in Jonathan Edwards's reproach to his congregation: "You object against your having a mortal hatred against God; that you never felt any desire to dethrone him. . . . - But if the throne of God were within your reach, and you knew it, it would not be safe one hour."[17]

Projecting it was one way of dealing with hostility; reconsidering the basic situation that generated it was another. Beneath the hostility Greven describes is, undoubtedly, the terrible fear of death – what the Puritans called "the King of Terrors" – and the damnation that for most followed hard upon it. If Jehovah could not be dethroned, his terrifying alter ego might.

In this regard David Stannard has argued convincingly that a significant shift in American attitudes toward death was ushered in by the Great Awakening in the early 1740s. An almost uncontrollable fear of death in the first century of American history gave way by midcentury to a more confident hopefulness of heaven.[18] In the earlier period a sense of security, an assurance of salvation was seen as the height of presumption and self-delusion. Because the only true assurance lay paradoxically in the presence of an anguishing doubt, such security was itself, ironically, a convicting sign of damnation. In the course of the great revivals, however, Stannard concludes, quoting a contemporary source: "It was becoming the norm, the accepted norm, for the godly to die 'in Raptures of Holy Joy: They wish and even long for Death, for the sake of that happy state it will carry them into'" (p. 150).

Both responding to and contributing to this shift was a substantial literature of consolation that personified death as the "heavenly Bridegroom," (a sacred version of the sentimental hero) rather than as the "King of Terrors." The Father is reconceived in the image of the compassionate and mediatorial Son. The death's heads on the gravestone give way to cherubim. And by the late 1760s the ominous "Duty of Children to Parents," which threatened the disobedient child with damnation, is replaced as a standard item in the *New England Primer* by Isaac Watts's "Cradle Hymn." The latter opens with this couplet: "Hush my dear, lie still and slumber./ Holy angels guard thy bed." Those holy angels embody the spirit of the child's loving parents who assure him how near and easy salvation is:

> Twas to save thee, child, from dying
> Save my dear from burning flame,
> Bitter groans, and endless crying,
> That thy blessed redeemer came.
>
> Mayst thou live to know and fear him,
> Trust and love him all thy days!
> Then go dwell forever near him,
> See his face and sing his praise.

The mother offers "a thousand kisses" to encourage the child to do so.[19]

Watts's "Cradle Hymn," though composed fifty years earlier, is central to the shift in attitudes toward children in America at mid-century. The poem is primarily a comparison between the sleeping babe whose "food and raiment, / house and home, thy friends provide" and the Blessed Babe who was forced to dwell in a lowly manger "with brutal creatures." The lesson of the poem is not that children should appreciate their earthly and heavenly blessings but that parents must appreciate their child, protect and recognize his or her birthright. For those who would not provide comfort to the newborn are no better than those who turned away the Christ Child. Watts rediscovers the divinity in infant innocence by analogizing all children to Christ. The most popular lullaby of the period, "Hushabye, Baby," which echoed Watts's views, was sung to a tune made popular by a song of the Revolution of 1688. The new parenting and the new constitutional government were intimately related.[20]

If Watts's "Cradle Hymn" displaced "The Duty of Children to Parents" in the 1760s and 1770s, Noah Webster's blue-backed speller (1787) would in time end the sovereign reign of the *New England Primer* itself. In the speller, Webster replaced the Westminster Catechism with one of his own, stressing mercy over justice; his neologism "happify" epitomizes the values of the new age for which he spoke, an age that required a new vocabulary.

> What are the advantages of this virtue [mercy]? A. The exercise of it tends to happify everyone. Parents and masters will not abuse their children and servants with harsh treatment . . . the more love the more society will be happy.[21]

No longer was it necessary to divide the Godhead into the just person of the Father and the merciful person of the Son; for God was as merciful as he was just.

⊁ In the same decade that Watt's hymns became a standard feature of the *New England Primer,* a very different work of religious consolation appeared in the colonies, an English translation of Salomon Gessner's *Der Tod Abels* (The Death of Abel). Originally published in German in 1758, Gessner's fictional treatment of the biblical story of Cain and Abel went through ten American editions between 1760 and 1770 (more than any other continental work) and twenty-five by the end of the century. Written by a Swiss writer of idylls and a painter of pastoral landscapes, *The Death of Abel* offered a fictionalized account of the introduction of death into the world. It articulated all the new Arminian emphases of midcentury Protestantism: the benevolent image of God, the benign character of death, and the complexity of moral accountability. But more important, it offered a sympathetic and psychologically acute analysis of filial anger and evangelical anxiety. Gessner's extremely influential and widely read work tells us much about the issues that interested Christian readers in the colonies in the decade before the Revolution.

As the volume opens, Adam and Eve are shown fully reconciled to the Fall and gloriously happy. They have built a new bower of bliss and bask in the certainty of God's love. "How could we know," asks Adam of Eve, "when . . . we took leave of Paradise that so much felicity was to be found on earth?"[22] Offering a version of Milton's "Wedding Hymn" (now sung on earth rather than in Eden), the couple praise God for the mercies he has shown in the midst of his judgment. Abel is true to his parents' nature. He and his wife Thrize (also fathered by Adam and Eve) praise God for his bounty, the beauties of nature, and for the "conjugal tenderness" (p. 12) he has granted them. They share with their parents a faith that a heart at ease makes possible a heaven on earth. Moved by his son's worship, Adam joyfully embraces Abel.

At a distance Cain watches this tender scene and is consumed with jealousy of a brother who he believes has "with his softness and effeminacy stolen the hearts of Adam and Eve" (p. 41). Though first born, Cain envies Abel who idly reclining "watches his flocks sport," while his brother endures the "rugged labour" of plowing (p. 13). It seems as if Adam's curse has fallen inequitably. "What advantage to me is the rank of first born," Cain asks, "misery is my inheritance, disdain my portion" (p. 50). Unlike Abel, who does not long for the paradise his parents have lost, Cain cannot take pleasure in a world cursed with labor and death. He "arraigns the dispensations of the Most High" (p. 15) and holds his father's primal sinfulness responsible for his painful fate. Like the eighteenth-century sentimental father on whom he is modeled, Adam tries to console Cain's "tortured heart" in the faith that "reason and parental love" will combat his son's obstinacy (p. 20).

But Cain will not be consoled. He lashes out against Adam in the manner a contemporary reader anguishing over his spiritual accountability might secretly have wished to address his own father:

> What need of all these exhortations? Do I not know that was my heart at ease everything around me would give me delight? But can I silence the storm, or bid the impetuous torrent flow in a placid stream? I am born of woman and from my nativity sentenced to misery. On my unhappy head the Almighty, has pour'd forth the cup of malediction. It is not for me nature displays her beauties (p. 156).

To this speech Adam responds not with anger, but with a plea for forgiveness no less satisfying to contemporary readers than Cain's outburst: "O Cain! Cain! I have deserved these cutting reproaches." He beseeches his son to indulge his "filial love" and "forbear this cruel charge which like a clap of thunder shakes my tortured soul" (p. 17). In this moment more than ever before, Adam becomes aware of the eternal consequences of his first sin. He darkly envisions a time when "all future generations will rise up against my dust and curse the first sinner." Adam's obvious pain touches Cain who refrains from reproaching "such a tender parent" (p. 17). But later the anger wells up again. Now aware how much anguish a son's rejection can cause a sentimental father, Cain must banish the fantasy of patricide from his mind: "Revenge not, unhappy man, revenge not thyself on another; by bringing before his eyes a spectacle of such horror, seiz'd with terror, he would expire at my sight" (p. 53).

In the meantime Satan has learned of Cain's misery and dispatches his minion Anamelech to recruit his soul. Anamelech sends Cain a vision in which he sees his children toiling in pain and Abel's children enjoying luxury and ease. By the end of the vision the former have become the servants and slaves of the latter. Awakening from this terrifying dream Cain fiercely confronts Abel who, seeking mercy, wraps himself around Cain's feet. In this posture he reminds Cain of the deadly serpent. Cain then smotes Abel and, immediately overwhelmed with despair and anguish, flees into the wilderness.

Having discovered Abel's body some time later, Adam blames himself for the murder rather than his eldest son: "From a trunk empoison'd by sin what can be produced but sinners . . . I have killed my posterity" (p. 47). Though God will not forgive Cain for the violent and unnatural death he has caused, he sends an angel to earth to relieve Adam of the guilt he feels for making death the curse of earthly existence. In a speech that reflects the mid-eighteenth-century shift in the perception of death, the angel assures Adam that when it comes to a good man or woman, death is not a punishment but a divine opportunity to return to a loving father: "The pale King of Terrors will assume a different form to each of you, but you will receive him as becomes the candidate for future happiness and welcome him as a friend long expected" (p. 70). With this speech "desolation fled," and Adam praises God as Cain continues his desperate flight from his own conscience.

Gessner's book offers an extraordinarily powerful message: The essence of sin lies in discontent, not in natural corruption. The "origins of inequality" Rousseau had sought out three years before are to be found in the skewed perceptions of that discontent. The earthly misery man experiences derives from a perverseness of heart, not from an inherited sinful nature. Thus Gessner insists man need not rail against either heavenly or earthly father; for God in his benevolence has ensured that a heart at ease makes possible a paradise regained both on earth and in heaven. Happiness and salvation are in the hands of those who can see in God's actions what Cain is unable to see in his father's face: "love" and not "reproach" (p. 14). For those, the knowledge of death does not compromise human happiness but contributes to it. Trust in God's love will banish forever the frightening image of Jehovah that haunts the discontented.

The enormous appeal of *The Death of Abel* is, however, only partially explained by the comforting doctrines of its sentimental and optimistic Arminianism. What makes Gessner's book so powerful is not its effort to diffuse filial anger, but its dramatic acknowledgment of that anger and of the fantasies and fears of the troubled sinners who presumably turned to it. Not only does it forcefully present the son's case against God and Adam, but it shows Adam accepting that filial judgment and anguishing in paternal guilt. Gessner makes clear that though Adam and Eve have from the first declared it their delightful task "to instruct the infant mind" of their son (p. 37), they have little psychological insight into Cain's discontent. Only *after* the still undiscovered fratricide do they resolve to bring "a present to their first born to erase from his mind the idea that he is not beloved of us with the same affection that we love his brother" (p. 68). Though Cain is accountable for his act because of his failure to rule his "tyrant passions" (p. 13), Gessner clearly acknowledges the problematic character of his moral accountability. In a volume dedicated to "tracing the motives of actions to their source" (p. v), Gessner seems to suggest that Satan who seeks his soul, Adam who first blesses only Abel, and God who refuses Cain's belated offering have each aggravated the "inward dejection" (p. 15) that propels Cain to murder.

The opening scenes of the book encourage a reading of that fratricide as a displaced enactment of the even more forbidden sins of patricide and deicide. Cain has turned outward against a scapegoat brother the anger that the evangelical temperament often turned inward in the form of self-hatred. It is not surprising that Goethe (and later Wordsworth and Byron) should have enjoyed Gessner; for Cain's sinful rejection of his fate offered the first generation of Romantics what Milton's Satan offered the next generation, a potentially heroic model of defiance. If a disobedient Adam and the prodigal son stand behind Crusoe and Clarissa, Gessner's Cain may lurk behind Werther. The scriptural sinner's defiance of God is all too easily transformed into the secular hero's defiance of tyranny.

HUMAN ACCOUNTABILITY AND THE MORAL
CHARACTER OF GOD

The power of orthodox Protestantism, under attack by Arminians and sentimentalists like Watts, Gessner, and others, had always resided in the vast internal logic of the doctrine of God's sovereignty. But that logic—despite even the magisterial efforts of an Edwards—fell apart if one refused to accept the paradoxes that underlay it. Shortly after completing divinity training at Yale, the newly ordained minister, Medad Rogers, found himself unable to deal with the most basic concerns of his parishioners. Edmund Morgan has brought to light Rogers's anxious letter to his mentor, Benjamin Trumbull.

> What to say to those under concern for a future existence, when they enquire how they shall come to the foot of a sovereign God. They try to but can not. They would bow to Christ's sceptre but are not able. How are we to blame, say they. We would be saved but can't be saved. How are such to be dealt with? Also, if God hath decreed all things, why is he not the Author of sin? How can any man do otherwise than he does?[23]

And on and on. Morgan has rightly seen in this 1771 letter evidence of the degree to which the orthodox clergy on the eve of the Revolution had lost contact with the real needs of the people. Trumbull is unable to give his parishioners what Gessner and Watts sought to give them: a more moral and rational understanding of accountability. At last, to use David Stannard's distinction, the tension between the rhetorical Christianity that implied one might participate in one's own salvation and a deterministic vision of history that denied participation had become unbearably acute. Either Christianity had to be made more reasonable and less repugnant or a new charismatic mythos, such as patriotism or national destiny, had to be offered in its place.

As the war drew to a close in late 1782, a pamphlet addressing the first alternative appeared in Boston entitled *Salvation for All . . . A Scripture Doctrine*. It was the first work printed in America devoted exclusively to arguing the doctrine of universal salvation. Its author was a local minister by the name of John Clark who, marshaling numerous authorities ancient and modern, argued that the good news that the angel announced at the birth of Christ was not the promise of redemption for some, but the fact of an ultimate redemption for all. All men would ultimately "join in enjoying the felicity of the sons of God."[24]

The pamphlet was a brief epitome of a much longer unpublished treatise written some twenty years earlier by Clark's friend, Charles Chauncy, who had been Edwards's antagonist during the Awakening and was now an ardent patriot. Fearing the professional consequences of publication, Chauncy had chosen simply to circulate his manuscript among a select group of liberal divines. In 1784, two years after Clark's trial run, the treatise was at last published in London under the title *The Mystery Hid for Ages*. Neither Chauncy nor Clark denied that some men will be damned and some saved. Rather the primary contention of both works was that the damned will only have to "suffer God's wrath for a season" (p. 7). After that time they will join the saved in heaven.

Shortly after the publication of Clark's pamphlet, Samuel Mather "of American Boston" picked up the gauntlet in behalf of the orthodox ministry. The doctrine of universal salvation, he argued in his public rebuttal, not only represented a misreading of Scripture, it called into question God's sovereignty. Reversing Shaftesbury's argument, Mather insisted universal salvation encouraged "libertinism" by removing the fear of absolute damnation, and that it resurrected the greatest of Popish heresies: "Here are some persons, that would be thought . . . Protestants, who however, are represented as declaring for the Popish doctrine of purgatory, though not in plain or explicit terms, yet in truth and reality; for they think, that the wicked by passing through a state of unutterable misery are to be prepared for a state of perfect happiness."[25] As Mather points out, what Clark and Chauncy are arguing for is to reconceive hell as a purgatory, to make damnation but a season in a progress whose end point is universal brotherhood in God, the reestablishment of a single family of man. The "rediscovery" of purgatory, a doctrine that would be widely popularized by Universalists at the very end of the century, was in effect another application of the concept of a progressive personal growth. It represented yet another triumph of nurture over absolute nature.

The debate ultimately centered on the character of Jehovah. Clark argued that to deny the concept of eternal damnation was to be rid at last "of that monstrous representation of God" – once again the issue is representation versus reality – and to render orthodox Christianity consistent with the tenor of the New Testament (p. 2). "God is love" and the knowledge that that love will be extended to all men, argued Townsend Shippen in a 1783 rebuttal to Mather's rebuttal, "will create a sense of obligation and gratitude to obedience which will do more than the terror of the doctrine of eternal damnation to render men righteous. For what is worse than to call a man ungrateful?"[26] Thus are the mechanics of moral sense offered in the place of the politics of coercion, God's example in the stead of his sovereignty. Shippen concludes his pamphlet, whose appearance almost exactly coincides with the signing of the Peace of Paris:

> If I could paint out greater affliction than any I have mentioned it must be the disastrous case of the poor prodigal children, from their father's house ladened with guilt, oppressed with shame, afflicted with a stubborn loathness to return. Even this painting has a bright side when we consider that in all their distress there is a design of love in over reaching all the misery as a means to bring them to themselves and to return to their father's house (p. 30).

The divine father, justly represented, will by the power of his love ensure the prodigal's return – to him and not to the earthly father who is said to represent him.

⇥ Chauncy's treatise culminated an attack on Calvinism that had begun from within its own ranks a generation earlier by the Arminian wing of the Congregationalist ministry. A growing number of such ministers were becoming uncomfortable with the essential Protestant paradox that though God is absolutely sovereign, man's will remains sufficiently free to render him completely responsible for his sinfulness. For many, Edwards's magisterial effort to save the paradox by arguing that man's will is free to do as it pleases but his pleasures are determined did not satisfactorily answer the greater question of accountability: If the sinner is unable to free himself from an innate and inherited sinfulness except by the gift of a free and unconstrainable grace, how may he be held accountable for his sinfulness? For Joseph Bellamy and Samuel Hopkins, disciples of Edwards who built the so-called New Divinity movement of the fifties and sixties, the answer was simple. Man himself was evil by nature and deserved damnation. His inability was not natural and hence excusable like that of an infant child who if he cannot yet walk cannot be blamed for it. His flaw was in his *moral* nature. Bellamy made the position of the new orthodoxy perfectly clear: "All our inability arises merely from the bad temper of our hearts and our want of a good disposition and that therefore we are wholly to blame and inexcusable. Our impotence is not natural but moral."[27]

Outspoken Arminian Calvinists like William Hart, Moses Hemmenway, and Jedidiah Mills – all writing in the late sixties after the Stamp Act crisis – insisted, on the contrary, that man's inability, indeed his sinfulness, was a matter of natural and not moral inability, of insufficient learning and not a depraved character. As such it did (as with the Vicar of Wakefield's "child of simplicity") "in some measure, if not wholly, excuse" him.[28] In his 1772 pamphlet *A Vindication of the Power, Obligation and Encouragement of the Unregenerate,* Hemmenway argued that Adam's fall lost man neither his moral nature nor his natural propensity to good, only "the habit or principle of righteousness disposing him to holy affections and actions." He was capable of a saving goodness but needed to be rehabituated to it until it was once again "secondary nature."[29] Salvation was a matter, William Hart argued, of a progressive moral understanding of the divine will, not a miraculous gift of a new heart. In brief, man was not so corrupt as to require a second birth, but rather needed only a spiritual education that would allow once again his understanding to be "rectified and rightly informed" and "misapprehensions" removed. His natural faculty to distinguish good and evil needs only that "these objects are seen by the mind in their true lights or as being what they truly are."[30] The issue was, in this regard, epistemological and not moral, a matter, as Locke would have it, of "mental" corruption. The divine message must be clarified and made self-evident, rather than the auditor given, as Edwards had argued, a new sixth sense with which to receive it. Here was the great principle of the American revolution against patriarchy Christianized. The sinner is like the impressionable Lockean adolescent not yet fully formed. He needs not to be renatured but rather to have the seeds of grace within him nurtured. To believe otherwise, Hart concluded, is to believe the creator a "hard-hearted, arbitrary cruel tyrant" and thus to lose sight of his essentially "paternal kindness."[31]

Those who argued that man's sinfulness was rightly understood as a natural and not a moral inability that thus diminished rather than magnified his accountability went right for the soft spot in the logic of orthodox Protestantism. What of children and idiots and the heathen who have not heard of the gospel, should they be damned for their credulity, their want of understanding? Must the newborn child who dies stillborn be sent to hell on the strength only of the sin imputed to him from Adam? If he must, as the orthodoxy declared, and inherited sin is thus acknowledged sufficient to damn, how can any man be held accountable for his damnation? The new sentimentality would triumph over the unfeeling doctrines of the old orthodoxy. Samuel Webster of Salisbury was one of its tear-jerking spokesmen. Of still-born infants he wrote in 1757: "How can you reconcile it to the goodness, holiness or justice of God, . . . to send them to hell from their mothers womb before they have seen the light of life, to make them first open their eyes in torment, a sin which if it comes upon them at all, certain is without any fault."[32] Even the New Divinity minister John Smalley would be obliged to concede the great point of the new pedagogy, the new novel, the new politics, and now the new theology: "man's present duty cannot exceed his present strength."[33] When Arminians inquired of the orthodox Clergy if "the disposition to love [God] is a thing supernatural . . . beyond the powers of nature, how can I, therefore be wholly to blame?"[34] they anticipated Paine's argument in *Common Sense*. How can the parent who does not inspire love (i.e., "create" the power he requires) with any justice demand it? Sin must be a matter of real and personal ability, not an imposed and inherited obligation.

The rejection of the damning character of the Adamic imputation was a rejection of the power of the first parents to control and determine the eternal life of their children. As such it paralleled a revolutionary rejection of absolute parental sovereignty over the next generation in the natural sphere. In *The Rights of Man* (1791), Tom Paine defined the new era of republican religion and politics that had so recently dawned:

> All men are born equal, and with equal and natural rights, and in the same manner as if posterity had been conceived by creation instead of generation . . . and consequently every child being born into it must be considered as deriving its existence from God. The world is as new to him as it was to the first man that existed, and his natural right in it is of the same kind. Each generation must be as free to act for itself . . . as the age and generations which preceded it.[35]

The facts of natural generation must not obscure the greater fact that each and every individual is as much the immediate creation of God as had been Adam and Eve. Each generation must be considered a new nation, a new world, yet a world with the same single parent. By denying the very concept of inheritance, Paine's declaration of human and generational equality freed mankind not only from parental tyranny but from the "sins of the father" and the necessity of a patrimony. In addition, it augured a second liberation – that of the sons of the Puritans from their own filio-pietistic myth of generational declension.

Charged with "misrepresenting" both the character of the unregenerate and the true character of the Deity, the New Divinity was obliged to make concessions. Though unwilling to compromise the orthodox stand on innate depravity and moral inability, Bellamy offered a new theory of the atonement that presented God not as "the offended party" who seeks recompense for the violation of his sovereign and arbitrary will, but as "the moral governor of the universe" who is enforcing and acting in accordance with the moral law.[36] The mediatorial scheme of Christ's death is to do honor to the divine law, not to God's sovereignty. In other words, man is punished for a violation of law not of private will, by a God concerned as much with the just administration of his government and the moral reformation of his creatures as with his own glory. Bellamy moved New England theology in the direction of the new politics – away from will and toward law. He imposed on God the same expectations the Glorious Revolution imposed on the monarchy and the new pedagogy on parents. Such would be the great contribution of the New Divinity.

Finally, however, it was not only the issues of accountability and the divine character on which the Arminians confronted the more orthodox, but the issue of freedom itself. In 1772, as colonists were beginning to call attention to the "despotism" of England, James Dana of New Haven published the most serious attack on Edwards to date. Far from securing for man free will, Edwards's famous accommodation conceded to man, Dana vehemently concluded, nothing more than "animal will."[37] The call for political independence could be heard in Dana's theological insistence that man be at last considered an "efficient cause" unto himself.

➤ The eighteenth-century rejection of patriarchal family or-ganization in favor of a new affectional family model paralleled an ever-growing sense of the incompatibility of the Old Testament with its insistence on man as God's obedient servant and the New Testa-ment with its insistence on man as God's loving son. Contrary to the returned prodigal's protestation that he be treated as "one of thy hired servants," sons must be distinguished from servants. From 1777 (when the English copyright was no longer observed) to 1800 there are only thirty-three American editions of the entire Bible, but in the same period there are nearly eighty separate printings of the New Testament.[38] Whereas "The Bible" was slowly becoming identified with the New Testament alone, the Old Testament, on the other hand, was becoming identified with the Book of Psalms. Though the Old Testament had no separate printings in the last three decades of the eighteenth century, the Psalms in various translations were fre-quently so printed.

Significantly, however, the most popular eighteenth-century edition of the Psalms in America was Isaac Watts's *The Psalms of David Imitated in the Language of the New Testament and Applied to the Christian State and Worship*. As the title indicates, the radical innovation of Watts's edition was that the Psalms were not translated but freely adapted to reflect the promise of the New Testament. Watts offers this justification:

> I have long been convinced, that one great occasion of this evil arose from the matter and words to which we confine all our songs. Some of them are almost opposite to the spirit of the gospel: many of them are foreign to the state of the New Testament and widely different from the present circumstances of Christians.[39]

His imitations are always theologically orthodox but they consistently eliminate the darker sayings of David and emphasize in their place Christian consolation and comfort. Watts's vision of the Deity is per-haps best expressed in this couplet from his version of the 119th Psalm, a psalm in which he substituted in his "imitation" the words "gospel, word, grace, and truth" for "law, commands, judgments, and testimo-nies" respectively: "Indulgent God with pitying eyes / the sons of men survey."[40] The God of the Old Testament is refashioned in the image of the God of the New. One additional clue to the popularity of Watts's *Psalms,* which went through an incredible twenty-eight separate print-ings in the colonies between 1770 and 1783, is given by the editor of the 1785 Hartford edition. He emphasized that these psalms are recommended because they are, in the Lockean fashion, "adapted to the capacities of common assemblies."[41] The psalmist is as indulgent as his God.

Watts's new psalmody paved the way for his hymnody. Though they usually have scriptural sources, Watts's hymns were apparently the first nonscriptural verse to be sung in eighteenth-century American congregations. The closed world of the revealed word had at last been opened to a new human voice and text. In one popular hymn Watts asks: "Of whence do our mournful thoughts arise?"

> Has restless sin and raging will
> Struck all our comforts dead
> Have we forgot the almighty name
> That form'd the sea and earth?

In another he offers this even more comforting vision:

> Rivers of love and mercy here
> In a rich ocean join
> Salvation in abundance flows
> Like floods of milk and wine.[42]

In his examination of Watts's adaptation of the 90th Psalm, Donald Davie concludes about Watts's strategy of consolation that "every time the ancient Hebrew poet looks back ('Lord, thou hast been our dwelling place in all generations'), our English poet looks back with him, but then immediately looks forward; thus, 'O God, our help in ages past,' but then, immediately, 'our hope for years to come.' "[43] Many of the Psalms ask, in effect, if God will desert his chosen people. Watts answers that He will not. The poet's looking forward, however, is more than simply a strategy of consolation. It is his way of insisting that the Old Testament must be read in light of the promises and dispensations of the New Testament. For all the originality of its language and emphases, the method of Watts's "Divine Songs" was but an extension of the conjunctive typological exegesis that orthodox Puritan divines had always used to accommodate the Old Testament to the New, to make the history of the Jews teach the history of salvation.

Watts's assertion that the Psalms were no longer "suited to the present circumstances of Christians" and (like Franklin) his consequent rewriting of them imply an understanding of the Bible that would a generation later become explicit in Gotthold Lessing's *Education of the Human Race,* one of the central texts of the European Enlightenment, written in that *annus mirabilis,* 1776. For Lessing the earliest form of divine education was revelation. It conveyed a version of the truth that, with more effort and training, man would be able to get from within himself.[44] The subsequent course of history has been the ongoing replacement of revelation with more rational education. The earliest peoples like the Israelites, "so raw . . . and so entirely in their childhood," could only receive a moral education "adapted to the age of children, an education of rewards and punishments addressed to the senses" (p. 357). Later races would be vouchsafed a new education.

The Old Testament then is best understood as a child's primer, designed to teach not by rational argument but through fear and the telling of engaging stories of miracles and battles. But, as Lessing continues in his account of Christian history as education, "every primer is only for a certain age. To delay the child, that has outgrown it, longer at it than was intended is harmful. . . . A better instructor must come and take the exhausted primer from the child's hand" (p. 364). Thus came Christ, "the first reliable and practical teacher." But still the Gospels, "the second better primer" (p. 366) *preached* the great truths – such as the immortality of the soul – rather than taught them by an address to human reason and through experience. Assuredly, Lessing concludes, there must be yet to come a third age of the world in which a new eternal gospel will be granted man and will succeed in "educating him to become a man, who when the prospects of honor and well-being have vanished, shall be able to do his duty" (p. 368).

It was precisely such an education that the colonists were accusing Britain of failing to provide and that the critics of New Divinity were calling essential. If Franklin was to declare the final tutor of man to be man himself, Paine was to argue in the *Age of Reason* some fifteen years after Lessing's work that the new gospel, the instrument of man's final education, is God's creation itself. The book of nature and not scripture is "the real and ever existing word of God." In this universal living gospel that must neither be interpreted, nor preached, nor translated into the languages of men, "We can not be deceived."[45] In nature nothing is misrepresented; for it is experienced, not taught. The great eighteenth-century anxiety is thus removed. Educated by the unmediated experience of God's creation, by its beauty, sublimity, and moral character, America would become, so the Romantics a generation later would declare, "nature's nation." The problem of moral education would be conveniently resolved and parental and ministerial mediation dispensed with altogether.

⊁ The rationalist dismissal of large parts of the Old Testament that insist affliction is the most beneficial and merciful form of instruction made explicit those objections to the character of Jehovah, which Puritans were accused by their ministers of sinfully fostering. Yet, Puritanism in no way denied the conflict between the morality of the Testaments to which critics insistently called attention. On the contrary, it addressed the issue directly. But rather than resolve the conflict by denying the divine character of the first Testament, orthodox theology sought to reconcile the Testaments. Whereas typology permitted the Puritan ministry to deal with the problem of the Old Testament's historicity, the doctrine of the two covenants addressed itself to the problem of the seeming discrepancy in morality between the Testaments. Watts and Lessing in their different ways simply extended the logic of this central doctrine of orthodox Protestantism, a doctrine whose implications ultimately allowed eighteenth-century evangelicals and rationalists to share similar ideological beliefs about liberty and sonship.

The relationship between man and God in the Old Testament is that of a servant bound to his master by a covenant of works. According to that first covenant made with Adam (and later extended to Abraham) man is required to do the impossible: to walk perfectly before his God. Through Christ, however, a new dispensation, whose saving agency is faith rather than works, is offered in the New Testament. Faith in the efficacy of Christ's sacrifice will not only free man from the killing letter of the Mosaic law, but will transform man's relationship with God from that of servant and master – the primary relationship of the Old Testament – to that of child and parent – the primary relationship of the New Testament. According to the Westminster Catechism that stage of grace preceding final sanctification is "adoption."[46] The true believer surrendering himself up to God will be "adopted" and will receive all the privileges of sonship. All of God's sons will join the redeemed family as firstborn with Christ. There will be no servants and no second sons.

In his *History of the Work of Redemption* first published posthumously in 1774, Jonathan Edwards reminds his readers that the meaning of Christ's birth and death is best expressed in the opening verses of Galatians 4:

1 Now I say, that the heir, as long as he is a child, differeth nothing from a servant, though he be lord of all;

2 But is under tutors and governors until the time appointed of the father.

3 Even so we, when we were children, were in bondage under the elements of the world:

4 But when the fulness of the time was come, God sent forth his son.

5 To redeem them that were under the law, that we might receive the adoption of sons.

....

7 Wherefore thou art no more a servant, but a son; and if a son, then an heir of God through Christ.[47]

In *Paradise Lost* Satan expressed his jealousy of the favor Jehovah showed Christ by insisting that the Only Begotten Son was, in fact, no different from others of the angelic host who were all begotten sons. He would not brook there being but one son and others who must slavishly obey. "That Glory never shall his wrath or might / Extort from me. To bow and sue for grace / With suppliant knees and deify his power."[48] Milton's point, of course, is that the tyrannical God against whom Satan rages is a projection of the arch-fiend's own rebellious pride and a reflection of the limitations of his perception. Milton has Satan view God apart from Christ, justice apart from mercy, works apart from faith, service apart from obedience. Contemporary detractors of Calvin claimed that he, too, read the Old Testament without the Gospel light that illuminated the types of Christ and set in shadow the Mosaic code.

Yet Satan's rebellious desire to be son and not servant and Christ's offer of a new dispensation of sonship (which silently acknowledged that rebellion) are ultimately related. They are both part of a similar reaction against the covenant of works that eighteenth-century Christian rationalists would later describe Calvin's God as having harshly enforced. Both are affirmations of that part of the Christian tradition that insists upon benevolence as a primary attribute of the Deity. Christian evangelicalism, rational theology, and revolutionary politics – each deeply affected by that antipatriarchal tradition – all concerned themselves with redefining sonship. Thus did all three move in the sweep of the seventeenth and eighteenth centuries toward a heretical union. That union would give the ideology of the American Revolution its distinctive character. The redefinition of divine authority both paralleled and reflected the redefinition of political authority.

PROTESTANT POLITICS: LIBERTY AND SONSHIP

The Protestant Reformation had defined "liberty" as freedom from an enslaving and deterministic original sin, which is achieved by a surrender of one's will and self to the will of God and to the person of Christ. In its Christian sense, liberty is the fruit of incorporation and renunciation and not of separation and self-assertion. The choice is always between true and false masters, never between a mastered and masterless condition. Accordingly, weakness is identified as strength, dependence as liberty, identity as selflessness, vulnerability as true security.

These identifications were repeated with a great degree of literalness in colonial sermons in which "that monster independence" spawned by the "rising of self" is set in opposition to selfless and glorious dependence. The cause of revolution, however, which encouraged the understanding of dependence as a political rather than as a religious posture, declared dependence anathema. The highest religious virtue, often anguishingly achieved through the stages of conversion, had become the greatest national vice. Declaring that independence was synonymous with slavery, Tory propaganda spoke directly to Christian values. Those who supported the war, particularly the rebel ministry, had, as a primary task, relieving the consciences of those parishioners who, having accepted literally the teachings of Scripture, believed "a rebel . . . indeed, is a monster in nature, an enemy not only to his country, but to all mankind."[49] Whereas Tory ministers sought to create guilty consciences by insisting that "Christianity was a religion which encouraged submission . . . even to tyrants,"[50] those Congregational and Presbyterian ministers sympathetic to the war responded by identifying political liberty with spiritual and moral liberty, freedom from the tyranny of George III with freedom from the tyranny of sin. By collapsing the distance between human and divine history, salvation and separation become part of one another.[51]

As one of the new breed of Arminian Congregationalists, Jonathan Mayhew believed that man might be active rather than passive in his salvation. On August 15, 1765, applying his understanding of moral activity, Mayhew preached against unlimited submission in civil affairs. "I would they were even cut off which trouble you. For, brethren, ye have been called to liberty, only use not liberty for an occasion of the flesh, but by love serve one another."[52] In an earlier sermon on the first verse of Galatians, addressing the problem of schism within the Congregationalist Church and echoing John Winthrop's famous address to the General Court one hundred and thirty years before, Mayhew declared:

> Let us all stand fast in the liberty wherewith Christ has made us free: and not suffer ourselves to be entangled with any yoke of bondage. If we have submitted to the yoke hitherto and ingloriously subjected ourselves to any human impositions in religious matters; it is better to throw off the yoke even now, than to let it gall us all our lifetime. It is not too late yet to assert our liberty.[53]

The original sense of Christian liberty as that freedom from the bondage to sin and self-love to which one is born is here significantly extended to include civil and religious liberties, to include "freedoms to" as well as "freedoms from." Once the cause of American independence had been identified with substituting God's yoke for Britain's, rather than with the suspect virtue of self-dependence, the Tory arguments for the necessity of a protective parent were turned back on themselves.

The Episcopalian minister who delivered the opening prayer to the first Continental Congress, Jacob Duché, preached in 1775 on the same verse Mayhew had chosen from Galatians. His sermon, "Standing Fast in Our Liberties," made direct reference to the imminent war:

> If *spiritual liberty* calls upon its pious votaries to extend their views far forward to a glorious hereafter, *civil liberty* must at least be allowed to secure in a considerable degree our well being here. . . . liberty, traced to her true source, is of heavenly extraction, that divine virtue is her illustrious parent, that from eternity to eternity they have been and must be inseparable companions. . . . when man lost his virtue, he lost his liberty too; and from that fatal period became subject to the bondage of corruption, the slave of irregular passions.[54]

As the patriarchal connection between divine and civil authority was being challenged, the connection between divine and civil liberty was becoming strengthened. As postlapsarian man's most pressing need is to be delivered from his own sinfulness, civil liberty was championed as a kind of secular grace.

Applying the formula of the jeremiad and of the captivity–conversion narrative to the immediate situation, many Congregationalist ministers declared that God had placed the tyrant George over his people in punishment for their backsliding and sinfulness, as he once had placed the Pharaoh over the Israelites. A month before Lexington and Concord, Samuel Langdon, President of Harvard College, declared: "But alas! have not the sins of America, and of New England in particular, had a hand in bringing down upon us the righteous judgment of Heaven? Wherefore is all this evil come upon us? Is it not because we have forsaken the Lord?"[55] To leave off sinning and to be freed of George are made synonymous. Thus, as both Perry Miller and Gordon Wood have pointed out, the great refrain of Whig rhetoric would be the necessity of embracing virtue[56] – which itself was the product of the right education.

In *Common Sense*, Paine also advanced the theological Whig argument but differed with Langdon as to the moment in Jewish history analogous to the present state of affairs. For unlike Langdon, Paine declares he knew the one specific sin for which both old and new Israel had been punished:

> Near three thousand years passed away, from the Mosaic account of the creation, till the Jews under a national delusion requested a king. . . .
>   The children of Israel being oppressed by the Midianites, Gideon marched against them with a small army, and victory through the Divine interposition decided in his favor. The Jews elated with success and attributing it to the generalship of Gideon, proposed making him a king, saying *'Rule thou over us, thou and thy son, and thy son's son.'* Here was temptation in its fullest extent; not a kingdom only, but an

hereditary one; but Gideon in the piety of his soul replied, '*I will not rule over you, neither shall my son rule over you.* THE LORD SHALL RULE OVER YOU . . . a prophet charges them with disaffection to their proper sovereign, the King of Heaven' (p. 10).

Here the deity does not punish his people's sinful backsliding and loss of faith by raising up a king or pharaoh. In Paine's illustration Israel's original *desire* for a king, her willingness to surrender a republic for a monarchy, is her original and only sin. Israel like Clarissa has fallen victim to a false understanding of the debt of gratitude that she presumes she owes Gideon and not God. When and if the American Israel will replace king with God once more (though the true "king of America" (p. 23) quickly modulates from God to Law), it will then, in effect, have redeemed itself from the original sin of monarchy. From that sin all its subsequent sinfulness and afflictions have proceeded. Thus Paine succeeds in suggesting that the formidable task of both personal and national reformation need not be achieved by the receipt of grace and a life of faith and good works but merely by a single act of renunciation. To unseat monarchy is to unseat sin, which Paine, following Locke and Rousseau, identifies with an external corruption of a natural purity. Here was the most radical formulation of Christian liberty.

Paine's "Children of Israel" oppressed by their own self-destructive monarchalism are versions of the child oppressed, in the political metaphor, by the exactions of an unnatural father. And both are related, in the evangelical language of the Revolutionary ministry, to the child of grace bound in sin, unable to return to his true parent:

> No sooner does the child of grace, the offspring of heaven, come to feel the bondage of the infernal usurper; no sooner does he find himself harrassed and oppressed by the obedience which he exacts to his unrighteous laws; no sooner is he convinced that such an obedience must terminate in everlasting slavery and wretchedness, than he awakens from his sleep of security . . . [an awakening] which his Redeemer is ever at hand to impart. . . .
>
> These glorious privileges being once obtained, the sinner is justified and adopted into the family of God.[57]

As republicanism transformed men into kindred "sons of liberty" and subjects into citizens, God's embrace and divine adoption made servants sons and prodigals pilgrims. The image of the liberated son embraced by a new parent stood in 1776 at the heart of evangelical Christianity and Revolutionary ideology. The two liberties and two redeemed sonships were ultimately one.

Preaching in 1783, the year the Peace of Paris was signed and the war concluded, a Connecticut minister spoke of Christ in His passion as opening "a treaty of peace" and raising up a "ministry of reconciliation."[58] The end of the war, like the end of the Babylonian captivity, completes a theological as well as a political era. The Treaty of Paris was a new dispensation of grace, freeing man from bondage to sin as well as from the tyrant who had been sent to punish that sin; the Christian ministry would replace the ministry of George III.

The Treaty opens with a most unusual formula for the period: "In the name of the holy and indivisible Trinity."[59] It then goes on, article by article, to announce America's political and commercial independence and to discuss boundaries and geographical separation. The opening formula seems a psychological compensation in the light of the whole document. The assertion of one sacred union permits the guiltless severing of a union more profane. The God in three persons replaces the three legal persons of the monarch: the King, the King in Parliament, the King in Privy Council.

Though Christianity historically had insisted on submission to earthly kings, it had also declared that the entire thrust of divine history was a separation of the holy from the "unclean thing," the winnowing of the chaff from the wheat. Such a view of history that stressed active purification rather than passive obedience permitted a critical distinction to be drawn between kings and God. This distinction would ultimately provide a common ideological ground for rationalists and more orthodox Christians. As long as the American Revolution was agreed to be a war to isolate God's holy remnant for its own moral protection, rather than a political rebellion against God's anointed and the image of his paternity, the Revolution became justifiable by all Christian lights and the cause of all Christendom. In 1798, Timothy Dwight prefaced a sermon with a scriptural text, which he developed as an argument against both Jacobinism and, retrospectively, British tyranny: "Come out, therefore, from among them and be separate, saith the Lord, and touch not the unclean thing; and I will receive you and will be father to you."[60] Earlier, rebels had been told by numerous sermons that they were directed by Scripture "to separate unto evil" those Tories who, like the Biblical citizens of Meroz, refused their own deliverance.[61] The child of grace, freed from his term as a slave, would be declared again a child and permitted his true sonship.

The political children of grace were not escaping the oppression sent to punish the sinful, but rather the contaminating sinfulness and luxury of a declining empire. The escape was essential to their virtue and, in more pietistical terms, their salvation. Repeatedly until 1776, as Bernard Bailyn has shown, the accusation is made that England is in an "old rotten state." In England "luxury has arrived to a great pitch and it is a universal maxim that luxury indicated the decline of a state."[62]

Oliver Goldsmith's *The Deserted Village* (1770) very poignantly described the way in which the rural and innocent pleasures of the English country life were being destroyed by a national obsession with luxury and acquisitive trade, the baleful consequences of which were land enclosures, corrupting dependence on foreign nations and, finally, the flight of the nation's children.

> Sweet smiling village, loveliest of the lawn.
> Amidst thy bowers the tyrant's hand is seen
> And desolation saddens all thy greed;
> One only master grasps the whole domain
> And half a tillage stints thy smiling pain. . . .
> And trembling shrinking from the spoiler's hand,
> Far, far away, thy children leave the land.

Goldsmith then looks backward:

> A time there was, ere England's griefs began
> When every rod of ground maintained its man;
> Just gave what life required, but gave no more:
> His best companions, innocence, and health
> And his best riches, ignorance of wealth.
>   But times are altered; trade's unfeeling train
> Usurp the land and dispossess the swain.[63]

The same self-dependence Locke had declared the goal of education and Richardson had hailed as "the noble principle of independence" essential to moral purity is invoked in Goldsmith's poem as an argument for agrarianism against mercantilism and luxury. Fearing that governments will surrender to what Adam Smith would seductively envision six years later as the "wealth of nations" and a free trade with a world purged of its dangers, Goldsmith champions, in contrast, the self-sufficient "virtue" of nations that provides every citizen, not just the firstborn, with his own self-sufficient plot of land. For agriculture is, as Rousseau declares in *Emile,* the true profession of free men. The image of "the cell," the figure of the hermit, and the theme of solitude in the late eighteenth-century pre-Romantic literature of England and America (the "Panther Narrative" is one example) suggest one dimension of the moral and ideological resistance to a self-aggrandizing, competitive, and interdependent world envisioned by Smith as the ideal embodiment of "natural liberty." American postwar isolationism would represent another. The praise Defoe lavished on Robinson's island isolation and for which he felt obliged to apologize in 1721 was to find a more receptive audience a half-century later.

Obliged to leave the old world land now turned over to "trade's proud empire," enemy of all "self-dependent power" (p. 303), Goldsmith's children must be provided with an asylum. That asylum, Paine dramatically concludes in the third section of *Common Sense,* can only be found in America.

> Every spot of the old world is overrun with oppression. Freedom hath been hunted round the globe. Asia and Africa have long expelled her. Europe regards her like a stranger, and England has given her warning to depart. O receive the fugitive and prepare in time an asylum for mankind (pp. 30–31).

It is, however, not only the republican child, the prodigal pilgrim or the expelled Adam who seeks asylum but the Daughter of Zion, the prefigurative type of the Protestant Church in the Book of Revelation who has fled into the wilderness to protect herself from the dragons of paganism. Thomas Bray was but one of many in 1775 to strike the millennial note:

> God Almighty, with all the powers of heaven, are on our side, to encounter the dragon. God brought His church, the daughter of Zion into his wilderness on eagle's wings, and He has tenderly nourished and cherished her from the cruel hand of oppression . . . by leading her to Canaan, for an everlasting inheritance.[64]

Virtue, the colonial child who has attained the age of reason, and the Protestant church all have deserted the English village to find tender parenting and adoption in America. "O England," declared Ezra Stiles in 1783:

> how did I once love thee! how did I once glory in thee! how did I once boast of springing from thy bowels. . . . And yet even now methinks in such an exigency, I could leap the Atlantic, not into thy bosom but to rescue an aged parent from destruction, then return on the wings of triumph to the asylum of the world, and rest in the bosom of Liberty.[65]

➤ If God regenerated man supernaturally, the new world asylum was capable of regenerating naturally those parents and children who had "leapt the Atlantic" to its virtuous soil and gracious atmosphere. Liberty would serve the function of grace. For if, as Crèvecoeur declared in his 1782 *Letters from an American Farmer,* "men are like plants" and "the goodness and flavour of the fruit proceeds from the particular soil and exposition in which they grow," transplanted Europeans would soon discover that in America "everything tended to regenerate them."[66] Freed from a life of servile dependency and enjoying the "immunities of a freeman," the new American farmers will at last be able "to become men." In Europe "they were so many useless plants wanting vegetable mould and refreshing showers" (p. 38). But transformed by "the love of this new adoptive parent" – it is parental love that is always the ultimate influence – Europeans will feel the effects of a "sort of resurrection" (p. 55).

Regeneration, resurrection: Here was the millennium of nurture. Like the regenerate sinner who takes off "the yoke of bondage" and puts on "the easy yoke" of Christ, in the new world men will shed their feudal bonds and put on "the silken bands of mild government," the "symbol of their adoption" (p. 38).[67]

Crèvecoeur's vision extends to the human species the popular claims of contemporary landscape designers that men in America had at last achieved sufficient power over nature such that they could transform a bog into a place of agrarian splendor and "rear the Valley into a lofty mountain."[68] The choice of "rear" makes clear the connection between landscape design, gardening, and education: the arts of natural transformation. "Before the establishment of the American states," wrote Jefferson to Adams, "nothing was known to history but the man of the old world, crowded within limits either small or overcharged, steeped in the vice which that situation generates."[69] Nurtured by the uncorrupt influences of the republic, the new American would for the first time in history show man to the world as God intended him to be. And though Americans might not remain eternally uncorrupted, "many hundred years must roll away before we shall be corrupted."[70] His perfectibility "proved by Price, Priestley, Condorcet, Rousseau, Diderot and Godwin," as Jefferson insisted, man would achieve his perfect cultivation in America.[71] Of Crèvecoeur's list of influences that form a man – the air he breathes, the climate of his region, the work he does, the religion he professes, the government under which he lives – only the first seemed incapable of control, of being chosen. In 1775, however, Joseph Priestley, the English scientist in Jefferson's list who would later emigrate to America and support the cause of the French Revolution, published the first treatise on oxygen. He had discovered, he claimed, a new purer air in which candles burned brighter and presumably in which men might, as with Mesmer's fluid, be invigorated with a purer spirit. Thus did it seem in the year of Lexington and Concord that even the atmosphere itself might be purified.[72]

What ultimately regenerated and transformed the old world man into the new world man, however, were the new habits his new life obliged him to acquire. Locke had declared that the "great Thing to be minded in Education is, what *Habits* you settle," for habits work with "greater Facility than Reason."[73] To make an action habitual was to make it more than a reasoned act or an emotional response, it was to make it instinctual, "woven into the very Principles of his Nature" (p. 146), second nature. It was by habituation that education more than formed man, it renatured him. New habits and new habitual connections, the central concept of associationalist philosophy, made new men. In his 1772 attack on the New Divinity position, Moses Hemmenway of Wells,

Massachusetts, spoke not only for the Arminians but for all those who subscribed to the new understanding of the human mind when he declared that man's sinfulness indicated no more than the failure to acquire the right "habits."[74]

Norman Fiering has demonstrated convincingly the operation of habituation to be the principle underlying Franklin's faith that "outward acts can cause inward changes," the faith that informs Franklin's project for moral perfection, his version of Crèvecoeur's vision.[75] Franklin's project is not to acquire the virtues he lists, but to acquire "the Habitude" of them (p. 180). And toward that end he must first keep "constant Vigilance" and maintain a guard "against the unremitting Attraction of ancient Habits" so that "contrary Habits" may be broken and "good ones acquired and established" (pp. 150, 148). Here was Franklin's version of the purging of the Old Adam.

In a passage from Marmontel we have examined in another context, the heroine declares of her adopted father: "Natural affection between him and me has become so habitual that it has acquired the force of natural attachment and the ties of adoption have connected us with the same strength as if they were the bonds of consanguinity."[76] The habit of true affection, the habit encouraged by the new world, creates a bond between child and adopted parent, between immigrant and adopted land as natural as any bond of birth and so permits the creation of a new set of naturalized domestic relations. Paine's belief in the regenerative character of the antimonarchical revolt, Crèvecoeur's insistence that "the cultivation of earth purifies man" (p. 49), Franklin's Lockean faith in the power of habitude, Jefferson's fascination with the moral influence of the pure forms both of nature and of neoclassical architecture,[77] the orthodox clergy's belief in the purgative value of the affliction of war, the Arminian assumption that civil liberty facilitates spiritual liberty and finally, the overarching cultural faith in the power of education and nurture – all reflected a belief that in America, delivered from the spiritual and moral corruption of Europe and ultimately, perhaps, of sin itself, man would become pure and would regenerate. Here would arise the new order to replace the dying order of Europe.

In his excellent work on late eighteenth-century art, Robert Rosenblum observes that the motif of the "deathbed surrounded by mourners . . . is so prevalent from the mid-century on that examples may well run into the thousands."[78] Such scenes depicted not only the deaths of heroic figures – Germanicus, Hector, Raphael, Leonardo, Du Guesclin, Seneca, Socrates, and Wolfe – but also of bourgeois fathers. Taken together with the popular depictions of ruins (Piranesi's are but the best known), of noble monuments transformed into unrecognizable shapes and overgrown and overtaken by nature, these deathbed scenes suggest that at the heart of European art of the mid- and late century is a haunting preoccupation with "the physical expiration of a dead civilization," with the imminent death of the ancien régime and an older set of values.[79] The grieving widows and orphans who fill contemporary canvases are mourning not only loved ones but the death of the old order. Whether orphans, prodigals, pilgrims, or parricides, the children of that now moribund order will find new and tender parenting in America where, as Paine declared in *Common Sense,* "we have it in our power to begin the world again" (p. 45), to rebuild "the Bowers of Paradise" on whose ruins the "palaces of kings" were first constructed (p. 4–5).

THE COMMON GROUND: THE NECESSITY OF REBIRTH

Alan Heimert has remarked that "There were in substance only two parties on the American religious scene in the period after the Great Awakening."[80] The Liberal Old Light, or Rationalist Party, believed that "man is or should be a rational being, one who derives his standards of virtuous behavior from an observation of the external world" (p. 5). In contrast, evangelical, or New Light, Protestants ascribed the virtuous conduct of men to "the inward operation of the holy spirit." According to this view, without a rebirth in the spirit there could be no virtue in the man. Heimert argues that the "ideologies" or value systems of these two parties represented a sharp split in the culture. The controlling imagery of the two suggests, however, that they were not so far apart. Though disagreeing on the role of transformational grace, both sides concerned themselves with the same overriding issue: the necessity of giving man a new nature.

The new birth that was believed by some to be occasioned by the natural development of reason and virtue, thus making it the end point of education and habituation, was believed by yet others to be occasioned by the operation of the Holy Spirit. Each construction, in a real sense, was a version of the other. More particularly, becoming a rational adult and becoming a child of God were, as we shall see, intimately related events. An understanding of their relationship is essential to an appreciation of the unity of the American cause and of the character of what would become the new American family.

Rationalists – Deists, Arminians, and Old Light Protestants – and Evangelicals – New Lights, Baptists, Methodists – differed on such issues as the efficacy of natural revelation, the depravity of man, and the divine authorship of evil. But they agreed upon the central assumption that makes deistical objections to the authoritarian nature of the Deity compatible with the most orthodox formulations of the Protestant faith: the voluntaristic character of any true faith and, consequently, the intimate connection between faith and reason. Even those who believed faith to be affectional or a divine gift insisted on the necessity of rational consent after the fact. Thus did both parties insist that the privilege conferred on man by the "age of reason" was the right to choose to join a new family, to participate in a new spiritual union. It is not surprising that such assumptions provide a common ground, for they are the primary legacy of the Protestant Reformation.

What Calvin, Luther, and Tyndale all agreed to be the great heresy of Rome was her insistence that only "the faith of the Church (by which thyn assent is made thyn faith) did make thee safe."[81] That is, they repudiated her insistence that faith resided not in the man but in the Church, which alone was bride to Jesus Christ. What the Reformation sought was to permit man to own (in both senses of the word) his faith, to return it to its true sense of *fiducia* rather than *assensus,* to remove the mediate church from between man and the Word. Thus did Calvin translate the holy writ into French, Luther into German, and Tyndale into English. To free the holy word from its bondage to the Latin tongue was the first step in freeing man from blind and inherited faith.

A century later in the wake of the English Civil War, Milton reiterated the Reformational message that it is God's wish that faith be experiential. In his *De Doctrina Christiana,* Milton wrote: "And as he requires that he who would be saved shall have a personal faith of his own, I resolve not to rely on the faith and beliefs of others."[82] But not only must faith be individualistic, it must be voluntaristic. Thus does Milton develop in *Paradise Lost* the argument that God made man free to fall so that man could have the freedom to choose to obey God, for only in such obedience is God glorified. To guide man in his faith and his freedom, the Deity has impressed upon man's nature right reason, "law to man." Though that reason was impaired by the Fall and in the post-lapsarian world must be supplemented by revelation, it is essential that man "choose" to receive faith.

In 1741, Isaac Watts elaborated such a sentiment in his important pedagogical volume entitled *The Improvement of the Mind:*

> It is hard to say at what exact time the child is exempted from the Sovereignty of parental dictates. Perhaps it is much justice to suppose that this sovereignty diminishes by degrees as the child grows in understanding and capacity, and is more capable of exerting his own intellectual powers.
>
> When childhood and youth are so far expired that the reasoning faculties are grown up to any . . . measure of maturity, it is certain that a person ought to enquire into the reasons of his own faith and practice in all the affairs of life and religion.[83]

The child who had attained an age of reason in Watts's view had also attained an age of faith. If reason were, indeed, the divine signature of the human character, becoming an adult conferred on one the possibility of becoming a child of God. Just such a view is set forth in Edward Young's contemplative *Night Thoughts on Life, Death and Immortality,* another poem so widely read in imported editions as to demand its first American impression in the midst of the war in 1777:

> All-sacred Reason! source and soul of all Demanding praise on earth,
> or earth above!
> . . . .
> Wear I the blessed cross, by Fortune stamp'd
> On passive Nature before Thought was born?
> My birth's blind bigot! fir'd with local zeal!
> No; Reason rebaptiz'd me when adult;
> Weigh'd true and false in her impartial scale;
> My heart became the convert of my head,
> And made that choice which once was but my fate.[84]

If, as Locke has insisted, the attaining to reason is a discernible and transformational moment in human growth, the receipt of reason becomes from Young's perspective a converting sacrament, a "rebaptizing" built into that morphology. The first moment one is loosed from the paternal yoke becomes identified with the first moment one may *choose* to seek the divine yoke and, if one is properly educated, with the moment one will. It is ultimately for *this* choice that a Christian parent has prepared his child for independence. One must never lose sight of the fact that Locke's view of the mind as a tabula rasa has as an antecedent Richard Hooker's view of grace as "imprinted on the soul as a book."[85] Education secularized the operation of grace.

As the above discussion may suggest, no single colonial accusation against Britain would be more charged with significance than that she was impeding the adolescent rite of passage of her child colonies and failing to educate them for a full participation in the world. For to impede that passage was virtually to interfere with a necessary stage of the salvational process. Young's passage continues:

> Wrong not the Christian: think not reason yours:
> 'Tis reason our great Master holds so dear;
> 'Tis reason's injur'd rights his wrath resents;
> 'Tis reason's voice obey'd, his glorious crown:
> To give lost reason life, he pour'd his own.
> Believe, and shew the reason of a man;
> Believe, and taste the pleasure of a god;
> Believe, and look with triumph on the tomb.
> Thro' reason's wounds alone thy faith can die (p. 68).

Young's lines illuminate the vast theological dimension to such complaints as we have heard Revolutionary spokesmen make. Though we have seen Paine brilliantly apply the affectional model of the Scots to the Revolutionary situation, he did not fail in *Common Sense* to invoke the rationalist model as well. By arguing that "to talk of friendship with those *in whom our reason forbids us to have faith* . . . is madness and folly" [(p. 30) emphasis added], Paine masterfully turns the basic Protestant formula against Great Britain, whose demands are thus implicitly identified with the Catholic principle of *assensus*. It is not surprising that Young's poem was first published in 1742 at the height of the Great Awakening in England and America. For once again the new birth occasioned by the receipt of reason and that occasioned by the operation of the Holy Spirit were versions of one another.

Cushing Strout has recently called attention to "the role of Awakening preaching in resolving emotional issues generated by parental rule over the lives of young people." His argument builds on William James's insight that "conversion is in its essence a normal adolescent phenomenon, coincidental to the passage from the child's small universe to the wider intellectual and spiritual life of maturity" and on Erik Erikson's contention that late adolescence is a period particularly "susceptible to the propaganda of ideological systems that promise a new world perspective at the price of total and cruel repudiation of the old one."[86] In the context of such insights, Strout finds it significant that virtually all the important New Light ministers of the postrevival generation were "between seventeen and twenty-five at the peak of the Awakening" and that, in five parishes examined, the average age of conversion dropped during the revivals from "thirty-one to the early twenties." This, he believes, confirms what Jonathan Edwards himself said of the Northampton revival: It was almost "wholly upon a new Generation; those that were not come to years of discretion in that wonderful season nine years ago" (p. 41). Both the Awakening and the Revolution drew on and gave expression to the morphological emphasis of the educational revolution. It is not at all surprising that one theme stressed by nearly all Awakening ministers was the necessity for greater family education.[87]

In the language of the Puritans, when one had undergone a conversion experience, it was said that "the old man was dead"; that is, that the old Adam had been replaced by the new Adam, Christ. Conversion effected a rhetorical patricide. The Awakening provided many young adults with a new and glorious identity based on an affectional experience of a new Father's grace. A generation later the Revolution would provide a similar identity for the nation at large. Both Young's account of reason rebaptizing him and Strout's reading of the Awakening as a rite of passage into adulthood take on an increased significance in light of one of the most important controversies raised by the first great wave of religious revivals in America: the proper understanding of the meaning of baptism, the prefiguring ritual of rebirth.

Shortly after the major phase of the great revivals had subsided, some members of the fast-growing Baptist community became especially vehement in their insistence that the Congregational church's baptizing of infants was a direful misapplication of that ordinance. The sacrament, argued the so-called Separate Baptists, should be reserved exclusively for those old enough to be able to give evidence of professing their own faith. Infant baptism in effect compromised the voluntaristic principle of the faith. As William McLoughlin has so effectively shown, the great Baptist minister Isaac Backus took the antipaedobaptist objection to its furthest extreme. Insofar as the time-honored covenant theology of New England Protestantism sanctioned infant baptism, Backus declared, it was in effect preaching the false doctrine of the fallen covenant of works. In that first covenant God not only promised glory to Abraham in exchange for his obedience but to his "seed" forever. As grace could in no way be inherited, however, that covenant was terminal according to Backus and others. It had necessarily to be superseded by the covenant of grace that the Deity, having sacrificed his son to make it possible, offered to each and every *individual* soul independent of the beneficiary's connection to the previous generation. As the Deists denied the continuity of the Testaments, so the new Baptists denied the continuity of the Old and New Testament covenants and the typological relationship between them that had been asserted so long. The generational covenant with Abraham and his seed had been abrogated by a covenant with the individual who must rationally choose to enter that covenant before the sacrament of baptism.[88] Only *he* may be symbolically reborn. Once again in the new value system of the age, the importance of birth and origin is subordinated to that of personal virtue and merit. The only true new birth must be correlated with the birth of reason. The American Revolution offered precisely such a ritual rebirth into adulthood.

In 1762 in *Emile*, Rousseau would take the theological metaphor of a new birth one step further by identifying puberty itself, that is, the arrival of one's full sexual identity, as man's true second birth:

> Man, if I may use the expression, is born twice, first to exist and then to live; once as a species and again with regard to sex.
>
> . . . .
>
> But man in general was not born to remain in a state of childhood; nature marks a time when he emerges from infancy, and this critical moment, though short, is attended with a long train of consequences.

> As the roaring of the sea precedes the tempest, so the murmur of rising passions portends this stormy revolution. . . . His eyes, those organs of the mind hitherto inexpressive learn to speak; animated with a lively fire.
> . . . .
> This is the second birth I was speaking of; at this age man is truly born to live and enter into the full possession of the human nature.[89]

Rousseau defines "that stormy revolution" puberty as the birth of self-love, a "passion," which as it generates "love of those about him" is prerequisite to true Christian behavior.

Whereas Evangelicals were concerned that man be free to pursue the welfare of his soul and create a Christian community, Rationalists were concerned with the social and political welfare of the individual. Both their ends, however, could only be achieved from the vantage point of adulthood. All the parties who eventually supported the war, in one way or another, insisted that the privilege conferred on man by the age of reason was the right to choose to join a new family, to participate in a new union – be that union political or spiritual.[90]

THE TRIUMPH OF NURTURE

The observation that a man's childhood and adulthood are virtually two different, though continuous, lives requiring two separate births had enormous implications for the development of eighteenth-century liberal Protestant thought. The triumphant popularity of that thought represents a crucial stage in the antipatriarchal revolution. Responding in part to the Lockean equation of experience and knowledge, a new generation of Christian apologists turned from Scripture to nature to offer a new set of rational and experiential proofs of the truth of Christianity. If man can live, asked these new apologists, one kind of existence and be born into another within his natural life, does this not serve as a proof by analogy of the possibility, if not the probability, of his being reborn again into an eternal afterlife? If nature obeyed regular and discernible laws, might not those very same laws, if properly understood, reveal the inherently rational character of such divine mysteries as the afterlife? Might not the visible world be one great analogy for the invisible?

In the greatest and most influential of the analytical works of midcentury, *The Analogy of Religion* (1757), Bishop Butler addressed two questions: "what the effect of death may or may not have on us" and "whether it be not from there probable that we may survive this change and exist in a future state of life and perception." Butler began by isolating what he saw to be the most general law of nature:

> From our being born into the present world in the helpless imperfect
> state of infancy, and having arrived from thence to mature age, we
> find it to be a general law of nature in our own species that the same
> creatures, that the same individuals should exist in degrees of life and
> perception with capacities of action, of enjoyment and suffering, in
> one period of their being, greatly different from those appointed them
> in another period of their being.[91]

The difference between the human states of infancy and of maturity is
no less a transformation "than the chrysalis into a butterfly, a worm
into a fly. Thus can not it in all reasonableness be supposed that we are
to exist hereafter in a state as different from our present as this is from
our former?" (p. 68). As the adult is the same individual as he was
when a child, so the transformation effected by both death and grace is
also a change in state not in identity. We remain the same living agent
as does by analogy a man who loses not his life, but his eye or his leg.

Given the primary analogy that the afterlife is to this life as maturity
is to childhood, from the vantage point of the afterlife all of human life
becomes a single childhood, a state of probation and ongoing education. Thus, it is natural that God behaves toward man as a good Lockean parent would toward a young child: "As the correction of children,
for their own sakes and by the way of example when they run into
danger or hurt themselves is a part of right education, so God rules man
in his infancy with severity" (p. 112). Because man is not born qualified
for his mature state, "nature has endowed us with a power of supplying
those deficiencies, by acquired knowledge, experience and habits; so
likewise, we are placed in a condition in infancy, childhood and youth
fitter . . . for our acquiring those qualifications." Butler's *Analogy* once
again makes clear the underlying assumption behind the eighteenth-
century obsession with parental responsibility. If all life is "a state of
education" (p. 77), the success of that education determines the disposition of the afterlife. The two lives are but stages in the same development. The final triumph of the morphological–progressive paradigm
was to deny the radical break between life and death.

In an essay entitled "Of Personal Identity," often printed with *The
Analogy,* Butler condemned those who believe man in his afterlife to be
reborn to a new identity rather than simply to a new stage of life.[92]
Locke's assertion that the perception of an object at two different moments cannot be the same perception led some to conclude that the very
identity of the perceiver was not fixed but shifted from moment to
moment. Butler saw such an assumption as particularly pernicious; for
not only did it potentially free man from taking responsibility for his
own previous actions, but it denied the developmental relationship of

the various stages of life. For Butler, as for so many of his contemporaries, the essential fact was that to nurture was to renature. One is educated by life into a final stage of a continuous progress. *That* is to be reborn. The history of redemption and the history of personal growth become part and parcel of one another. Doddridge best stated the essential message of Butler's *Analogy:* Christians who have been raised on "the sincere milk of the word" will each "come unto a perfect man." They who grow in grace will achieve the "fullness of Christ" and "henceforth be no more children."[93] True nurture is saving.

In 1772, the year of Dana's and Hemmenway's attacks on Edwards and four years before Paine's work of the same name, a pamphlet entitled *Common Sense* appeared in New York. It addressed itself to the question: "whether if at the moment sin entered the world there occurred a total destruction of God's image in man or if some degree of right morality remains in man." The substance of the pamphlet is a systematic attack on those who, taking the latter view, conclude that regeneration rather than effecting an absolute moral transformation in man is "but an improvement, increase, gradation of preexisting disposition."[94] The anonymous author finds intolerable the view that grace is "a circumstantial alteration," a kind of special nurture. Man must not "be flattered but regenerated," reborn into a new identity (p. 24). "All must change or man must be miserable"; for regeneration has nothing to do with "suasability" (p. 29). Such a shrill defense of regeneration suggests the threat the new model of growth (as applied to salvation) was presenting to the older view of grace as transformation in the years before the war.

The conviction that salvation consists in "the gradual nurture of the sense of goodness in the soul," or, to use Lockean rather than Scottish terms, in the development of a rationality that allows "the enlarged contemplation of the wisdom of the Deity," underlies what Ernest Tuveson has called "the cosmic progressivist optimism of the age as a whole."[95] That optimistic faith in a divinely designed program of human growth finds a theological parallel, he argues, in the emergence in mid-eighteenth-century Protestant thought of a postmillennial reading of Scripture. Postmillennialism is the denial of the more orthodox premillennialist position that the resurrection of the dead will occur before the millennium, or 1,000-year reign of peace predicted in Revelation. The postmillennialist believes, reversing the terms, that the earthly paradise will occur before the resurrection as the last, culminating state in "the series of progressive stages which can be discerned in history."[96] The millennium is, one popular English theologian asserted, only a better version of "our present state of probation which by our exertions we may improve."[97]

The postmillennial insistence that the 1,000-year reign of peace would precede the Second Coming, that it would be achieved within human history rather than after the apocalyptic end of history, had its roots in the Reformational idea of progressive revelation, the view that each generation would be vouchsafed a fuller and fuller vision of God's will until the final triumph of the Protestant Church. The postmillennialism Jonathan Edwards embraced during the Great Awakening took the form of believing that that triumph would occur in America:

> God has made as it were two worlds here below, the old and the new . . . two great habitable continents, far separated one from the other; the latter is but newly discovered . . . and is as it were newly created . . . that God might in it begin a new world in a spiritual respect when he creates the new heavens and new earth.[98]

Whether the site would be America or not, the primary article of faith for the postmillennialist was that God had placed it within man's assisted power to redeem society, to create and nurture and educate his kingdom on earth.[99]

A generation later the American Revolution would be fought, in part, to ensure that the new world would remain new, would be forever freed from the taint of the old world, and would remain a ready stage for the generation and nurture of the ultimate Christian community. The educational revolution fueled the postmillennial vision. In an allegorical oration delivered to American troops in 1778 on the subject of Noah and his ark, Hugh Henry Brackenridge described how "the family of Cain, early driven to the land of Nod and deprived of the instruction of their father Adam, sunk down into the deepest ignorance . . . and every vice." The British sons of Cain would now be destroyed and the new race of Americans, committed to parental instruction, would outlast the flood, and triumph.[100] In 1783, just as the war ended, Charles Turner declared: "But, if all the youth were educated, in the manner we recommend, *The Kingdom of God* would appear to have come . . . and we might be induced to think of that *Millennial state,* the approach whereof, does perhaps at this time appear, by several prognostic symptoms, to be in some degree probable."[101]

➤ By the early nineteenth century the primary doctrines and assumptions of the revolution against patriarchal authority and the triumph of nurture had generated what would become, at least in New England, a new Christian orthodoxy: Unitarianism. By denying Christ a divine nature, Unitarianism sought to return to the Deity a single unified character at once merciful and just. In 1805, David Tappan would be succeeded as Hollis Professor of Divinity at Harvard by Henry Ware, the first Unitarian to hold that chair. Though thirty years later Emerson would attack the Unitarian regime for its dust-dry rationalism and lack of spirituality, in 1800 reason (man's spiritual guardian) and benevolence (the rediscovered principle of divinity in mankind) were deemed the most glorious of spiritual entities.

The first Unitarian congregation was formed in London by Theophilus Lindsay in the year before Lexington and Concord and was attended in its first session by Benjamin Franklin. From the end of the Revolution to the second decade of the nineteenth century, a growing number of ministers who embraced the doctrines of English Unitarians like Lindsay quietly preached in the Boston churches. Most were as yet unwilling to make explicit either their objections to Congregational polity or to the doctrine of the Trinity. But by 1815, the accommodation had become too problematic and uncomfortable. In that year William Ellery Channing took the occasion of the ordination of Jared Sparks to preach a sermon that was in effect a declaration of theological independence. His sermon, a masterpiece of exposition, makes clear the degree to which the Unitarian revolt carried forth the eighteenth-century revolution against patriarchy. It seems fitting to end this chapter with a brief consideration of that sermon, for it, better than any other contemporary document, summarizes and gives definitive expression to the half-century of liberal Christian thought that preceded it.

Channing begins his sermon with a rebuttal to the most prevalent contemporary criticism of the Unitarian position: "We are said to exalt reason above revelation, to prefer our own wisdom to God's."[102] It is not reason that is being elevated over revelation, Channing points out, but rather it is revelation that is being argued to be rational. He dismisses as pernicious and untenable the view that "God, being infinitely wiser than men, his discoveries will surpass human reason" and thus that "in a revelation from such a teacher we ought to expect propositions that we cannot reconcile with one another and that may seem to contradict established truths" (pp. 67–8). On the contrary, Channing asserts, "the Bible is a book written for men. . . . We believe that God when He condescends to speak and write, submits to the established rules of speaking" (p. 61). Resembling a good Lockean parent or tutor "who knows the precise extent of our minds," Channing's God "discovers His wisdom in adapting Himself to the capacities of His pupils, not in perplexing them with what is unintelligible" (p. 68). Though some of Scripture is surely obscure, "all that is necessary for us and for salvation is revealed too plainly to be mistaken" (p. 69).

Agreeing with Lessing that the two testaments were written to address two different stages of the development of the human race, Channing makes clear that "the dispensation of Moses compared with that of

Jesus, we consider as imperfect, earthly, obscure, adapted to the child-hood of the human race" (p. 60). Though the authors of the Bible were inspired, they were not "freed from the peculiarities of their own mind or the prejudices of the historical period out of which they were writ-ing" (p. 62). Rational readers of the nineteenth century must look then from the letter to the spirit of such passages of Scripture as those that attribute human passions to God or those in the New Testament, for example, in which Christ declares that he came not to send peace but a sword and that we must hate father and mother. For the Unitarian no doctrine may be inferred from Scripture that calls into question the prior truth of "God's moral perfection" or denies that "God is infinitely good, kind, benevolent . . . good in disposition as well as in act, good not to a few but to all" (p. 83).

At the heart of the sermon one finds Channing invoking the central doctrine of the antipatriarchal tradition: "to give our view of God, in a word, we believe in His Parental character. We ascribe to Him not only the name, but the dispositions and principles of a father. We believe that He has a father's concern for His creatures . . . a father's joy in their progress. We look upon this world as a place of education, in which He is training men by mercies and sufferings." To substitute for God a being "whom we cannot love if we would" is to deny the most self-evident and glorious truth of Christianity (pp. 84–85). Drawing on the critical antipatriarchal distinction between credulity and guilt, Channing concludes that a God who "regards us with displeasure be-fore we have acquired power to understand our duties and reflect on our actions" is no God (p. 85).

Central to the Unitarian purpose is to prove that the source of love and the source of authority could be one; indeed, that true authority was conferred by the power to love. Edmund Burke's distinction be-tween "the Sublime and the Beautiful," between, to invoke Isaac Kramnick's formula, the masculine realm "associated with pain and terror" and the "feminine realm of friendship and love, associated with pleasure and compassion," suggests how alien this idea was to the conservative temperament of the eighteenth century.[103] The psychologi-cal assumption of that temperament was that true authority must, by definition, ultimately and terrifyingly, derive from brute force rather than the ordering force of love. Power and affection were incompatible terms. Such an assumption had always represented the greatest obstacle to the antipatriarchal revolution. Unitarianism sought to quell that great unspoken anxiety of the age.

Once the character of God is redefined as simultaneously merciful and just, powerful and loving, it is no longer necessary to cling to the mystery of the Trinity. The Doctrine of the Trinity suggests, in effect, that God has two natures, one just and powerful embodied in the Father, and one merciful and compassionate embodied in the Son; the latter nature often forced to plead with the former. In the true God, however, the two natures are one. If understanding the true character of God makes the Doctrine of the Trinity repugnant, so does understanding the true character of Christ.

To elevate Christ to a person in the Godhead is to make "a fiction of Christ's humiliation, it almost wholly destroys the impressions with which His cross ought to be received" (p. 8). According to the Trinitarians, "Christ was, comparatively, no sufferer." It is the Unitarian belief, however, "that His humiliation was real and entire. . . . As we stand round his cross, our minds are not distracted, or our sensibility weakened, by contemplating Him as composed of . . . differing minds" (pp. 81–82). The real significance of Christ lay in the power of his example on man's sensibilities and on human character; for ultimately a religious system must be judged by its effects on character – its power to educate in the largest sense. Thus is God made over in the image of the Lockean father and religion redefined to serve the ends of moral education as well as salvation.

At the center of Unitarianism is the reaffirmation of the idea of rational and spiritual growth and the radical moral inference drawn from that idea:

> Now if there be one plain principle of morality, it is this, that we are accountable beings, only because we have consciences, a power of knowing and performing our duty, and that in as far as we want this power, we are incapable of sin, guilt, or blame. We should call a parent a monster, who should judge and treat his children in opposition to this principle, and yet this enormous immorality is charged on our Father in Heaven (p. 85).

So had it been "charged on" George III. In Channing's sermon we see in full flower one of the great themes of the Revolution: a father who judges nature and ignores the responsibilities of nurture is no father. As the nineteenth century dawned, this idea in its multiple forms resided at the heart of American culture. Whereas the insistence on the primacy of nurture over nature was an essential element in eighteenth-century Revolutionary ideology, Unitarians made clear the deeper antirevolutionary implication of that doctrine. To insist on education over miraculous rebirth and nurture over supernatural renaturing was to insist on reform rather than revolution. Having ushered in the great age of revolution, the new faith in nurture would no less usher in the subsequent great age of reform with its parental benefactors and beneficent parents and its Lamarckian belief in the mutability of the species.

PART III

THE CHARACTER OF THE NATIONAL FAMILY

7

GEORGE WASHINGTON AND THE RECONSTITUTED FAMILY

According to the Puritan morphology of salvation, the stage of grace following the receipt of grace is "adoption." As adoption frees man from service to the family of sin, its "particular fruit" is "the perfect law of liberty."[1]

The Christian doctrine, which required all children to look beyond their natural parents to their heavenly parent and insisted that all men be born again into a new family and to a new father for their own salvation, provided the kernel of a revolutionary insight: the title of father was transferable. Such an insight was reinforced by the new definition of a true parent as one who forms a child's mind rather than one who brings that child into the world. It permitted colonial Christians to consider abandoning one father without having to deny either their deep-seated desire for a father surrogate in general or their self-image as children.

One of the most extended descriptions of divine adoption is found in Samuel Willard's 1726 volume, *The Compleat Body of Divinity*. Willard lists the ways in which God's adoption of those who will become his heirs differs from the pattern of inheritance familiar to seventeenth-century America:

> 2. Among men the adopted must wait for the death of the adopter, in order to [receive] his inheriting. . . . Whereas in this, there is no succession. God lives, and yet though Christ died to purchase the inheritance for us, yet he is alive, and lives forever; and we live and have a joynt participation with him, hence John 14.19. Because I live ye shall live also.
>
> 3. The adopted hath no assurance, but is at uncertainty, and may on the least disgust be discarded. . . . But God's adoption is immutable, if once he puts any into the number of his children.
>
> 4. For those men do act spontaneously, and without compulsion, yet they see something in the person so chosen, which is the motive and determines them, either nearness of kindred, or winning natural

197

endowments, or virtuous inclination. . . . Whereas God saw no difference, between those whom he purposed to adopt and others, and
when he comes actually to apply the adoption to them, there is nothing in them at all to commend them to him more than others: He doth
not find but makes the difference there is between his adopted children
and others.[2]

Willard's description of the heavenly family addresses the great human
fantasy that was to find a focus in the American Revolution: the desire
to have both the father and the inheritance – to be absolved of having to
make the choice between them, to be at once free and bound, enfran-
chised and dependent. The related fantasy is to inherit along with an
estate the character deserving of it, to become at once internally as well
as externally the member of a new propertied social class. The son will
walk his own acre: the adopted child like Crèvecoeur's immigrant will
miraculously become a child of blood. The adoptive parents, the for-
giving parents, and the benefactors of eighteenth-century fiction are all
types of the benevolent deity who disinterestedly adopts his heavenly
family.

In Irving's tale "Rip Van Winkle," Rip awakens from a twenty-year
sleep to find the world "metamorphosed." Returning to the tavern –

> He recognized on the sign, however, the ruby face of King George,
> under which he had smoked so many a peaceful pipe; but even this
> was singularly metamorphosed. The red coat was changed for one of
> blue and buff, a sword was held in the hand instead of a sceptre, the
> head was decorated with a cocked hat and underneath was painted in
> large characters, GENERAL WASHINGTON (p. 48).

The spiritual family described by Willard will become the model for the
new American family, and Washington, the embodiment of the new
understanding of paternity, will be at once her deliverer and father. By
delivering America from the "British Pharaoh" he would give it birth.
"His presence like order moving over the face of chaos, brought harmony out of confusion, confidence from despair, He separated the new
world from the old and gave liberty to the world," declared one early
Fourth of July oration.[3] But Washington not only brought the new
world to life, he sealed it off from corruption, formed its character by
the force of his virtuous example, and brought his nation to manhood.

"With what language shall I recall," asks Thomas Savage, "that filial
confidence with which in those perilous times, we rested upon him as
the rock of our safety . . . as wall of fire round about us and the glory
in the midst of us?"[4] The "language" Savage chooses and for which he
is obliquely apologizing is the scriptural language with which colonial
sermons, particularly the election sermons of Massachusetts, had so
often described the Old Testament Deity and his relationship to his
American people. Washington had become America's new center and

circumference – a naturalized version of both the Old Testament father and New Testament savior. But Washington was at once both more and less than America's tutelary deity.

Recently the eulogies delivered on Washington's death and the late eighteenth- and early nineteenth-century literature that mythologized him have received much attention. Most of this scholarship treats the material from a mythic or psychohistorical or purely rhetorical perspective. Washington is the "father figure" who serves to bring the new nation together. His is the "sacred story of the divine man and his heroic friends who had in a mighty act of power effected the foundation of the republic" thus making him "a *theios aner* in the pattern of a charismatic founder."[5] He is the American antitype of Joshua and Moses.[6] His mythologization serves the psychological need of the new nation to "reconcile their quest for perfection with their urge for roots."[7] Or in the sinister rather than benign reading of Washington's national paternity, patriotic eulogists are argued to have held up "the revolutionary leaders to the youth of the country not as insurgent sons but rather as symbols of paternal authority" in an effort to ensure "the permanent loyalty of future generations," and forestall subsequent generational revolutionary conflict.[8] A version of this latter view of "the mystique of the founding fathers" informs the recent Freudian accounts by George Forgie and Michael Rogin of what they argue to be the revolt of the post-Revolutionary generation against the stifling myth and tyrannical example of their Revolutionary fathers.[9]

As useful and stimulating as these studies are, all are flawed by an overreliance on the apparatus of psychohistory at the expense of sufficiently coming to terms with the relevant eighteenth-century intellectual history. As Freudian and archetypal paradigms are imposed, the historical character of the language of the contemporary documents is lost and left unexamined. Far from betraying the Revolutionary ideology, the mythologization of Washington as founding father enthroned the antipatriarchal values that made up that ideology. The point is not that he is described as America's father, but rather what kind of father he is described as being. He would at last be the parent who would provide the forming example Britain had failed to provide and for which failure she had been reviled and rejected. The call to imitate his example was an attempt to apply to the national character the Lockean prescriptions, so central to Enlightenment thought, for forming a virtuous and independent man. If Unitarianism represented the triumph of the antipatriarchal values in the theological sphere, the myth of Washington represented its triumph in popular culture and the sphere of the national imagination. A careful examination of the contemporary idealization of Washington makes clear that the glorification of Washington was intimately related to the glorification of the new parenthood. It is not only Washington who will preside over the new nation; it is also the antipatriarchal ideal he is made to embody. Unlike George III, Washington would be not only "First in war, first in peace," but also "first in the hearts of his countrymen."[10]

Washington is first referred to as "Father of his country" in *The Lancaster Almanack* for 1778. In the references to Washington in the last quarter of the eighteenth century, however, that famous phrase is more often to be found in one of two expanded forms: "Father and friend of his country," or "Father, friend and guardian of his country."[11] As we have seen, by the third quarter of the eighteenth century "father" no longer had unequivocally positive connotations, so that these complementary terms make clear the specific, Lockean nature of Washington's paternity. One eulogist declared, "whosoever applies for redresses of grievances to Washington finds a father and, thus, we see the father consistently displaying not to the dutiful only but to the forward, not to friends only but enemies." In pointed contradistinction to George III and Jehovah, Washington answers all grievances. Joseph Tuckerman, applying Lockean categories, made it clear Washington is a parent "who has sacrificed his own, to prove our enjoyment, our father, who has found his highest satisfaction in promoting our felicity."[12]

At an early age Washington was rendered sterile by a case of mumps. To many, his childlessness had the same significance as Christ's. "Hear the instructive lesson of your parent's life," declared the playwright Royall Tyler. "But in reality he was not childless but the parent of millions like Christ and who is there among you that is not of that happy number?"[13] Like Goldsmith's Vicar or the evangelical God of the Second Great Awakening, the revival movement sweeping the nation in the last years of the 1790s, Washington never would turn away a returning child. His family is the family of all Christians. Gouverneur Morris speculated that Washington's sterility was divinely intentioned: "Was it in mercy, lest the paternal virtue should triumph (during some frail moment) in the paternal bosom?"[14] For the father of a nation, a discriminating concern for his natural children over the children of his nation, would, indeed, be a vice. In the new fraternity not only the firstborn and secondborn of one family, but the sons of all families must be leveled. Washington's sterility freed America permanently from the hereditary monarchy that some Federalists, if Republican propaganda may be believed, wished to make from the Washington line. Through his "great example" Washington himself and not his generation would remain America's parent.

Providence was assisted in preparing Washington for his role as national father by Washington's own father, Augustine, who had brought up his son according to the most advanced notions of childrearing, taking more pains with his son than had "Ulysses with his beloved Telemachus." At least this is the thesis of Parson Weems, the enterprising minister and publicist whose *Life of Washington* established the myth of the ideal family whose ideal son becomes his nation's ideal father.[15] It is their relationship, father to young son, that is the crux of the book. Weem's childraising theories (for they are presumably Weems's and not, as they are made to seem, Augustine's) reflect the post-Lockean perception of the nature of children that attributed a child's disobedience to accident and credulity rather than to original sin and moral inability. In the ideal parent–child relationship of George and Augustine, honesty and not obedience is the organizing ethic.

Significantly departing from the dictum of *The New England Primer*, "Foolishness is bound up in the heart of a child, but the rod of correction shall drive it from him," Augustine expands on a theory of childrearing that is drawn directly from Locke:

> Many parents, indeed, compel their children to this vile practice [lying] by barbarously beating them for every little fault, hence, on the next offence, the little terrified creature lets out the lie just to escape the rod. But as to yourself, George, you know I have always told you and now tell you again that whenever by accident, you do anything wrong, which must often be the case, you are but a poor little boy without experience or knowledge, you must never tell a false story or conceit. . . . I will but more honor and love you for it (p. 15).

The tyrannical expectation of perfection, a type of the original tyranny of the first covenant, gives way to an understanding of the limitations of youthful capacity. The republican child is at once excused for his age, never obliged to dissemble his feelings, and comforted with boundless parental solicitude.[16]

Weems's famous cherry-tree episode extends parental indulgence to its farthest point, a radical justification of filial rebellion. As the passage represents the most popular epitomization of the new antipatriarchal ideology, it should be quoted in full:

> When George . . . was about six years old, he was made the wealthy master of a hatchet! of which, like most little boys, he was immoderately fond, and was constantly going about chopping every thing that came his way. One day, in the garden, where he often amused himself hacking his mother's pea-sticks, he unluckily tried the edge of his hatchet on the body of a beautiful young English cherry tree, which he barked so terribly, that I don't believe the tree ever got the better of it. The next morning, the old gentleman, finding out what had befallen his tree, which, by the by, was a great favorite, came into the house; and with much warmth asked of the mischievous author. . . . Presently George and his hatchet made their appearance. "George," said his father, "do you know who killed that beautiful little cherry tree

yonder in the garden?" . . . Looking at his father with the sweet face
of youth brightened with the inexpressible charm of all-conquering
truth, he bravely cried out, "I can't tell a lie, Pa; you know I can't tell
a lie. I did cut it with my hatchet." "Run to my arms, you dearest
boy," cried his father in transport, "glad am I, George, that you killed
my tree; for you have paid me for it a thousand fold. Such an act of
heroism in my son is worth more than a thousand trees, though
blossomed with silver, and their fruits of purest gold" (p. 16).

Having received his hatchet at the same age as all the other little boys,
Washington had to experiment with his new instrument. After trying it
against his mother's pea-sticks, he lays its blade into the beautiful "English" body of his father's "great favorite." But rather than provoking
his father's furious anger, George's violation of his father's "favorite"
miraculously inspires the opposite reaction. Like Adam's fortunate fall,
George's sin permits him to rise higher in his father's estimation than he
had stood previously in his innocence. Here again is the heroic prodigal
whose disobedience in this idealized scenario secures rather than alien-
ates the father. And as the tree was English, the praised sin of disobedience becomes both the psychological and patriotic theme of the
biography.[17]

Editorializing on the childraising techniques imputed to Augustine,
Weems is congratulatory: "This you say was sowing good seed. Yes it
was and the crop, thank God, was what I believe it ever will be where a
man acts the true parent, that is, a guardian angel by his child" (p. 15).
Less a father in his own right than an agent of nature's paternity, the
ideal parent cultivates "his crop" by silently watching over his charge,
neither obliging nor constraining specific obedience. He is like "the
holy angels" that "guard thy bed," in Watts's "Cradle Hymn." The
perfect model for Weems's ideal father was the recently deceased Washington himself, who was declared America's "GUARDIAN ANGEL" in the
year of Weems's book.[18] The American Revolution had sought to restore paternity to Heaven; with the father of the nation installed in
Heaven as a permanent parent, natural and supernatural paternity are at
last identified.

THE POWER OF EXAMPLE
It is universally acknowledged that example serves better than
precept –

The Life of Lord Chesterfield (Philadelphia, 1775)

Preaching in 1783, Charles Turner recalled that before the war America
"imbibed false maxims and the vices of that which we called the parent
state with a thirst and avidity which was truly amazing." Yet, having
been reborn a new nation after the war, America had the opportunity

"at present" to look to new examples "to stem the passion for innovation."[19] "We are at present," declared Benjamin Rush, "in the forming state. We have as yet few habits of any kind, and good ones may be acquired by fixing a good example and proper instruction as easily as bad."[20] If in childhood the mind was a tabula rasa, it was of the first importance to hold up examples that would properly form the American mind or, as Rush echoing Franklin's emphasis suggests, "habituate" it to virtue. To such an end had Providence designed the life of Washington:

> Let us devoutly glory in the thought, that our great Countryman was lent to mankind, to instruct them both how to live and how to die; that, while his spirit still lives . . . he also survives on earth in his excellent pattern and counsels. . . .
>
> What matter of thankful joy, that in addition to the other means of education, with which this age abounds, Providence has opened to our children a volume so pure and instructive, as THE LIFE OF WASHINGTON! Ye American PARENTS, and TEACHERS of youth! Study this volume; become masters of its important contents; transcribe them into your own hearts and lives; and thus convey them with happiest effect to your children and pupils.[21]

Eulogist after eulogist stressed the necessity of parents' teaching their children to read Washington's "volume," of their ensuring that "the first word he lisps be Washington."[22] That "volume" constitutes a new revelation, a national scripture. "Let us all of whatever age, rank and station, remember to imitate the virtues and deeds which have immortalized his name," urged Thomas Thatcher, adding the Lockean qualification "according to our respective abilities and opportunities."[23] Here available to all was the education that both Franklin's subscription libraries as well as his own *Autobiography* sought to provide. The power of the heroic or virtuous example to command imitation had by midcentury become a commonplace not only of pedagogy but aesthetics. Joshua Reynolds would build his aesthetic theory on "man's observed capacity to 'raise' his nature by contemplating heroic images."[24] In their different ways Jefferson's account of the natural bridge in Virginia and Peale's exhibits also were intended as such images.

"Having been raised up," in Levi Frisbie's words, "to assist the birth, nourish the infancy and to direct and defend the childhood of our member empire," Washington freed the "infant country from a state of childhood and weakness to that of manhood and strength."[25] He did what England and the old order had failed to do. And if, as David Ramsay declared, "his example . . . now complete will teach wisdom and virtue to magistrates, citizens and men not only in the present age, but in future generations,"[26] America would continue to be preserved in protective virtue till eternity. Thus the fundamental truth of Lockean pedagogy would be vindicated. Whereas the authority of a parent who forcibly and irrationally demands obedience dies with the enforcer, the parent who compels obedience by his parental example will be immortalized in his child, and that child though orphaned will never be parentless. Washington, "The Guardian of America," was ultimately, as had been Minerva, an icon of American "reason." His example serves the same governing purpose as that common sense which the common parent had implanted in all mankind. The catastrophic consequences of allowing a new nation to grow up without such a moral example were made clear by Mary Collyer in her popular work *The Death of Cain,* a sequel to Gessner's *The Death of Abel,* which went through multiple American editions in the 1790s. "Notwithstanding the joint attempt" by Cain and his wife "to inculcate precepts of filial duty and piety in [their children's] growing years," their sons grow up so wanton and disobedient that God will decide to destroy their race. The reason for their obstinacy is not hard to find. Cain's sons were born and spent their infancy during the years of their father's "discontent."[27] No amount of subsequent precepting can compensate for the failure to provide that first moral example.

The government of imitation had, however, one fatal flaw in that man "learns more easily to imitate their [great men's] vices than their virtues."[28] In a letter to Washington, Paine caustically observed: "As the Federal Constitution is a copy, though not quite as base as the former of the British government, an imitation of its vices was naturally to be expected."[29] After the revolutionary violence and guillotining of 1793, the French boast that their revolution had been in imitation of the American rebellion became a mortifying compliment; for they had imitated the defiance of authority without appropriating the ideology to restrain that defiance.

Because mankind could not be trusted to differentiate between virtues and vices in human example, ultimately only Christ's unadulterate example might safely be set before it. Though an earlier highly "Protestantized" adaptation appeared in 1749, the first true American edition of Thomas à Kempis's classic *Imitation of Christ* appeared, significantly, in 1783, the year of the peace.[30] Yet, a government based on the imitation of Christ was also flawed, since an inimitable example would make men despair of their own capacities rather than serve to inspire them. Because Washington was "the image as well as the production of Him, who is the great example and source of perfection . . . so finished a copy of a higher original as . . . human frailty would allow," he removed the fatal flaw from Christian government. Unlike Christ he was imitable and human and yet in his own sphere perfect, a perfect copy of the Godhead.

In 1747 Samuel Lee, a minister at Bristol, prefaced an anthology of reformational martyrologies that was directed to a juvenile audience. In his preface Lee objects, in the spirit of Gilbert Stuart, to some martyrologists as "limners who would shadow over a wrinkle," and paint their subjects so perfectly as to discourage rather than encourage their imitation. But here the reader would find real men, not saints:

> Man is led by nothing better than by Example. I know abundantly how this lazy formal Age is ready to look on Scripture worthies, as men unimitable, as Giants, to whose stature, they despair ever to arrive. . . . here is no excuse left for frailty, which we are ready to make against obedience; for these Presidents, in all ages, abundantly testifie, that we frail men, by the power of the same grace of God, may reach to the same perfections.[31]

Lee's spelling of "precedent" with "si" is an accepted eighteenth-century variation and as such suggests a neglected dimension of the word "president." If, following Montesquieu, the three branches of republican government were respectively to partake of the character of the three acknowledged types of government – monarchy, oligarchy, republic – the executive branch was to reflect the character of a monarchy. As it suggested "Presiding spirit," "President" embodied the monarchial concept of "the one" without connoting the repugnant principles of exclusive power or the pure agency of a true monarchy; in addition, however, the term suggested a record of previous possibility or, in Washington's case, a testimony to the extent of human capacity, an "example" of what was possible.

Historically, the Protestant tradition had declared man might successfully imitate Christ only in his passive obedience and his human suffering; for his divine character was beyond imitation. Thus was the martyr whose death witnessed the divine truth of the Protestant cause held up to be the perfect imitation of Christ, and the Marian martyrs proclaimed the paternal aristocracy of English Protestantism. The popular martyrologies of Eusebius and Foxe promulgated the view that God reveals heaven to the martyr in his final moments of agony, antedating the dying man's glory and permitting him to achieve, at least momentarily, a Christ-like double nature on earth.[32]

By the early eighteenth century, however, rationalist Christians and optimistic sentimentalists alike agreed that "God-like virtue" and the benevolent character of the Deity were indeed imitable. Men not only could but should strive to attain the double nature once reserved for martyrs. By demonstrating that the double nature of the martyrs could, indeed, be achieved by man, the exemplum of Washington may be said to have completed a process begun centuries before: the redefining of Christian heroism as active benevolence rather than passive obedience. In its own way the Revolution of 1776 was part of that redefinition, for among the God-given rights Americans most coveted were the right and the opportunity to do good. Shortly after the war, Ezra Stiles wrote: "We should live henceforth in amity as brothers inspired with and cultivating national benevolence united by glorying in the name of a Columbian or American."[33]

Having perfectly embodied the divine original, Washington joined Christ as a standard by which to judge human achievement; and as that standard had now become an earthly one, so too had virtue's reward:

> Furthermore, the life of Washington points out the true path to the Temple of Fame. The expanded genius of Columbia may exert all the emulous powers in imitation of the great exempla. The man who approximates nearest to the original will ever be the boasted Hero of America in the proportion as the life and virtue of Washington shall be transcribed, so will the just tribunal of popular approbation and praise be conferred.[34]

Here there is no mention of the divine exemplum of whom Washington is a copy. For Americans, Washington had himself become enshrined as that original. As invisible grace becomes replaced with visible virtue, the tribunal of heaven is replaced by the tribunal of "popular approbation" or public opinion and the divine mansion by the "Temple of Fame." In a world capable of recognizing and rewarding virtue, the divine function is appropriated. Of Washington's immortal soul no one speaks; rather, it is his "immortal name" that is hailed.

Once "common school" education could be made available to all—a cause promoted by Jefferson and others—Washington's example might ultimately be institutionalized. A national public school system serving in loco parentis to form the minds of Americans would eventually take Washington's place as a national parent. In his seminal work *The Spirit of the Laws*, Montesquieu had declared:

> The laws of education are the first impressions we receive; and as they prepare us for civil life, each particular family ought to be governed pursuant to the plan of the great family which comprehends them all.
> . . . The laws of education will be therefore different in each species of government; in monarchies they will have honor for their object; in republics, virtue; in despotic governments, fear.[35]

Though despots and monarchs must in some degree keep education from their subjects; those who administer republics must ensure that it is made universally available. To instill in its citizenry the "virtue" essential for the survival of a republic, "the whole power of education is required":

This virtue may be defined, the love of the laws and of our country. As this love requires a constant preference of public to private interest, it is the source of all the particular virtues. . . .

Everything therefore depends on establishing this love in a republic, and to inspire it ought to be the principal business of education: but the surest way of instilling it into children, is for parents to set them an example (I, 48–49).

Those who most seriously pondered the question of the nature and significance of education in the early republic agreed in accepting Montesquieu's first principles. Many, however, took him one step further. In his *Remarks on Education* (1798), Samuel Harrison Smith declared:

> Previously to any prospect of [a republic's] success, one principle must prevail. Society must establish the right to educate, and acknowledge the duty of having educated, all children. A circumstance so momentously important must not be left to the negligence of individuals.[36]

Because error is "never more dangerous than in the mouth of a parent" (p. 208), Smith urged that "the mind of a child must be withdrawn from an *entire* dependence on its parents" (p. 206). Hence the need for the example of Washington. Here was the Protestant-antipatriarchal anxiety about dependence carried to its furthest limits, but with one difference: the final unmediated dependence was to be on the republic, not on God. Amable de Lafitte Courteil's *Proposal to Demonstrate the Necessity of a National Institution in the United States of America* (1797) extends Smith's sentiments:

> To say to fathers and mothers that their children are subjects of the state and were born to become members of the republic is what they know and what nobody pretends to deny. But to tell them that the consequence of this principle is that the direction and immediate inspection of the education of children belongs to the jurisdiction of government will not be perhaps so generally avowed. 'It is my child' and all the cries of nature which command attention even in their weakness . . . are considerations to which it is not permitted to answer with the stoical coldness of a presentation of principles.[37]

But a means must be found to calm these too sensible mothers. For the true nursery of an individual's mind is not one's home, but the government under which one lives. "The soil is to plants," declared Robert Coram in yet another contemporary essay on education, "what government is to man."[38] Though God created all men equal, they might only remain so if public education raised them all "to the same level of cultivation."[39] Government is the primary agent of nurture. Just as the mantle of paternity and its attendant responsibilities were being passed from a deceased Washington to the federal government, a new literary genre made its first appearance on the American scene: the textbook written exclusively for institutional use. It, too, would become an icon of a new paternity. The title of John Hamilton Moore's popular late eighteenth-century volume recommends it as a Lockean parent: *The Young Gentlemen and Ladies Monitor and English Teacher's Assistant . . . Calculated to Improve the Understanding, rectify the will; purify the passions; direct the minds of youth to the pursuit of proper objects.*[40] Before the government of the new nation could inspire the same filial affection as had the figure of Washington, it had to become, in the eyes of its people, an ideal parent. To achieve this purpose the government, no less than its citizenry, was obliged to imitate the character of America's first father and preceptor.

THE CHARACTER OF THE FATHER

As Washington was both "friend and father" to his nation, so too was he repeatedly styled "good and great."[41] Just as "friend" was meant to suggest the true nature of paternity, so "good" was meant to suggest the essential quality of greatness. If Washington was to be distinguished from "the fabulous heroes of paganism in fictional portraits,"[42] from "the race of heroes who while terrible in war are as destructive in peace,"[43] from those whose "greatness was vulgarly assumed to mean royal parentage,"[44] from the "ghastly trash of Roman intercession,"[45] from military geniuses such as Bonaparte or martyred deities such as Marat,[46] eulogist after eulogist declared Washington's greatness to be specifically Christian greatness, his heroism a Christian heroism, his glory not in his deeds but in the motive force behind his deeds, his virtuous goodness. Declared one minister from Rhode Island, "Let us remember that in the estimation of God it is not greatness but goodness that is rewarded with bliss."[47] In a sermon entitled *Greatness the Result of Goodness,* Samuel West reminded his parishioners of the Pauline position on which the distinction rested: "The savior of the world found greatness in service performed. If any man will be great among you, let him be your servant. I am among you as one who serves."[48] The republican insistence that sovereignty resides in the people and is delegated to magistrates who, though they seem to be rulers, are in fact servants, secularized this position. The Christian-Republican paradox permitted Washington, "our earthly benefactor who saved one nation and set an example for all," to become a new model of Christ; for insofar as he, too, had served all mankind he, too, had become mankind's master.[49]

If, as nearly all the philosophers of the eighteenth century agreed, both divine and human virtue consisted in "disinterested benevolence to being in general," a love of "beauty's virtue not its rewards,"[50] Washington then epitomized such virtue. His example refuted Hobbesians who declared disinterested benevolence to be alien to the self-serving character of man as well as Edwardsians who proclaimed it an ideal to which unregenerate man might aspire but might never attain. Ezra Stiles wrote:

> [Washington] convinced the world of the beauty of virtue; . . . There is a glory in thy disinterested benevolence which the greatest characters would purchase . . . and which may excite indeed their emulation, but cannot be felt by the venal great who think everything, every virtue and true glory may be bought and sold and trace our every action to motives terminating in self.[51]

Because Washington had convinced the world of the beauty of virtue, David Tappan, Hollis Professor of Divinity at Harvard, concluded:

> that the life of Washington has in some degree changed the dialect of mankind. We now almost instinctively apply the epithet Great to high moral excellence rather than to superiority of intellect or fortune. The best Eulogists of our Hero almost always appropriate this title to his self-denying and exalting virtue. . . . May we not hope that the time is at hand when this dignified appellation will be wholly alienated from exalted libertines and villains.[52]

Though Tappan exaggerated in attributing the shift in meaning of the word "great" to the example of Washington, the fact is that such a shift did originate in the eighteenth century. According to the *Oxford English Dictionary,* prior to 1700, "great" as applied to persons denoted either "large in size or physical bulk" or, by extension, "full or 'big' with courage . . . anger or pride," or finally, "eminent by means of birth, rank, wealth, power or position." Not until 1709 was the word used to signify "eminent in point of mental or moral attainment or magnitude of achievement." And it is not until 1726 that the word is used specifically to indicate an individual's character as being "lofty," "magnanimous," or "noble." Of special interest is the fact that in the eighteenth century the word takes on a new and particular significance in the lexicon of natural history. When preceding the name of an animal species, the adjective indicates the "full grown or adult" variety of that species, as in the phrase "a great hare." Thus in more than one eighteenth-century sense of the word would the newly independent nation be glorying in its "greatness."[53]

An interesting light is shed on the shifting significances of the term "greatness" by one particular verse of *The New England Primer.* The numerous changes in emphasis and content found in the 325 editions of the *Primer* serve as a delicate barometer of alternating moral and theological sentiments in New England in the eighteenth and early nineteenth centuries. In 1793, Washington's policy of neutrality held firm against the machinations of Citizen Genêt and saved America from involvement in a "European holocaust." A year later in a Newton,

Massachusetts, edition, one of the most familiar, if dissonant, of the *Primer*'s alphabetical couplets disappeared for the first time. The verse representing the letter "W," "Whales in the sea, God's voice obey," gave way to "By Washington great deeds were done."[54] The intention of the original verse had been to moralize that even the greatest and most puissant of God's creatures still served His will and not its own. It had as its scriptural antecedent the encounter of Moses and the Pharaoh in the Book of Exodus. There the point is made that, though the Pharaoh is, as he is later described in Ezekiel 32:2, "a whale in the seas," even *his* supreme act of human willfulness, his hardening his heart against the deliverance of God's people, is still the work of God.

Though it is now Washington who replaces the whale as the greatest of God's creatures, the passive construction of the new verse retains the Christian moral of the old. Though hidden in syntax, the *deus absconditus* is still glorified. It is God through the agency of Washington who does great deeds. Not until 1825 does the construction change and an ambiguous assertion of human efficacy and achievement give way to a proud and explicit boast: "Great Washington brave, his nation did save."[55] In the first example Washington replaces the whale; in the second, efficient and formal causes telescoped, he replaces the Deity. In the first verse the whale's size implies his greatness; in the second, "great" modifies God's deeds; and in the third, it describes the human actor. The idea of a great man is discovered, acknowledged, and glorified. Man displaces God and Christ as the "hero" of his own life. As the sailing ship was giving way to the great invention of the age, the self-propelled steamboat, James Dana's insistence in 1772 that the human will be considered as its own motive force at last found a final vindication.[56]

Though the nineteenth century would free him from the referential greatness of the Deity, Washington's greatness would never be exclusively his own. "Pari Paribus," declared Benjamin Orr in a sermon entitled *The Rising Pillar of Our Republic*, "great things to great is the rule she [Nature] delights in. Where, for example, do we look for the whale, 'the Biggest Born of Nature' not, I trow, in the mill-pond but in the main ocean."[57] A great man was proof of a great nation. He was also its model. Hobbes had said it long before: "For *by art* is created that great *Leviathan*, called a *Commonwealth* or *State*, in Latin *Civitas*, which is but an artificial man."[58]

The new understanding of greatness as goodness reflected an essential theme of the antipatriarchal revolution that would replace patriarch with benefactor, precept with example, the authority of position with the authority of character, deference and dependence with moral self-sufficiency, and static dichotomies with principles of growth: Sovereignty and power were no longer glorious in and of themselves. Rather, they were glorious, as Washington had demonstrated, only as opportunities to do good. God delegates his authority only to those, in Jonathan Mayhew's words, whom he has "ordained to be his ministers of good."[59] By 1800, God himself was everywhere acknowledged to be, in Pope's phrase, "a universal benefactor." In 1782, as the war neared its end, Charles Chauncy tentatively set forth the ultimate theological implication of that appellation: universal salvation. A decade after the war, Universalists such as Hosea Ballou turned to itinerancy to spread the message, and Unitarians everywhere declared God's power to be his love, his greatness to be his goodness.[60]

Taking as his verse Jehovah's address to the Kings of Israel in Psalms 82:6–7, "Ye are Gods on earth; but ye shall die like men," David Tappan called attention to the larger implications of his observation about the shifting meaning of greatness:

> I am sensible that as the Hebrew word, translated God, strictly denotes the power and authority of the Most High, rather than his whole character; so the same title, when given to rulers, may primarily refer to that portion or image of divine power, with which they are invested. But as the omnipotence of the Supreme Ruler is ever employed by goodness, and governed by rectitude; so his vice-regents fulfill the object of their commission, and the true import of their title, only by copying the moral character and measure of their sovereign (p. 35).

Once divinity had been reformulated not as a sovereign will but as the capacity to do good, Jehovah as well as Christ became imitable. All men, thus, might aspire to what Washington had achieved: "god-like beneficence," "divine virtue."[61] Such phrases, commonplace during the eighteenth century, were more than hyperbole. They suggested a new understanding of Christian imitation. Fruitless was it for kings and magistrates to lay claim to the divine authority of God by simple right of their analogous earthly office. For, in truth, such authority could only be secured by means of a successful imitation of the divine character. Tappan continues:

> I have said ye are gods. The name God usually connoted the underived and all perfect Being . . . whose infinite greatness imparts light, strength, a majesty to his goodness; while his unbounded goodness gives equal beauty and dignity to his greatness. . . . Since the character of the Supreme Divinity thus combines the greatest ability and disposition to communicate happiness with regular and constant exertion of both; the title of Gods, by a bold and significant figure, is conferred on those subordinate beings, who inherit from Him large portions of these Godlike qualities and employ them for the divine purpose of extensive good (p. 37).

If God's authority lay in his perfect example of benevolent solicitude, in his goodness rather than in his greatness, then the authority of his vice-regents must be rooted equally in their own exemplary character. In his Massachusetts election sermon for 1800, Joseph McKeen took as his verse Matthew 5:12, "A city on a hill can not be hid." "As it is the general disposition in people to imitate the conduct of their superiors," McKeen encouraged the governor and his deputies "to remember their responsibility to set good examples";[62] for "the most efficient and benevolent form of government is by example since it reproves without upbraiding" (p. 10). In accordance with the great eighteenth-century ideal such government exerts its binding power silently and at a distance, by conduction rather than old-style Newtonian collision. It is not, he argued, the assembly or the vote of the franchised that ultimately serves as a check on magisterial behavior, but magisterial "visibility." In a post-Lockean world McKeen's verse from Matthew, which John Winthrop had made a signature of the American enterprise, took on a new ideological life. The "city on the hill" that cannot be hid referred to the new power of example to reform the world in opposition to the old power of force and revolution – the light under the bushel. The Marquis de Condorcet made the point succinctly: "The example of one great nation where the rights of man are respected is invaluable to all the others."[63]

⋊ An important result of the view that a man's example was more important than any title or office was the realization that the examples of a pre-Christian pagan or a Mohammedan might in their own particular ways instruct a Christian as much as the example of Christ. Neoclassicism bore testimony to the preceptorial powers of the former, while the popularity of Oriental tales in eighteenth-century America gave credence to the latter. Though appalled at deistical attempts to reduce world religions to a common denominator, Timothy Dwight, grandson of Jonathan Edwards and reigning pope of Congregationalism, made this concession to Washington (whose twenty volumes of correspondence reveal not a single mention of Christ): "That if he was not a Christian he was more like one than any man of the same description whose life has hitherto been recorded."[64] Such a concession is little less than an epitaph to an age of denominational authority and an admission that Christian examples need not be Christian.

The decline of preceptorial instruction and the rise of exemplary instruction historically paralleled an increasing subordination of Scripture to the book of nature, of the revelation of the word to the revelation of creation. Weems tells the story of Martha Custis in church preferring to look at the "mind-illumined face" of Washington than listen to "the cold reading preacher" (p. 58). The sight of God at work in his creation is experienced as more powerful than his immediate presence in his word. If in the deistical view God had revealed himself in his creation, and one could look up through creation to the creator, the lionizing of Washington, his greatest creature, was a form of worship and not, as some contended, a kind of idolatry.

At the turn of the century it was often acknowledged that there were three great man-made wonders in America: Dr. Rittenhouse's world-famous Orrery; Charles Willson Peale's Museum; and the character of Washington. One was a working model of the universe (i.e., the solar system); the second was an attempt to represent in a single great hall all the known species of nature in taxonomic form; and the third was pronounced to be the perfect imitation of the Deity. With reference to Rittenhouse's Orrery, Jefferson declared: "As an artist he has exhibited as great a proof of mechanical genius as the world has ever produced. He has not indeed made a world; but he has by imitation approached nearer its Maker than any man who has lived from the creation to this day."[65] From Rittenhouse's achievement Paine inferred the metaphysical truth of which so many late eighteenth-century *philosophes* were enamored: "We know that the greatest works can be represented in model and that the universe can be represented in the same means."[66]

According to the fundamental doctrine of scientific deism, the glory of God is revealed in the order and harmony of his creation; it is only in discovering and appreciating that harmony that the Deity is properly worshiped and man rendered most satisfyingly happy. Though unable to rise above the earth and wonder at the unity of the whole creation, man would be able to appreciate that unity were it to be represented to him in miniature. Peale was so convinced that exposure to the harmonies of nature displayed in his museum produced a supernal serenity in the visitor that he recommended it to Jefferson as an ideal site for the signing of national treaties. Jefferson was sufficiently convinced to arrange at least one such signing on Peale's premises.[67]

If the Orrery and the Museum were scale models of the creation, Washington was a working model of the divinity, performing on the greatest scale known to man the divine function of making men happy. The examples of Washington, the Museum, and the Orrery permitted mankind to understand better the constitution of the creation (the "more perfect union" the national Constitution sought to reflect) and, thus, the character of the Creator. The truth proclaimed in both the book of nature and in the life of Washington was that the universe was but one family under God. Upon looking up at heaven, Lorenzo in Edward Young's *Night Thoughts* cries out emotionally:

> O what a root! O what a branch is here!
> O what a father! what a family.
> Worlds! Systems! and creations! – And creations
> In one agglomerated cluster hung.
> Great Vine! on Thee, on thee The cluster hangs,
> The filial cluster! infinitely spread
> In glowing globes, with various beings fraught;
> Or, shall I say (for who can say enough)
> A constellation of ten thousand gems! . . .
> Dread Sire, accept this miniature of Thee (pp. 241–42).

The poet, no less than the astronomer and natural scientist, offers up his miniature of God, his vision of the familial tree of life.

THE DEBT OF HONOR AND THE GREATER GOOD

There is another dimension to the universal insistence that Washington's example be followed that has not yet been touched upon. If the gratitude and affection of its citizenry that Montesquieu had declared to be the motive forces to obedience in a republic could not by definition be constrained, they could, however, once a proper education had prepared the way, be excited. This had been Paine's point in *Common Sense*. The republican form of government both derives from and depended on the spontaneous operation of gratitude. Polybius long before had made this clear in his account of the origins of the Roman republic.

> For the people moved with present gratitude toward those who had delivered them from tyranny, resolved to invest them with the government, and submitted themselves to their guidance and dominion. And these, being on their part also not less satisfied with the honour that was bestowed upon them regarded the good of the community as the only rule of their administration. . . . Everything was calculated to attract the attention, to allure the consideration and excite the congratulations of the people; to attach their hearts to individual citizens according to their merit; . . . And this was in the true spirit of republics (p. 416).

The test of the republican experiment would be whether or not America would continue to show gratitude toward its rulers, for gratitude was the barometer of a republican people's virtue. Joseph Allen in his Washington eulogy encouraged public shows of gratitude "in defiance of a doctrine which Despots have taught their slaves, that ingratitude is the vice of a Republic."[68] Jedidiah Morse pointed to the remorse over Washington's death as "a most remarkable instance in support of those who contend Republicans can be grateful."[69]

In his widely read *Elements of Criticism*, Lord Kames urged all playwrights and poets to include at least one scene of gratitude in each of their works; for, as we have heard him comment earlier: "A signal act

of gratitude produceth in the spectator or reader a feeling which disposeth the spectator or reader to acts of gratitude."[70] William Charles White
was one of many American playwrights who heeded Lord Kames's
advice. In *Orlando or Parental Persecution* (1797) the protagonist responds
to an offer of assistance:

> That's bravely spoke, I excuse the tide howev'r,
> The overflowing current, that then swell'd
> My soul, and prompted it to gratitude.
> Who could withstand such kindness, without
>   bursts of grateful rapture?[71]

The moral of *Orlando* is that it is not the exercise of authority that
secures obedience, but kindness. Against kindness the sensible heart has
no defense. To disinterested benevolence the debt of gratitude is paid
involuntarily. It receives what it does not seek.

    ⟼ Because it assumed that one's benefactor was one's true
father, sentimental theory elevated the moral obligation to repay kindness above the natural obligation owed one's parent. This assumption
permitted Americans to transfer both their filial affection and the title of
parent from King George to President Washington. Yet, in an important instance, the doctrine of gratitude complicated rather than simpli-
fied that transfer. That instance was the execution on October 2, 1780,
of Major John André, the British intelligence officer responsible for
enlisting the services of Benedict Arnold.

On his way to a final rendezvous with Arnold, André was discovered
in disguise and brought before General Washington. Ignoring the usual
custom of according a firing squad to an officer, Washington sentenced
André to the death prescribed for spies: hanging. Public sympathy
sprung up for Major André, who, though a duty-bound officer to the
king, sympathized with the rebels by his own admission. His kindness,
compassion, and fairness shown rebel prisoners had become legendary,
and in deference to his personal honor and virtue many Americans
objected strenuously to the execution, several even going so far as to
criticize publicly the sacred Washington.

The execution of Major André raised important questions about
the nature of the war with Britain. Everywhere the claim had been
made that America had resisted Britain because of her unnatural conduct, her unresponsiveness to the obligations of nature. But here was
an Englishman, an avowed enemy, who had repeatedly responded to
the will of nature, who had demonstrated that he could, in the then
popular phrase from Pope's "Universal Prayer," "feel another's
woe."[72] André's execution forced Americans to confront the moral
complexities of the war.

Hamilton reported in a letter that André's last words were acknowledgments of generosity made in a "tone of manly gratitude."[73] André himself wrote a heartrending letter to Washington that was reprinted later in several colonial newspapers challenging the general, and by extension the American nation, to prove himself a creature of sensibility by granting his simple request that he be shot rather than hanged.

> Buoyed above the fear of death, by the consciousness of a life spent in the pursuit of honor, and fully sensible that it has at no time been stained by any action which, at this serious moment, could give me remorse, I have to solicit your Excellency, if there is any thing in my character which excites your esteem, if aught in my circumstances can excite you with compassion, that I may be permitted to die a death of a soldier.[74]

More stoical than sensible, Washington defaulted on the challenge. He had failed the parental test: His compassion had not been "excited." The ballads, broadsides, and press reaction following André's death suggest that Washington's default produced a feeling of widespread guilt and shame. *The Pennsylvania Packet* for October 10 reported:

> This day at twelve o'clock it took place, by hanging him by the neck. Perhaps no person (on like occasion) ever suffered the ignominious death, that was more regretted by officers and soldiers of every rank in our army, or did I ever see any person meet his fate with more fortitude and equal conduct.[75]

The most popular of the contemporary André ballads versified:

> Andre was executed, he look'd both meek and mild;
> Around on the spectators most pleasantly he smiled;
> It moved each eye to pity, and every heart there bled,
> And everyone wished him releas'd and Arnold in his stead.[76]

The elevating of André to the status of sacrificial lamb (a meek and mild Christ) was one way by which Revolutionary America relieved its guilty awareness that, in some cases, it must deny gratitude to those truly deserving of it in order to complete deliverance from the larger claims of a falsely extorted gratitude.

No document better reveals how Americans finally dealt with the guilt induced by André's execution than William Dunlap's 1798 play, *André*. Colonel Bland, the play's protagonist, is exercised by the need to discharge a debt of gratitude whose weight he passionately feels; for once as a prisoner of war he had been saved by André's kindness and ministrations. Bland sues for André's release and, in a scene booed by the first-night Philadelphia audience,[77] reviles General Washington to his face. M'Donald, an Irish rebel full of stoical Federalist wisdom – and

Dunlap's spokesman in the play – engages Bland in a debate over the obligations of gratitude:

> *Bland:* I know his value; owe to him my life;
> And gratitude, that first, that best of virtues,
> Without the which man sinks beneath the brute,
> Binds me in ties indissoluble to him.
> *M'Donald:* That man-created virtue blinds thy reason.
> Man owes to man all love; when exercised,
> He does no more than duty. Gratitude,
> That selfish rule of action, which commands
> That we our preference make of men,
> Not for their worth, but that they did *us* service,
> Misleading reason, casting in the way
> Of justice stumbling-blocks, cannot be virtue.
> *Bland:* Detested sophistry! T'was André saved me.
> *M'Donald:* He sav'd thy life, and thou art grateful for it.
> How self intrudes, delusive, on man's thoughts.
> He sav'd thy life, yet strove to damn thy country;
> Doomed millions to the haughty Briton's yoke.
> . . . .
> His sacrifice now stands the only bar
> Between the wanton cruelties of war
> And much-suffering soldiers; yet when weigh'd
> With gratitude, for that he sav'd thy life.
> *Bland:* Cold-blooded reasoners, such as thee, would blast
> All warm affection; asunder sever
> Every social tie of humanized man (p. 33).

Immediately before this colloquy, Bland had revealed to M'Donald the disastrous news that the British had taken his father, also an officer under Washington, as hostage and intended to kill him were André executed. Thus it is that Bland desperately seeks not only to save André but also his parent – both the man who gave him life and the man who had preserved that life. Consequently, what M'Donald is urging with "cold-blooded reason" is that Bland not only disavow the false debt of honor but the debt owed blood. Believing that the elder Bland "with smiles" will undoubtedly yield up his glorious life for his country and "count his death a gain," M'Donald insists that the son imitate the stoicism of his father and take the risk of losing his father by refraining from urging Washington to free André. The identification of André with Bland's father is crucial to the Revolutionary-sentimental message of the play. Though Bland's father will be liberated eventually by a rebel ruse, the son is forced by sanctioning André's death to order the death of his own father. The symbolic significance of the figure of André in the postwar period is dramatically revealed. If the American children are to be liberated from their British parent, the good aspect of parent (embodied by André) must be sacrificed along with the evil (embodied by George III). André serves as such a sacrificial figure and the honors accorded him posthumously memorialize that sacrifice.

Earlier in the play, Bland, overcome with passion, dares to lecture Washington on the nature of true virtue. He compares André with Arnold:

> The country that forgets to reverence virtue;
> That makes no difference 'twixt the sordid wretch
> Who, forewarned, risks treason's penalty,
> And him unfortunate, whose duteous service
> Is by mere accident, so chang'd in form
> As to assume guilt's semblance, I serve not;
> Scorn to serve (p. 21).

According to Bland's code of honor, one must discriminate among en-emies – between those who are virtuous and those who are not; between those who are obeying orders out of a sense of duty and those who are actively sympathetic to such orders. Most important, one must discrimi-nate between the treacherous friend who exploits the distinction between appearance and reality and the avowed and undisguised enemy. The latter must finally be considered noble; the former worse than contempt-ible, for his sins – the false engagement of feelings and betrayal of trust – are the more heinous. Though André may be morally superior to Ar-nold, as even M'Donald concedes, he remains an officer of an enemy army and, thus, it is Dunlap's message, can neither be true friend nor, in the symbolism of the play, true father. There is but one true friend and father, and his name is Washington. Shortly after his outburst before the Commanding General, Bland is overcome with remorse:

> My tongue, unbridled, hath the same offence,
> With action violent, and boisterous tone,
> Hurl'd on that glorious man, whose pious labors
> Shield from every will his grateful country,
> That man, whose friends to adoration love,
> And enemies revere.
> . . . .
> How shall I see him more? (p. 41).[78]

What Bland finally comes to realize is that, although owing his life to both André and his father, he also owes his life to that greater savior, Washington. By saving his nation's life, Washington, in effect, had saved Bland's life as well. But as Washington's merciful act was not ad hominem but in service of the greater good, Bland has no specific debt to discharge. Though freed from the obligation to embody his gratitude in action, he still, however, is obliged to feel and revere Washington in his heart.

⊰ Two years earlier in his play *The Archers,* Dunlap had made much more explicit the generational dimension of the moral obligation issues presented in *André.* *The Archers,* which features a revolutionary setting of a different sort, interprets the popular story of William Tell. His thirteenth-century leadership of the Swiss Helvetic league against the Catholic forces of Austria made Tell, according to the late eighteenth-century historical imagination, a pre-Reformational prototype of the defender of the sacred cause of Protestant liberty, the cause of the American Revolution. Having occupied Switzerland, the Austrian army has sent its recruiters into the countryside. Though claiming only to want volunteers, they are engaged in impressment. The conflict between force and voluntarism provides the thematic backdrop for all the subsequent action of the play.

Tell is thwarting Austrian efforts by trying to awaken the Swiss to the threat to their liberty. Unwilling to tolerate any more interference, Governor Gesler (an Austrian version of the hated colonial governor of the Revolutionary period) arrests Tell. He is charged with failing to bend his knee before the governor's hat, which has been placed on a pole in the middle of town as a test of obedience. Rather than executing Tell, as a mock gesture of his mercy Gesler sets him another test. He is to shoot an apple off his son's head. If he succeeds, both will be set free. If he fails, Gesler, sardonically speaking the language of the sentimentalist, will be forced to put to death a parent who so unfeelingly has drawn "innocent blood from yonder helpless child."[79]

Tell's crime of failing to bend the knee to the governor's cap is a rejection of the empty rituals of deference, of the pure claims of office. His punishment is a sadistic test of his fatherly love for his child, of the paternal benevolence Tell charges Austria with lacking. In effect, it creates a situation whereby Tell, Gesler hopes, will unwittingly be obliged to join Austria in committing the sin of tyrannically abusing "parental" power. Complementarily, it is a test of his son's willingness to trust that his father's power will be used to protect rather than destroy him, a test of republican faith. The climactic moment in which the apple is shot through confirms the son's trust and the father's claim to the character of a loving parent. Tell's sure aim frees his son not only from the authority of the tyrannical Austrians (the apple on the head is the structural equivalent to the cap on the pole), but from, as the Edenic significance of the apple suggests, the inherited sins of the father.

The Archers epitomizes the eighteenth-century preoccupation with

Plate 3. Painted when William Dunlap was twenty-two, and ten years before *André* was written, *The Artist Showing a Picture from "Hamlet" to his Parents* (1788) announces the controlling theme of Dunlap's future work, filial ambivalence toward parental expectations. The painting of Hamlet and his father's ghost serves as a dark mirror image of the anxious relations between father and son suppressed in the presentation of the larger family group. (Courtesy of the New-York Historical Society.)

displacing the father who enslaves with the father who liberates, with discovering a figure of authority who can be trusted with the power conferred on him by those over whom it will be administered. The popularity of the figure of Tell in eighteenth-century art and early nineteenth-century drama – Schiller's play is the most notable example – suggests the power with which it addressed the most pressing issues of the age.[80]

These issues were obviously of vital personal interest to Dunlap himself. In one of the more revealing self-portraits by an eighteenth-century American, *The Artist Showing a Picture from "Hamlet" to his Parents* (1788), Dunlap, a portrait painter as well as a playwright, depicts himself displaying a painting of Hamlet on the ramparts of Elsinore castle awaiting his father's ghost, who will ask the Prince to avenge his murder[81] (Plate 3). The painting seems Dunlap's tortured way of sharing with his parents his Hamlet-like fear of being unable or unwilling to fulfill parental expectations; his overwhelming sense, demonstrated in all his plays, of the problematic and burdensome character of filial obligation. The ostensible subject of the painting – the recently returned artist demonstrating to his parents that his three years of study have in fact improved his skills – no less reflects his anxiety about parental expectations and judgment. The choice of *Hamlet* to make his larger point is less unusual than it may first appear. In 1787, a production of *Hamlet* advertised as a "moral and instructive tale" was presented at the Southwark Theater in Philadelphia under the title of *Filial Piety*.[82]

Washington was for America its William Tell, its loving parent who liberated his children by the force of arms and virtuous example and who, as Tell brought the Swiss city-states into a confederation, united the thirteen colonies into a new and glorious family. He would banish forever the ghost of the father king, the dead hand of the past with its onerous demands that the present generation set right "the original sin." And the nation, his children, would be then like young Tell – freed from Adam's sin thereafter the better to enjoy their new life.

DISSENT AND CONFIDENCE

There were, however, dissenting voices on the subject of Washington's glorification. A few eulogists discussed the sin of idolatry and at least one feared that to "raise Washington up any more would be to unseat the omnipotent."[83] Others, such as Charles Brockden Brown, Dunlap's friend, saw in the deification of Washington a national act of self-abasement. Unable to find a sufficient number of other American literary productions to review in the year 1800 for his journal, *The Monthly Magazine,* Brown was obliged to review some fifty sermons and orations on Washington's death. In exasperation, he wrote a parody, "Advice to the Writers of Eulogies":

> You must so conduct yourself that it shall not appear that any one besides Washington possessed an intelligence or moral character during or since the revolution. You must hang not only the success of the war but the safety of our present political system upon his single life. Without him nothing could have happened that did happen and with his departure the energies that kept us together as one nation have taken their flight.[84]

Tom Paine, the great demystifier, restated Brown's objections with philosophical seriousness in an attack he published in the popular press:

> Mr. Washington had the nominal rank of Commander in Chief, but he was not so in fact. He had, in reality, only a separate command. . . . The nominal rank, however, of Commander in Chief served to throw upon him the luster of those actions and to make him appear as the soul and control of all military operations in America.[85]

Paine had undisguised disdain for the man who had refused to negotiate his release from a French Jacobin prison, but his criticism was much more than personal bitterness. Indeed, it was consistent with the argument of much of his later writing. Operations in nature, as well as on the battlefield, need not be referred to a superintending power. To attribute a victory of Greene's or Gate's to Washington suggested the slavish habits of superstitious Christianity that insisted on attributing to a supernatural Deity what might better be attributed to secondary causation within nature and which, by exclusively glorifying God, cheated man of a glory God intended for him. All the evils of scriptural Christianity could be traced, Paine declared in *The Age of Reason*, to the pernicious doctrine of "proxyism,"[86] which, declaring that one great man might save all mankind, obliged all mankind to suffer another man's single sin.

In his eulogy on Washington, *The Agency of God in Raising Up Instruments*, William Williston placed Paine's objection in an evangelical Christian context. One single man may move in so large and useful a sphere as to render his services uniquely important, but God, declared Williston, concerned himself no more with Washington than with any other man. Truly Washington was, indeed, a raised-up man, a deliverer, an instrument of God, but so were all American patriots:

> The hand of God was, no doubt, as really employed in raising up every soldier who fought in the American army . . . as in raising up the great commander. We do not say but he moved in a great and more important sphere but none of them could be spared without making a chasm.[87]

The word "chasm" suggests Williston's frame of reference. If the glory of God lay in the unity and order of his creation, each link in the chain (as Pope and Shaftesbury and numerous others had asserted for over a century) was as important as the next in serving the function for which it was designed. As the balanced and ordered drawers of a Chippendale highboy iconographically suggested, each part in its place contributed to a glorious whole. This was the rule of nature. In God's eyes, Williston concluded, all men were equally important.

What Brown, Paine, and Williston all neglect to acknowledge, however, is that in exalting Washington the nation was glorifying itself, its power to nurture and cultivate greatness. Washington was not being set apart but was made representative of his nation, made representative of the spirit of the Lockean age. Was this not the ultimate significance of the call to imitate him? With characteristic insight, informed by more than a little jealousy, it was John Adams who, anticipating Emerson's distinction, most explicitly recognized that Washington's greatness, his national significance, was to be discovered in his representativeness and not in his transcendence. Here was the birth of nineteenth-century Whig history:

> I glory in the character of a Washington because I know him to be only an exemplification of the American character. . . . If his character stood alone, I should value it very little. . . . I should wish it never existed, because, although it might have wrought a great event, yet that event would be no blessing.[88]

The fact that all natives had a character such that, given the right circumstances, they might grow up to be a second Washington, reaffirmed the ultimate power of nurture to create Crèvecoeur's "new man."

In addition, by positing that "our history is little more than his [Washington's] biography,"[89] Americans could take comfort in the illusion that rather than being an infant nation they had, like Washington, already achieved manhood. David Tappan of Harvard observed that Washington's chronology and his nation's were one. "At his birth, a nation was virtually born and the Pharaoh's question is resolved: 'Shall a nation be born at once?' At his birth the grave of old tyranny was dug."[90] The Pharaoh had asked Moses if he were so foolish as to believe that removing his people would make them a nation. Unlike a child, a nation could not be born at once or miraculously brought forth, the pharaoh implied; it must be slowly made. Jehovah refuted the Pharaoh in Isaiah: "Shall a land be born in one day? Shall a nation be brought forth in one moment? For as soon as Zion is in labor, she brought forth her sons."[91] The identification of ontogeny with phylogeny, of Washington with America, of biography with history, permitted America to boast that a nation could be born at once and, like a man, attain to greatness in one generation. Preaching on this verse in 1783, George Duffield commented:

> This passage, it must be confessed, has a manifest respect to that happy period generally termed the latter-day glory, when the various nations of the earth, formerly styled Gentiles, and yet in darkness, shall, in a sudden and surprising manner, be converted to the knowledge and obedience of Christ, and the Jews, so long rejected of God, shall, by an admirable display of Divine power and grace, be gathered home from their dispersion as in one day; and being formed into a people in their own land . . . being born to God at once . . . will constitute that joyous state of affairs which the apostle terms life from the dead.[92]

The spiritual model for the new nation "born at once" was the miraculous gathering of the diaspora, the formation of the new Israel. And the model for both was the Christian become regenerate by a second birth, reborn by embracing a new father of grace.

If America was an infant nation, then it was a "young Hercules breaking chains and playing with snakes in his cradle."[93] Having left the British parent as a child, America miraculously becomes capable of its own nurturing; independence transforms the son into his own parent, a child into an adult. At the age of twenty, concluded Enos Hitchcock, Washington "gained the meridian of ordinary life. Perhaps no young man had so early laid up a life's store of materials for solid reflection nor settled so soon the principles of and habits of his conduct."[94] So, too, may a nation reach "the meridian of its life" without passing through the epochs of history. The period of the nation's vulnerable infancy, so went the wishful thinking, would be no longer than that of a man's. A full-flown greatness was just within reach.

Completing a comparison of America and Rome, Samuel Tomb boasted, "Rather than developing to provide him, our civilization began with a great man."[95] America's first fruit was already its finest. According to the conservative prejudices of neoclassical thought, the ancients were superior to the moderns. As America, however, was a new nation among the nations of the world, Washington was its "ancient," its *first* hero, a unique ancient modern, suited both for "the *toga virilis*" of the precocious infant Hercules and the uniform of the commander of the Continental Army. Other nations in the eighteenth century who had not the records of such ancestors had to invent them. By "discovering" the poems of Ossian and the lost history of the heroes of Valhalla, James McPherson had done just that for Scotland. "Some people," asserted one of Ossian's early editors, "have thought that Mr. Robertson, Mr. Hume and Mr. Smith were ingenious men, but quite the contrary. They are only a few degrees above profound ignorance." They are, that is, when compared to the ancients, with "the holiest men, Moses and Solomon, the greatest lawgivers, Lycurgus and Solon and Alfred, the greatest warriors, Alexander and Augustus."[96] Washington was not only a contemporary of Hume and Adam Smith but also an ancient on the model of Augustus and Moses, an original and an imitation. Thus was the ancient–modern conflict resolved: Washington represented both a link to tradition and the severing of that link.

As an "ancient," Washington served the need of the Congregationalist Federalist alliance to have an oracle of ancient wisdom, an imitable exemplum, an argument for aristocracy, and after his death, fuel for the jeremiad's assertion of the moral decline of the new generation. As a "modern" he would serve the Republicans, in contrast, as a refutation of the jeremiad's assumptions. Jefferson would cite his example – as Franklin had used various flora and fauna to do – to disprove the degeneration theories of DePauw, Buffon, and others.[97] The influences of the American climate – moral, political, and natural – had combined to form the greatest of men. To the Federalists, he was a tutelar deity, inspiring patriotism, who properly cautioned against "entangling foreign alliances"; to others, he was both a source of national pride and a paternal link with the rest of Christendom, father to his nation and the world. But most important, his idealization as the nation's father served to complete the transformation of the antipatriarchal ideology into a national dogma.

⋊ In a letter to Edmund Pendleton dated August 13, 1776, Jefferson betrayed his fears about the inherent weaknesses of Republicanism. Admitting the possibility of "a reacknowledgment of the British tyrant as our king," he went on to recall the disastrous course of Cromwell's "Republican" experiment: "Remember how universally the people ran into the idea of recalling Charles II after living many years under a Republican government?"[98] Beset by postwar depression and social unrest, burdened with the unlegislatable Articles of Confederation, terrified by their nation's fragility, Americans had moments of regretting their independence.

From the vantage point of 1800 one of Washington's eulogists, Charles Summer, reflected on the period of the confederation, particularly late 1786 and early 1787; for these were the months during which Daniel Shays aroused the nation's conscience by leading a violent and protracted insurrection of 1,200 debt-ridden farmers, most of whom had not yet been paid for service in the Revolutionary Army.

> Faith was worn out, credit had been swollen till it burst; justice not only blind, but deaf and dumb, with scales reversed and blunted sword, could neither help her votaries, nor protect herself, the defenders of their country almost addressed themselves to her compassion; the poor soldier begged his bread through the land he had served and the fair but trembling fabric of society almost threatened ruin to those it scarcely sheltered.[99]

Shortly after Shays's insurrection ended, the Abraham Panther narrative appeared in print. Without "guide to direct or friend to protect [her]" and having fled for days from her Indian captors, the heroine of the narrative feels she can no longer endure her desperate and exhausting freedom; she wishes only "a place to dwell until a period be put to my miserable existence; to find and deliver myself a prisoner to those Indians, to whose cruelty I had so lately been a witness and, had I seen them, I certainly should have delivered myself into their hands" (p.

171). She cannot but entertain the dark thought: "Had I continued with him [her father], possibly I might have been happy" (p. 170).

The Declaration of Independence had recognized implicitly the possibility that America might wish to return to the care and custody of its powerful first parent. It had declared that "all men were endowed by the Creator with certain inalienable rights" – rights that could not be transferred, rights that could not even voluntarily be surrendered. But as long as Washington and the new paternity he represented remained the appropriate object on which to lavish their filial obedience, Americans would never be tempted to surrender those rights to another lesser parent, to trade their "easy yoke" for the "yoke of bondage."

8

THE SEALING OF THE GARDEN, OR THE WORLD WELL LOST

Emending Polybius's account of the origins of civil society, John Winthrop described in 1630 the process by which the perfect Christian community in America would be achieved. The passage from *A Modell of Christian Charity* describes the ancient Christian principle of *simile simili gaudet,* which posits that one loves those in whom one perceives one's own image:

> This is the cause why the Lord loves the Creature, soe farre as it hathe any of his Image in it . . . soe a mother loves her childe, because shee thoroughly conceives a resemblance of herself in it. Thus it is betweene the members of Christ. Each discernes, by the worke of the Spirit, his owne Image and resemblance in another, and therefore cannot but love him as he loves himselfe: Now when the soule, which is of a sociable nature, finds anything like to it selfe, it is like Adam when Eve was brought to him . . . this is flesh of my flesh . . . and bone of my bone.[1]

Winthrop assumes that the love between generations (the instincts of blood) and the "sociable" instincts of the soul are complementary, that the allegiance owed to the natal family and to the Christian community are part of one process. By 1800, Winthrop's principle of *simile simili gaudet* combined with the Scottish logic of the expanding social bond had developed into a species of Christian and Republican Universalism, which stood in opposition to American nationalism and the allegiance to the "city on the hill."

THE NATIONAL FAMILY OR
THE CHRISTIAN FAMILY OF NATIONS?

One form of the "paternal virtue" of which Washington was *absolved* by the Protestant ministry was patriotic chauvinism. He was father to his nation but not to his nation alone. For to favor one's own nation over the good of the whole Christian world was, finally, as unchristian, tyrannical, and idolatrous as the blind fondness of Marmontel's "bad mother" for one child over another. One's true nation was the entire Christian family. Washington had cut the Gordian knot of unnatural attachment but only in order to permit a new union. "No," declared David Leonard, "a divided world could not locate his benevolent mind."[2] "Though he had severed worlds, he was aware," added Aaron Wigglesworth, "that mankind are brethren, however separated by mountains or divided by seas."[3] Washington himself had declared in a letter to Lafayette in 1786: "I am a philanthropist by character and . . . a citizen of the great republic of humanity at large."[4]

In an article dealing with the character of Christian charity that appeared in the February 1789 issue of *The Columbian Magazine*, the doctrine Jonathan Edwards called "Self-love extended" and Washington "philanthropy" (literally love for mankind) is schematically represented by an illustration of six concentric circles. The center circle is labeled "self" and is surrounded by larger and larger orbits labeled: "Self-love Reflected – Family"; "Public Spirit – city, village, township or country"; "Patriotism – nations of the same religion"; "Imperfect Philanthropy – nations of the same color"; "Christian Charity or Perfect Philanthropy, constituting the Duty, Interest, and Supreme Happiness of Man – the whole world."[5] The family of the charitable Christian, as the design suggests, is not opposed to the world but is only the most immediate part of a world that *is* his family, a family even larger than the collective Christian nation to which he owes his "patriotism," for it includes non-Christians as well as Christians, to both of whom charity and friendship are owed. In this light it is not surprising that the fast and the thanksgiving sermons of the postwar period are full of attempts at reconciling the self-interested nature of patriotism with the Christian ethic of disinterested benevolence. That ethic declared all sin and depravity the result of selfishness and limited love. It insisted that to love being in general was the truest way of loving God, the ultimate principle of being.

In his most important essay on education, Benjamin Rush sought to remove the stigma from patriotism by arguing that when embraced by the young, the patriotic sentiment would in fact not only deliver them from the prison of selfishness but from the temptation to idolatrize their families as well.

> Next to the duty which young men owe to the creator, I wish to see a supreme regard to their country inculcated upon them. When the Duke of Sully became prime minister to Henry, the first thing he did, he tells us, was to subdue and forget his own heart! . . . Let our pupil be taught he does not belong to himself but he is public property. Let him be taught to love his family, but let him be taught at the same

time, that he must forsake and even forget them, when the welfare of his country requires it.[6]

Yet, though the doctrine of the greater good established patriotism as a higher obligation than filial obedience to the natal family, what was to keep Rush's logic from being extended to an argument for Christian duty over patriotism? Was there a way in which patriotism might be hailed as an unqualified virtue?

In his sermon *The Duty and Reward of Loving Our Country and Seeking Its Prosperity,* Joseph Dana is cautionary: "Our natural attachment to the country which gave us birth, like that to our parents or children, may properly be indulged as long as it serves to stimulate us to our duties at home, without interfering with what we owe abroad."[7] The last phrase is the key one. One may pray for the prosperity of one's own nation, but not at the expense of the prosperity of another. But as self-interest is best served by disinterested benevolence so, too, is patriotism. Reminding his parishioners that patriotism is not among the moral virtues taught by Scripture, John Lathrop suggests a middle road: "We may, however, possess a virtuous attachment to our country without thinking it the best on earth."[8] The most thoughtful discussion in the period of the circumscribed virtue of partial connections is, however, to be found in David Kellogg's *The Nature of Christian Compassion:*

> But we are not confined to the Christian family, in our benevolent wishes. Particular societies with which we are connected by some particular bonds, have a right to a special share of our attention, and friendly assistance. Those to whom we are allied by consanguinity, reason and Christianity point to our view that partial connections are necessary in the present imperfect state. The great family can not be in the same circle, but is unavoidably formed into detached parts; each select portion can best attend to their own improvement. . . . The wants of the great whole cannot fall under particular observation, neither can there be a mutual covenant through so extensive a body.[9]

Kellogg's treatise defends the obligations of consanguinity and partial connections as necessary – because of the fallen and divided state of the world – not as ideal. The obligation owed "the country which give us birth" and that owed the larger Christian family, part and parcel of one another in Winthrop's passage, remain in opposition. The rebel rhetoric of the war had called into question the significance of accidental natal attachments, had insisted on the glory of a new voluntaristic adopted family, and had argued independence to be the essential first step toward becoming citizens of a more glorious Christian union. That rhetoric and ideology had by 1785 rebounded so as to have undermined, to some extent, the new nation's assumption of its own intrinsic and self-contained worthiness. Though America's demands for allegiance were just, as opposed to those of Britain, still such allegiance threatened once again to cut one off from the world. Here in another guise was Scottish communalism chiding the glories of autonomy.

Though the American nation might well be God's chosen empire that he will protect with his wall of fire from foreign contamination, it does not constitute all of Christendom. The holy remnant must remain pure, but it must also join with all the other scattered sons of God to bring about the reign of peace announced in the Book of Revelation.

In secular terms such a universalism was necessitated by the fact that it alone would end the reign of the great enemy of republicanism and Christian fraternity: the power of birth. The accidents of birth and the divisive allegiances they obliged set family against family, eldest against secondborn, class against class, and nation against nation. In a late letter to Jefferson, who believed the abhorred power of birth would eventually be eradicated, John Adams, who ruefully believed such an eradication impossible, reminded his friend that their concern had been shared by Plato himself: "no Man expressed so much terror of the Power of Birth. His Genius could invent no remedy or precaution against it; but a Community of Wives, a confusion of Families, a total extinction of all Relations of Father, Son and Brother."[10] The ideal eighteenth-century republic, like Plato's republic, could brook no families, no partial attachments. The choice between family and larger world (whether defined as God, society, or Christendom) was, as the heroes of the puritan picaresque made clear, always an absolute choice. One could never have it both ways. If, through the Revolution, the whole (the British Empire) had been surrendered to preserve its best part (American purity and liberty), so eventually must that best part be surrendered for a new whole. The French Revolution, which sought to make all men citizens of the world, would ironically, however, postpone that second surrender indefinitely. Its violence and ultimate failure made clear the terrifying consequences of the surrender to a universal sympathy.

THE DANGERS OF SENTIMENTAL FRATERNITY:
THE HARDENING OF THE HEART

The universalist sympathy that disdained partial connections and extolled the sociable instincts of the soul was but one expression of the larger phenomenon of eighteenth-century sensibility, which Sterne had defined as "the Eternal fountain of our feeling . . . the divinity which stirs within."[11] Sentimentalists and moralists subscribed to an optimistic view of human nature, which presumed that human behavior was regulated by what Shaftesbury and later the Scots called "a natural moral sense" and Adam Smith "an internal monitor activated by the sympathetic attachments."[12] From a rationalist perspective sentimentality was a dangerous doctrine, insofar as it led to a delight in emotion for its own sake and an unwillingness to face harsh realities or unpleasant truths.[13] By abjuring stoicism and making a virtue of the vulnerability of the heart, it encouraged flattery and seduction in human relations and enthusiasm in religion. Whereas Locke's internal monitor, reason, suppressed or social-ized the passions, the moral sense posited by sentimentalists purified and intensified them. Sentimentality implicitly deprecated rational love in favor of purer attachments of the heart.

If sympathy was automatic as the early moral sense philosophers suggested, then, argued their rationalist opponents, it was not worthy of moral approval. One must look to man's rational action and not to his instinctual or habitual compassion to answer the perplexing question about the goodness or evil of his natural character. Instinctual behavior could be claimed to be neither moral nor immoral. Responding to such criticism, Adam Smith, Abraham Tucker, and other moralists writing in the 1760s and 1770s sought to redefine compassion as an active rather than passive virtue involving a deliberate moral projection or identifica-tion, an active attempt "to feel another's woe." Such a redefinition sought to compromise the assumption of post-Lockean skepticism that each human mind is sealed off from a precise understanding of the thinking and feeling of another human mind and heart.[14] Yet to accept the principle of moral projection, to believe that man could indeed experience another individual's pain, was to do more than facilitate the advent of a new age of compassion. It was to make the human mind and heart vulnerable to a new kind of invasion.

By providing access to the province of another's private thought and feeling, a sentimentalized sympathy or compassion compromised in a seemingly benign, but no less radical, way man's rational and emo-tional autonomy. For a nation concerned with independence, "negative capability" involved an unsettling blurring of the definitional bounda-ries of self and other. In the first American novel, *The Power of Sym-pathy* (1789), the heroine, drawn by the pull of an enormous sympathy, falls in love with a man who turns out to be her brother. Taken to its extreme, Winthrop's *simile simili gaudet,* like sentimental identification, leads to incest. Rather than rationally accepting the impossibility of their plight, the two form a suicide pact and become victims of the power of sympathy, the non-Newtonian attraction of likes.

The didactic fiction of the eighteenth century, which followed Locke in preaching a rationalist pedagogy, warned as vehemently against the fatal effects of sentiment – particularly excessive self-lessness – as it did against the abuse of parental authority. Such a warning is contained in the history of Mr. Thornhill recounted in Goldsmith's *Vicar of Wakefield:*

> He carried benevolence to an excess when young; for his passions
> were then strong, and as they all were upon the side of virtue, they led
> it up to a Romantic extreme. . . . He was surrounded with crowds,
> who showed him only one side of their character; so that he began to
> lose a regard for private interest in universal sympathy. He loved all
> mankind; for fortune prevented him from knowing that there were
> rascals. Physicians tell us of a disorder in which the whole body is so
> exquisitely sensible that the slightest touch gives pain: what some have
> thus suffered in their persons this gentleman felt in his mind. The
> slightest distress, whether real or fictitious, touched him to the quick,
> and his soul laboured under a sickly sensibility of the miseries of
> others (p. 20).

The analogy of sentimentality to a disease was not a facetious one. By
the middle of the eighteenth century the older humoral theory of disease that stressed the need to balance the humors (blood, phlegm, black
bile or melancholy, and yellow bile or choler) by purging or diet was
quickly being replaced. A newer environmental theory of disease domi-
nated, which, following Locke's emphasis on influence, stressed excitation, irritability, and the deleterious effects of external stimulation. Disease, according to Dr. Benjamin Rush, was less a matter of internal
malfunction than it was of external interference.[15] Sympathy made man
vulnerable not only to the misrepresentations of fraudulent beggars and
petitioners playing on the automatic moral sense, but to the tyrannical
"disease" of draining excitations and constant feeling and sensation. By
making the heart sensitive, it had become as vulnerable as the impressionable mind to the enthrallments of the world. Like laughter or
yawning, sympathy and compassion were seen as "contagious."[16] Governor Keith of Franklin's *Autobiography* was one who had caught the
contagion and couldn't shake it. Mr. Thornhill was another.

Later in *The Vicar* Goldsmith makes his point about a sickly sensibility in yet another context. The Vicar asks of his recently recovered
daughter:

> "But tell me, my child, sure it was no small temptation that could
> thus extinguish all the impressions of such an education, and so virtu-
> ous disposition as thine?"
> "Indeed sir," replied she, "he owes all his triumph to the desire I
> had of making him, and not myself, happy" (p. 177).

In a world where the character of mankind is far from virtuous, to
allow one's emotions to be played upon, to choose to follow the heart
rather than educated reason, is to call for one's own destruction. To
become a citizen of the world one must transcend rather than indulge
the enslaving, and necessarily partial, attachments of the heart by being
vigilant of autonomy rather than promiscuous of it. For only on a plane

of universal reason reached through rational love may mankind establish a unity, and the greater good be served.

Whether formulated as an involuntary constitutional response or as the constraint of a code of honor, sentimentality obliged men and women of feeling to respond unhesitatingly to misery with benevolence and to benevolence with gratitude. Thus, if the villains of a pre-Lockean world were those who constrained obedience by force, the villains of a post-Lockean world were those who, by boasted acts of heinously calculated benevolence, imposed upon a sentimental heart a debt of gratitude so sacred as to require its being discharged even though the benefactor's motives were impure. The new villain, to quote from yet another revealing essay amongst *Cato's Letters,* by "false bounty" gained "the Hearts of the manly, who saw not into his design of bribing and feeding them, in order to enslave them" (IV,106).

M. d'Etanges in Rousseau's *La Nouvelle Héloïse* traces his daughter's undoing to her tutor St. Preux's manipulation of the family's gratitude:

> Unhappy youth! Not to perceive that to suffer himself to be paid in gratitude, what he refused in money, was infinitely more cruel. Under the mask of instruction, he corrupted her heart; instead of nourishment he gave her poison and is thanked by a delusive mother for the ruin of her child (II,79).

Sounding like the American pamphleteers of the early 1770s, an alert Clarissa addresses Lovelace early in the novel:

> And pray, sir, said I, let me interrupt you in my turn; why don't you assert, in still plainer words, the obligations you have had me under by this your boasted devotion. Why don't you let me know, in terms as high as your implication, that a perseverance I have not wished for, which has set all my relations at variance with me, is a merit that throws upon me the guilt of ingratitude for not answering it as you seem to expect? (I, 216–17).

For all her bold talk, Clarissa's fastidious attempt to avoid the damning charge of ingratitude will become the immediate cause of her downfall. She confesses to Miss Howe that she has agreed to meet Lovelace in the garden since, having responded to his initial attentions, to deny him in "this particular" would be to convict herself of being "tyrannical." Clarissa's understanding of tyranny follows closely that of the pedagogical rationalists who warned parents against thwarting the development of their child's reason by suddenly and irrationally denying privileges long acceded to.[17] Yet, in choosing to subordinate self-interest to blameless consistency, Clarissa avoids one Lockean sin only to convict herself of yet another – one we have heard denounced vehemently in Dunlap's *André* – prideful enslavement to personal honor.

In the 1790s, the reigning Federalist party believed that the same false sense of gratitude that had been Clarissa's downfall was threatening to rend the fabric of American society. They feared the republican appeal to "the sacred debt of gratitude" owed France for the part she had played in the American Revolution. Talleyrand, Citizen Genêt, and other representatives of the French government along with ardent francophile Republicans urged the American government to advance the cause of the French Revolution by supporting France in what might become a war against Britain. The Federalists especially singled out Jefferson and Madison for their irrational and "womanish attachment to France and womanish resentment" to Britain. Federalist spokesmen declared that such an indulgence of sentimental principle would involve America inevitably in "a European holocaust"[18] that would destroy the infant nation. In addition, the Federalists contended that France, the boasted "Saviour of America,"[19] was not deserving in the least of gratitude, since, like Lovelace, she had sought to isolate the child only later to destroy her morals. Fisher Ames pointed to the recently spawned Jacobin clubs, "those impure offspring of Genêt . . . conceived in sin"[20] as proof that France's motives in assisting America's deliverance from parental tyranny had been, from the very beginning, far from disinterested. To the same point Timothy Dwight commented ironically that "No knight Errant rushed more speedily to the assistance of a damsel, than they to our assistance." And as for Talleyrand's contemptible demand for aid and tribute, was it not an attempt to extort what nature demanded must freely and unrestrainedly be given? "Tribute, when and what? Tis an exaction."[21] Talleyrand, he might have said, was no better than the blackmailing Barbary pirates.

The Federalist party and its sympathizers were in profound agreement with the opinions of Chesterfield:

> The season of youth is the season of attachments. The heart is then susceptible to the finest impressions, and is too little concerned about the objects of its attachments, or the circumstances in which they ought to be formed. This makes counsel the more necessary.[22]

Consistent with this view of the heart's vulnerability, Washington issued in 1793 a Proclamation of Neutrality (the "great" deed ascribed to him in *The New England Primer* the following year). Later, addressing his own children in his Farewell Address of 1796 he restated the warning of the sentimental parent to the sentimental heroine:

> 'tis folly in one nation to look for disinterested favors from another –
> that it must pay with a portion of its independence for whatever it
> may accept under that character – that by such acceptance, it may place
> itself in the condition of having given equivalents for nominal favours
> and yet of being reproached with ingratitude for not giving more –
> There can be no greater folly than to expect, or calculate upon real

favours from Nation to Nation – 'Tis an illusion which experience must cure, which a just pride ought to disregard.[23]

Seeking to foster conciliation with England and to stem the tide of sympathy for Jacobin France, Washington reiterated the great psychological insight of Locke's that, a generation earlier, had so well served the ideology of the Revolution. Here, boldly put, was Marmontel's attack on parents who favored one child over another: "The nation which indulges toward another habitual hatred or a habitual fondness is in some degree a slave. It is a slave to its animosity or to its affection either of which is sufficient to lead it astray from its duty and interest." Arguments gilded "with the appeal of a virtuous sense of obligation" (p. 320) must be heard only with extreme caution. What in 1776 had been an argument for separation and self-determination became in 1796 a justification for a national policy of neutrality and self-interest.

The news of the horrors perpetrated by the French Assembly and especially of the guillotining of Louis (the ultimate patricidal crime Revolutionary America so wished to dissociate itself from) confirmed for many Americans the Federalist reading of the French character. It also confirmed the appropriateness of a policy of self-interest in a fallen world, even if such a policy betrayed the Christian idealism of the American Revolution.

VENTRILOQUISTS, COUNTERFEITERS, AND THE SEDUCTION OF THE MIND

The revolutionary events of the decade following the fall of the Bastille radically intensified the fear of corruption of mind and morals so much a part of the predominant Lockean world view and epistemology of the eighteenth century. The multiple editions of Franklin's *Autobiography* published in the 1790s and the calls at the end of the decade to imitate the great Washington were attempts to ensure that the national character would be formed before the course of violent events – to invoke Noah Webster's neologism describing the effects of the French Revolution on the impressionable mind – "demoralised" it forever. Before, that is, the contagious power of sympathy implicated Americans in the French madness.[24] The Alien and Sedition Acts of 1798 attempted to do by law what Washington was to do by example: protect the American character from Jacobin seduction.

Such seduction threatened not only the individual mind by misrepresenting the world to the informing senses, but also the collective national mind. In a republic that sought to implement the general will by relying on public opinion as the expression of that will, the republican experiment would be radically jeopardized if public opinion were manipulated rather than informed. How secure public opinion was against such seduction and, by extension, how much faith might be accorded the great formula of the age, the voice of the people is the voice of God (*vox populi, vox Dei*) were among the most important issues that divided Federalists and Republicans. Jefferson, on the Republican side, declared that newspapers without government was a choice preferable to government without newspapers, those instruments necessary to inform the public mind.[25] The properly educated mind rendered invulnerable to seduction would speak with the authority of God. "On the basis of sensation, of matter and motion, we may erect the fabric of the certainties we can have or need," he confidently wrote Adams late in his career and added in conclusion: "A single sense may indeed be sometimes deceived, but rarely; and never all our senses together, with their faculty of reasoning. They evidence realities; and there are enough of these for all the purposes of life, without plunging into the fathomless abyss of dreams and phantasms."[26] Even if the mind is, as Locke declared, a "dark room" receiving only shadowy reports of the world, Jefferson believed it was fully capable of judging the reliability of those reports.

Federalists, a less sanguine lot, were far less convinced of that reliability, however, as Thomas Fessenden made especially clear in 1803: "We are informed that the general will cannot err (*vox populi, vox Dei*) and that it ends invariably to the public advantage. Yet we are told almost in the same breath that the people are often deceived and that the expressions of the will of a fallible body are always fallible."[27] Fessenden's fear of corruption reflected a realistic perception of the new political world. Because it declared true authority to be incompatible with the obnoxious shows of power, the antipatriarchal revolution obliged authority to go underground. This fact introduced a new set of anxieties into Anglo-American culture about the manipulation of will, reason, motivation, and the affections of the heart. In one set of terms, these anxieties achieved their fundamental expression in the Richardsonian novel of seduction.

Caught between her father's tyranny and Lovelace's manipulation, Clarissa is victim of two kinds of tyranny: one, pre-Lockean, seeks to control her person, and one, post-Lockean, attempts to control her mind and affections. If Mr. Harlowe represents the abuse of patriarchal authority that rules by the imposition of will, Lovelace, an eighteenth-century anti-tutor, seeks to rule by deception, artfully justifying his actions with the claim that he is serving his victim's own best interests. Having escaped the parental tyrant, Clarissa must contend with the libertine who charms her with a dream of happiness and independence from the constraints of filial obligation. Elaborating on Fessenden's point, John Adams identified his Jeffersonian opponents with Richard-

son's great villain and their Francophile idealism with the illusory
dream Lovelace proffers:

> The awful spirit of Democracy is in great progress. It is a young rake
> who thinks himself handsome and well-made, and who has little faith
> in virtue. . . . When the people once admit his courtship, and permit
> him the least familiarity they soon find themselves in the condition of
> the poor [seduced and pregnant] girl. . . .
>   Democracy is Lovelace and the people are Clarissa. The artful vil-
> lain will pursue the innocent lovely girl to her ruin and her death. . . .
> The time would fail me to enumerate all the Lovelaces in the United
> States. It would be an amusing romance to compare their actions and
> character with his.[28]

Whereas Jefferson believed in the power of education, Adams feared
that "human reason and human conscience are not a match for human
passion, human imagination and human enthusiasm,"[29] All power must
be restrained and balanced, or America will embrace Clarissa's fate.

In 1798, the year of the Alien and Sedition Acts, Charles Brockden
Brown's *Wieland or the Transformation,* the first important American
novel, took up the debate over the fragility and credulity of the human
mind. Rather than merely implying the epistemological dilemmas implicit in the Richardsonian novel of seduction, Brown made those dilemmas his primary subject. Therein lies the crucial importance of the
novel as a reflection of American culture in the wake of the French
Revolution. The novel's primary assumption is vintage Locke: "The
will is the tool of the understanding, which must fashion its conclusions
on the notices of sense. If the senses be depraved, it is impossible to
calculate the evils that may flow from the consequent deductions of the
understanding."[30] Thus Brown declares it is the didactic purpose of his
novel to "inculcate the duty of avoiding deceit. It will exemplify the
force of early impressions, and show the immeasurable evils that follow
from an erroneous or imperfect discipline" (p. 5).

The story takes place in Pennsylvania "between the conclusion of the
French and the beginning of the Revolutionary war" and concerns
Clara Wieland and her brother Theodore. Some years before, they had
been left orphans when their father, a religious enthusiast, was killed,
perhaps in fulfillment of his fear of divine punishment in a fire of
spontaneous origin. Their grieving mother died shortly after. The pair
were then raised by their maiden aunt at home and saved "from the
corruption and tyranny of colleges and boarding schools" by being
"left to the guidance of our own understanding, and the casual impressions which society might make upon us" (pp. 207–8). Wieland (as
Theodore is called) marries a young woman named Catherine Pleyel
whose brother Henry comes to live with them and Clara to round out

the foursome. Having inherited his father's enthusiasm, Wieland is a religious determinist who seeks the revelation of a higher will by which he may be guided; Henry, on the contrary, is a rationalist who rejects all guidance but that of his own reason. These two figures are somewhat crudely meant to represent the temperamental division of the age.

After a period of peaceful fraternity, strange things begin to happen to this little community whose security hitherto "had never been molested" (p. 56). Disembodied voices are heard – one warning Wieland of dangerous things to come and another, even more ominous, overheard in Clara's closet plotting her death. Shortly after these occurrences there appears at the Wieland's home an old acquaintance of Pleyel's by the name of Carwin who ingratiates himself into their rural society. Though ungainly and awkwardly dressed, he is possessed of a strangely hypnotic voice that – "combining sweetness and force," the ideal of the age – seemed as if "a heart of stone would not fail of being moved by it" (p. 52). The resonant tones of his voice seem to exert an almost mesmeric influence on Clara, who even momentarily believes she may be in love with the stranger. It is, of course, Carwin who is responsible for these voices. He has mastered the new eighteenth-century science of biloquism or ventriloquism, like mesmerism a profane embodiment of Locke's principle of the inner voice and Rousseau's of the hidden hand, those earlier surrogates for Christian conscience through which the *deus absconditus* performed his ventriloquism.

Carwin's motives are never made fully clear. But the reader does learn that, having heard from Clara's maid admiring accounts of her mistress's courage and rationality, Carwin feels compelled to test that courage, to determine how accessible to wonder and panic she really is. He will test the age of reason's faith in itself. As part of his plan Carwin arranges things such that Pleyel overhears from within Wieland's bedroom what he believes to be Clara's voice declaring her love for the strange visitor. Believing the evidence of his senses, Pleyel (secretly in love with Clara himself, as she is, indeed, in love with him) reviles her for what he imagines to be her promiscuity and banishes her from his affections. Thus has Carwin, an updated Lovelace, succeeded in destroying Clara's reputation, not in fact but in appearance. He is seducer less of women than of opinion, that sacred entity to which the Declaration of Independence addressed itself with "a decent respect." As her virtue was unable to protect her from misrepresentation, so truth and the "consciousness of innocence" are not enough to vindicate her (p. 113). In this postsensationalistic world Clara lacks what has become most essential: demonstrable evidence. Her character is no longer evidence enough. Thus she is obliged to confess despairingly with her age:

I used to suppose that certain evils could never befall a being in possession of a sound mind; that true virtue supplies us with energy which
vice can never resist; that it was always in our power to obstruct . . .
the designs of an enemy who aimed at less than our life. How was it
that a sentiment like despair had now invaded me? (pp. 90–1)

But it is not only Pleyel who is misled. Even more tragically, Wieland, himself, is convinced that he has heard a voice – the voice of God
obliging him to sacrifice his family as a testimony of his absolute acceptance of the divine will. Believing that obedience is the truest test of
virtue and that by serving a higher will he will no longer be but "mere
man" (p. 173), Wieland unhesitatingly obeys what he imagines is "an
unambiguous token of God's presence": He slays his wife and children
(p. 167). The pilgrim's choice of God over family is travestied and
transformed into Gothic horror. Though it is never clear whether the
voice is Carwin's or is of Wieland's own enthusiastic imagining, Carwin seems to confess in the very act of denying responsibility: "I am
not this villain; I have slain no one; I have prompted no one to slay, I
have handled a tool of wonderful efficacy without malignant intentions,
but without caution; ample will be the punishment of my temerity, if
my conduct has contributed to this evil" (p. 198). So the novel ends
with the mystery of agency unresolved and, as Carwin is himself to
some degree a victim of "the empire of mechanical and habitual impulse" (p. 159), the question of moral accountability is intractably problematic. Brown's novel of authority misrepresented and authority imagined is a terrifying post–French Revolutionary account of the fallibility
of the human mind and, by extension, of democracy itself. Ventriloquism and religious enthusiasm, its central dramatic devices, seem with
a sardonic literalness to call into question all possible faith in the republican formula *vox populi, vox Dei*. In the year of the Alien and Sedition
Acts here were embodied the larger fears that informed the Jacobin
anxiety. Even Jefferson insisted that only *some* truths were self-evident.

Upon seeing the corpses of her brother's family, Clara exclaims: "I
was not qualified by education and experience to encounter perils like
these" (p. 150). No education can really prepare one for the horrors of
the world, nor can one successfully seal oneself off from the world. "I
had vainly thought that my safety could be sufficiently secured by
doors and bars," Clara declares (p. 110). But Carwin's post-Lockean
"invisible power," like the power of love, its benign but no less en-
thralling counterpart, is a foe from "whose grasp no power of divinity
can save me" (p. 109). The fall into experience is inevitable. The only
real question is whether the fall will be fortunate. "Be the maker of
your fortune," Pleyel advises Clara, "and may adversity instruct you in
that wisdom, which education was unable to impart to you" (p. 135).

Wieland is, in effect, the dark flip side of Franklin's *Autobiography*. Here the same post-sensationalist world is invoked, but in all its terror rather than its freedom and glorious opportunity. A generation after the first part of the *Autobiography* the story is told from the point of view of the victim, rather than that of the self-satisfied and winning opportunist. Gone is the Franklinian optimism of the 1770s; in its stead are epistemological terror and moral confusion. Carwin is Franklin corrupted or, in eighteenth-century terms, the "projector" has become the "designer." The book's subtitle, *The Transformation*, refers not only to the transformation of Wieland but to a broad historical transformation, the shift from a world that assumed stable forms and fixed relations between appearance and reality and between man and society to a world sensitive to shifting values, deceptive appearances, mixed motives and, most significantly, the tyranny of language over things, rhetoric over logic. A secure world has been made insecure and that, Brown announces, is the price of its having become "free." By placing his novel in the decade before the American Revolution, Brown suggests, by implication, that the great conflict for American independence, rather than merely being a result of that larger "transformation," decisively hastened it.

In this transformed world both freedom of rational inquiry and the enthusiast's belief in religious determinism lead to fatal consequences. The insistence of Edwards and Rousseau that the manipulation of human motivation was not a violation of human freedom, that the "willing" slave was, in fact, free, no longer seems tenable. The very principle of guidance itself has been perverted and must be guarded against rather than surrendered to. The first American novel, *The Power of Sympathy*, written nine years before *Wieland*, opens with the Lovelace figure announcing his seduction scheme in these terms: "I will shew you my benevolent scheme; it is to take this beautiful sprig, and transplant it to a more favourable soil, where it shall flourish and bloom under my own auspices."[31] Here the "benevolent scheme" of nurture and cultivation, the great enterprise of the Enlightenment, is mocked and perverted. Significantly, that perversion serves as the point of departure for American literature, which for the next hundred years will be concerned in its greatest works with both the character and the betrayal of the American promise of liberty.

In this transformed though presumably enlightened world in which Carwin declares himself "a friend, one come, not to injure, but to save you" (p. 63), liberators cannot be distinguished from seducers, the "pseudo-aristoi" of charm from the "natural aristoi" of virtue,[32] and those that promise you the world cheat you of it. Religion itself seems a great confidence game and revelation no more than, in Paine's word, "hearsay," inadmissible evidence. Faith in the involuntary actions of the moral sense, in the self-evidence of truth, and in the power of reason to discover that truth has been radically shaken. All is deception. Even compassion is built on it. One verse that adorns eighteenth-century American samplers is the opening couplet of Pope's "Universal Prayer": "Teach me to feel another's woe / To hide the fault I see."[33] Such deception appeared benign in the earlier part of the century, but in the context of the world of *Wieland* Pope's lines seem strangely ominous.

The necessary fall of man from familial security into a deceptive and competitive social world – the great story and history of the eighteenth century – created a new species of man: "the man of the world" who superimposes onto his original familial identity a new self-made identity based on his relationship to society. In *Emile* Rousseau described that new man and the transformation of his appearance: "The man of the world is entirely covered with a mask; he is so accustomed to disguise, that if, at any time he is obliged for a moment to assume his natural character his uneasiness and constraint are palpably obvious. . . . Reality is no part of his concern, he aims at nothing more than appearance" (II, 183). Like Franklin he preferred his personae.

Rousseau is both horrified by and attracted to such a vision of the social world. Though deception was a central element in his own pedagogy, Rousseau believed he spoke for nature. Yet he, nearly as much as Franklin, recognized that the displacement of the limited "natural world" by the infinite "imaginary world" (II, 104) was, in one respect, more comforting than frightening. For in the masked world of appearances one great dilemma is resolved: man may become familiar and intimate with the world without jeopardizing the integrity of his personal identity. The grand tour was safe if conducted as a masquerade. By the 1790s however, the world appeared considerably more frightening than comforting, or so at least is the suggestion of the prodigal son engravings of the period.

In 1792, the printer Carington Bowles, whose earlier engravings we have examined, offered a new prodigal son series. In 1775, *The Prodigal Son Taking Leave* showed father and son out of doors just as the son is about to mount his horse. In the background was the outline of a beckoning city (Plate 4). Seventeen years later the scene has moved indoors. A low door to the outside world is open revealing nothing but a long serpentine path – in contrast to the orderly pattern of the indoor carpet – that leads to a distant carriage flanked by two lounging drivers. The carriage obscures all view of a world beyond (Plate 5). The "world" in the 1792 engraving is further away and, as the anguished

Plate 4. This 1775 engraving of *The Prodigal Son Taking Leave* printed and distributed by Carington Bowles optimistically depicts the departure of this second son of an English gentry family. Accompanied by his servant, he sets forth to make his fortune, as his elder brother, whose patrimony has allowed him to marry, watches. (Courtesy of The Library Company of Philadelphia.)

look of one family member suggests, infinitely more dangerous. Indeed, those who would venture out into such a world are no longer merely young men who wish to embrace a universal fraternity, who seek the liberty to exercise their social nature, but opportunists like Montraville, Charlotte Temple's seducer, whose name, like that of his French collaborator, Madame La Rue, suggests the dangers of being "shown the city." Because Chesterfield's advice, unlike say Watts's, stressed lessons necessary to rising in this world rather than being saved in the next, "Chesterfieldian" had become by the end of the century an adjective describing one who is unscrupulously concerned with social position.[34] The great work read in the 1770s as a text for preaching moral independence becomes more widely perceived in the 1790s as a primer for opportunists.

The transformed world of the 1790s held horrors more philosophical and metaphysical than merely the threat of designers. In 1758, Poor Richard taught that the loss of a nail led to the loss of a shoe and of a shoe to the loss of a horse and then finally to the loss of life in battle. A

Plate 5. In the engraving of *The Prodigal Son Taking Leave* offered by Carington Bowles in 1792, the rite of passage from family to world is more fateful than in earlier depictions and the passage beyond the wall of private life more ominous. (Lewis Walpole Library.)

half-century later John Adams proposed a more ominous Newtonian sequence to his friend Benjamin Rush: "Did not the American Revolution produce the French Revolution and did not the French Revolution produce the Calamity and Desolation for the human race?"[35] In a world where actions initiate a chain of often unforeseeable and uncontrollable consequences, the very prospect of action, even the most glorious action, becomes frightening and the question of moral responsibility exquisitely complex.

The only response to such a world was to be, to use Franklin's favorite word, "careful." But for Poor Richard writing at midcentury, the word meant simply "vigilant". By the 1790s, its more literal sense, full of cares, was more acutely felt. The French Revolution had introduced the modern age of anxiety. The tabula rasa was now less a foundation on which to build and more a vulnerable fortress under siege, a fortress even the power of education could not protect. Of all of *Wieland*'s lessons, this was the darkest; for it undermined the central assumption of the eighteenth-century ideology of independence. Carwin himself, "English by birth and Protestant by education," had moved to Spain and converted to Roman Catholicism. There "the impressions of his youth" had been "obliterated" (p. 69).

Perhaps the greatest fear, however, engendered by this new world was that the Christian paradox that defined freedom as a function of restraint and self-control, a paradox endorsed by Locke, Rousseau, and the authors of *The Federalist*, could no longer be sustained. The new Gallic understanding of liberty seemed to threaten to eclipse the older Protestant understanding. In his eulogy on Washington, Fisher Ames made clear the contrast:

> Here liberty is restrained, there it is violent, here it is mild and cheery, like the morning sun of our summer, brightening the hills. . . . There it is like the sun when its rays dart pestilence on the sands of Africa. They had led the citizen to look for liberty where it is not and consider the government which is its castle, as its prison.[36]

The French Revolution demanded not only that the "yoke of bondage" be cast off, but the "easy yoke" as well.

In this regard, an infinitely greater account of the "transformation" Brown records is set forth by Burke in his *Reflections on the Revolution in France* (1790), written three years before the guillotining of Louis. The passage is as important as it is familiar.

> But the age of chivalry is gone – That of sophisters, oeconomists, and calculators, has succeeded; and the glory of Europe is extinguished for ever. Never, never more, shall we behold that generous loyalty to rank and sex, that proud submission, that dignified obedience, that subordination of the heart which kept alive, even in servitude itself, the spirit of an exalted freedom . . . which ennobled whatever it touched, and under which vice itself lost half its evil, by losing all its grossness.[37]

The age of reason is the age of sophisters who have fatally severed the glorious link between submission and freedom:

> But now all is to be changed. All the pleasing illusions, which made power gentle, and obedience liberal, which harmonized the different shades of life, and which, by a bland assimilation, incorporated into politics the sentiments which beautify and soften private society, are to be dissolved by this new conquering empire of light and reason (p. 114).

"The empire of light and reason" that insists on seeing "things as they are" – the wishful subtitle of Godwin's *Caleb Williams,* the major literary influence on *Wieland* – destroys all the necessary fictions that hold society together. The "pleasing illusions" the Reverend Zubly called for in his discussion of taxes and "benevolences" are destroyed.

It is not nature that is glorious, Burke suggests, but what man creates to improve it:

> All the decent drapery of life is to be rudely torn off. All the super-added ideas, furnished from the wardrobe of a moral imagination, which the heart owns, and the understanding ratifies, as necessary to cover the defects of our naked shivering nature, and to raise it to dignity in our own estimation, are to be exploded as a ridiculous, absurd, and antiquated fashion (p. 114).

What the demystifiers, Paine in his sphere, Gilbert Stuart in his, neglect to see is that, contrary to antipatriarchal assumptions, it *is* the office and not the natural man that is essential. Men change and die, but the office remains forever, its meaning and significance fixed, its glory undiminished. The issue is not the force of character over the mind, but the power of symbols and the ancient code of chivalry such symbols embody. Truth resides not in naked facts and self-evident truths, but in the fictions of the moral imagination.

To attempt to pierce to the nakedness of men is to force them to trade their symbolic garments for the infinitely more deceptive masks and costumes of Rousseau's man of the world, or to trade, as Rousseau observes in *Emile*, "the external marks of dignity" for the spectacle of armies "in readiness to see their order executed" (III, 79). The power of symbols must either be replaced with duplicity or with force, which itself creates what Locke so feared in the *Education*: "a counterfeit Carriage, and dissembled Out-side" (p. 146). The very effort of uncovering "truth" ensures its being hidden, ensures the survival of that deceitful and duplicitous world revolutionary rationalists sought to destroy. In its sometimes crude but powerful way, *Wieland* makes this point unforgettably. Without those fictions of the moral imagination, the world is chaotic and "the murder of a king . . . or a father," Burke concludes, is "only common homicide" (p. 115).

    ➤ Of the literary works of the American 1790s, only one book seems to keep alive the spirit of Franklinian optimism against the prevailing vision of Burke and Brown, and continues to see in the chaos the image of freedom and unlimited opportunity. That the dissenting voice should be that of an impostor convicted as a counterfeiter during the public credit crisis of the early 1790s is wonderfully fitting. A book Robert Frost believed to reveal so much about the American character that it should be kept on one's shelf between Franklin and Edwards, *The Memoirs of Stephen Burroughs* (1798) reads, in its shamelessly self-interested way, as a plea to the new nation to embrace the new age of deception and invention.[38]

Having left Dartmouth College because of what he claims to have been a constant round of unmerited reprimands, Burroughs moves to Pelham, Massachusetts. There, like Franklin and Carwin in their different ways, he makes the great discovery of his rhetorical powers, but rather than turning to ventriloquism or journalism, he chooses to impersonate a minister. Only after delivering a successful run of sermons is he finally discovered and forced to flee town. Burroughs gamely defends his "counterfeiting of a name, a character, and a calling" (p. 96) in a passage whose concluding question catches up the double-edged spirit of the post–Bastille era:

> The name imposter, is, therefore, easily fixed on my character. An imposter, we generally conceive, puts on feigned appearances, in order to enrich or aggrandize himself, to the damage of others. That this is not the case with me, in this transaction, I think is clear. That I have aimed at nothing but a bare supply of the necessaries of life, is a fact, never taken advantage of that confidence which the people of Pelham entertained to me . . . is a truth acknowledged by all. Under these circumstances, whether I ought to bear the name of imposter according to common acceptation, is the question (p. 68).

Burroughs's insistence that it is intention and not action, the spirit and not the letter, that must be judged, informs the defense of counterfeiting offered by Lysander, Burroughs's associate. Given the terrible postwar scarcity of cash, Lysander argues, to counterfeit money is but to reestablish "that due proportion between representative property and real property" and thus do a patriotic deed (p. 85). The issue is, as always in a political world obsessed with epistemological questions, a matter of restoring a just "representation." At the center of Lysander's defense is his own sophisticated expostulation on the idea of representation:

> Money, of itself, is of no consequence, only as we, by mutual agreement, annex to it a nominal value, as the representation of property. Anything else might answer the same purpose, equally with silver and gold, should mankind only agree to consider it as such. . . . We find this verified in fact, by those bills of credit which are in circulation through the world. Those bills, simply, are good for nothing; but the moment mankind agrees to put a value on them, as representing property, they become of as great consequences as silver and gold, and no one is injured by receiving a small insignificant piece of paper for an hundred bushels of wheat. . . . Therefore, we find the only thing necessary to make a matter valuable, is to induce the world to deem it so; and let that esteem be raised by any means whatever, yet the value is the same (p. 81).

"To induce the world to deem it so," makes it so, no matter what means are employed to raise that "esteem" – the Lockean touchstone revisited. Burke's fictions of the moral imagination, now no longer workable, must be replaced, as Rousseau's pedagogy suggested, by a new set of fictions – perhaps moral, perhaps not, but no less necessary. Like Franklin, Burroughs and his friends see paper money as the symbol of a new age of invention and reconceived values, as the great new fiction of the age.

But whereas Franklin's *Autobiography* would be universally applauded, Burroughs's version of the new gospel lands him in jail. In a society obsessed with misrepresentation and the deception of the senses as ultimate threats to liberty, the counterfeiter, like the Jacobin for whom he is an analogue, cannot be tolerated. In 1790, the first Congress made counterfeiting a crime. In 1792, Britain made the giving of a "false character" (reference) a felony.[39] For Burroughs, however, his imprisonment for counterfeiting "a character" represented a betrayal of the cause of American liberty that was, he insisted, intended to allow every man to form his own character:

> How is this, said I to myself, that a country which has stood the foremost in asserting the cause of liberty, that those who have tasted the bitter cup of slavery, . . . should so soon after obtaining that blessing themselves, deprive others of it. I know that it will be said, that for my crimes I am deprived of liberty, which is according to every dictate of justice; whereas America was only struggling for her natural rights, when exercising the principle of virtue (p. 98).

In this age when sinners are declared more sinned against than sinning, Burroughs demands to know why he is not vouchsafed that dispensation. One answer may be that the new nation feared counterfeiting out of a deep concern lest America itself was counterfeit: an impostor in a world of genuine nations. Another is that for the eighteenth century his was the one unpardonable sin: the seduction of mind.

To imprison men like Burroughs was one way of ensuring the mind's chastity; to attempt to thwart the passage of mesmerism across the Atlantic as Jefferson sought to do was another; education, of course, still another.[40] Yet just as no measure of protection seemed adequate, some were claiming none were necessary. In 1783, the year of the Peace, the *Annual Register* published an extract from a new book on taste by Hugh Blair, the popular Scottish rhetorician and aesthetician. Blair defines the concept that preoccupied virtually all late eighteenth-century writing on aesthetics: "A man of correct taste is one who is never imposed on by counterfeit beauties; who carries always in his mind that standard of good taste which he employs in judging of everything."[41] Taste, like the moral sense a generation earlier and Coleridgian "reason" a generation later, was a faculty conjured up to comfort the man of the new age, to give him the pleasing illusion of moral certainty and infallible judgment in a chaotic and subjective world.

One such comforter was the eighteenth-century German novelist and belle-lettrist Cristoph Martin Wieland, whose name and reputation Brockden Brown very consciously sought to invoke in his novel of the same name. One of Wieland's most important essays (and one Brown surely had in mind) was a defense of enthusiasm published in 1775. The defense turned on the distinction in German between *Enthusiasmus,* the result of the "immediate perception of the beautiful, the good, the perfection and the divine in nature, in our own souls," and *Schwärmerei,* "an excitation of the soul by objects which either do not exist in nature or are at least not those things which the intoxicated soul thought them."[42] Wieland's essay reflects the optimistic faith of the 1770s that the two could be easily distinguished. By the time Brown is writing, several years after Paine had insisted that the book of nature should supersede Scripture because no "counterfeit" could be made of the former, that faith had been called into question decisively.

The loss of that faith and the transformation in perspective symbolized by the contrast between Franklin's *Autobiography* and *Wieland* are dramatically reflected in the contrast between American relations with France first during America's revolution and later during France's. Perry Miller has observed that "The French Revolution brought home to the devout an immediate realization of the need for disassociating the Christian concept of life from any blind commitment to Revolution."[43] The story of that disassociation, of the transformation of America's great ally of 1778 into America's greatest threat – a story taken up earlier in the chapter – must now be returned to in greater detail. For it dramatically helps clarify both the final fate and ultimate significance of the American revolution against patriarchal authority.

FROM POLITICAL TO MORAL INDEPENDENCE:
THE TRIUMPH OF NEUTRALITY

The affections Britain had alienated were transferred to France, which served an emotional as well as a military function in the American Revolutionary period. France's Minister for Foreign Affairs, Count Vergennes, wrote in his account of the period: "The American people turned to France deliberately and gave her their affection."[44] The "Treaty of Amity," concluded in 1778, declared: "There shall be a firm, inviolable and universal peace, and a true and sincere friendship between the Most Christian King, his heirs and successors, and the United States of America."[45] Here was the "sincere friendship," the "amity," America had been unable to secure from Britain, the fraternal bond that would replace the abrogated bond of blood. As Minerva, the national symbol of France, was cast as a surrogate parent in the iconography, "the good and great" Louis XVI, "the protector of the rights of humanity against tyranny," was hailed in language later to be applied to Washington.[46]

In a letter to Patrick Henry written in 1778, Richard Henry Lee announced "the salvation to America depends on our holding fast" to France.[47] Defoe's *The True-Born Englishman* (originally written in 1701 as a rebuttal to the parliamentary resolution to limit the British Army to "natural born subjects") significantly appeared for the first time under an American imprint in 1778.[48] Defoe's contention that the only "True-born Englishman" was "that man a-kin to all the universe" seemed addressed to the anxious fears of those who opposed the French connection. An alliance with a Catholic and monarchical nation would not corrupt American purity, for that Catholic and monarchical nation was America's friend.

A national Francophilia following the Treaty of 1778 was reflected in the choice of French names for children and towns, in advertisements for French singing and dancing masters.[49] But perhaps no instance of the acceptance of French culture in America during the years following the Great Alliance is more symbolically significant than the decision of the Harvard faculty in 1782 to allow undergraduates to substitute French for Hebrew in satisfaction of the final language requirement.[50] If there was one nation with which colonial America identified almost as strongly as it did with Britain, that nation was Israel. To join the fraternity of "moderns," America was obliged not only to sever her filial attachment to an aging parent but also her typological attachment to the most ancient of nations. France served as surrogate for both Israel and Britain. France was Naomi to America's Ruth.

As early as 1775, however, there were dissenting voices to the proposed alliance. Not only was France monarchical and Catholic, but as late as 1763 it had been the avowed foe of the British colonies in the fight for control of the continent. Tories such as Joseph Galloway accused the colonies of committing the fatal error of the prodigal and the sentimental heroine in believing a "truer friend" than one's parent might be found "abroad": "Do you wish to exchange the mild and equal rule of English custom and manners and your inestimable religion for the tyranny of a foreign yoke and the bloody superstition of popery?" asked Galloway in *A Candid Examination of the Mutual Claims* (1775).[51] The previous year, Samuel Sherwood had warned against "the temptation to succumb to the old filthy harlot" and, mixing his metaphor, he announced to France that "the Daughters of Zion despise you."[52] Anti-Catholic anxieties were not the only prejudices advanced against the French Alliance. Daniel Dulany in his *Discourse of the Times* declared the entire idea of a protector to be idolatrous and heretical; for was it not declared in Romans 8:31: "If God be for us, who can be against us? Surely, if God be for us, we need not apply to France, Spain or Prussia for protection, for the blessed God will protect us."[53] In the context of a providential view of history the argument was a powerful one. But the fact remained that America was without a navy in 1778. French ships on the waters were more reliable than the hand of God.

Most of the dissent prior to the Treaty of Alliance abated after 1778, and Francophilia (with its attendant Anglophobia) held a portion of the nation in its sway for the whole of the next decade. The news of the storming of the Bastille in 1789 intensified the sense of spiritual fraternity, inspiring Americans to sentiments akin to those expressed by one Pennsylvanian: "By this and yesterday's papers France seems travailing in the birth of Freedom. Her throes and pangs of labor are violent. God give her a happy delivery."[54] In that same year, however, the Federalist administration led by Washington but controlled in large part by Hamilton had formulated a neutralist foreign policy, which declared that a fraternal attachment to one country to the exclusion of others was inconsistent with the self-interest of the nation. In the sphere of international trade, friends and allies must not be given special privileges, lest politics interfere with the national prosperity. Thus, at the first session of the First Federal Congress, convened in New York in April of 1789, an amendment was proposed and passed that did away with the discrimination in trade between foreign nations in and out of treaty and the official designation of a "most favored nation" status. Yet, as we know from the journal kept by William Maclay, a senator from Pennsylvania, no issue was passed over more strident opposition. The great point of contention between "the party of interest and its opponents . . . of principle" was the role that gratitude should play in international relations. As the following entries from his journal make clear, Maclay led the forces for "principle":

> I asked, if we were not called on by gratitude to treat with discrimination those nations who had given us a helping hand in the time of distress. . . . I was, however, answered from all sides. All commercial treaties were condemned. It was echoed from all parts of the House that nothing but interest governed all nations.
> . . . .
> I alleged . . . that nations in treaty were on terms of friendship; that strangers had no right to be offended at acts of kindness between friends. She might be a friend, if she pleases, and enjoy these favors. On the contrary, I thought our friends were the people, who had a right to be offended if no discrimination took place. It had been asserted that interest solely governed the nation. I was sorry it was so much the case. . . . The conduct of France to us in our distress, I thought was founded, in part, on more generous principles. Had the

principle of interest solely governed, she would have taken advantage of our distress.

. . . .

The answer 'no' has been given to the calls of gratitude in this business.[55]

In the eyes of Maclay and his party, the passing of such "villainous amendments" was practically a repudiation of the theory of republicanism. For, as we have observed in an earlier section, Montesquieu and others had set forth gratitude as the only viable motive for obedience in a republican government and, consequently, its sacred principle. The Scots, positing a more involuntary model, had suggested the same thing. Maclay, whose "gratitudinarian" party was later to evolve into the Democratic party (the party of sentiment), mockingly speaks in the voice of his opponents:

> Gratitude no governing principle among the *humanum pecus*. Fear only the parent of obedience among the herd of mankind. The hangman in this world and the devil in the next. Republican theories are well enough in times of public commotion or at elections; but all sensible men once in power know that force is the only effectual means to secure obedience (p. 118).

Ultimately what had been renounced in the vote of April 1789 was a view of mankind as innately good and benevolent and possessing a trustworthy moral sense. The alternate view of man as *humanum pecus* would remain, at least for the next dozen years, the legislative assumption of the government of the new nation. To the question "What is the best lesson in moral philosophy?" Farrago, the hero of Hugh Henry Brackenridge's *Modern Chivalry* (1792–1815), declares: "To expect no gratitude."[56]

The debate between gratitudinarians and the party of interest, however, had only just begun in 1789. In fact, the proper relationship of America to France was to become the most important political issue of the 1790s and the focus of a larger debate as to the character of the American nation. After the execution of Louis in 1793 and its consequent alienation of American sympathy, the issues of the debate shifted and the pressing theoretical question became whether or not a debt of gratitude was owed to a nation or to a nation's leader. For if such a debt were ad hominem, the death of Louis would have absolved America effectively from any such debt believed to be owed its "ancient friend."

Joseph Lathrop was one of the many who found such a view unacceptable and made his thinking clear in his July Fourth sermon of 1796. "To France we owe," he declared,

> unbounded gratitude . . . she burst in all the radiance of her power, upon our dreary situation and illumined our passage to the haven of

> freedom. . . . Can we check the tears that gratitude claims, when in mournful idea, we visit the dank dungeon of Lafayette and listen ˙ ˙ the clinking of his chains?[57]

In his Thanksgiving sermon delivered some months earlier, John McKnight, despising the partial politics of interest, voiced similar sentiments; though Louis had been beheaded, the debt is still owed his nation:

> I am one of those who believe that there are such things as national as well as individual honor. . . . I believe that the argument against our obligation to France is palpable and absurd sophistry and it is the office and not the man, the nation and not the regime which is owed.[58]

"The office not the man." Here was the English view of gratitude and of inherited obligation against which the antipatriarchal revolution had been fought, come back to make new demands of the American moral conscience.

The party of interest, of Lockean contractualism, had the longer memory. The politics of affection and gratitude were too dangerous to be embraced. They had to be resisted. In his passionate July Fourth oration of 1799, John Lowell, an arch anti-Jacobin, argued persuasively that the debt of gratitude was not absolute, but must be evaluated by a higher moral criterion. He sought to turn the moral argument of the gratitudinarians back on themselves:

> From the treaty of 1778 to the present, these Gratitudinarians have stunned our ears with the magnanimity, the disinterested benevolence of monarchial and anti-monarchial France.
>
> In former times, gratitude was considered as a relative, personal and National virtue. It was a generous sentiment flowing from the tenderest feelings of the heart of the person who received, towards one who conferred a benefit. In the vocabulary of modern philosophy it has a directly opposite meaning. Accordingly in this new light, an inhuman doctrine, we are to love the persecutors of our parents. . . . Are we to cherish murder and thievery as fresh stimulation to . . . grateful sentiments?[59]

What was owed Louis XVI must not be paid to Robespierre. Gratitude is an emotion excited by a particular individual. As it is not a debt, it cannot be transferred. America must not be victim again of a new emotional blackmail.

Two years later, William Dunlap used identical logic to make the corollary Federalist point: As gratitude must not be transferred, so neither must animosity. The new and unborn generations of Britons who had taken no part in the war must be forgiven.

> Still may our children's children deep abhor
> The motives, doubly deep detest the actors;

Ever remembering that the race who plann'd
Who acquiesced, or did the deeds abhor'd,
Has pass'd from off the earth; and, in its stead,
Stand men who challenge love or detestation
But from their proper, individual deeds.
Never let memory of the sire's offence
Descend upon the son.[60]

[handwritten margin note: Generation versus creation]

The Federalist argument for conciliation with Britain drew upon the same distinction between generation and creation that Paine had made twenty years earlier. Having fought to free the colonial son from the sins of the father and to establish the principle of the autonomy of each generation, Americans ironically were urged – in their first application of the revolutionary principle of political affairs – to absolve the sons of their former enemy. The politics of interest demanded, in Washington's phrase, that both "habitual hatred" as well as "habitual fondness" be banished from international relations. All emotional bonds must be broken. Here were the issues of Dunlap's *André* come alive.

In his "Pacificus" papers written in defense of Washington's Neutrality Proclamation, Hamilton, then Secretary of the Treasury, argued that Republicans who favored an alliance with America's old ally France had confused the issue by collapsing two very different arguments: the moral demands of gratitude and the obligation to support the cause of liberty. He like so many others sought to clarify the true nature of gratitude:

> Between individuals, occasion is not unfrequently given to the exercise of gratitude. Instances of conferring benefit from kind and benevolent disposition . . . without any other interest on the part of the person who renders the service, than the pleasure of doing a good action, occur every day among individuals. But among nations they perhaps never occur. It may be affirmed as a general principle, that the dominant motive of good offices from one nation to another is the interest or advantage of the nation which performs them.
>
> Indeed the rule of morality in this respect is not precisely the same between nations as between individuals.[61]

Here is the crux of the issue: Were nations to be considered a species of being wholly distinct from individuals and thus free from the moral code by which men must live, or as individuals writ large and individuals with an excitable moral sense at that? For Hamilton, quoting Dryden, gratitude in politics was "this shrine" at which "we are continually invited to sacrifice the true interests of the country: as if 'All for love and the world well lost' were a fundamental maxim in politics."[62]

Though the rhetoricians of the Revolution denounced the patriarchal version of the parent–child metaphor that sought to bind colonists with the claims of gratitude, their denunciation was intended to affirm rather than to deny the necessity of natural affections as a motive force in international relations. The adolescent must be permitted to become an adult, but adult nations must then interact with feeling and honorable sentiment. Federalists stood aghast at the naiveté of such a view. Had not the lesson of the war been that nations must stand vigilant against the enslavement of affectional politics? For Hamilton, the war had freed America not only from habitual debts and false bonds of gratitude but from the very obligation to act disinterestedly. In the Federalist view, what educated reason was to individuals, self-interest was to nations. "The science of policy," Hamilton wrote, "is the knowledge of the human nature. . . . Take mankind as they are, and what are they governed by? Their passions. . . . Our prevailing passions are ambition and interest; and it will ever be the duty of a wise government to make them subservient to the public good."[63]

➚ Only if self-interest were allowed to serve as a fence to national virtue and national autonomy might America safely participate in the international trade that Federalists declared essential to her survival. In *The Deserted Village,* Goldsmith had bemoaned the decline of England as a self-dependent power and the rise of "trade's proud empire." But no nation in the mid-eighteenth century realistically could remain, as had the village of "Sweet Auburn," a self-sufficient entity. In a mercantilist world, national wealth was measured not by internal resources but a favorable balance of trade. The necessity of international trade now rendered the nations of the world dependent on one another while, at the same time, obliging them to seek their own preservation in self-interest. Even Goldsmith himself was to draw such a conclusion in *Letters from a Citizen of the World.* The luxury he had condemned earlier is identified by "The Citizen" with the positive values of growth and prosperity:

> Examine the history of any country remarkable for opulence and wisdom; you will find they would never have been wise had they not been first luxurious; . . . The reason is obvious: we then only are curious after knowledge when we find it connected with sensual happiness. . . . In short, we only desire to know what we desire to possess. . . .
>
> But not our knowledge only, but our virtues are improved by luxury. . . . The greater the luxuries of every country, the more closely, politically speaking, is that country united. Luxury is the child of society alone . . . it is more likely, therefore, that he should be a good citizen who is connected by motives of self-interest with so many, than the abstemious man who is united to none.[64]

Rather than corrupt them, luxury makes men virtuous and social. Here was an argument that turned the Puritan ethic on its head and seemed to some to jeopardize America's future.

Captain Seward, the passionate rebel of Dunlap's play *André*, prays to God that "impassable barriers" seal forever the severed worlds of America and Europe so that America may never again "by villainy seduc'd" be laid waste by Europe's "mercenary son" (p. 21). M'Donald, an older and wiser officer, points out his naiveté:

> Prophet of ill,
> From Europe shall enriching commerce flow,
> And many an ill attendant; but from thence
> Shall likewise flow blest science. Europe's knowledge,
> By sharp experience bought, we should appropriate;
> Striving thus to leap from that simplicity,
> With ignorance curst, to that simplicity
> By knowledge blest; unknown the gulf between. (p. 22)

Whereas Seward fears that mercantilism and self-interested politics will precipitate a national fall from innocence, M'Donald, the spokesman for stoical Federalism, argues that, on the contrary, "sharp experience" can be bypassed and the unknown gulf avoided by pursuing a national policy of self-interest unrestrained by false debts of honor. As long as irrational affections are not admitted to the national heart and sympathy for the favorite nation, facilitating the illusion of an imaginary common interest guarded against, the American garden may open itself to intercourse with the world and yet remain uncorrupt. No longer could the dissemblers and seducers – the Lovelaces, the Talleyrands, the Arnolds, and the Carwins – pose a threat in a world where self-interested motives were assumed; no longer could American affection be alienated.

Believing the only true unity in the world to be the unity of the human species, Republicans in the decade of the nineties were far less concerned than Federalists with the cause of a powerful and self-sufficient national union. The Republicans clung to the hope that America, now freed from Britain, might participate in a republican harmonization of the world – in the cultivation of a world family. Federalists agreed with their opponents that harmony and liberal intercourse with all nations were recommended by policy, humanity, and interest. But the point was *how* to cultivate peace and harmony with all. In an international context, affectional or sentimental attachments were necessarily political attachments, and political attachments necessarily divisive. Whereas European nations must depend on one another, Washington observed: "Our detached and distant situation invites and enables us to pursue a different course." The intention of Providence in providing America with her geographical detachment was to oblige her to "steer clear of permanent alliances" and to "resort to temporary alliances" only for "extraordinary emergencies."[65] The great cause of the nation was the unity, purity, and liberty of its own union and not the unity, purity, and liberty of the world – America was not a part but a whole.

In 1798, the Alien and Sedition Acts were signed into law and the 1778 Treaty of Alliance officially dissolved. On the first anniversary of that dissolution – July 17, 1799 – Robert Treat Paine, prosecutor at the Boston Massacre trial and signer of the Declaration of Independence, delivered the most powerful oration of his career. If dissolution with Britain had marked America's birth, then, Paine declared,

> the period, which sundered our alliance with France, may be pronounced the day of our nation's manhood; when the Genius had become a Hercules who, no longer amused with the coral and bells of "liberty and equality," no longer "pleased with the rattles, tickled with the straws" of "health and fraternity," . . . boldly invested himself in the *toga virilis* and assumed his place in the forum of nations.
>
> . . . .
>
> The Fourth of July will be celebrated by our latest posterity as the splendid era of our national glory, but the Seventeenth will be venerated as the dignified epoch of our nation. The one annihilated our colonial submission to a powerful, avowed and determined foe; the other emancipated us from the oppressive friendship . . . of a treacherous ally. The first asserted our political supremacy . . . the latter . . . a declaration of our moral superiority.[66]

Having been delivered from the "ecstatic rapture" of her "hug fraternal" and France's "syren charms," the American Hercules might now set about his own chosen labors and offer thanks to "Our guardian Washington, who like Uriel descending on the sunbeam, discerning the latent fiend enter our paradise, had called an alarm" and purged the garden.[67] American foreign policy of the next quarter century sought to secure the garden, to permit America to develop that economic self-sufficiency requisite to its eventual progress into a safe and confident reengagement of the world. But how was America to know with assurance at what point it had attained to such self-sufficient manhood? Washington had fatally neglected to describe to his children the signs that might be trusted. And in the meantime in a world where trade agreements necessitated political agreements, a policy of neutrality and isolationism was, in its own way, as naive and dangerous to national survival as blind engagement. The security of "bars and doors" was, as *Wieland* made clear, no more than a dream.

⋇ During the first decade of the new century, France and England once again engaged in a war for European trade. In the course of that conflict both nations insisted that America not trade with the other, and both abused the rights of American seamen. In retaliation and in an effort to remain neutral, the United States cut off trade relations with both nations. But such neutrality proved self-destructive. One historian narrates the story this way:

> After holding out a promise to trade with whichever belligerent would repeal its obnoxious measures, Congress in May, 1810, resolved to trade with both; it authorized the President, if either France or Great Britain should reform its practices, to revive the non-intercourse against the other. On the strength of what appeared to be an assurance from Napoleon, that the objectionable decrees were revoked in so far as they affected the United States, Madison on November 2, 1810 naively issued a proclamation of non-intercourse against Great Britain. The error was not the only cause of the War of 1812.[68]

But it was among the most important. American trust had once again been betrayed.

Among the posthumous papers of Madison was discovered a note entitled "Advice to My Country." Perhaps compelled by a haunting guilt over his tactical error of 1810, Madison restated the great Washington caution: "The advice nearest to my heart and deepest in my conviction is that the Union of the States be cherished. Let the open enemy of it be regarded as a Pandora with her box opened and the disguised one as the serpent creeping with his deadly wiles into Paradise."[69] War had to be avoided at all cost, because, as Henry Adams was to observe in his history of the period, the dominant conviction of the nation was that war caused irrevocable harm to the morals of mankind: "The reign of brute force and brutal methods corrupted and debauched society, making it blind to its own vices and ambitions only for mischief."[70]

To keep Satan from entering Paradise, all foreign powers, friendly or otherwise, must be excluded from the American continent. But even that was not security enough. When it seemed possible in 1823 that a Franco–Spanish alliance was about to send an expeditionary force to South America, President Monroe promulgated the doctrine that bears his name opposing further colonization of the Americas. The old world serpent was to be excluded from the shores of the *entire* Western Hemisphere – at least until America had achieved its political and economic manhood.

Washington's Farewell Address with its opposition to alliance and treaty had closed the garden, but was it the father's wish that it be closed permanently? The answer was clearly "no," as the address itself made explicit:

> With me, a predominant motive has been to endeavor to gain time for our country to settle and mature its yet recent institutions and to

progress without interruption, to that degree of strength and consistency which is necessary to give it, humanely speaking, the command of its own fortunes (p. 237).

Notwithstanding Hamilton's attempt to make neutrality a permanent policy, America might, indeed, once again embrace international alliance *and* freedom. But it must await its manhood before attempting the fall. Yet the question remained: At what point would intercourse with and attachments to the Old World be safe? Or, put another way, how was America to know when it had reached its maturity and manhood? The test was unspecified. The Farewell Address, that sacred legacy of the nation's father and the ideology it reflected, left the first generation of Washington's children insecure and fearful about its own manhood, unsure of the term of its adolescence. Adolescence and America, those kindred eighteenth-century "inventions," had perhaps in some fundamental manner become overidentified with each another. In Joel Barlow's *Columbiad* (1807), Hesper warns Columbus (the New World's Telemachus), and by extension nineteenth-century America:

> Man is infant still; and slow and late
> Must form and fix his adolescent state,
> Mature his manhood and at last behold
> His reason ripen and his force unfold.[71]

Here was no nation "born at once" capable of achieving manhood in a generation. America was still an untried infant.

Prepared or not, America was obliged to unfold its force in 1812, and its inordinate fear of the moral consequences of war was counterbalanced by a new sensation. Henry Adams describes the American response to the news that their ship the *Constitution* had defeated the British *Guerriere:*

> With the shock of new life, they awoke to the consciousness that after all the peace teachings . . . they could still fight. The public had been taught, and had actually learned to doubt its own physical courage; and the reaction of delight in satisfying itself that it still possessed the commonest and most brutal of human qualities was the natural result of a system that ignored the possibility of war (p. 270).

Yet still, as the Monroe Doctrine suggests, the fear of European corruption and engagement remained too deeply ingrained to be dispelled. Consequently, America remained confused as to the proper definition of its national manhood. Was manhood synonymous with self-sufficiency or the ability to live interdependently with the world? Was it achieved, as Robert Treat Paine suggested, the moment all worldly attachments were broken or in the moment the nation once again had become confident enough to embrace fully and ardently yet another relationship? The former ideal was Edenic and separatist; the latter, rational and Lockean. It was to be the latter to which Washington ultimately subscribed, but it was to the former view his orphaned child-nation in its own self-glorifying defense had chosen to subscribe. Or so at least seems to be the suggestion of our national literature.

There are two great and complementary morals that permeate much of nineteenth-century American prose: One may be said to be epitomized in the career of Fenimore Cooper's Natty Bumppo, who was introduced to America during the year of the Monroe Doctrine; the other epitomized in the fate of Henry James's Daisy Miller, that latter-day sentimental heroine who fatally chose to do "what she liked."

Natty leaves family behind and flees the progress of civilization by venturing forth into the forest where he undergoes a wilderness initiation into self-sufficient manhood. Like Bunyan's Christian fleeing the wrath to come, he has broken "the cords with which men of my race are bound to their lodges" and demonstrated that as long as there is a frontier, American innocence, supplemented by a good heart and extricated from both family and world, might survive in the wilderness.[72] The Roman death of Daisy Miller testified to the supplemental truth. It is *only* in the wilderness or in a self-contained provincial America that such innocence may survive; for once abroad or in society innocence can survive neither its intercourse with the world nor the contaminating touch of European history.

Written during the centennial of the French Revolution, Herman Melville's *Billy Budd,* a meditation on the meaning of that revolutionary era, places that direful discovery in the 1790s. Born in 1776 Budd, the quintessential innocent whose birth date associates him with the idealism of the American Revolution, must be sacrificed in 1797, in the year of his majority. Impressed from the *Rights of Man* onto the *Bellipotent* and, subsequently, falsely accused of fomenting a mutiny among the impressed men, he is sentenced to death. The sight of Budd's hanging, the death of the "peace maker," so awes the crew that they were "without volition, as it were." For at least a moment the force of character and innocent virtue is proven a greater "impressment" than the force of law and a rigorous discipline.[73] Yet only in death is Budd allowed his greatest glory. Only neutrality and isolation will preserve American innocence and virtue in a world at war.

THE NEW FAMILY AS THE NEW WORLD

The ultimate legacy of Lockean rationalism for the Western world was an intensified fear of the power of sympathy, of noncontractual or affectional relations – relations based on trust and involuntary fellow-feeling rather than on declared and calculated common interest. Such relations led to a dependence that compromised rational autonomy and violated the Puritan insistence that one rely on the Creator and not the creature. In his eulogy on Washington, John Tyler reminded his audience that since all men must die, to place one's trust in even the most perfect earthly creature cannot but lead to renewed anxiety: "Impress Dependence on thy will; that we may learn to cease from him whose breath is in his nostrils. . . ."[74] Both definitions of national manhood suggested above – as self-sufficiency and as self-assurance – followed Lockean theory in assuming a world that must be distrusted lest heart and mind be seduced, one into which a child may be allowed to enter only after his reason has been developed by the ministrations of a tutor or parent committed to preparing him for that world.

Yet at the same time, Lockean pedagogy encouraged a new parental solicitude, an engaged and emotional commitment to one's children and their future, which militated against both rational relations between generations and the final parental letting go. In violation of its own rationalist emphasis, it encouraged the manipulation of heart and mind as well as manipulation of will. Thus did it, especially in its Rousseauistic modification, suggest the terms of a new emotional or affectional authoritarianism by which the old-style family might, in effect, be reconstituted. Parents who could manipulate their children's emotions and bind their hearts need not resort to more overt imposition of their will. The new and more benign Mr. Harlowes would learn their strategy from Lovelace.

J. H. Plumb has noted in this regard that an "exceptionally common theme" in eighteenth-century English children's literature is "cruelty to a mother bird by the taking or destruction of her eggs."[75] If seventeenth-century children's literature preached the Fifth Commandment by threatening death and damnation to the disobedient, its eighteenth-century counterpart made the scriptural injunction all the more terrifyingly immediate by dramatizing the vulnerability of the parental heart. One finds this sentiment in *The Happy Family . . . Intended to Shew the Delightful Effects of Filial Obedience,* published in Philadelphia in 1799: "I would rather do anything than offend my papa and mama for they do look so unhappy when we are naughty, so cheerful when we are good, that I cannot bear to disobey them."[76] Though the new sensibility conferred upon children "the power to make your parents and yourself happy or sad" (p. iv), it impressed upon them the terrifying responsibility attendant on that power. No longer might filial disobedience result only in the damnation of a child, but now, too, in the death of a parent. Such was the guilt-inducing message of more than several of those eighteenth-century deathbed paintings. Filial disobedience becomes a species of parricide, a heartbreaking betrayal of love.

The scriptural proof text for this new version of the Fifth Commandment is Genesis 42:38. When famine had come upon his land, Jacob had sent his grown sons to Egypt where, unbeknownst to them, Joseph, their brother whom they had sold into slavery, had won his freedom and become prosperous. Pretending that he feared them to be spies and not petitioners for grain, Joseph demanded that his brothers return home and bring to him their youngest brother Benjamin as surety. Though he later relented, Jacob adamantly refused to surrender his youngest son. His already broken heart could not endure the prospect of losing another son. "But," he said, "my son shall not go down with you, for his brother is dead, and he is left alone. If mischief befall him by the way in the which ye go, then shall ye bring down my gray hairs with sorrow to the grave." No single biblical verse was to have more influence on eighteenth-century familial fiction than Jacob's final statement. It would become the argument of a new parental tyranny or overprotective solicitousness – the hidden hand reaching for the vulnerable heart. As the following examples will demonstrate, Jacob's verse would be echoed in French, English, and American literature.

In Rousseau's *La Nouvelle Héloïse,* Julie's mother dies shortly after Julie has revealed that she has fallen in love with her tutor. In a role reversal that could never have appeared in Richardson, M. d'Etanges perversely plays the returned prodigal in order to accuse his daughter of matricide.

> He found that I was determined and that he should make no impression on me by dint of authority. For a minute I thought myself freed from his persecution. What became of me when I suddenly saw the most rigid father softened into tears and prostrate at my feet? Without suffering me to rise, he embraced my knees and fixing his streaming eyes on mine, he addressed himself to me in a plaintive voice which still murmurs in my ears: O my child have some respect for the gray hairs of your father. Do not send me with sorrow to the grave of her who bore thee. Will Eloisa be the death of all her family? (III, 102)

Having learned of her daughter's seduction, the wife·of Goldsmith's Vicar cannot restrain herself:

> "She is an ungrateful creature," cried my wife, who could scarce speak for weeping, "to use us thus. She never had the least constraint put upon her affections. The vile strumpet has basely deserted her parents without provocation, thus to bring your grey hairs to the grave and I must shortly follow" (p. 86).

When confronted with her suitor's demand to leave the parental roof with him, Charlotte Temple, the heroine of the most popular eighteenth-century American novel, declares: "But I can not break my mother's heart, Montraville; I must not bring the grey hairs of my doting grandfather with sorrow to the grave, or make my father perhaps curse the hour that gave me birth."[77] When Tom Sawyer was younger, Aunt Polly would whip him, but now that he is older, rather than addressing him rationally, she reverts to another tactic.

> After breakfast his aunt took him aside and Tom almost brightened in the hope that he was going to be flogged; but it was not so. His aunt wept over him and asked him how he could go and break her old heart so, and finally told him to go on and ruin himself and bring her gray hairs with sorrow to the grave, for it was no use for her to try anymore. This was worse than a thousand whippings and Tom's heart was sorer now than his body.[78]

There may be said to be two varieties of parental tyranny in the sentimental novel—one patriarchal, one Lockean. So may there be said to be two varieties of heroine—martyr. Caught between the ingratitude of seducer and the severity of parents, the Richardsonian heroine receives too late the pardon of her penitent parents and thus dies in heroic isolation, a death of sorrow and faith. A later incarnation of the seduced and abandoned heroine is forgiven her credulity by benevolent parents but is either so terrified of grieving the guardians of her infancy or so reproached by a parent's kindness that she either dies of shame or chooses, as does the heroine of Hannah Foster's *The Coquette* (Boston, 1797), to end her own life:

> Oh Madam! Can you forgive a wretch, who has forfeited your love, your kindness, and your compassion? Surely, Eliza, said she, you are not that being! No, it is impossible. But however great your transgression, be assured of my forgiveness, my compassion and my continued love. . . . Oh, this unmerited goodness is more than I can bear. . . .
>   Yes, Madam, your Eliza has fallen. . . . She flies from you, not to conceal her guilt, that she humbly and penitently owns but to avoid what she has never experienced, and feels herself unable to support, a mother's frown; to escape the heartrending sight of a parent's grief occasioned by the crimes of a guilty child.[79]

It is a parent's grief, not anger, authority, or indifference, that is feared in the postpatriarchal family. Eliza's mother asks rhetorically: "Where can she find that protection and tenderness, which, notwithstanding her great apostasy, I should never have withheld. From whom can she receive those kind attentions which her situation demands?" (p. 224). She is soon given her answer. Eliza writes:

> This night, therefore, I leave your hospitable mansion! This night I become a wretched wanderer from thy paternal roof. Oh, that the

grave were this night to be my lodging – then should I let down and be at rest trusting in the mercy of God, through the mediation of his son. I think I could meet my heavenly father with more composure and confidence than my earthly father. (p. 236).

Eliza kills both herself and the child she is carrying, the "monument of her sin." She embraces the Deity not because she has no one else to call by "the tender name of parent" but because she *has*. It is the sensitive parent, not Paine's "unfeeling" parent, from whom one now must flee.

Ultimately, however, both varieties of martyrs – Richardson's Clarissa and Foster's Eliza – are victims of a sentimental code that elevated children to such a sacred position as to make their honor identifiable with the honor of their family. They are victims of what Philippe Ariès has described as the tyrannical character of the "new" family relations of the eighteenth century:

> Family and school together removed the child from adult society. The school shut up a childhood which had hitherto been free within an increasingly severe disciplinary system. . . . The solicitude of family . . . deprived the child of the freedom he had hitherto enjoyed among adults. It inflicted on him the birch, the prison cell . . . in a word, the punishments usually reserved for convicts from the lowest strata of society. But this severity was the expression of a very different feeling from the old indifference: an obsessive love which was to dominate society from the eighteenth century on.[80]

The eighteenth-century family organized "itself around the child and raised the wall of private life between the family and society." It thus "satisfied a desire for privacy and also a craving for identity: the members of the family were united by feeling, habits, and their way of life. They shrank from the promiscuity imposed by the old sociability" (p. 413). As the loss of the family had been the price of choosing the world in Puritan picaresques like *Crusoe,* so the price of choosing the family is the loss of the world, a sense of anxious separateness from it. In 1775, the year whose events we have spent so much time examining, the British Patent office issued the first patent for an indoor water closet. As America was about to declare its independence of Britain, the family was about to be permitted to sever yet one more link with the world out-of-doors.[81]

The wall enclosing the parental garden beyond which the prodigals and fallen daughters of eighteenth-century fiction dared not tread is, in a real sense, identical with what Ariès describes as "the wall of private life between the family and society." The power of sympathy against which both Locke and Washington warned as a threat to independence is no less than the forbidden impulse to embrace once again "the old sociability." Yet, as the eighteenth century extolled the closed garden of the family, it also longed for the sense of community, of whose loss it was deeply aware. The preoccupation with sentimentality, benevolence, self-love extended, stewardship, republican fraternity, the sociable instincts of the soul, and, in the world of music, the "philoharmonium" or symphony orchestra with its utopian harmonization of disparate instrumental voices,[82] all attested to this profound sense of loss. That loss was not only of the organic society Burke eulogizes, but of the assurance of reality as well as that easy commerce of minds, which the new philosophical skepticism so sharply called into question. Embittered at the acquisitive machinations of her family, Clarissa spoke the silent sentiment of her age: "And yet, in my opinion the world is but one great family. Originally it was so. What then is this narrow selfishness that reigns in us, but relationship remembered against relationship forgot?" (I, 41).

Surely it is Richardson's point that if the "one great family" has been lost it cannot be rediscovered on earth. Clarissa must go to heaven to find it; on earth, the part must serve as the whole. Now one great masked ball, the public world can never be returned to its once familial character. The family becomes its own world, a world both unlost and perfectible. As the dream of a postmillennial universal family must be surrendered to achieve the safer, more practical goal of perfecting the nuclear family relationship, so piety must give way to moralism in religion and universalism to nationalism in politics. Having escaped a false parent to embrace a true one, having sworn allegiance to a universal reason under God, the American nation had only to seal itself off from the temptations of sociability and cherish its glory, its imprisonment of independence. The cost of that independence would be the failure to learn what Rousseau in *Emile* described as the "one art absolutely necessary to a civilized man, the art of living among his fellow men" (IV, 204).

In his Farewell Address, Washington concluded:

> It is of infinite moment that you should properly estimate the immense value of your national Union to your collective and individual happiness; – that you should cherish a cordial, habitual, and immovable attachment to it; . . . watching for its preservation with jealous anxiety; discountenancing whatever may suggest even a suspicion that it can in any event be abandoned, and indignantly frowning upon the first dawning of every attempt . . . to enfeeble the sacred ties which now link together the various parts (p. 219).

The sacred national union isolated from the world recapitulated the sentimental nuclear family isolated from society. Yet whereas the former was, at first, contractual, the idealization of the latter silently undermined the dream of a voluntaristic family. The point is made

descriptively in "Amelia," a tale published within months of the ratification of the Federal Constitution, the document that bound the states
in a union so sacred that three-quarters of a century later thousands
would be killed to preserve it:

> Around the smiling swain, are ranged a happy family: his wife, fair as
> a rose, when first the blushing spring sprinkles the balmy leaf with
> moistening dew, sat near him decked in the rural robe of native ele-
> gance; she scorned the wanton dress of luxury high pampered; her
> simple garb proved what modest nature lent, and heightened graceful
> charm; smiling on her knee, an infant played and laughed at the gay
> wrens, singing on aerial boughs; pleased, he joins the strains' response
> and in his little notes salutes the feathered strangers; both parents clasp
> the prattler to their breast by turns, and melt away in raptures of
> supernal bliss, and elder branches of the tree parental, sport around
> their fire or quaff maternal smiles.[83]

Here is the sealed garden of the nuclear family for which the world is
well lost. At its heart is the paternal tree sporting its filial branches. The
organic metaphor of a rooted, interdependent, and hierarchical society
so central to the conservative vision has triumphed over Locke's contractual paradigm for family and society.[84] The image of the familial tree
suggests the immutable and "immovable attachment" to union Washington had called for in the Farewell Address, while at the same time
denying the possibility of subsequent filial revolution or future dis-
union. For parents and children are organic parts of one another: the
branch cannot be cut off and survive. And what the branch is to the
tree, the tree is to a larger, infinitely benign natural world. The only
strangers are the wrens with whose song the child is easily able to
harmonize his own song. As children "quaff" their mother's smile, so
too, one imagines, does the wren sip his morning dew. Nature is parent
and parental love and nurture no more than the processes of nature.
There is no corrupting luxury here, only rural simplicity; no serpent
with hypnotic charm, only graceful charm and recaptured prelapsarian
bliss; no designing art but nature's own, and, in the dark sense of the
word, no designer at all, only the familial tree of life.

The idyllic picture of the self-contained and naturalized family reflects
the optimistic mood of the year of the Constitution's ratification. After
the establishment of the new "national family," it is not surprising that
American literary journals began to be more critical of, rather than
sympathetic to, the attack against parental excesses conducted by sentimental fiction. In 1798, *The Weekly Magazine* condemned novels in
which "parents are described as cruel and obdurate, thwarting the inclinations of their children." Four years earlier another journal asked how
children were to reconcile depictions of parents who "are daily offering

up the honor and happiness of their children at the shrine of interest and ambition" with their own presumably very different American experience of the parental garden.[85]

Having fought the Revolution in order to break the familial bond and to escape the enforced separation from the world, the liberated colonies embraced another familial bond in order to separate yet again from the world. Rejecting Dr. Pangloss's optimism – the tutor is exposed a fool – the new nation concluded with Candide that as the world is a moral disaster "we must cultivate our gardens."[86] Many years later as it was becoming clear that the bonds of national union might not long endure, Nathanial Hawthorne would argue in his troubling story, "Rappacini's Daughter," that the new Edenic garden, far from being tended by God and directed by the hidden hand of nature and nature's laws, had become, like Dr. Frankenstein's laboratory in Mary Shelley's earlier work, a place of dark experimentation and deviance from nature, a place where nurture had gone mad.[87] But the garden in the passage above has no hidden hand and the new nation, far from believing itself Hobbes's "artificial man," will protest itself "nature's nation" with the power to "naturalize" its immigrants.

⊁ On the twenty-fifth anniversary of the American Revolution and a year after Washington's death, William Richardson of Amherst in his July Fourth sermon looked back over the whole course of American history. He suggested an analogy between the Puritan departure in 1630 to find freedom "amid the wolves and wilds"[88] of America and the departure of Adam and Eve from Eden. Altering "world" to "wilderness," Richardson applied the penultimate lines of *Paradise Lost* to the Puritan enterprise as Defoe, Fielding, and Samuel Richardson had applied them to the garden expulsions of their heroes and heroines the century before: "The wilderness all before them, where to choose / The place of rest, and Providence their guide" (p. 6). The winning of the Revolution, Richardson suggested, had made clear the fortune in the Fall, the liberty made possible by separation.

> But the arduous labors of the sons of liberty found not here an end.
> They had torn the branch from the parent trunk, but to make it
> flourish, independent of that trunk and relying only on its own
> strength for the sap and the nurture, was still a task of much diffi-
> culty (p. 7).

By 1801, however, that task of self-nurture had, in Richardson's view, been all but completed. The self-sufficient paradise had now been regained. The transplanted branch miraculously surviving its separation from what Crèvecoeur calls "the parent roots" (p. 52) becomes the new familial tree, emblematic of the new nation. It has at last found its proper nurture.

The rising glory of America had proven to be the fortune long promised and now provided the earliest European prodigals, the first fallen. America was the Canaan to which God's providence had led. It was a macrocosm of the rehabilitated nuclear family, that original ideal of the antipatriarchal revolution, that great compensation for the fall from universal sociability. It was Crusoe's island, Clarissa's heaven, the Panther heroine's cave; at once a vast wilderness garden made continent by sea and shining sea, an asylum from the world where a new society could be begun, and a city of God whose children of God were charged with the preservation of virtue.

For some, however, that Edenic garden was also imprisoning, the "parental clasp" confining, and the "supernal bliss" stifling: the world ill-lost. The pantheon of Revolutionary heroes, the godlike founding fathers, intimidated subsequent generations too young to remember the war and yet raised to reverence the nation's saviors. Feelings of filial inferiority contributed to the desire many felt to be free of the demands of filiopietism and to find a stage for their own heroism. Denying that it could be taught, Emerson defined the new self-reliance as the substitution of tuition with intuition, imitation with self-expression, and habit with genius.[89] Like the new idealist philosophy, the West itself beckoned with its frontier promise of a new independence and an original relation not to family or to nature but to the universe itself.[90] Laden not only with hopes and dreams but also with anger, frustration, and guilt for leaving home, millions responded, thus enacting yet another antipatriarchal revolt.

The American revolution against patriarchal authority in the second half of the eighteenth century provided the paradigm by which Americans for the next two hundred years would understand and set forth the claims of both individual and national independence. Whether that glorious independence necessitated separation from the world or encouraged communion with it would remain, however, a question with which each generation would have to struggle. Only by understanding the overarching revolution of the eighteenth century, which formed the infant character of American culture, can we begin to appreciate the profound historical significance of that ongoing struggle.

NOTES

INTRODUCTION

1 Kenneth Lynn, *A Divided People* (Westport, Conn.: Greenwood Press, 1977), p. 68.
2 The most thorough recent treatments of this phenomenon are Lawrence Stone's *The Family, Sex and Marriage in England, 1500–1800* (New York: Harper & Row, 1977), esp. Parts III and IV, and Randolph Trumach, *The Rise of the Equalitarian Family: Aristocratic Kinship and Domestic Relations in Eighteenth-Century England* (New York: Academic Press, 1978). Philip Greven's *The Protestant Temperament: Patterns of Child-Rearing, Religious Experience, and the Self in Early America* (New York: Knopf, 1978) attempts a similar analysis of American materials. Greven, however, rather than arguing a fundamental shift in the nature of the family and family relations in the eighteenth century, calls attention to what he sees to be the simultaneous presence throughout the colonial period of three distinctive modes of childrearing that correlate with three very different attitudes toward the self and its importance and, finally, with what he describes as the three fundamental American temperaments – Evangelical, Moderate, and Genteel (see esp. pp. 12–14). Though full of fascinating analysis and insights, Greven's book is severely hampered by his insistence on viewing the primary data of American family history apart from the intellectual and cultural history of the period. See also John Walzer, "A Period of Ambivalence: Eighteenth-Century American Childhood," in Lloyd deMause, ed., *The History of Childhood* (New York: Psychohistory Press, 1974), pp. 351–82; and Carl N. Degler, *At Odds: Women and the Family in America from the Revolution to the Present* (New York: Oxford University Press, 1980), pp. 86–110. Still further documentation of the new parent–child relations is to be found in Mary Beth Norton's *Liberty's Daughters: The Revolutionary Experience of American Women, 1750–1800* (Boston: Little, Brown, 1980), pp. 71–109, and Daniel Blake Smith's *Inside the Great House: Planter Family Life in Eighteenth-Century Chesapeake Society* (Ithaca: Cornell University Press, 1980), pp. 25–54. Noting the similarity of findings in the work of Degler, Norton, and Smith, Lawrence Stone concludes a review of the latter volume: "It therefore seems an established fact that there was a fundamental

psychological and social change in family life in this gentry sector of the Anglo-Saxon world in the mid-eighteenth century." *The New York Review of Books,* vol. XXVIII, no. 1 (February 5, 1981), p. 35.

3 Alexander Pope, "Moral Essay," First Epistle, lines 149–50, in *The Works,* 9 vols., (London, 1751), III, 182.

4 William Cowper, *The Task: A Poem in Six Books,* Bk. II, lines 771–9 (Philadelphia, 1787). The lines are applied to the American scene in Robert Coram, *Political Inquiries: To which is Added, a Plan for the General Establishment of Schools throughout the United States* (Wilmington, 1791), p. 84.

5 Stone, *The Family, Sex and Marriage,* pp. 225–39.

6 Immanuel Kant, "What Is Enlightenment" in *The Enlightenment: A Comprehensive Anthology,* ed. Peter Gay (New York: Simon & Schuster, 1973), p. 383.

7 Immanuel Kant, *Education* (Ann Arbor: University of Michigan Press, 1971), p. 6.

8 See Saul K. Padover, ed., *The Complete Jefferson* (New York: Tudor Publishing Company, 1943), p. 29, for a facsimile of the revised manuscript page. For a superb treatment of the generational issue in Jefferson's writing see Harold Hellenbrand, "The Unfinished Revolution: Education and Community in the Thought of Thomas Jefferson," Diss. Stanford University, 1980.

9 William Blackstone, *Commentaries on the Laws of England,* 4 vols., (1765–1769; rpt. University of Chicago Press, 1979), I, 441.

10 Of *Some Thoughts concerning Education,* J. H. Plumb has commented: "This was by far his most popular book; it was reprinted nineteen times before 1761 and was as well known in America as it was in England." "The First Flourishing of Children's Books" in *Early Children's Books and their Illustration,* comp. Charles Ryskamp (Boston: Godine, 1975), p. xvii.

11 Kenneth Silverman, *A Cultural History of the American Revolution* (New York: Crowell, 1976), pp. 82–4. See also Gordon Wood's classic argument that especially in revolutionary situations "it does seem possible that particular patterns of thought, particular forms of expression correspond to certain basic social situations" in "Rhetoric and Reality in the American Revolution," *William and Mary Quarterly,* ser. 3, XXIII (1966), 3–32.

12 Henry F. May, *The Enlightenment in America* (New York: Oxford University Press, 1976), pp. vii–xix. The contents analysis is contained in Henry F. May and David Lundberg, "The Enlightened Reader in America," *American Quarterly,* XXVI (1976), 262–72. See Chapter 2, n. 7. My emphasis throughout this book on the intimate relations between education and politics follows the lead of the final chapter of Peter Gay's *The Enlightenment: An Interpretation,* 2 vols. (New York: Knopf, 1960–9), II, 497–555.

13 James Axtell, ed., *The Educational Writings of John Locke* (Cambridge University Press, 1968), cf. p. 148. All future citations in the text to Locke's *Education* are from this edition.

14 Leslie Fiedler, *Love and Death in the American Novel* (New York: Criterion, 1960), p. xvii.

15 My book may be seen as offering a case study of Thomas Kuhn's concep-

tion of a complex paradigm revolution or fundamental shift in world view. In Kuhnian terms my study presents an interdisciplinary account of the interaction and conflict between a new affectional paradigm of social relations and an older patriarchal paradigm. The rhetoric of the American Revolution and of many of the great eighteenth-century texts of Anglo-American culture (as well as the emergence of the novel as a new literary form) are part of the same project of articulating that new paradigm and responding to the anomalies of the old. See Thomas S. Kuhn, *The Structure of Scientific Revolutions,* 2nd ed., enlarged (University of Chicago Press, 1970), esp. pp. 66–92. See also two important applications of Kuhn, with respect to the world view assumed by historical language: J. G. A. Pocock, *Politics, Language and Time: Essays on Political Thought and History* (New York: Atheneum, 1973), pp. 3–42 and 104–48, and Gene Wise, *American Historical Explanation: A Strategy for Grounded Inquiry* (Homewood, Ill.: The Dorsey Press, 1973). Michel Foucault's concern with historical discontinuities has much in common with Kuhn's arguments. See, for example, *The Archaeology of Knowledge and the Discourse on Language,* trans. A. M. Sheridan Smith (New York: Harper & Row, 1976), esp. pp. 3–17.

1. EDUCATIONAL THEORY AND MORAL INDEPENDENCE

1 Samuel Richardson, *A Collection of the Moral and Instructive Sentiments, Maxims, Cautions and Reflections Contained in the Histories of 'Pamela,' 'Clarissa,' and 'Sir Charles Grandison,' Digested under Proper Heads* (London, 1755), p. vi.

2 These subject heads have been drawn from Richardson, *A Collection,* but similar ones may be found in *Miscellanies for Sentimentalists* (Philadelphia, 1786), *The Beauties of Sterne* (Philadelphia, 1789), *The Beauties of Fielding* (Boston, 1792), and *The Beauties of Poor Richard's Almanack* (Boston, 1760).

3 These findings are summarized from James A. Henretta, *The Evolution of American Society, 1700–1815* (Lexington, Mass.: Heath, 1973), pp. 23–31, 132–4. See also Degler, *At Odds,* Chapter 1.

4 Henretta, *Evolution of American Society,* p. 30.

5 David Hackett Fischer, *Growing Old in America* (New York: Oxford University Press, 1978), p. 96. Fischer argues that there was a substantial loss of social status suffered by the elderly in America in the period 1770–1820. He cites among other evidence "the invention of a new language to express contempt for old people." Words like "fogy" and "greybeard," he claims, emerge in this period. See pp. 77–112 and, as a caution, 253 n30.

6 Raymond Williams, *Keywords: A Vocabulary of Culture and Society* (New York: Oxford University Press, 1976), pp. 108–10. Mills is quoted on p. 110.

7 Philippe Ariès, *Centuries of Childhood: A Social History of Family Life,* trans. Robert Baldick (New York: Random House/Vintage Books), 1962, p. 411.

8 Christopher Hill, *Society and Puritanism in Pre-revolutionary England* (New York: Schocken Books, 1972), p. 466. On this subject in general see also Michael Walzer, *The Revolution of the Saints* (Cambridge: Harvard Univer-

sity Press, 1965), esp. pp. 49 and 55, and Stone, *The Family, Sex and Marriage*, pp. 83–119.

9 Alleine quoted by Hill in *Society and Puritanism*, p. 450.

10 The best and most comprehensive account of Locke's educational theory is to be found in James Axtell's introduction to his edition of *The Educational Writings*, cited above. On the Puritan background to Locke's writings see Richard L. Greaves, *The Puritan Revolution and Educational Thought: Background to Reform* (New Brunswick: Rutgers University Press, 1969). In "Of Education," Milton anticipates Locke's insistence on accommodating the specific capacities of youth. He directs his attack against "The scholastic grossness of barbarous ages, that instead of beginning with arts most easy . . . present their young unmatriculated novices . . . with the most intellective abstractions of logic and metaphysics." Merritt Y. Hughes, ed., *John Milton: Complete Poems and Major Prose* (Indianapolis: Bobbs-Merrill, 1957), p. 632. All citations to Milton are from this edition.

11 John Locke, *An Essay concerning Human Understanding*, ed. A. S. Pringle-Pattison (London: Oxford University Press, 1953), p. xii. Professor Pringle-Pattison problematically argues that what Locke is objecting to is less a theory of innate ideas than more particularly the principle of self-evidence. It is, as we shall see, this experiential bias of Lockean thought that, when linked to an intense Protestant emphasis on the "experimental" character of efficacious faith, would help eventually expedite the development of a revolutionary ideology in America.

12 Axtell, ed., *The Educational Writings*, p. 111.

13 For a contemporary account of the degree to which the denial of divine right found its moral basis in a preexisting constitutional tradition, see *The New Cambridge Modern History*, vol. VI, ed. J. S. Bremley (Cambridge University Press, 1970), p. 217.

14 See the entries for "govern" and "governour" in the *Oxford English Dictionary*.

15 Quoted in Gay, *The Enlightenment: An Interpretation*, II, 512.

16 Leslie Stephens quoted in A. D. Nuttall's *The Common Sky: Philosophy and the Literary Imagination* (Berkeley: University of California Press, 1974), p. 19.

17 John Trenchard and Thomas Gordon, *Cato's Letters*, 4 vols. in 2 (New York: Russell & Russell, 1969), III, 330–1.

18 See Book III, "Of Words," of *An Essay concerning Human Understanding* and Locke's opposition to education based on memorization in Axtell, ed., *Educational Works*, pp. 157–8, 285–6.

19 In his authoritative volume *American Education: The Colonial Experience* (New York: Harper & Row, 1970), Lawrence Cremin cites the relevant *Spectator* and *Tatler* numbers in the course of his brief account of Lockean ideas. He concludes: "the journals were full of Lockean exhortations about proper parental training and Lockean criticism of the tyranny of schooling" (p. 367).

20 Daniel Defoe, *The Family Instructor in Three Parts* (1715–1718; New York, 1795), p. 5.

21 Peter Earle, *The World of Daniel Defoe* (London: Weidenfeld & Nicolson, 1976), p. 210. Earle's chapter "The Making of the Individual" is most valuable. See also Levin L. Schucking's useful *The Puritan Family: A Social Study from the Literary Sources,* trans. Brian Battershaw (New York: Schocken Books, 1970), pp. 89–90.

22 On Watts's influence in America see Cremin, *American Education,* p. 506. On Watts's hesitant Calvinism see Paul Ramsey's intoduction to Jonathan Edwards, *The Freedom of the Will* (New Haven: Yale University Press, 1957), pp. 91–4.

23 Isaac Watts, *The Improvement of the Mind* (1741; Edinburgh, 1801), pp. 376–7.

24 Locke's understanding of the stages of growth to rational adulthood drew on Roman distinctions between *infantia* (to age 6), *pueritia* (7 to 13), and *pubertas* (14 to 20).

25 Isaac Watts, *Logick or The Right Use of Reason* (1725; London, 1760), p. 3.

26 Philip Doddridge, *The Rise and Progress of Religion in the Soul . . . also subjoined A Plain and Serious Address to a Master of a Family* (1745; Northampton, Mass., 1804), p. 338. For a more political presentation of Doddridge see Caroline Robbins, *The Eighteenth Century Commonwealthman; Studies in the Transmission, Development and Circumstance of English Liberal Thought from the Restoration of Charles II until the War of the Thirteen Colonies.* (Cambridge: Harvard University Press, 1959), pp. 218–19.

27 James Burgh, *Thoughts on Education* (London, 1747), p. 3.

28 James Burgh, *The Dignity of Human Nature* (1754; Hartford, Conn., 1802), 68.

29 James Burgh, *The Art of Speaking* (1762; London, 1768), pp. 2–3.

30 James Burgh, *Britain's Remembrancer or The Danger Not Over* (London, 1746), p. 3.

31 Thomas Sheridan, *British Education* (1756; Dublin, 1766), p. 384.

32 Burgh, *Thoughts on Education,* p. 58.

33 Milton, *Paradise Lost,* Bk. XII, lines 586–7. See James Burgh, *Youth's Friendly Monitor* (1754; Hartford, 1787), p. 3.

34 Bernard Bailyn, *Education in the Forming of American Society* (New York: Norton, 1972), p. 49.

35 Francis Hutcheson, *A System of Moral Philosophy* (Glasgow, 1755), II, 112. My discussion draws on the excellent introductory essay to Louis Schneider, ed., *The Scottish Moralists on Human Nature and Society* (University of Chicago Press, 1967). Also see Gladys Bryson, *Man and Society: The Scottish Inquiry of the Eighteenth Century* (Princeton University Press, 1945), and D. H. Monro's useful anthology, *A Guide to the British Moralists* (London: Fontana Books, 1972).

36 Hutcheson, *Illustrations Upon the Moral Sense,* in Monro, *A Guide,* p. 264. Hutcheson goes on to argue the inadequacy of "assigning as the ultimate Reason both exciting to and justifying the Pursuit of publick Good" the proposition "It is best that all should be happy." "Best," he continues, "is most good; good to whom? To the whole or to each individual? If to the former, when this truth excites to action, it must presuppose kind affections. If it is good to each individual, it must suppose self-love."

37 Hutcheson is building on Hume's earlier insistence that reason chooses the means by which our ends are achieved; passion determines the choice of those ends. See David Hume, *A Treatise of Human Nature,* 2 vols., ed. T. H. Green and T. H. Grese (London, 1898), II, 195.

38 Ferguson and Stewart both cite the passage. See Schneider, *Scottish Moralists,* pp. 78, 92.

39 "Moral Philosophy" (unsigned), in *Encyclopaedia Britannica or a Dictionary of Arts and Sciences,* 3 vols., by a Society of Gentlemen in Scotland (Edinburgh, 1771), III, 270.

40 Garry Wills, *Inventing America: Jefferson's Declaration of Independence* (New York: Doubleday, 1978). See especially Part III. For example, Wills's opposition might fruitfully be applied to an analysis of the parties favoring and opposing the Great Awakening in New England. The opposition is further testified to by the crucial congressional debate between "gratitudinarians" and "men of interest," described in Chapter 8 of this work. Wills's argument has been severely called into question by Ronald Hamowy in "Jefferson and the Scottish Enlightenment: A Critique of Garry Wills's *Inventing America: Jefferson's Declaration of Independence,*" *William and Mary Quarterly,* 35, no. 4 (October 1979), 503–23.

41 On this general subject see Schucking, *The Puritan Family,* Chapters III and IV.

42 Henry Home, Lord Kames, *The Elements of Criticism,* 2 vols. (1762; Boston 1796), I, 55.

43 Samuel Richardson, *Pamela or Virtue Rewarded,* 2 vols. (London: Dent, 1962), II, 399. All citations to *Pamela* are from this edition. On the popularity of *Pamela* in America, James Hart comments: "*Pamela* was by far the most popular of all fiction, followed by his other novels. . . . [even] Jonathan Edwards read *Pamela* and gave it to his daughter." *The Popular Book: A History of American Literary Taste* (New York: Oxford University Press, 1950), p. 55.

44 Robert A. Feer, "Imprisonment for Debt in Massachusetts before 1800," *Mississippi Valley Historical Review,* 48 (1961), 256. See also Peter J. Coleman, "Insolvent Debtors in Rhode Island, 1745–1828," *William and Mary Quarterly,* ser. 3, 22 (1965).

45 Leonard W. Labaree; ed., *The Papers of Benjamin Franklin,* 21 vols. (New Haven: Yale University Press, 1959–), VII, 341.

46 Arthur Friedman, ed., *The Collected Works of Oliver Goldsmith,* 5 vols. (Oxford University Press, 1966), IV, 101.

47 "The Puritan Ethic and the American Revolution" collected in Edmund S. Morgan, *The Challenge of the American Revolution* (New York: Norton, 1976), pp. 95–6.

48 Quoted in Christopher Hill, "Clarissa Harlowe and Her Times," in *Essays on the Eighteenth Century,* ed. Robert Donald Spector (Bloomington: Indiana University Press, 1965), p. 34.

49 For a fuller treatment of Richardson's novel and its reception in America, see Chapter 3, "Two Views of the Fall: *Clarissa* in America."

50 Robert Adams Day, *Told in Letters: Epistolary Fiction Before Richardson* (Ann

Arbor: University of Michigan Press, 1966), p. 49. On this point see also
Ian Watt, *The Rise of the Novel: Studies in Defoe, Richardson and Fielding*
(Berkeley: University of California Press, 1957), p. 189.

51 Patricia Spacks, *Imagining a Self: Autobiography and Novel in Eighteenth Century England* (Cambridge, Mass.: Harvard University Press, 1976), pp. 313,
25.

52 Rousseau, *Emilius and Sophia, or a New System of Education*, 4 vols. (Lon-
don, 1762–3), I, 125. All citations are from this edition and translation.
On the impact of *Emile* in America see Paul Merrill Spurlin, *Rousseau in
America 1760–1809* (University, Ala.: University of Alabama Press), p. 75:

> No book of Rousseau's appears to have been advertised more often by
> American booksellers than *Emile*. The survey in the second chapter
> makes this clear. It was available in English in Philadelphia as early as
> 1763, in Williamsburg in 1765, and in New York City in 1773. At one
> time or another, it could be purchased from Rhode Island to Georgia.
> The book was on the shelves of Library Societies. Harvard had it by
> 1774.

Spurlin also mentions the degree to which *Emile* influenced the second
American novel, Hitchcock's *The Memoirs of the Bloomsgrove Family*, from
which we have quoted earlier. David Lundberg and Henry May in "The
Enlightened Reader in America" report that thirty-eight percent of the
library holdings and bookseller's catalogues they investigated for the period
1777–90 included *Emile*.

53 Lester Crocker, *Jean-Jacques Rousseau*, 2 vols. (New York: Macmillan,
1973), II, 135. My reading of Rousseau throughout is much indebted to
Crocker's treatment. On "la main cachée" see II, 136. For the darker side
of eighteenth-century "social engineering" and the new theories of control
see the brilliant but overstated arguments of Michel Foucault in his chapter,
"The Correct Means of Training," in *Discipline and Punish: The Birth of the
Prison*, trans. Alan Sheridan (New York: Random House/Vintage Books,
1979), pp. 170–94.

54 Gordon S. Wood, *The Creation of the American Republic* (Chapel Hill: University of North Carolina Press, 1969), pp. 40–1.

55 In his *Origin and Progress of Language* (1773–92), Lord Monboddo uses Peter
to illustrate his theory of the progressive development of man.

56 Carole Fabricant, "Binding and Dressing Nature's Loose Tresses: The Ideology of Augustan Landscape Design," in *Studies in Eighteenth-Century Culture*, vol. 8, ed. Roseann Runte (Madison: University of Wisconsin Press,
1979), p. 132.

57 *The Spectator*, 4 vols. (London: Dent, 1950), III, 406.

58 Robert Darnton, *Mesmerism and the End of the Enlightenment in France* (New
York: Schocken Books, 1970), pp. 3–4.

59 Brissot, quoted in ibid., p. 96.

60 Quoted in Crocker, *Jean-Jacques Rousseau*, II, 74.

61 Rousseau, *Eloisa: Or, a Series of Original Letters*, 4 vols. (London, 1776), I,
xlix. All citations are from this edition.

62 Ronald Paulson, "A Chapter from Tobias Smollett," *Tobias Smollett: Bicen-*

tennial Essays Presented to Lewis M. Knapp, ed. G. S. Rousseau (New York: Oxford University Press, 1971), p. 78.

63 Rousseau, *Political Writings,* ed. F. Watkins (London: Nelson, 1953), p. 4.

64 *The Papers of Benjamin Franklin,* VII, 342–3.

65 Charles Coleman Sellers, *Mr. Peale's Museum: Charles Willson Peale and the First Popular Museum of Natural History and Art* (New York: Norton, 1980), p. 22.

66 Ibid., pp. 26, 48.

67 For the best account of Edwards's position, which has affinities with the Scottish insistence on excited affections as antecedent to rational choice, see Paul Ramsey's Introduction to Jonathan Edwards, *Freedom of the Will,* pp. 11–47.

68 Quoted in Crocker, *Jean-Jacques Rousseau,* II, 139.

2. THE TRANSMISSION OF IDEOLOGY AND THE BESTSELLERS OF 1775

1 Though Watt surprisingly makes no mention of the *Education* or the educational theory context, the best treatment of the novel's emergence is still to be found in Ian Watt's *The Rise of the Novel,* pp. 35–59.

2 These titles are drawn from the bibliographical listings in Robert Mayo, *The English Novel in the Magazines, 1740–1815* (Evanston: Northwestern University Press, 1962), pp. 440–620, and Henri Petter, *The Early American Novel* (Columbus: Ohio State University Press, 1971), pp. 403–63.

3 Cited in Petter, *The Early American Novel,* p. 81.

4 Mrs. Patterson, *The Unfortunate Lovers and Cruel Parents . . . The Seventeenth Edition* (Boston, 1797), p. 11.

5 In their seminal study "The American Revolution: The Ideology and Psychology of National Liberation," Edwin G. Burrows and Michael Wallace cite over two hundred examples of familial language drawn mostly from the critical year, 1775. They conclude that:

> Colonial Americans accepted British authority because they saw themselves as the children of a powerful and protective mother country, an image which at once provided an ideological justification for obedience in natural law and an emotionally acceptable resolution of their feelings of inferiority and inadequacy. . . . A hardening of imperial policy in the early 1760s broke the spell of familial comity, however. . . . The colonists in America, bitterly disappointed with the mother country, discovered that the idea they were children of England could also be used to legitimate, still in natural law, their opposition to her policies; in a remarkably short time they were prepared, except for a Loyalist minority, to reject British rule altogether on the grounds that they had at last come of age, this belief, too, affording them the ideological sanction of natural law at the same time that it represented their emerging sense of collective and individual maturity.

Perspectives in American History 6 (1972), 287.

6 For the influence of Locke himself (as opposed to the popularizations of his

ideas) on eighteenth-century American education, and childrearing, see
Cremin, *American Education* pp. 370, 374; Greven, *Protestant Temperament,*
p. 160; and James Axtell's excellent volume, *The School Upon a Hill: Education and Society in Colonial New England* (New York: Norton, 1974), pp.
50–2. One contemporary comment that Greven misses about childrearing
techniques in revolutionary America is the following passage in Edmund
Quincy's biography of his father Josiah Quincy (1772–1863). The scene
described takes place in the year 1775:

> Josiah Quincy was not quite three years old when his father went
> away to die. His mother . . . was so scrupulously careful lest the
> passionate fondness of a young widow for her only son should over-
> flow in a hurtful indulgence, that she even refrained, as he used to tell,
> from the caresses and endearmei t which young mothers delight to
> lavish upon their children. This self-command was attended by no
> harshness or severity of manners. . . . He attributed the excellent
> health which he had during his long life to his good early training, and
> the correct physical habits he acquired under his mother's tuition. . . .
> Locke was the great authority at that time on all subjects which he
> touched, and in conformity with some suggestion of his, as my father
> supposed, Mrs. Quincy caused her son, when not more than three
> years old, to be taken from his warm bed, in winter as well as sum-
> mer, and carried down to a cellar-kitchen, and there dipped three
> times in a tub of water cold from the pump. She also brought him up
> in utter indifference to wet feet, – usually the terror of anxious mam-
> mas, – in which he used to say that he sat more than half the time
> during his boyhood, and without suffering any ill consequences. This
> practice, also, he conceived to have been in obedience to some sugges-
> tion of the bachelor philosopher.

Quoted from *The Life of Josiah Quincy* (Boston: Ticknor & Fields, 1865),
pp. 18–19.

7 Representative of scholarly thinking on this subject is Wilson Ober
Clough's *Intellectual Origins of American National Thought: Pages from The
Books Our Founding Fathers Read* (New York: Corinth, 1955). If one were
to judge from Clough's volume, our founding fathers read nothing but
political science and liberal religion. Even more disturbing is the reluctance
of Lundberg and May to consider literary texts as transmitters of Enlightenment ideas. In their description of the contents of eighteenth-century
American libraries they chose to ignore the frequency of appearance of
most literary texts:

> We are not attempting to determine which were absolutely the most
> popular books in America, but rather to find out which were the most
> popular among a selected list. We have not dealt for instance with the
> extremely popular works of novelists like Samuel Richardson, Lau-
> rence Sterne and Smollett. The list of books to be checked, the intel-
> lectual categories in which they are arranged and the checking periods
> were those which seemed most relevant to a study of the spread of the
> European Enlightenment in America.

"The Enlightened Reader," p. 164. Of the nine figures dealt with at some length in this section and the next section, May's *Enlightenment in America,* based on a selective contents' analysis, allots only Chesterfield more than a passing reference.

8 James D. Hart, *The Popular Book;* Frank Luther Mott's *The Golden Multitudes: The Story of Bestsellers in the United States* (New York: Macmillan, 1947). Narrower but equally useful are Howard Mumford Jones's two articles: "The Importation of French Books in New York, 1750–1800," in *Studies in Philology,* XXVIII (1931), 235–51, and its revealing companion, "The Importation of French Books in Philadelphia, 1750–1800," in *Modern Philology,* XXVIII (1934), 157–77. Jones is complemented by Bernard Fay, *The Revolutionary Spirit in France and America* (London: Allen & Unwin, 1928). May and Lundberg's article was, of course, not available to Burrows and Wallace. See also C. R. Kropf, "Availability of Literature to Eighteenth-Century Georgia Readers," *Georgia Historical Quarterly,* 63 (Fall 1979), 360–3. Kropf's examination of Georgia importation records shows literature and education titles steadily gaining on history and theology until the former categories constitute nearly 50 percent of *all* titles advertised by certain dealers.

9 Frank Luther Mott, *Multitudes,* p. 304; Charles Evans, *American Bibliography,* 14 vols. (Chicago: Blakely, Press, 1903–59), lists over 500 different titles published in the year 1775. See vol. 5. Because Mott's figures represent cumulative sales rather than those exclusively for a twelve-month period, James Hart has cautioned that the works on Mott's list are not necessarily the bestselling volumes of the year of their publication. Yet Hart's own analysis of "books most widely read in America" in the years immediately following their first (usually British) publication confirms the large scale popularity of all but one of the dozen volumes examined in this chapter. The only "bestseller" on Mott's list, which curiously he makes no mention of, is Gregory's *Letters,* the only book of the group having a separate edition in five of the eight war years. Indeed, in the year 1775 it had the highly unusual honor of having simultaneous editions in New York, Philadelphia, and Annapolis. See the entries under "Gregory" in Clifford K. Shipton and James E. Mooney, eds., *National Index of American Imprints Through 1800: The Short-Title Evans,* 2 vols. (American Antiquarian Society and Barr Publishers, 1969), which updates and alphabetizes Evans, American *Bibliography.* All future references to the printing record of titles appearing in eighteenth-century America draw on *The Short-Title Evans.*

It is not essential to the argument of this chapter that the volumes discussed are demonstrably the "absolute" bestsellers of the period, but rather that they fairly represent the character of Revolutionary reading taste. May, for example, argues that Pope and Addison were the most revered English writers in the colonies. Addison's "Spectator Papers," perhaps more than any other volume, gave Locke's ideas a wide audience. In their different ways, Pope and Addison no less than others discussed here popularized the values of the new pedagogy. Richard Beale Davis's *A Colonial*

Southern Bookshelf: Reading in the Eighteenth Century (Athens: University of Georgia Press, 1979) further confirms the popularity of the figures with whom I deal. Without footnotes Davis's book is, however, of limited use.

10 See Lord Chesterfield, *Principle of Politeness* (Boston, 1795), to which is annexed *A Father's Legacy*. Another anthologization of Chesterfield's maxims whose title is extremely suggestive is *The American Chesterfield or Way to Wealth . . . with Alterations and Additions Suited to the Youth of the United States* (Philadelphia, 1853). The title posits a composite preceptor – part Chesterfield and part Franklin.

11 On Goldsmith's and Sterne's popularity see Mott's *Multitudes*, pp. 40–1, 304, and Hart's *Popular Book*, pp. 60–1.

12 Fay, *Revolutionary Spirit*, p. 39. Of French books imported in the period immediately before the war, Fay concludes: "The most popular books were Marmontel's stories, the memoirs of Sully and above all, Fénelon's *Télémaque* and Rollin's histories, which were in current use in the English colonies and were everywhere praised for their right thinking." Whether the volumes to be examined were popular *because* of their "ideological" content cannot, of course, be demonstrated. Yet it may be safely assumed that such popularity presupposes a sympathy with their enunciated values.

13 Lord Chesterfield, *Letters to His Son* (London: Dent, 1929), p. 38. This *Everyman* edition – with some clearly indicated additions from later editions – reprints the original series of letters published by Chesterfield's wife in London in 1774, reprinted the following year in America.

14 Henry Fielding, *The Beauties of Fielding* (Philadelphia, 1792), p. iii.

15 L. H. Butterfield et al., ed., *The Book of Abigail and John: Selected Letters of the Adams Family* (Cambridge, Mass.: Harvard University Press, 1975), p. 88 and passim.

16 Edward Young, *Night Thoughts on Life, Death and Immortality* (Hartford, Conn., 1820), pp. 32–3.

17 Rousseau, *Eloisa*, IV, 108.

18 *The American Chesterfield*, p. 105.

19 The crucial tensions between the degenerative, the millennarian-progressive, and the cyclical views of history (the three views held in eighteenth-century·America) have been much too little investigated. One early study is Stow Persons's rebuttal to Carl Becker: "The Cyclical Theory of History in Eighteenth Century America" in *American Quarterly*, VI (1954), 147–63. Constantin Francois Volney's very influential *The Ruins or Meditations on the Revolutions of Empires* (1791) popularized a spiral theory of history that mediated between the cyclical and progressive views. Joel Barlow, Jefferson's associate, published a translation in 1795.

20 J. Logie Robertson, ed., *The Complete Poetical Works of James Thomson* (London: Oxford University Press, 1908), p. 45. The following antimonarchal couplet from Thomson appears on the title page of the first edition of *Common Sense* (Philadelphia, 1776): "Man knows no master save creating Heaven / Or those whom Choice and common good ordain." Franklin tells us he solicited God's assistance for his scheme of perfection by reciting

a prayer he took from Thomson's "Winter." See Leonard W. Labaree et al., eds., *The Autobiography of Benjamin Franklin* (New Haven: Yale University Press, 1964), p. 154. All future citations to the *Autobiography* are from this edition.

21 Charles Rollin, *Ancient History of the Egyptians* . . . (New York, 1796), p. 3. All citations are from this edition. On Rollin's popularity and influence see Lundberg and May, "The Enlightened Reader," appendix, n.p.

22 John Gregory, *A Legacy to His Daughters* (London, 1797), p. vi. All citations are from this edition. Gregory was a London physician. His *Lectures on the Duties and Qualifications of Physicians,* which had a London edition in 1775, has passages that make one suspect that his prototype for the good father was the physician who ministered to his patients until they were well enough to do without him – a version of Doddridge's teacher who seeks to make his students independent of him.

23 For the political dimension of eighteenth-century attitudes toward marriage and divorce see "Wedded Love and Revolutionary Ideology" in Chapter 4.

24 Bernard Bailyn, *The Ideological Origins of the American Revolution* (Cambridge, Mass.: Harvard University Press, 1967), pp. 144–59.

25 The phrase is from Alexander Garden's *Regeneration and the Testimony of the Spirit* (1741), which attacks Whitefield's theatrical style in Alan Heimert and Perry Miller, eds., *The Great Awakening* (Indianapolis: Bobbs-Merrill, 1967), p. 47.

26 *Cato's Letters,* II, 3.

27 Padover, ed., *The Complete Jefferson,* p. 35; Paul de Rapin-Thoyras, *The History of England,* 5 vols. (London, 1732–45), I, ii.

28 Julian P. Boyd, ed., *The Papers of Thomas Jefferson,* 19 vols. (Princeton University Press, 1950–), X, 309.

29 For, respectively, a rebel and Tory use of Sully see "Candidus," *Plain Truth* (Philadelphia, 1775), p. 14, and the *Pennsylvania Magazine* for December 1775, p. 189. For the Federalist appropriation of Sully as a "new Ancient" with whom to beat Republican moderns over the head, see Joseph Dennie, *The Lay Preacher* (New York: Scholars' Facsimiles and Reprints, 1943), p. 175:

> I look into the memoirs of Sully and into the age of Louis XIV. I read there interesting narratives of an illustrious prince, magnanimous nobles, erudite clergy and a gay people. . . . I lay aside my books and look at modern Paris. It is like peeping into the show-box of the vagrant Savoyard. Everything shows fantastic and puerile.

30 *The Beauties of Telemachus* appeared in eighteen parts in the *Universal Magazine of Knowledge and Pleasure,* LX (January 1777)–LXVI (February 1780). A full reprinting of the entire 153,000-word Hawkesworth translation appeared in another London journal, *The Novelist's Magazine,* XVII (1784). Salignac de la Mothe-Fénelon, *The Adventures of Telemachus, The Son of Ulysses,* 2 vols. (New York, 1800). All future citations are to this edition that reprints the 1769 English translation by the popular literary figure John Hawkesworth.

31 An account of Fénelon's Quietism may be found in the article devoted to

the author by the Viscount St. Cyres in the *Encyclopaedia Britannica,* 11th ed. (Cambridge University Press, 1910).

32 Kenneth Lynn has stressed the importance of the successful search for a second father in Jefferson's life. Having been orphaned at fourteen, "Thomas still felt the need for parental guidance." The figure who would satisfy that need was William Small, Jefferson's professor of natural history at William and Mary. Lynn concludes:

> Like the fathers of John Adams, Anthony Wayne, and other future leaders of the American Revolution, Professor Small believed that young personalities required a mixture of freedom and authority. It is no wonder that Jefferson regarded Small as "like a father" to him.

A Divided People, p. 73. Small was himself a student of John Gregory. The ideal father both guides and sets free.

33 Fénelon, *The Adventures of Telemachus* (Boston, 1794), title page. Nancrède was also an admirer of Rousseau and his *L'Abeille François ou nouveau recueil de morceaux brillans, des auteurs François les plus célèbres . . . à l'usage de l'université de Cambridge* (Boston, 1792) featured "extraits" from Rousseau's *Emile* as well as several other works.

Fénelon's popularity continued well into the nineteenth century. Writing in 1829, William Ellery Channing saw in the writings of Fénelon a version of the proto-transcendentalism he was drawn to embrace. For him, Minerva symbolized not so much human reason as a divine inner voice. He sets forth what he sees as Fénelon's essential lesson:

> The mind . . . is perfect, only in so far as it is self-formed. . . . The great aim of instruction should be to give the mind the consciousness and free use of its own powers. The soul often owes its best acquisitions to itself . . . glimpses of its own nature which it cannot trace to human teaching, from the whispers of a divine voice.

The Works, 6 vols. (Boston: James Munroe, 1848), I, 174.

In retrospect it seems far from surprising that when Andrew Jackson, the orphan who came to symbolize the self-made man in America, should choose to cover the walls of his Hermitage with wallpaper, he should choose imported French papers depicting scenes from Fénelon's *Telemachus.* See Plate 65 in Kate Sanborn, *Old Time Wall Papers* (New York: Literary Collector's Press, 1905).

34 Bernard Bailyn, *The Ordeal of Thomas Hutchinson* (Cambridge: Harvard University Press, 1974), p. 273.

35 The cartoon by John Singleton Copley is reproduced in Michael Wynn-Jones, *The Cartoon History of the American Revolution* (New York: Putnam, 1975), p. 25. For a brilliant reading of the relationship of this cartoon to Copley's later painting, *Watson and the Shark,* and to his anxious politics of neutrality, see Ann Uhry Abrams, "Prints, Politics and Copley's *Watson and the Shark,*" *The Art Bulletin,* 61, no. 2 (1979), 265–76.

36 Francis Hutcheson, *A System of Moral Philosophy* (London, 1755), II, 192; Anon., *The Hapless Orphan; or, Innocent Victim of Revenge* (Boston, 1793), p. 116; Madame de Genlis, *The Seige of Rochelle or the Christian Heroine,* 3 vols. (London, 1808), II, 132.

37 St. Preux, it must be noted, initially is reluctant to abuse his position of trust:

> What shall I in reality be to your father, in receiving from him a salary for instructing his daughter? Am I not from that moment a mercenary, a hireling, a servant? and do I not tacitly pledge my faith for his security, like the meanest of his domestics? Now what has a father to love of greater value than his own daughter?

Rousseau, *Eloisa or a Series of Original Letters,* I, 78.

38 Reprinted in *The Augustan Reprint Society Publication,* 48 (1954), xix.

39 As quoted in Sainte-Beuve's essay on Marmontel reprinted as a preface to Jean-François Marmontel, *The Memoirs* (New York: Dial Press, 1930), pp. xii–xiii. The following from the first chapter of Marmontel's *Memoirs* is sufficient to suggest to the reader the degree to which his autobiography and his fiction are related, both in fact and in his own mind:

> But what in my memory makes the charm of my home is the impression that remains of the early sense, filling and penetrating my soul, of the inexpressible tenderness my family had for me. If there is any goodness in my character, I think I owe it to these gentle feelings, to the constant happiness of loving and being loved. Heaven is indeed kind when it gives us good parents. I learned to read in a little convent of nuns who were good friends of my mother. They educated girls only, but made an exception to their rule for my sake. A well-born lady, who had lived for a long time in retreat in their asylum, was kind enough to take care of me. I ought to cherish her memory and that of the nuns dearly; for they loved me as their own child (pp. 2–3).

It was, of course, the reading of Marmontel's *Memoirs* that effected the famous conversion John Stuart Mill records in his *Autobiography.*

40 Marmontel, "The Errors of a Good Father," reprinted in *The Universal Magazine* XC (April–May, 1792), 319.

41 Mayo, *The English Novel,* p. 376.

42 Marmontel, *Moral Tales,* 2 vols. (1766; London, 1776), II, 6. All future references to Marmontel's *Tales* will be from this edition. One reason for Marmontel's popularity has to do with the genre in which he wrote. The concision of the "conte moral" must have found a ready audience among those who were sated with the multivolume didactic novels popular during the earlier part of the century.

43 Marmontel, *The History of Belisarius* (1767; Burlington, 1770). All future citations are to this edition. Two other American editions of Marmontel's novel appeared in the same year. In his essay "Marmontel et Belisaire" in *Jean François Marmontel,* ed. J. Ehard (De Bussac: Clermont-Ferrais, 1970), Jean Renwick makes the important observation that many contemporary readers of Marmontel's novel believed "Belisaire devait être le Telemaque du futur Louis XVI" (p. 60).

44 Quoted in Monica Keifer, *American Children Through Their Books* (University of Pennsylvania Press, 1948), p. 83.

45 The phrase is quoted in J. H. Plumb's Afterword to *The Vicar of Wakefield*

(New York: New American Library/Signet, 1961), p. 188. All future cita-tions to *The Vicar* in the text will be to Friedman, ed., *The Collected Works of Oliver Goldsmith*, vol. 4.

46 Fielding, *The Beauties of Fielding*, p. 59.

47 Henry Fielding, *Joseph Andrews*, ed. Martin Battesin (Boston: Houghton Mifflin, 1961), p. 265. It is worth noting that in the preface to his novel Fielding compares the "epic" form of his "romance" to that of Fénelon's *Telemachus* (p. 7).

48 *The Happy Child, or a Remarkable and Surprising Relation of a Little Girl* (Boston, 1774), p. 30.

49 On the subject of children's deaths, Mary Beth Norton deals briefly with "the conflict colonial parents felt between their own emotions and tradi-tional teachings of religion." *Liberty's Daughters*, p. 90.

50 Axtell, ed., *Educational Writings*, p. 165.

51 On inoculation debate see pp. 98–99.

52 J. H. Plumb, "The New World of Children in Eighteenth-Century En-gland," *Past and Present*, 67 (1975), 88.

53 Joseph Addison, *Cato*, in John Hampton, *Six Eighteenth-Century Plays* (New York: Dutton, 1928), p. 26; *The American Chesterfield*, pp. 108–9. See reprinted in the same volume "Dr. Watts' Advice to a Young Man on his Entrance into the World," pp. 224–31. Written a half-century before Chesterfield's *Principles of Politeness*, Watts's "Advice" opens with the fol-lowing conceit about its discovery. After the death of a particularly pious man named Curino, "a paper was found in his closet, which was drawn up by his kinsman in holy orders, and was supposed to have had a large share in procuring his happiness" (p. 224).

54 The observation is Martin Battesin's in his Introduction to *Joseph Andrews*, p. xxiv. Fielding's antagonism to Methodism and particularly to evangeli-cal itinerants such as Whitefield opposes his version of the eighteenth-cen-tury picaresque to the earlier Puritan picaresque of Defoe, which we shall discuss at length.

55 Berkeley's *New Theory of Vision* quoted in E. H. Gombrich, *Art and Illusion* (Princeton University Press, 1960), p. 297.

56 Laurence Sterne, *The Works*, 5 vols. (Philadelphia: Humphreys, 1774), IV, 237.

57 Laurence Sterne, *A Sentimental Journey Through France and Italy*, ed. Ian Jack (Oxford University Press, 1968), p. 11.

58 Quoted in W. B. Carnochan, *Confinement and Flight: An Essay on English Literature of the Eighteenth Century* (Berkeley: University of California Press, 1977), p. 191. Carnochan explores the philosophical-epistemological impli-cations of imprisonment motifs in eighteenth-century fiction and poetry.

59 Quoted in Daniel George's Introduction to Laurence Sterne, *A Sentimental Journey and the Journal of Eliza* (London: Dent, 1975), p. v.

60 *The Journal of John Woolman* (Gloucester, Mass.: Peter Smith, 1971), p. 3.

61 Wills, *Inventing America*, p. 273. He adds, "Sterne was taken far more seriously in the eighteenth century than we can readily believe at present."

62 On the subject of millennialism see pp. 190–191.

63 Noah Webster, "On the Education of Youth in America" (as well as other essays reproduced), in *Essays on Education in the Early Republic,* ed. Frederick Rudolph (Cambridge: Harvard University Press, 1965), p. 81.

64 Hector St. John de Crèvecoeur, *Letters from an American Farmer* (1782; New York: Dutton, 1957), letter 3.

65 Cited in Richard Seaver and Austryn Wainhouse, eds., *The Marquis de Sade* (New York: Grove Press, 1965), p. 69.

66 Sterne, *The Life and Opinions of Tristram Shandy, Gentleman,* ed. James Aiken Work (New York: Odyssey Press, 1940), pp. 5–6. All future citations from this edition. On Sterne and Lockean psychology see John Traugott, *Tristram Shandy's World: Sterne's Philosophical Rhetoric* (Berkeley: University of California Press, 1954).

67 *The Papers of Thomas Jefferson,* I, 178–82.

3. THE FAMILIAL POLITICS OF THE FORTUNATE FALL

1 *Emilius,* II, 63.

2 Cited in Keifer, *American Children,* p. 131.

3 *The Novels of Samuel Richardson,* 19 vols. (New York: Croscup & Sterling, 1902), IV, 211. All citations to the unabridged *Clarissa* are from this edition.

4 *The Works of Daniel Defoe,* 16 vols. in 8 (New York: The National Library, 1903), I, 14. Citations to all three volumes of *Crusoe* are from this edition, except where otherwise noted. For a related study of *Crusoe* in its Puritan context see G. A. Starr, *Defoe and Spiritual Autobiography* (Princeton University Press, 1965), pp. 74–125. See also Watt, *Rise of the Novel,* pp. 82–3.

5 Cited in Perry Miller, "The Moral and Psychological Roots of the American Rebellion," in *The Reinterpretation of the American Revolution, 1763–1789,* ed. Jack P. Greene (New York: Harper & Row, 1968), pp. 251–2.

6 Ibid., p. 157.

7 Henry Steele Commager, *The Empire of Reason: How Europe Imagined and America Realized the Enlightenment* (New York: Doubleday, 1978), p. xi.

8 Defoe, *The True Born Englishman* (Boston, 1778), p. 7. In light of my earlier discussion of the significance of "friendship" to rationalist ideology, it is worth noting Defoe's charge that England is a nation whose aristocratic acquisitiveness makes it unable to appreciate the sacred relation: "Friendship th' abstracted Union of the Mind / Which all men seek, but very few can find: / Of all the nations in the Universe, / None talk on't more, or understand it less: / For if it does their Property annoy / Their Property their Friendship will destroy" (p. 11).

9 The broadside is reproduced in Mason I. Lowance and Georgia B. Bumgardner, eds., *Massachusetts Broadsides of the American Revolution* (Amherst: University of Massachusetts Press, 1976).

10 Defoe, *The Wonderful Life . . . of Robinson Crusoe* (New York: Hugh Gaine, 1774), p. 97. In the same year as his *Crusoe,* Gaine issued a "juvenile" that in many respects may be said to serve as its "female" counterpart. The long title makes clear why: *The History of Little Goody Two-Shoes with the*

means by which she acquired her Learning, and Wisdom and in Consequence
thereof her Estate, set forth at large for the Benefit of Those
>*Who for a State of Rags and Care,*
>*And having Shoes but half a Pair*
>*Their Fortune and their Fame would fix,*
>*And Gallop in a coach for six.*

11 Defoe, *The Wonderful Life . . . of Robinson Crusoe* (Boston: R. Coverly, 1779), p. 31.

12 For example, *Tom Jones* appeared in a three-volume, 800-page edition issued by Johnson and M'Kensie in Philadelphia in 1794–95, a 131-page abridgment from Hall in Boston in 1797, and a 28-page chapbook from Thomas in Worcester in 1799. *The Short-Title Evans* lists a comparable range of editions of *Pamela*. For abridgments of *Clarissa* see my discussion below. In the *Autobiography* Franklin remarks that as a youth he sold his Bunyan volumes to buy "R. Burton's Historical Collections . . . small Chapman's books, . . . 40 or 50 in all" (pp. 57–8).

13 Defoe, *The Travels of Robinson Crusoe* (Worcester: Isaiah Thomas, 1786), p. 29.

14 See Charles Clarence Brigham's "Bibliography of American Editions of Robinson Crusoe to 1830" in *The American Antiquarian Society Proceedings* 67 (1958), 137–83. The virtues of Defoe's brand of Puritan stoicism would continue to be preached in nineteenth-century American fiction through the exemplary figure of the noble Red Man.

15 Johann Wyss, *The Swiss Family Robinson* (London: T. Nelson, 1871), p. 13. In his introduction to the above volume Charles Nodier makes the acute observation about the original *Robinson Crusoe*: "Of the three chief duties of an intelligent creature towards God, towards himself, towards the creatures who resemble him, Robinson Crusoe discharged the first two with admirable and touching fervor: he is tormented by the need of fulfilling the third."

16 Quoted in the unsigned article on Godwin in *The Encyclopaedia Britannica*, 11th ed.

17 Quoted in Pauline Maier, *From Resistance to Revolution: Colonial Radicals and the Development of Opposition to Britain, 1765–1776* (New York: Random House/Vintage Books, 1974), p. 47.

18 Paulson, "Tobias Smollett," p. 67.

19 Hill, "Clarissa Harlowe," p. 144.

20 Quoted in Paulson, "Tobias Smollett," p. 67.

21 For the popularity and colonial reception of *Clarissa*, see Mott, *Multitudes*, pp. 32, 38; Hart, *Popular Book*, pp. 52–9; and especially R. E. Watters, "The Vogue and Influence of Samuel Richardson in America; A Study of Cultural Conventions, 1742–1825" (Ph.D. diss., University of Wisconsin, 1941).

22 My account of editions follows the entries in *The Short-Title Evans*. The advertisement for the 1772 chapbook, though not cited as a "ghost" there, is so cited in Harry B. Weiss, "American Chapbooks, 1722–1842," *Bulletin of the New York Public Library*, 49 (1945), 590.

It is worth noting here that William Godwin in an autobiographical frag-
ment indicates that as an adolescent in the 1770s he occupied himself by
abridging Richardson. See William Godwin, *Italian Letters,* ed. Burton R.
Poulin (Lincoln: University of Nebraska, 1965), p. xii. No *English* edition
with the revised title I discuss appears in the National Union Catalogue. (The
British Museum Catalogue gives short titles only.) Those catalogues suggest
that the earliest English abridgments of *Crusoe* and *Clarissa* designed specifically for youth begin to appear in the late 1760s as, given the argument of this
book, one might expect. My point here and above is not to deny that
comparable British redactions exist – most American abridgments presumably had British sources. My point is that *only* such abridgments are published
in eighteenth-century America and that the American interest in these great
works coincides, most noticeably, with the phenomenon of editions "adapted
for youth." Scholars like Mott and Hart fail to recognize that their "popular
books" are popular in formats very different from what they imagine.

23 Richardson, *Clarissa* (Boston, 1795), p. 1.

24 William Hill Brown, *The Power of Sympathy* (Boston: New Frontiers Press,
1961), p. 38. Like Clarissa, Brown's heroine "Knew there was a God who
will reward and punish: She acknowledged she had offended him, and
confessed her repentance." Once again the reader is reminded that the
separation of parent and God is at the thematic heart of the sentimental/
Puritan tradition.

25 *Paradise Lost,* IX, 644.

26 Edward Gibbon, *The History of the Decline and Fall of the Roman Empire,* ed.
J. B. Bury, 7 vols. (London: Methuen, 1896–1902), II, 29–36.

27 Philip S. Foner, ed., *The Complete Writings of Thomas Paine,* 2 vols. (New
York: Citadel, 1945), I, 19. All future citations to Paine in the text are to
volume I of this edition. Of interest in this connection is the libretto of *The
Disappointment: or, the Force of Credulity* (New York, 1767), the first opera
written in America. H. Wiley Hitchcock, *Music in the United States: A
Historical Introduction* (Englewood Cliffs, N.J.: Prentice-Hall, 1974), p. 35n.

28 Quoted in Watters, "The Vogue of Richardson," p. 197. See also the
comment of Stephen Burroughs in his *Memoirs* (1797; Albany, 1811):
"Critics of Clarissa and Edward Young say they are too gloomy, that our
compassion is wounded but never gratified; that our disgust is excited
against certain characters; that the rewards of vice are set forth, but nothing
on the pleasing side; that virtue is not rewarded . . . " (p. 228).

29 *The United States Magazine,* I (March 1779), 123. Clarissa awakes just as she
imagines she is about to embrace Abigail Adams.

30 John Adams to William Cunningham, March 15, 1804, in *Correspondence
between the Hon. John Adams and the Late William Cunningham, Esq.* (Boston,
1823), p. 19. For the entire passage see below, p. 237.

4. THE DEBT OF NATURE RECONSIDERED

1 Francis Hopkinson, *A Pretty Story* (1774) (New York: Books for Libraries
Press, 1969), p. 51. Pages 93–98 of this section are indebted to and build on
the argument of Burrows and Wallace in "Ideology and Psychology."

Several of my illustrations are, in one form or another, to be found in their excellent monograph, but without the contextual framework necessary, I believe, to fully illuminate them. For a provocative nonideological treatment of the generational dimension of the revolutionary conflict, see Peter Shaw's recent *American Patriots and the Rituals of Revolution* (Cambridge: Harvard University Press, 1981).

2 Paul Leicester Ford, *The New England Primer* (New York: Dodd, Mead, 1899), n.p. Ford reproduces the earliest known complete copy, that of 1727, and includes a great number of variants.

3 Blackstone, *Commentaries on the Laws,* I, 442.

4 The first appeared in Philadelphia, the second in Boston.

5 "Miss Thoughtful," *Instructive and Entertaining Emblems* (Hartford, Conn., 1795), p. 7.

6 Polybius, *General History of the Wars of the Romans* (London, 1764), Book VI, 414. This is the second edition of John Hampton's famous translation. See also John Adams, *A Defence of the Constitutions of Government of the United States of America* (Boston, 1787–1788), I, 112.

7 Peter Oliver, *The Origin and Progress of the American Revolution,* ed. Douglass Adair and John A. Schutz (Standard University Press, 1967), p. 3.

8 Jonathan Boucher, *A View of the Causes and Consequences of the American Revolution* (London, 1797), pp. 360–1.

9 Quoted in Burrows and Wallace, "Ideology and Psychology," pp. 195–6.

10 William Eddis in *The American Tory,* ed. Morton and Penn Borden (Englewood Cliffs, N.J.: Prentice-Hall, 1972), p. 32.

11 The ode is printed in *The Annual Register . . . for the Year 1776* (London, 1788), p. 203.

12 Filmer quoted in Gordon J. Schochet, *Patriarchalism in Political Thought: The Authoritarian Family and Political Speculations and Attitudes Especially in Seventeenth-Century England* (Oxford: Blackwell, 1975), p. 262.

13 Jacob Duché, *The Duty of Standing Fast in Our Liberties* in *Patriot Preachers of the American Revolution,* ed. Frank Moore (New York: Published for the Subscribers, 1860), p. 83.

14 "Letter from a Member of the Virginia Convention," in *Diary of the American Revolution,* ed. Frank Moore (1860; New York: Washington Square Press, 1968), p. 98.

15 John Morgan, *A Recommendation of Inoculation* (Boston, 1776), p. 16.

16 Cited in Charles W. Akers, *Called Unto Liberty: A Life of Jonathan Mayhew* (Cambridge: Harvard University Press, 1964), p. 202. For the principle in action see Mercy Otis Warren's explanation to John Adams that her three sons had left home because they "had attained an age that makes it proper they leave the parental roof." Quoted in Norton, *Liberty's Daughters,* p. 99.

17 John Adams, *Dissertation on the Canon and Feudal Law,* in *Political Writings of John Adams,* ed. George A. Peck (New York: Bobbs-Merrill, 1954), p. 18. Compare with Blackstone's remark cited in C. K. Allen, *Law in the Making* (London: Oxford University Press, 1964):

> Justice is not derived from the King, as from his free gift, but he is the steward of the public, to dispose it to whom it is due. He is not the

spring, but the reservoir from whence right and equity are conducted by a 100 channels to each individual. (p. 15)

The fountain–reservoir dichotomy, often to be found in the constitutional literature of the eighteenth century, permitted an easy distinction between absolute and constitutional monarchy. In the case of the latter, no man is dependent on one breast or one will.

18 From "Moral Philosophy," *Encyclopaedia Britannica* (1771), III.

19 C. Labaree, ed., *The Papers of Benjamin Franklin*, XIII, 24.

20 Print reproduced in Wynn-Jones, *The Cartoon History*, p. 33. See also Kenneth Silverman, *A Cultural History*, p. 81. For a Loyalist treatment of Belisarius see Hector St. John de Crèvecoeur's sketch, "The American Belisarius," first discovered and published in 1925 with eleven other sketches. See *Sketches of Eighteenth Century America* (New York: Benjamin Blom, 1972), pp. 228–50. The story recounts the trials of a kindly Loyalist farmer victimized by his rebel brothers' jealousy of his prosperity. In his *Letters of an American Farmer* (written before the Revolution), Crèvecoeur idealized the life of the American farmer liberated from his servile European existence – liberated, that is, by emigration and not revolution. Terrified by the violence and madness he associated with revolution and by the threat he believed it posed to human virtue, Crèvecoeur opposed the revolutionary break with England's paternal authority. In his understanding of the familial drama, the death of the father, rather than liberating the sons, cheats them of a restraint and guidance essential both to their moral development and to the staving off of eventual civil strife. Or at least such seems the moral of Crèvecoeur's unpublished political parable, "A Happy Family Disunited by the Spirit of Civil War," in which the patriarch, depressed at being unable to reconcile his two Tory sons with his two Whig sons, dies only to leave his sons to turn on one another. In a recent article A. W. Plumstead, having summarized the sketch, concludes that the dying pioneer is "symbolic of the country, grown through the youth of its frontier innocence and prosperity into its first old age only to find that in handing down the fruits of the colony to the sons, there is discord where unity should prevail, war in a land of peace." "Hector St. John de Crèvecoeur," in *The Revolutionary Years*, ed. Everett Emerson (Madison: University of Wisconsin Press, 1977), p. 227. Crèvecoeur's sketch offers a revealing complement to Hopkinson's *A Pretty Story*. For the Tory attitude toward authority, with its insistence on "the denial of a natural unruly spirit" and its "acceptance of a divine order as things are constituted," see Robert McCluer Calhoon, *The Loyalists in Revolutionary America, 1760–1781* (New York: Harcourt, Brace & Jovanovich, 1973), pp. 218–43. See also Bailyn, *The Ordeal of Thomas Hutchinson*, pp. 70–108. I hasten to add at this point that the ideology described in the present book becomes the dominant ideology in the period under consideration, but it is not the only ideology. Its success, however, has to do, in part, with its co-opting large parts of the competing ideology. The two phrases above from Calhoon's book, read in different lights, might be said to characterize the Whig as well as the Tory position.

21 John Joachim Zubly, *An Humble Enquiry into the Nature of Dependence* (Charleston, 1769), p. 6.

22 See entry for "benevolence" in the *Oxford Universal Dictionary on Historical Principles,* ed. C. T. Onions (London: Oxford University Press, 1955).

23 Paine uses the image in an article published in 1776, quoted in Eric Foner, *Tom Paine and Revolutionary America* (London: Oxford University Press, 1976), p. 127.

24 Burlmaqui's *Principles of Natural and Political Law* (1747) in *The Ideological Origins,* p. 210n. The distinction opposes not only provincial-administered government to Parliament-administered government, but also government based on rational (literally, internal) consent to government based on habitual deference and superintending duty. The American constitutional government framed in 1789 would seek to effect a compromise between internal and external government. Federalist 51 argues acutely: "If men were angels, no government would be necessary. If angels were to govern men, neither external nor internal controls of government would be necessary. In framing a government which is to be administered by men over men you must first enable the government to control the government; and in the next place oblige it to control itself." *The Federalist* (Washington: National Home Library Foundation, 1937), p. 33.

25 Boyd, ed., *The Papers of Thomas Jefferson,* I, 178. Jefferson also asks in the same letter whether "the generosity of Blandford in Marmontel" does not "elevate his sentiments as much as any similar incident which real history can furnish."

26 Cordelia's remark is made in *King Lear* I.1.92–4.

27 Foner, ed., *The Complete Writings of Thomas Paine,* I, 30. Winthrop Jordan discovers in *Common Sense* images not only of parental rejection but symbolic regicide. See his "Familial Politics: Tom Paine and the Killing of the King, 1776," *Journal of American History,* LX, no. 2 (September 1973), esp. p. 294.

28 *Encyclopaedia Britannica* (1771), III, 277. Paine's pamphlet gave expression not only to the new moral philosophy but to the new "sensibility" – a word that by 1776 had become identified less with the head than with the heart. Rousseau's insistence that compassion as much as reason distinguishes man from animal and "monster," that man must do no harm to his fellow man "less because he is a reasonable being than because he is a sensitive being," made clear the assumptions of that new sensibility. *The First and Second Discourses,* pp. 98, 132.

29 Ibid., III, 275.

30 Adam Ferguson, *The Principles of Moral and Political Science* excerpted in Schneider, ed., *The Scottish Moralists,* p. 84.

31 *Pennsylvania Gazette* article described in Meritt Ierley, *The Year that Tried Men's Souls: The World of 1776* (South Brunswick: A. S. Barnes and Company, 1976), p. 328. Ierley's book is a month-to-month accounting of events as culled from newspapers and magazines. Franklin was the first to use "positive," "negative," and "charge" as relating to electricity. See I. Bernard Cohen, *Benjamin Franklin: Scientist and Statesman* (New York:

Scribner, 1975), p. 41. In some ways the Leyden jar (or capacitator), which fascinated the eighteenth century with its inner and outer conductors, may be seen as a scientific correlative to the period's understanding of the heart and affections.

32 Gilbert Tennent, *The Danger of an Unconverted Ministry* (1741) in Heimert, ed. *The Great Awakening*, p. 89.

33 Ezra Stiles, "The United States Elevated to Glory," in *The Pulpit of the American Revolution*, ed. John Wingate Thornton (Boston: Gould & Lincoln, 1860), p. 441.

34 The famous phrase appears in an 1815 letter to Jedidiah Morse in Charles Francis Adams, ed., *The Works*, 10 vols. (Boston, 1850–56), X, 182.

35 Old South Church Pamphlet Series No. 53, pp. 4–5. Winthrop anticipates Rousseau by turning around the argument of his accusers. He asks his brethren at home not to desert him, reminding them that separation is a test of the bond and not a threat to it. Indeed, separation made more stringent the terms of nature's laws. The stipulation in Hopkinson's *Pretty Story* had been: "Though they should be removed, they should be considered as Children of his family."

Another example of "non-separation" is the appearance of George III on at least three state coins (whose obverse depicts Liberty) as late as 1789. His image presumably served as iconographic support for "the Protestant succession in the house of Hanover." See Frank H. Sommer, "The Metamorphoses of Britannia" in Charles H. Montgomery and Patricia C. Kane, eds., *American Art: 1750–1800 toward Independence* (Boston: New York Graphic Society, 1976), pp. 46–47. Marcus Lee Hansen has made clear how for many later immigrants the love of democracy and love of monarchy were far from inconsistent. Having fled oppressive conditions, many European immigrants hung portraits of the kings of their respective countries for the purpose of maintaining cultural identification. *The Immigrant in American History* (New York: Harper & Row, 1976), p. 80.

36 On non-separatist Congregationalism see Perry Miller, *Orthodoxy in Massachusetts, 1630–1650* (Boston: Beacon, 1959), pp. 73–101.

37 On "party" vs. "faction" see Alison Gilbert Olson, *Anglo-American Politics, 1660–1775* (New York: Oxford University Press, 1973), pp. v–vii. On "loyal opposition" see William Safire, *Safire's Political Dictionary* (New York: Random House, 1978), p. 388.

38 Gibbon, quoted in Gay, *The Enlightenment: An Interpretation*, I, 154; Jonathan Mayhew, *A Discourse Concerning Unlimited Submission* (Boston, 1750), pp. 49, 53.

39 James Thomas Flexner, *Gilbert Stuart* (New York: Knopf, 1955), p. 55. The enormous impact of David Garrick's naturalistic acting style on the British stage is another example of the mid-eighteenth-century challenge to conventional formalism. On his hostility to "affectation" see Kalman A. Burnim, *David Garrick, Director* (Carbondale, Ill.: Southern Illinois University Press, 1961), pp. 57 ff. Thomson's use of blank verse instead of heroic couplets in *The Seasons* is yet another.

40 See Martha Gandy Fales, *Early American Silver* (n.p.: Excalibur, 1970), p.

23. Revere is shown holding such a teapot in the famous Copley portrait of 1768.

41 Labaree et al. ed., *The Autobiography of Benjamin Franklin,* p. 135. In a recent article Hugh J. Dawson also examines the generational metaphor in the *Autobiography* and recognizes it as consistent with the language of contemporary politics. "Fathers and Sons: Franklin's 'Memoirs' as Myth and Metaphor," *Early American Literature,* 14 (Winter 1979–80), 269–92. It is interesting to note that the first part of the *Autobiography,* which is addressed to Franklin's son, is written in the same year (1771) as Jefferson's letter to Robert Skipwith concerning his education. Franklin had read widely in the pedagogical tradition we have examined earlier. After the famous passage in which he praises Bunyan as the first who "mix'd Narration and Dialogue" (p. 72), he cites *Pamela* and Defoe's *Family Instructor* as realistically exploiting the same innovation.

42 For an interesting brief account of the rigorous nature of eighteenth-century apprenticeship that undoubtedly politicized others besides Franklin – witness Beaumarchais's Figaro and Rousseau, himself – see Bailyn, *Education in the Forming of American Society,* pp. 29–36.

43 The controversy is treated insightfully by James Axtell who quotes the statute in his *School on a Hill* and summarizes the primary issue behind the violent opposition to eighteenth-century collegiate government in New England:

> New Englanders from twelve or fourteen to twenty-one years were expected to assume in imperceptible, evolutionary stages the manners, freedoms and responsibilities of adulthood. . . . When the other members of his age group were exercising their maturity in apprenticeship or military service, where the full force of legal and ecclesiastical sanctions operated, the college student was incarcerated in a moral stockade of special privilege and overweening, absolute paternalism. The tensions generated by his anomalous position became so acute in the eighteenth century that only rebellion in the colleges and revolution in the colonies could relieve them (p. 235).

On the confusion in early America over the character of adolescence as a distinct stage of life see Joseph F. Kett, *Rites of Passage: Adolescence in America, 1790 to the Present* (New York: Basic Books, 1977), pp. 14–50.

44 Maurice Cranston, ed., *Locke on Politics, Religion and Education* (New York: Collier Books, 1965), p. 240.

45 In 1729, Franklin published a pamphlet entitled *A Modest Enquiry into the Nature and Necessity of a Paper-Currency.* Paper money was originally a Massachusetts invention intended to relieve the debt and payment problems of the 1680s. In his *The Life of William Phips* (1697) later collected in his *Magnalia* (1702), Cotton Mather declares that the "Invention had been of more use to the New-Englanders, than if . . . the [ore-rich] Mountains of Peru had been removed into these parts of America." *Magnalia Christi Americana,* 2 vols. (Hartford, Conn., 1855), I, 191. Mather implicitly associates the new expedient bills of credit with the "self-made" character of Phips, himself, a second "Pizarro," and the new values he embodied. Such

bills that represent gold or land are also a benign form of the "spectral representation" Mather is so concerned with in the witchcraft portion of *The Life*. For another treatment of paper money see p. 246. On daylight savings see Mark Van Doren, *Benjamin Franklin* (New York: Viking Press, 1938), p. 702.

46 The relevant section of Buffon's *Histoire* is reproduced in *Was America a Mistake? An Eighteenth Century Controversy*, ed. Henry Steele Commager and Elmo Giordanetti (New York: Harper & Row, 1967), pp. 72–4.

47 See Commager, *Was America a Mistake?*, p. 20.

48 My account follows the publishing history of the print (from a collector's rather than a historian's point of view) in Edwin Wolf 2nd, "The *Prodigal Son* in England and America: A Century of Change," collected in *Eighteenth Century Prints in Colonial America*, ed. Joan D. Dolmetsch (Williamsburg: Colonial Williamsburg Foundation, 1979), p. 152. The midcentury popularity of the prodigal son prints reflects, in part, the earlier success of Hogarth's *Rake's Progress* sequence (1733).

49 J. M. Tompkins, *The Popular Novel in England, 1770–1800* (London: Constable, 1932), p. 91.

50 Wolf, "The *Prodigal Son*," p. 155.

51 *Annual Register . . . for 1776* (London, 1788), p. 184.

52 The Carter diary entries I quote all appear in Jack P. Greene's excellent introductory essay to *The Diary of Colonel Landon Carter of Sabine Hall 1752–1778*, 2 vols., ed. Jack P. Greene (Charlottesville: The University Press of Virginia, 1965), I, 54, 82, 16. For an interesting use of Fénelon's *Telemachus* (unattributed in Greene's note) see Carter's entry for February 21, 1777.

53 James Duane quoted in Bruce Granger, *Political Satire in the American Revolution* (Ithaca, N.Y.: Cornell University Press, 1960), p. 122. Pamphlets reproduced in H. Teerink, *The History of John Bull* (Amsterdam: H. Paris, 1925), pp. 163, 165.

54 Quoted in Granger, *Political Satire,* p. 21.

55 Cartoons in Wynn-Jones, *The Cartoon History,* p. 42.

56 Granger, *Political Satire,* p. 23.

57 Dickinson's *Letters* is reproduced in *Empire and Nation,* ed. Forrest MacDonald (Englewood Cliffs, N.J.: Prentice Hall, 1962). The Pitt quote is on p. 24. Rush is quoted by his biographer, Carl Binger, *Revolutionary Doctor: Benjamin Rush, 1746–1813* (New York: Norton, 1966), p. 51.

58 *The Remarkable History of Tom Jones* (Worcester, 1787), pp. 9–10.

59 *Universal Magazine of Knowledge and Pleasure* (July 1783), p. 2.

60 *Hibernian Magazine or Compendium of Entertaining Knowledge* (December 1783), p. 621.

61 Richardson, *A Collection of the Moral . . . Sentiments,* p. 169.

62 *The Pennsylvania Magazine,* I (June 1775), 265.

63 *Paradise Lost,* IV, 749–50.

64 See Jones, "Importation of French Books in Philadelphia," p. 159. All citations to Madame de Genlis's *The Siege of Rochelle* are to the London edition of 1808, which appears the same year as the first French printing. I have taken the liberty of representing Madame de Genlis's work with a

very late volume, but one that dramatizes the pedagogical theory set forth in her most popular book of the 1780s, *Adèle et Théodore, ou Lettres sur L'education* (1782). Genlis was tutor to Louis-Philippe but later became active in the Revolution. Steeped in the new education, she edited *Emile* and named her adopted daughter Pamela after Richardson's heroine.

65 See Revelation 12 and 13, and Isaiah 66.
66 Samuel Sherwood, *The Church's Flight into the Wilderness* (New York, 1776), p. 41. See also Samuel West, *An Anniversary Sermon* (Boston, 1778). West's text is Isaiah 66.

5. AFFECTIONATE UNIONS AND THE NEW VOLUNTARISM

1 Nancy Cott, "Divorce and the Changing Status of Women in Eighteenth Century America," in *The American Family in Social-Historical Perspective,* 2nd ed., ed. Michael Gordon (New York: St. Martin's Press, 1978), p. 116. See also Carl N. Degler, *At Odds,* pp. 15–17, 104–5, 165–6. Linda K. Kerber's *Women of the Republic: Intellect and Ideology in Revolutionary America* (Chapel Hill: University of North Carolina Press, 1980), which takes up the issue of divorce and other matters relevant to my book has, unfortunately, come into my hands too late for me to have profited from it.

2 *The Pennsylvania Magazine,* I (April 1775), 152. A month earlier, in a piece entitled "Cupid and Hymen," Paine insisted on the primacy of love over marriage. For a brief discussion of Paine's contributions and pseudonyms see Frank Luther Mott, I, 87–90. In 1775 the new magazine was described by a friend of the publisher as less important as a repository than as "a nursery for young authors, who may easily try their strength with little loss of time, and no great risk in point of reputation." Here was the morphological argument in yet another context. Peter J. Parker and Stephanie Munsing Winklebauer, "Embellishments for Practical Repositories: Eighteenth-Century American Magazine Illustration," in *Eighteenth-Century Prints in Colonial America,* ed. Joan D. Dolmetsch (Williamsburg: The Colonial Williamsburg Foundation, 1974), p. 76.

3 *The Pennsylvania Magazine,* I (June 1775), 264. The pseudonym "The Old Bachelor" is an allusion to Congreve's licentious 1693 play of the same name, popular on the London stage in the 1770s.

4 Martha Stohlman, *John Witherspoon, Parson, Politician, Patriot* (Philadelphia: Westminster Press, 1976), p. 153. On marital rights in general see Noel C. Stevenson, "Marital Rights in the Colonial Period," in *New England Historical and Genealogical Register,* 109 (1955), 84.

5 *The Pennsylvania Magazine,* I (December supplement 1775), 602. In Washington Irving's "Rip van Winkle," Rip, driven from home by the tyrannical "petticoat government" of his "termagant" virago of a wife, sleeps through the Revolutionary War and awakens to find his wife dead and George III deposed. Irving's tale in its stress on domestic politics is more historically acute than has perhaps been realized. Rip is a direct descendant of the plaintive persona of Tom Paine. See Washington Irving, *The Sketch Book* (New York: New American Library/Signet, 1961), p. 39.

6 Anon., *An Essay on Marriage or the Lawfulness of Divorce* (Philadelphia, 1788), Preface.

7 Cf. Rousseau, *Emilius,* IV, 104–6. Having been given her free choice, Sophia, Emile's sister, shrewdly declares that her liberal parents have "not educated her suitably for a man of the present age." Ideally she would marry someone like "Fénelon's Telemachus" (p. 116).

8 Franklin's famous cartoon depicting the colonies as the severed sections of a snake predated the great political controversies. It first appeared in *The Pennsylvania Gazetter* for May 9, 1754.

9 Mayhew quoted in Charles Akers, *Called Unto Liberty,* p. 74. Also see the chapter entitled "The Happy Effects of Union," in Alan Heimert, *Religion and the American Mind from the Great Awakening to the Revolution* (Cambridge: Harvard University Press, 1966) for a discussion of the degree to which Christian union and national union were related themes in the sermons of the Revolutionary period.

10 Ezra Stiles, quoted in James Woodress, *A Yankee Odyssey: The Life of Joel Barlow* (Philadelphia: Lippincott, 1958), p. 41.

11 *The Pennsylvania Magazine,* I (April 1775), 152.

12 *The Royal American Magazine* I (January 1774), 9. For the divorce petition alleging his wife's adultery see Annie Russell Marble, *From 'Prentice to Patron: The Life Story of Isaiah Thomas* (New York: Appleton, 1935), pp. 134–7.

13 *The Columbian Magazine,* I (January 1787), 244.

14 *The Royal American Magazine,* I (March, 1774), 9.

15 The verse is quoted in George Sensabaugh, *Milton in Early America* (Princeton University Press, 1964), p. 113. Sensabaugh's discussion of Milton's influence on literary attitudes toward marriage in Revolutionary America is on pp. 110–22. Sensabaugh's account is given further support by the anonymous pamphlet on divorce in note 6 above, which also quotes the "Wedding Hymn" in support of its argument.

16 John Salkend, *A Treatise of Paradise* (London, 1617), pp. 178–9.

17 David Humphreys, *The Happiness of America,* in *Miscellaneous Works* (New York, 1804), p. 37.

18 Hughes ed., John Milton, *The Complete Poems and Major Prose,* p. 631. The famous line appears in an early paragraph in "Of Education" (1644): "The end then of learning is to repair the ruins of our first parents by regaining to know God aright, and out of that knowledge to love him, to imitate him, to be like him, as we may the nearest by possessing our souls of true virtue." Later primitivistic fiction like Bernardin de Saint-Pierre's *Paul et Virginie* (1777) recast Adam and Eve as tragic innocents.

19 Reid's phrase is quoted in the *OED* entry for "grace."

20 Hill, "Clarissa Harlowe," pp. 61–2.

21 See Fiedler, *Love and Death in the American Novel,* chapter 4. Though overly schematic, Fiedler's distinction between the bourgeois and antibourgeois tradition is a valuable one.

22 *The Royal American Magazine,* I (August 1774), 298.

23 Burrows and Wallace, "Ideology and Psychology," p. 197.

24 See Arthur Loesser, *Men, Women and Pianos* (New York: Simon & Schuster, 1954), p. 472, and Silverman, *A Cultural History*, p. 185.

25 This quote and the information immediately following are drawn from Spurlin, *Rousseau in America*, p. 50.

26 Adams's marginalia in this and in numerous other important Enlightenment volumes are reproduced in Zoltan Haraszti, *John Adams and the Prophets of Progress* (New York: Grosset & Dunlap, 1952), p. 97.

27 The significant phrase is not Adams's but one that appears in the popular press in the 1790s. See the passage quoted by Watters, "The Vogue of Richardson," p. 164.

28 Quoted in G. Thomas Tanselle, *Royall Tyler* (Cambridge: Harvard University Press, 1967), p. 14.

29 Ibid., pp. 14–15.

30 Ibid., pp. 68–9.

31 Quinn, *Representative American Plays*, p. 72.

32 Jonathan Boucher, *Reminiscences of an American Loyalist*, ed. Jonathan Boucher (New York: Houghton Mifflin, 1925), p. 32. For a brief psychobiography of Boucher, see Lynn, *Divided People*, pp. 8–15.

33 This episode in Barlow's life is well told in James Woodress, *A Yankee Odyssey*. Barlow's letter is quoted on p. 69. An interesting comparison with certain aspects of the "ideology" of romantic love is provided by the parable of the ten virgins, recounted in Matthew 25. The parable likens Christ to a suitor-bridegroom who, coming in the middle of the night, finds five virgins prepared to elope with him and five unprepared. The former, according to Benjamin Colman in his important early eighteenth-century volume on the parable, were types of the regenerate, the latter, of the unregenerate. Colman's God is likened to a father-in-law, "a king that arranges a marriage for his son. . . . It is God's ardent desire to receive us into the embrace of a father and husband, to take possession of our heart." *The Parable of the Ten Virgins* (London, 1707), p. 21. As father-in-law, God is a "chosen" parent who chooses us.

34 Daniel Scott Smith, "Parental Power and Marriage Patterns: An Analysis of Historical Trends in Hingham, Massachusetts," *Journal of Marriage and the Family*, II (August 1963), 225.

35 Herman Lantz et al., "Pre-Industrial Patterns in the Colonial Family in America: A Contents Analysis of Colonial Magazines," *American Sociological Review*, XXXIII (June 1968), 414.

36 A good recent account of the incident is to be found in Fairfax Downey, *Indian Wars of the United States Army, 1776–1865* (Derby: Monarch Books, 1964), pp. 11–19.

37 *Boston Gazette* (18 August 1777), p. 3.

38 Burgoyne quoted in *Revolutionary Memorials*, ed. Rev. Stephen Dodd (New York, 1852), p. 55.

39 Burke quoted in Downey, *Indian Wars*, p. 16.

40 Ibid.

41 Ibid., p. 11. My treatment of Jane as a sentimental heroine here is in basic agreement with the brief speculations of Silverman in *Cultural History*, p.

330, who draws on a similar constellation of citations. See also Michael Kammen, *A Season of Youth: The American Revolution and the Historical Imagination* (New York: Knopf, 1978), p. 116.

42 Quoted in *Revolutionary Memorials,* pp. 37–8. The poem is by Rev. Wheeler Case.

42 Ballad reproduced in Oscar Brand, *Songs of '76* (New York: M. Evans, 1972), p. 97.

44 See Lewis Leary's edition of *Miss McCrea* (Gainsville: Scholars' Facsimiles and Reprints, 1958).

45 For a complete printing history of this narrative see the edition reprinted, with a bibliographical introduction, by R. W. G. Vail in the *American Book Collector,* II (1932), 165–72. All citations are from this edition.

46 Indeed one source or inspiration for the "Panther Narrative" may be another brief narrative that appeared the year before and also went through numerous editions: *An Account of the Death and Burial of a Hermit* (New Haven, 1786).

47 For an archetypal reading of the narrative see Richard Slotkin, *Regeneration through Violence: The Mythology of the American Frontier, 1600–1860* (Middletown, Conn.: Wesleyan University Press, 1975), p. 257. Slotkin fails to recognize the degree to which the narrative follows conventional sentimental formulas of late eighteenth-century fiction. Overall, however, Slotkin's work is enormously impressive and revealing. It has influenced my thinking in a number of matters.

48 David Humphrey, *The Miscellaneous Works,* p. 36.

49 "The Narrative of the Captivity of Mrs. Mary Rowlandson," in *Narratives of the Indian Wars,* ed. Charles H. Lincoln (New York: Barnes & Noble, 1913), p. 112. All future citations are from this text.

50 The best account of the changing character of the genre is to be found in Slotkin's *Regeneration,* chapter 10.

51 Mather's account of Hannah Dustin's captivity is in Lincoln's *Narratives of the Indian Wars,* p. 266.

52 Responding not to the text itself, but to Mather's subsequent insistence that the lesson of the narrative is the necessity of humility before God, Slotkin sees no difference in meaning between the Dustin and Rowlandson narratives. *Regeneration,* pp. 113–14.

53 J. M. S. Tompkins, *The Popular Novel in England, 1770–1800,* p. 84.

54 Johann Wolfgang von Goethe, *The Sorrows of Werter,* 2 vols. (Litchfield, 1789), I, 60. All future citations, except where noted, are from this two-volume edition.

55 *The Sorrows of Werter* (New York, 1795), p. 4.

56 Henri Petter in *The Early American Novel* lists four American novels published in the 1790s in which a protagonist kills himself or herself under the explicit influence of Werther's example. Petter's plot summaries of some fifty early American novels appended to the back of his volume provide numerous instances of the newly emerged figure of the suicide (p. 58n).

57 Robert Bage, *Mount Henneth* (London, 1781), p. 136.

58 *Sorrows* (Litchfield, 1789), p. iii.
59 See Frederic M. Litto, "Addison's Cato in the Colonies," *William and Mary Quarterly*, ser. 3, 23 (July 1966), 431–49.
60 Quoted in Silverman, *A Cultural History*, p. 81.
61 Joseph Addison, *Cato, A Tragedy* (Worcester, 1782), p. 59.
62 John Adams, *The Flowers of Ancient History* (Philadelphia, 1795), p. 182.

6. FILIAL FREEDOM AND AMERICAN PROTESTANTISM

1 The paragraph is from Shaftesbury's "Inquiry concerning Virtue," contained in his large miscellaneous work, *Characteristicks of Men, Manners, Opinions, Times* (1711), 2 vols, ed. John M. Robertson (London: Grant Richard, 1900), I, p. 312.
2 Harry Hayden Clark, ed., *Thomas Paine: Key Writings* (New York: Hill & Wang, 1961), p. iv. In his valuable introduction to this edition Harry Hayden Clark contends, perhaps naively, that Paine's benevolent view of the Creator reflected the influence of his Quaker father's convictions. In his journal the Quaker John Woolman does, for example, describe a deity "whose tender love of his children exceeds the most warm affections of natural parents" (p. 33).
3 Jonathan Mayhew in Akers, *Called Unto Liberty*, p. 72.
4 As quoted in O. I. A. Roche, ed., *The Jefferson Bible with the Annotations and Commentaries on Religion by Thomas Jefferson* (New York: Potter, 1964), p. 378. The letter was written when Jefferson was 80. Age did not lessen his rancor.
5 Chester E. Jorgenson and Frank Luther Mott, eds., *Benjamin Franklin: Representative Selections* (New York: Hill & Wang, 1962), p. 414.
6 St. John in Moore, *Diary*, p. xxvi.
7 Philip Freneau, *The Poems of Freneau*, ed. Harry Hayden Clark (New York: Macmillan / Hafner 1929), p. 24.
8 *Pennsylvania Journal* (17 July 1776) in Moore, *Diary*, p. 132.
9 Quoted in Jordan, "The Killing of the King," p. 304.
10 Oliver, *Origin and Progress*, p. 40.
11 In Burrows and Wallace, "Ideology and Psychology," p. 291.
12 Andrew Fuller, *The Gospel, Its Own Witness* (New York, 1801), pp. 47, 32.
13 Amos 3:6.
14 Michael Wigglesworth, *The Diary of Michael Wigglesworth*, ed. Edmund S. Morgan (New York: Harper & Row, 1965), p. 20.
15 Samuel Sewall, *The Diary of Samuel Sewall*, ed. M. Halsey Thomas (New York: Farrar, Straus, & Giroux, 1973), p. 35.
16 Proverbs 12:10. Compare Psalms 77:9, 103:4.
17 Edwards quoted in Greven, *Protestant Temperament*, p. 111.
18 David Stannard, *The Puritan Way of Death: A Study in Religion, Culture and Social Change* (Oxford University Press, 1977), pp. 141–161.
19 Because there are so many "ghosts" in Evans's microprint listings it is impossible to determine in which edition Watts's hymn first makes its appearance. It may be found, however, in the *New England Primer Improved* (Boston, 1767). Cotton's "Duty" reappears once or twice in the 1770s and

1780s, but is clearly on the wane. Watts's influence on Blake's *Songs* is particularly marked in this instance. On change in headstone iconography see Stannard, pp. 155–7.

20 The tune was that of "Lilliburlero." See Derek Jarrett, *England in the Age of Hogarth* (Frogmore: Paladin, 1976), p. 63.

21 Noah Webster, *The American Spelling Book* (Boston, 1798), pp. 145–6.

22 Salomon Gessner, *The Death of Abel*, trans. Mary Collyer (Boston, 1768), p. 15. I am indebted to Wyn Kelley for calling my attention to this important work. For Gessner's international popularity see John Hibberd, *Salomon Gessner: His Creative Achievement and Influence* (Cambridge University Press, 1976), pp. 127–42. American editions listed in *Short-Title Evans*.

23 Edmund Morgan, *The Challenge of the American Revolution*, p. 73.

24 [John Clark and Charles Chauncy], *Salvation for All . . . A Scripture Doctrine* (Boston, 1782), p. 1.

25 Samuel Mather, *All Men Will Not Be Saved Forever* (Boston, 1782), p. 8.

26 Townsend Shippen, *Some Remarks on a Pamphlet* (Boston, 1783), p. 15.

27 Bellamy quoted in Frank Hugh Foster, *A Genetic History of New England Theology* (University of Chicago Press, 1907), p. 110. My discussion of New Divinity theology and its opponents follows closely Foster's account and more especially the corrective treatment in Joseph Haroutunian, *Piety versus Moralism: The Passing of the New England Theology* (New York: Henry Holt, 1932).

28 Samuel Hopkins describing Mills's position in Foster, *Genetic History*, p. 143.

29 Hemmenway, *A Vindication of the Power, Obligation and Encouragement of the Unregenerate* (Boston, 1772), p. 24.

30 Hart's position is quoted extensively in Haroutunian, *Piety versus Moralism*, pp. 65–8.

31 Ibid., pp. 67–8. For Hart, the misrepresentation of God's character derives from sinners being blinded by their own false sense of self-interest, not some absolute constitutional inability. Hart thus rejects the view that the more "natural men" see the "moral beauty" and goodness of God, the more they abhor them. This is to make man "a moral monster" as well as God. On the contrary, when they are obliged "to see them as they are, they are reduced to silence, can object nothing to them, but justify and approve them as right and condemn themselves." Hart, *Brief Remarks on a number of False Propositions, and Dangerous Errors, which are spreading in the Country* (New Haven, 1769), pp. 37, 48–9, 66.

32 Quoted in Haroutunian, *Piety versus Moralism*, p. 22.

33 Ibid., p. 63.

34 Bellamy in his *True Religion Delineated* (1750) here summarizes the position of his Arminian opponents, quoted in ibid., p. 110.

35 Foner, ed., *The Complete Writings of Thomas Paine*, I, 274.

36 Haroutunian, *Piety versus Moralism*, p. 161. On Bellamy's understanding of God as "governor" see Foster, *Genetic History*, pp. 114–17, and Sydney E. Ahlstrom, *A Religious History of the American People* (New Haven: Yale

University Press, 1974), p. 407. In this regard see Bellamy's significantly entitled treatise, *The Law, Our School-Master* (New Haven, 1756).

37 James Dana, *An Examination of . . . Edwards's Enquiry* (New Haven, 1772), pp. 6 ff.

38 See entries under "Bible" in Shipton and Mooney, eds., *The Short-Title Evans*. Jefferson's remark to Adams in an 1813 letter provides one context for this fact: "The great principle of the Hebrews was the *Fear* of God, that of the Gentiles, *Honour* . . . that of Christians the *Love* of God." Lewis Cappon, ed., *Adams–Jefferson Letters: The Complete Correspondence between Thomas Jefferson and Abigail and John Adams,* 2 vols. in 1 (New York: Simon & Schuster, 1971), p. 380.

39 Watts quoted in Arthur Paul Davis, "Isaac Watts: His Life and Work." (Ph.D. diss. Columbia University, 1943), p. 199.

40 The hymn appears in *A Number of Hymns Taken from Dr. Watts' Scriptural Collection* (Boston, 1773), p. 84, appended to N. Brady and N. Tate, *A New Version of the Psalms of David* (Boston, 1773). Watts calls attention to the word shift in his own note to his "imitation" of the 119th Psalm in *The Psalms of David Imitated* (Newburyport, 1781), p. 252. See *The Short-Title Evans* for the printing history of Watts's *Psalms.*

41 *Psalms of David Imitated* (Hartford, 1788), sig. A2.

42 Watts, *Scriptural Collection,* p. 27.

43 Donald Davie, *The Gathered Church: The Literature of the English Dissenting Interest, 1700–1930* (Oxford University Press, 1978), p. 23.

44 Gotthold Lessing, "The Education of the Human Race" in Peter Gay, ed., *The Enlightenment: A Comprehensive Anthology* (New York: Simon & Schuster, 1973), p. 356.

45 Foner, ed., *The Complete Writings of Thomas Paine,* I, 512.

46 According to the Shorter Catechism, which was the version that appeared in *The New England Primer,* a child was obliged to respond to the question "What is Adoption?" with the words, "Adoption is an Act of God's Free Grace; whereby we are received into the Number, and have rights to all the Privileges of the Sons of God."

47 Jonathan Edwards, *A History of the Work of Redemption* (New York: American Tract Society, n.d.), p. 27.

48 *Paradise Lost,* V, 835–7.

49 Nathanial Whitaker, *An Antidote against Toryism, or the Curse of Meroz,* in Moore, *Patriot Preachers,* p. 206. Whitaker instructs his parishioners in the true meaning of "rebel." A rebel is one who opposes civil government founded in the consent of society, not one who insists upon it.

50 Ibid.

51 The two standard treatments of this subject are Heimert, *Religion and the American Mind,* and Perry Miller, "From the Covenant to the Revival," in *The Shaping of American Religions,* ed. James Ward Smith and A. Leland Jamison (Princeton, 1961), I, 322–50. This and the following chapter are indebted to Heimert's and Miller's convincing insistence on the importance of post-Awakening evangelicalism on the psychohistory of America in the last half of the eighteenth century. Recently Sacvan Bercovitch has further

clarified the connection in *The American Jeremiad* (Madison: University of Wisconsin Press, 1978), pp. 93–131.

52 Mayhew in Akers, *Called Unto Liberty*, p. 1.

53 Ibid., p. 71.

54 Duché in Moore, *Patriot Preachers*, p. 80.

55 Samuel Langdon, *Government Corrupted by Vice* in Moore, *Patriot Preachers*, p. 64.

56 On virtue, see Miller, "The Moral and Psychological Roots," and Gordon Wood, *The Creation of the American Republic*, pp. 65–70.

57 Duché, p. 78. On "sons of liberty" see Catherine Albanese, *The Sons of the Fathers: The Civil Religion of the American Revolution* (Philadelphia: Temple University Press, 1978), chapter 2.

58 John Rodgers, *Divine Goodness Displayed . . . preached December 11, 1780*, rpt. in Moore, *Patriot Preachers*, p. 314. For a fuller elaboration on Rodgers's analogies see David Tappan, *A Treaty of Peace* (1780), also in Moore.

59 *Treaties and Conventions Concluded between the United States of America and Other Powers* (Washington: Government Printing Office, 1889), p. 375. Another reminder of the conservative and compensatory character of the Revolution (which sought not freedom from authority but rather the ability to replace a secular authoritarian power with a divine authoritative one, a constrained obedience with a voluntaristic obedience) is the motto of Jefferson's personal seal that he would later suggest as an alternative motto for the state of Virginia: "Rebellion to Tyrants is Obedience to God." For the source of this inscription as the tombstone of a regicide judge see *The Papers of Thomas Jefferson*, I. 679. The filiopietism of the Revolutionary generation with regard to "the first fathers" who came over in the first "errand in the wilderness" in 1620 and 1630 also seems, in this light, a compensation for breaking the bond with a paternal England. On this point see Sacvan Bercovitch, *The American Jeremiad*, p. 123.

60 Timothy Dwight, *Triumph of Infidelity . . . The Duty of Americans* (New Haven, 1798).

61 Cf. Whittaker, *Antidote*, p. 194. See Heimert, *Religion and the American Mind*, pp. 454–510.

62 Cited in Bailyn, *Ideology*, p. 137.

63 Friedman, ed., *The Works of Oliver Goldsmith*, I, 162. For the contemporary popularity of Goldsmith's poems, see Mott, *Golden Multitudes*, p. 40, and Hart, *Popular Books*, p. 28.

64 Quoted in Sacvan Bercovitch, *The Puritan Origins of the American Self* (New Haven: Yale University Press, 1975), p. 144.

65 Ezra Stiles in Thorton, *Pulpit*, p. 431.

66 Crèvecoeur, *Letters of an American Farmer*, pp. 63, 35.

67 Rousseau's version of this is the substitution of the intolerable yoke of arbitrary will for the yoke of necessity.

68 John Adams's 1756 diary entry quoted in Cecilia Tichi, *New World, New Earth: Environmental Reform in American Literature from the Puritans through Whitman* (New Haven: Yale University Press, 1979), p. 76. Tichi quotes several American writers on "improved" landscapes.

69 Cappon, ed., *Adams–Jefferson Letters,* p. 391.

70 Ibid., p. 30.

71 Ibid., p. 338.

72 Though still clinging to the "phlogiston" theory, Priestley describes the character of oxygen in *An Account of Further Discoveries in Air* (1775) reprinted as an appendix to *The Autobiography of Joseph Priestley* (Teaneck N.J.: Fairleigh Dickinson University Press, 1970), pp. 143–52.

73 Axtell, ed., *The Educational Writings,* pp. 129, 215.

74 See n. 29 above.

75 The phrase is Fiering's in "Benjamin Franklin and the Way to Virtue," *American Quarterly,* XXX (Summer 1978), 212. Fiering's stress on Franklin's debt to Locke's *Education* gives further credence to the claim made at the beginning of this volume that Locke's work may well be the single most important influence on the American Enlightenment. An exact contemporary of Franklin's also enormously concerned with attaining "superiority over my habits" was Samuel Johnson. For Johnson on habits and "the discovery that human nature is able to remake and renovate itself" see Walter Jackson Bate, *The Achievement of Samuel Johnson* (University of Chicago Press, 1978), pp. 31–2, 100, 143–4.

76 See Chapter 2, n. 40.

77 Robert Rosenblum discusses the "geometric idealism" of Jefferson and others in his *Transformations in Late Eighteenth Century Art* (Princeton University Press, 1967), pp. 122 ff.

78 Ibid., p. 28.

79 Ibid., p. 114. These depictions, for the most part, mourn rather than revel in that death. In the case of Jean-Baptiste Greuze's 1778 painting *Le Fils Puni,* the deathbed motif is united with that of the prodigal son. The son having returned to his father's deathbed must confront the fact that his prodigality has hastened his father's demise. This, in essence, is the point of Crèvecoeur's "A Happy Family Disunited" discussed in an earlier footnote and the reversal of that made in the "Panther Narrative." Rosenblum reproduces the painting, plate 32, appendix.

80 Heimert, *Religion and the American Mind,* p. 3.

81 John Fisher quoted in William Clebsch, *England's Earliest Protestants* (New Haven: Yale University Press, 1964), p. 29.

82 Hughes, ed., *John Milton: Complete Poems and Major Prose,* p. 900.

83 Quoted in *The Beauties of the Late . . . Dr. Isaac Watts* (Newburyport, 1797), p. 133.

84 Edward Young, *Night Thoughts* (Hartford, 1810), p. 68. Hart tells the story of a woman who "upon hearing her home was burned down during the Revolution, remarked that if the Bible and *Night Thoughts* were spared she would not grieve for the rest of her books." *Popular Book,* p. 28.

85 Richard Hooker, *The Laws of Ecclesiastical Polity,* 2 vols. (London: J. M. Dent, 1969), I, 166.

86 Cushing Strout, *The New Heavens and the New Earth: Political Religion in America* (New York: Harper & Row, 1973), p. 39.

87 Ibid., p. 49.

88 My discussion of the "separate" position draws partially on William

McLoughlin, *Isaac Backus and the American Pietistic Tradition* (Boston: Little, Brown, 1967), esp. pp. 74–6.

89 Rousseau, *Emilius,* III, 134–135.

90 With regard to the Southern Awakening, Donald G. Mathews has recently reminded us that though Evangelicalism "did isolate the individual from his surroundings and demand an act that would validate his entire existence," it did not "celebrate his isolation," but rather brought him immediately into a new community. Mathews like Strout emphasizes the Evangelical insistence on family education. *Religion in the Old South* (University of Chicago Press, 1977), pp. 19, 44.

91 Joseph Butler, *The Analogy of Religion, Natural and Revealed* (Boston, 1793), pp. 67–8. For a discussion of related ideas see Greven, *Protestant Temperament,* pp. 226–33. The book was widely read by the Revolutionary generation. It was, for example, along with Doddridge's writings, Patrick Henry's favorite volume. See Alexander H. Everett, *The Life of Patrick Henry,* in *The Library of American Biography,* 15 vols., 2d ser., ed. Jared Sparks (Boston, 1844), I, 385.

92 Butler, "Of Personal Identity," appended to ibid., p. 347.

93 Philip Doddridge, *The Rise and Progress,* p. 284. Doddridge is linking I Peter 2:2 and Ephesians 4:13.

94 Anon., *Common Sense* (New York, 1772), p. 2.

95 Ernest Tuveson, *Millennium and Utopia: A Study in the Background of the Idea of Progress* (Berkeley: University of California Press, 1949), p. 128. See also on this subject two useful books: Nathan D. Hatch, *The Sacred Cause of Liberty: Republican Thought and the Millennium in Revolutionary New England* (New Haven: Yale University Press, 1977), and James W. Davidson, *Logic of Millennial Thought: Eighteenth Century New England* (New Haven: Yale University Press, 1977). The latter volume challenges the pre- and post-millennial distinction.

96 The definition is Tuveson's, who is drawing on numerous contemporary sources (p. 133).

97 Erasmus Darwin quoted in ibid., p. 194.

98 The passage appears in Heimert, *The Great Awakening,* p. 271.

99 Sacvan Bercovitch has recently offered a corrective to the view that in America an eighteenth-century postmillennialism triumphed over a seventeenth-century premillennialism by arguing "the common emphasis on process" in both formulations, *The American Jeremiad,* p. 98.

100 Brackenridge quoted in Daniel Marder, ed., *A Hugh Henry Brackenridge Reader, 1770–1815* (University of Pittsburgh Press, 1970), p. 94.

101 Charles Turner quoted in Hatch, *The Sacred Case of Liberty.* See also Edward Young quoted in Tuveson:
> since, this world is a school, as well for intellectual, as moral, advance; and the longer human nature is at school, the better scholar it should be; since, as the moral world expects its glorious millennium, the world intellectual may hope, by the rules of analogy, for some superior degrees of excellence to crown her later scenes (p. 151).

102 Channing, *The Works,* III, 61. For a recent treatment of Channing as an

Enlightenment figure see Donald H. Meyers, *The Democratic Enlightenment* (New York: Putnam, 1976), pp. 199–210.

103 Isaac Kramnick, *The Rage of Edmund Burke* (New York: Basic Books, 1977), p. 97.

7. GEORGE WASHINGTON AND THE RECONSTITUTED FAMILY

1 Hughes, ed., *John Milton: Complete Poems and Major Prose,* p. 1012. The relevant scripture is Romans 8:15: "Ye have not received the spirit of bondage again to fear; but ye have received the Spirit of adoption."

2 Samuel Willard, *A Compleat Body of Divinity* (Boston, 1726), p. 349.

3 Luther Richardson, *An Oration Pronounced July 4th, 1800* (Boston, 1800), p. 11. For an extended treatment of Washington as a second Moses see James H. Smylie, "The President as Republican Prophet and King: Critical Reflections on the Death of Washington," *Journal of Church and State,* 18 (1976), 232–52. The best general study of the mythologization of Washington is "The Flawless American" in Lawrence Friedman, *Inventors of the Promised Land: Patriotic Crusades in the White Man's Country* (New York: Knopf, 1975). Also, Albanese, *The Sons,* pp. 143–81.

4 Thomas Savage, *An Eulogy upon . . . Washington* (Salem, 1800), p. 13. Cf. Thomas Shepherd, *Eye Salve* (Boston, 1672): "Have you not been as an inclosed garden to me, and I a wall of fire round about you?" (p. 3).

5 Albanese, *The Sons,* p. 181.

6 Smylie, "The President as Republican Prophet and King," pp. 232–52.

7 Friedman, *Inventors of the Promised Land,* p. 77.

8 Michael Gilmore, "Eulogy as Symbolic Biography: The Iconography of Revolutionary Leadership, 1776–1826," in *Harvard English Studies* 8 (1978), 146.

9 George Forgie, *Patricide in the House Divided: A Psychological Interpretation of Lincoln and His Age* (New York: Norton, 1979); Michael Rogin, *Fathers and Children: Andrew Jackson and the Subjugation of the American Indian* (New York: Random House/Vintage Books, 1975).

10 The famous phrase is from the pen of Richard Henry Lee, who composed the official Congressional *Resolutions* on the death of Washington. See his *Funeral Oration* (Boston, 1800), p. 3.

11 *Lancaster Almanack* quoted in Dixon Wecter, "President Washington and Parson Weems," in James Morton Smith, ed., *George Washington: A Profile* (New York: Hill & Wang, 1969), p. 14. Examples of the expanded citation appear in, for example, Ezekiel Savage, *An Eulogy,* p. 18, and John Foster, *A Discourse* (Boston, 1800), p. 6.

12 Joseph Dana, *A Discourse on the Character . . . of Washington* (Newburyport, 1800), p. 18. Also, Joseph Tuckerman, *A Funeral Oration* (Boston, 1800), p. 7.

13 Royall Tyler, *An Oration Pronounced at Bennington* (Walpole, N.H., 1800), p. 7.

14 Gouverneur Morris, *An Oration Upon the Death of Washington* (New York, 1800).

15 Mason Weems, *The Life of George Washington* (1800; Philadelphia: Lippincott, 1858), p. 14. For a good brief psychological treatment of Washington's family relations see Lynn, *A Divided People,* pp. 73–7. For a reading of Weems and his importance for the nineteenth century see Forgie, *A House Divided,* pp. 34–49. Forgie anticipates my emphasis on Weems's biography as a childrearing text, but fails to appreciate it as the end product of perhaps the central Revolutionary and Enlightenment tradition in America.

16 In *The Child and the Republic* (Philadelphia: University of Pennsylvania Press, 1968), Bernard Wishy adds that "Complete rejection of the belief in depravity or innate tendencies of wickedness did not appear generally in popular literature until just before the Civil War" (p. 22).

17 In his introduction to the John Harvard Library edition of Weems's *Washington* (Cambridge: Harvard University Press, 1969), Marcus Cunliffe reports a derivative piece of apocrypha that appeared in the *United States Gazette* in 1826 and that attests to the continuing appeal of the new parental model of the cherry tree story. In this incident Washington rides his mother's horse to death, literally "breaking its noble heart." "The hectic of the moment was observed to flush the matron's cheek, but like a summer cloud, it soon passed away and all was serene and tranquil. She remarked . . . 'While I regret the loss of my favorite, I rejoice in my son who always speaks the truth.' "

18 Cf. Pliny Merrick, *Eulogy on the Character of Washington* (Brookfield, 1800), p. 20. The identification of Washington as angel reflects an emerging perfectionist critique of the chain of being. See Friedman, *Inventors of the Promised Land,* pp. 76–7. In his Freudian reading of Locke's *Second Treatise,* Norman O. Brown concludes:

> Procreative power itself is transferred from the earthly to the heavenly father. The parents are only guardians of the children they had begotten, 'not as their own workmanship but the workmanship of their own Maker, the Almighty.' . . . Parents are only the guardians of their children: fathers are not even fathers of their children.

Love's Body (New York: Random House/Vintage Books, 1962), p. 5.

19 Charles Turner, *Due Glory* (Boston, 1783), p. 12.

20 Rush quoted in Robert H. Bremner, *American Philanthropy* (University of Chicago, 1960), p. 36.

21 David Tappan, *An Oration* (Charlestown, 1800), appended to Joseph Willard, *A Latin Oration* (Charlestown, 1800). No separate Evans listing.

22 William Cunningham, *An Eulogy* (Worcester, 1800), title page.

23 Thomas Thatcher, *An Eulogy* (Dedham, 1800), p. 24.

24 Paul Fussell, "What Is Humanism?" in *Backgrounds to Eighteenth Century Literature,* ed. Kathleen Williams (Scranton: Intext, 1971), p. 71.

25 Levi Frisbie, *An Eulogy on George Washington* (Newburyport, 1800), p. 6. Second phase drawn from Josiah Dunham, *A Funeral Oration* (Boston, 1800). Though Frisbie uses "raised up" in the scriptural sense of "provided" (cf. Judges 3:9), the conventional sermonic term by 1800 has irrevocably taken on connotations of nurture.

26 David Ramsay, *The Life of George Washington* (New York, 1807), p. 314.

27 Mary Collyer, *The Death of Cain in Five Books after the Manner of The Death of Abel* (Philadelphia, 1796), p. 91.

28 Joseph McKeen, *A Sermon Preached before the . . . Council* (Boston, 1800), p. 9.

29 Foner, ed., *The Complete Writings of Thomas Paine*, II, 693.

30 Thomas à Kempis's *Of the Imitation of Christ* (Philadelphia, 1783). The 1749 version was published in Germantown, Pennsylvania.

31 Samuel Lee, "A Brief Account," in Thomas Mall, *A Cloud of Witnessess* (Boston, 1747), sig. A4 verso.

32 See John Flavel's introduction to ibid., sig. A4 verso. Because Mall's volume like all martyrologies argues the usefulness of a Christian "aristocracy," it is particularly interesting that it should appear in the wake of both the first and, reprinted in 1799, the second Great Awakening.

33 Thorton, *Pulpit,* p. 433. Bremner, *American Philanthropy,* pp. 20–41, gives an account of what Benjamin Rush called the "Humane Mania" of the Revolutionary period.

34 Tomb, *An Oration,* p. 16.

35 Baron de Montesquieu, *The Spirit of Laws,* 2 vols. (London, 1752), I, 42.

36 Samuel Harrison Smith in *Essays on Education in the Early Republic,* ed. Frederick Rudolph (Cambridge: Harvard University Press, 1965), p. 190. Rudolph's volume reprints eight contemporary essays.

37 Amable de Lafitte de Courteil in ibid., pp. 242–3.

38 Robert Coram, *Political Inquiries* (1791), in ibid., p. 13.

39 Ibid.

40 The earliest edition for which Evans records a surviving copy is the fifth edition published by Hugh Gaine in 1787.

41 Levi Hart, *Religious Improvement* (Norwich, 1800), p. 12. The paired terms are most elaborately developed in Samuel West, *Greatness the Result of Goodness* (Boston, 1800).

42 David Tappan, *An Oration,* p. 35.

43 Jeremiah Smith, *An Oration* (Exeter, 1800), p. 5.

44 Cunningham, *An Eulogy,* p. 11.

45 Tomb, *An Oration,* p. 13.

46 Weems's biography opens with Napoleon himself conceding: "Posterity will talk of him with reverence as the founder of a great empire, when my name shall be lost in the vortex of Revolutions" (p. 1). An interesting contemporary comment on Napoleon's character may be found in the *Baltimore Weekly Magazine* for July 12, 1800, pp. 25–7. On Marat see G. Adolph Koch, *Republican Religion* (New York: Henry Holt, 1933), p. 257.

47 James Wilson, *Substance of a Discourse* (Providence, 1800), p. 14.

48 West, *Greatness the Result of Goodness,* p. 9.

49 Tappan, *An Oration,* p. 35.

50 Ibid., p. 37.

51 Stiles in Thornton, *Pulpit,* p. 448.

52 Tappan, *An Oration,* p. 35.

53 See entry in the *OED.* Jefferson's neologism "belittle," which appears in *Notes on the State of Virginia,* suggests the opposite process.

54 Variant forms appear in Ford, *Primer*, p. 63.

55 Ibid.

56 Interestingly, the first experiments and trials with "self-propulsion" with steam-generated craft by John Fitch in America and A. L. Perier in France took place in the late 1770s and early 1780s. See James Thomas Flexner, *Steamboats Come True* (Boston: Little, Brown, 1980), pp. 38–63.

57 Benjamin Orr, *An Oration* (Amherst, 1800), p. 10. The phallic image conjured by such characteristic phrases of the period as "rising pillars" and "rising glory" may be seen as yet another aspect of the analogy between national independence and adolescence.

58 Thomas Hobbes, *Leviathan*, ed. Michael Oakeshott (New York: Collier Books, 1962), p. 19.

59 See Jonathan Mayhew, *A Sermon Preached in the Audience of His Excellency, William Shirley* (Boston, 1754), in Plumstead, *Wall and Garden*, p. 297.

60 See Charles Chauncy, *Salvation for All Men Illustrated* (Boston, 1782), and Hosea Ballou, *A Literary Correspondence* (Northampton, 1799).

61 Benjamin Pickman, *An Oration Pronounced* (Salem, 1797), p. 4. Benjamin Trumbull chose the same text as Tappan for his *The Majesty and Mortality of Created Gods Illustrated and Improved* (New Haven, 1800).

62 McKeen, *A Sermon*, p. 9.

63 Condorcet, *On the Influence of the American Revolution in Europe*, excerpted in Commager, ed., *Was America a Mistake?*, p. 188.

64 Timothy Dwight, *A Discourse Delivered at New Haven* (New Haven, 1800), p. 9.

65 Thomas Jefferson, *Notes on the State of Virginia*, ed. Thomas Perkins Abernathy (New York: Harper & Row, 1962), p. 76.

66 Foner, ed., *The Collected Writings of Thomas Paine*, pp. 602–3. Peale's remarkable and often reproduced painting, *The Artist in His Museum* (1822), which depicts Peale lifting the curtain on his museum as if he were Jehovah revealing a second creation, makes clear the power of the miniaturization idea.

67 See Charles Coleman Sellers, *Charles Willson Peale*, 2 vols. (Philadelphia: American Philosophical Society, 1947), II, 93.

68 Joseph Allen, *An Oration* (Brookfield, 1800), p. 3.

69 Jedidiah Morse in *The Monthly Magazine*, III (1800), 125.

70 Lord Henry Kames, *Elements of Criticism*, 2 vols. (Boston, 1796), I, 55.

71 White, p. 32.

72 The full quatrain of Pope's poem reads: "Teach me to feel another's woe/ To hide the fault I see/ That mercy I to others shew/ That mercy shew to me." *The Works*, I, 47.

73 Hamilton to Henry Laurens, October 20, 1780, in *The Works of Alexander Hamilton*, ed. Henry Cabot Lodge (New York: Putnam, n.d.), IX, 217.

74 Quoted in Moore, *Diary*, p. 450.

75 Ibid., p. 451.

76 Ibid., p. 454.

77 Dunlap rewrote the scene for subsequent performances. Both texts are reproduced in William Coyle and Harry Damaser, eds., *Six Early American*

Plays, 1798–1890 (Columbus, Ohio: Charles Merrill, 1968). On André's hold on the American imagination see Silverman, *Cultural History,* pp. 377–82, and Kammen, *A Season of Youth,* pp. 104–7.

78 These lines are from the revised text. See n. 98.

79 William Dunlap, *The Archers* (New York, 1796), p. 56. The Zurich Town Hall commissioned Henry Fuseli's famous painting of the *Oath on the Rütli* in 1778 as part of a commemoration of Swiss freedom. See Rosenblum, *Transformations in Late Eighteenth Century Art,* p. 69.

80 Schiller's *Wilhelm Tell* was first published in German in 1804. For an earlier example see Antoine-Marin Lemierre, *Guillaume Tell* (1766). All these works stress Tell's association with the forest (and its values), his marksmanship, and his commitment to freedom. The figure of Tell may thus lie somewhere behind Fenimore Cooper's Natty Bumppo, a figure whose European ancestry has been insufficiently investigated.

81 The picture is very briefly discussed in Harold E. Dickson, *Arts of the Young Republic: The Age of William Dunlap* (Chapel Hill: University of North Carolina Press, 1968), p. 27. On Dunlap's relation to his father see Joseph J. Ellis's fine study *After the Revolution: Profiles of Early American Culture* (New York: Norton, 1979), pp. 118–20. Ellis also briefly considers *André.*

82 George D. Seilhamer, *History of the American Theatre* (1889; New York: Greenwood Press, 1968), II, 219. The most powerful and psychologically acute late eighteenth-century depiction of a slain father's ghostly return in quest of revenge (a cultural complement to the parental deathbed and prodigal son motifs in eighteenth-century European art discussed above) is the last act of Mozart's *Don Giovanni* (1787), originally entitled *Il Dissoluto Punito* [The Rake Punished]. Mozart's domineering father died earlier that same year.

83 Seth Williston, *The Agency of God* (Geneva, 1800), p. 16. The larger passage reads: "He that can raise one Washington, can with infinite ease, raise up another. . . . It is impious, therefore, to say 'our loss is irreplaceable.' Let us respect the merits of the great man, but let us not limit the Omnipotent. Success is of the Lord, great generalship cannot command it." All men, Williston argues, are God's agents, none more so than any other. Similar sentiments are to be found in Peter Whitney's *Weeping and Mourning* (Brookfield, 1800). Though not making an important issue of it, numerous other eulogists such as James Wilson caution: "Let nothing that is done savour of idolatry, let not that tribute be paid to a creature that is due to God alone." *Substance of a Discourse* (Providence, 1800), p. 14.

All these sentiments are variants of the principle of radical Protestant monotheism that eventually would become formulated as Unitarianism. To some, like the early Unitarian Joseph Priestley, the view that God worked exclusively through secondary causes could too easily become perverted into the doctrine that he was dependent upon them, a doctrine that eventually led to the idolatrizing of men. The spheres of God and man must be kept separate in order to understand properly the character and nature of both. The scriptural doctrine of the "raised up" man made such an understanding virtually impossible. Amidst numerous reviews of eulogies on Washington's death, Charles Brockden Brown turned his attention to a new volume of Doctor Priestley's, *A Comparison of the Institutes of Moses with those of the Hindoos of Other Ancient Nations*. Brown quotes this passage that epitomizes early Unitarian values:

> The Hindoos, however, conceive that there is more of dignity in the Supreme Being doing nothing himself, but rather employing inferior agents. . . . But if a great prince could, with perfect ease and without the least fatigue, do all the business of a great prince, it would certainly give us a high idea of his power and capacity; and if the work had great utility for its object, that conduct would not suggest the idea of meanness, but of the greatest Benevolence. They are little minds that reason like the Brahmin. The Brahmins of Malabar told Mr. Lord that it did not become the majesty of God to demean himself so much as to make the creation when he could do it by his minions.

The Monthly Magazine, II (1800), 426.

84 *The Monthly Magazine*, II (1800), 104.

85 Foner, ed., *The Complete Writings of Thomas Paine*, II, 718.

86 Ibid., I, 480.

87 Williston, *The Agency of God*, p. 15.

88 Adams, ed., *The Works of John Adams*, IX, 541. Adams's comments must be seen, however, in the context of his considerable jealousy of Washington's national reputation.

89 Sumner, *An Eulogy*, p. 20.

90 Tappan, *An Oration*, p. 9.

91 Isaiah 66: 7–8.

92 George Duffield, *A Sermon Preached . . . 1783*, in Moore, *Patriot Preachers*, p. 348.

93 Dana, *A Discourse*, p. 19. See right relief panel on Horatio Greenough's statue of Washington for the same image.

94 Enos Hitchcock, *A Discourse on the Dignity of . . . Washington* (Providence, 1800), p. 7. Hitchcock develops these ideas in *The Parent's Assistant* (Providence, 1788). Quite a few orations have the double identification. Weems's biography about the son becoming a father unsurprisingly develops the image of Washington as "Columbia's first and greatest Son" (p. 8).

95 Tomb, *An Oration*, p. 21.

96 Hugh and John M'Callum, eds., *An Original Collection of the Poems of Ossian* (Montrose, 1816), p. xiv.

97 Jefferson asserts that Washington's memory "will in future ages assume its just station among the most celebrated worthies of the world, when that wretched philosophy shall be forgotten that would have arranged him among the degeneracies of nature." "Arrange" suggests the contemporary debate over the arrangement of Linnaeus's categories. *Notes on the State of Virginia*, p. 65. For the debate over the American habitat see Commager, ed., *Was America a Mistake?*

98 Jefferson in Wood, *The Creation of the American Republic*, p. 123.

99 Sumner, *An Eulogy,* p. 14. Of Lovelace, Clarissa declares:

But if I value him so much as you are pleased to suppose I do, the trial, which you imagine will be so difficult to me, will not, I conceive, be upon getting from him, when the means to effect my escape are lent me; but how I shall behave when got from him; and, if, like the Israelites of old, I shall be so weak as to wish to return to my Egyptian bondage (*Clarissa,* IV, 144).

8. THE SEALING OF THE GARDEN, OR THE WORLD WELL LOST

1 John Winthrop, *A Modell of Christian Charity,* in Edmund S. Morgan, *Puritan Political Ideas* (Indianapolis: Bobbs-Merrill, 1965), p. 87.

2 David Augustus Leonard, *An Oration* (New York, 1800), p. 16.

3 Aaron Wigglesworth, *An Extract from an Eulogium* (Albany, 1800), p. 3.

4 Cited in Saul K. Padover, ed., *The Washington Papers* (New York: Grosset & Dunlap, 1955), p. 101.

5 *The Columbia Magazine,* III, no. 1 (February 1789), 1.

6 Rush, in Rudolph, ed., *Essays on Early American Education,* p. 13.

7 Joseph Dana, *The Duty and Reward of Loving Our Country* (Boston, 1799), p. 31.

8 John Lathrop, *Patriotism and Religion* (Boston, 1799), p. 7.

9 David Kellogg, *The Nature of Christian Compassion* (Boston, 1796), p. 14.

10 *Adams–Jefferson Letters,* p. 377.

11 Laurence Sterne, *A Sentimental Journey,* p. 125.

12 Both Shaftesbury and Smith are quoted in Mildred Davis Doyle, "Sentimentalism in American Periodicals" (Ph.D. diss., New York University, 1941), p. 18.

13 For a brief illuminating history of the terms "sentimentality" and "sensibility" and of their rather confusing relationship in the eighteenth century see Williams, *Keywords,* p. 235.

14 Such a redefinition is argued in John B. Radner, "The Art of Sympathy in Eighteenth-Century British Moral Thought," in *Studies in Eighteenth-Century Culture,* vol. 9, ed. Roseann Runte (Madison: University of Wisconsin Press, 1979), pp. 189–210. See also Norman S. Fiering, "Irresistible Compassion; An Aspect of Eighteenth-Century Sympathy and Humanitarianism," *Journal of the History of Ideas,* 37 (1976), 195–218.

15 Richard Harrison Shryock, *Medicine and Society in America: 1660–1860* (Ithaca: Cornell University Press, 1960), p. 71.

16 Radner, "The Art of Sympathy," p. 204n.

17 *Clarissa,* II, 117. Clarissa's anxiety about seeming tyrannical recalls the popular eighteenth-century characterization of Charles I as one who, fearing to have such a charge leveled against him, fatally conceded too much ground to Cromwell, to Parliament, and to advisers urging conciliation. It is perhaps not far-fetched to suggest that in some degree the martyred figure of Charles (perceived as a tyrant *and* as a type of the crucified Christ) served as a model for the martyred heroine of the early sentimental novel. Her seduction recapitulated the great modern event: the English Revolu-

tion, from which proceeded the great debate over the nature of authority. Richardson does, as Christopher Hill has pointed out ("Clarissa Harlowe," p. 43), put some "curiously radical political views into Lovelace's mouth." The king corrupted by conniving ministers and the heroine seduced by one professing to serve her own good were analogous figures to a world that used the word "tyranny" as comfortably to describe domestic relations as it did political ones. The following passage from the preface to the first edition of Lord Clarendon's *History of the Rebellion and Civil Wars in England* (1702), the most influential eighteenth-century account of those events, suggests that the political drama can be best understood as a form of domestic drama. Charles's love for his nation, Clarendon asserts, was neither feigned nor scheming.

> Upon the whole matter, we have often wondered, and rest still amazed, that any prince should care to govern a people against their nature, their inclinations, and their laws. What glory can it be to a prince of a great spirit, to subdue and break the hearts of his own subjects, with whom he should live properly. . . . If two lovers, who should pass their time in renewing, repeating, and returning all the offices of friendship, kindness, tenderness, and love, were, instead of that, unluckily contriving always to cross, oppose, and torment one another, what could be the effect of such a conversation, but vexation and anguish in the beginning, a shortlived correspondence, and hatred and contempt in the conclusion?

Quoted from Edward, Earl of Clarendon, *The History of the Rebellion* (Oxford: Clarendon Press, 1888), I, xxiii.

18 Prescott, ed., *Hamilton and Jefferson,* p. xxxv. As psychological realism and conventionalized sentimentality were opposed strains in eighteenth-century fiction, so were they in contemporary politics.

19 Republican newspapers lauded France as such throughout the nineties. See Donald Stewart, *The Opposition Press of the Federalist Period* (Albany: State University of New York Press, 1969), p. 126.

20 Ames quoted in Alfred J. Beveridge, *Life of John Marshall,* 3 vols. (Cambridge, Mass,: Riverside Press, 1916), II, 40.

21 Timothy Dwight, *A Description of Some Events of the Last Century* (New Haven, 1801), pp. 27–8; Robert Treat Paine, *An Oration Written at the Request of the Young Men of Boston* (Boston, 1799), front. In this oration, preached on the first anniversary of the dissolution of the Alliance of 1778, Robert Treat Paine glories in the moment when "that memorable treaty which had linked two heterogenous nations in an unnatural, unequal, and hateful alliance, after an attenuated life of twenty years, was ignominiously committed to the grave" (p. 7).

22 *The American Chesterfield,* p. 159.

23 John C. Fitzpatrick, ed., *The Writings of Washington,* 39 vols. (Washington, D. C.: Government Printing Office, 1940), vol. 35, pp. 235–6.

24 For "demoralised" see the entry in Mitford M. Mathews, ed., *Americanisms: A Dictionary of Selected Americanisms on Historical Principles* (University of Chicago Press, 1966).

25 Remark quoted in Merrill D. Peterson, *Adams and Jefferson: A Revolutionary Dialogue* (New York: Oxford University Press, 1978), p. 79.

26 Cappon, ed., *Adams–Jefferson Letters* p. 567, 569.

27 Fessenden quoted in Linda K. Kerber, *Federalists in Dissent: Imagery and Ideology in Jeffersonian America* (Ithaca: Cornell University Press, 1970), pp. 203–4.

28 *Correspondence between the Hon. John Adams and the late William Cunningham,* p. 19.

29 Cappon, ed., *Adams–Jefferson Letters,* p. 461.

30 *The Novels and Related Works of Charles Brockden Brown* (Kent State University Press, 1977), I, 35.

31 Brown, *The Power of Sympathy,* p. 4.

32 The terms are Jefferson's. Cappon, ed., *Adams–Jefferson Letters,* pp. 388–9.

33 Having located and catalogued some several thousand surviving American samplers dating from the late seventeenth century through the early nineteenth century, Ethel Bolton and Eva Coe transcribed and ordered by subject matter all the sentiments, quotations, and verses appearing therein. In their volume *American Samplers* (1920; Princeton: Pyne Press, 1973), they conclude, "Of secular authors Alexander Pope leads all the rest" (p. 23). The lines above appear in a sampler sewn in 1787. At least one young girl chose in 1785 to sew into her sampler the famous lines from the first Epistle to Pope's *Moral Essay:* "Tis education form'd the tender mind / Just as the twig is bent the tree's inclin'd." In the original, "common" appears rather than "tender" (P. 267). Bolton's and Coe's work is an unfortunately neglected resource for the study of the transmission of eighteenth-century values.

34 For reproductions of additional such prints, see once again Wolf, "The *Prodigal Son* in England and America." "Chesterfieldian" is to be found in Royall Tyler's play, *The Contrast* (1789), in *Representative American Plays,* ed. Arthur Hobson Quinn (New York: The Century Company, 1927), p. 76. See also S. J. Pratt, *Pupil of Pleasure* (London, 1777), an early attack.

35 Quoted in Beveridge, *The Life of John Marshall,* III, 2.

36 Fisher Ames, *An Oration* (Philadelphia, 1800), p. 23.

37 Edmund Burke, *Reflections on the Revolution in France* (London, 1794), p. 113.

38 Stephen Burroughs, *The Memoirs of the Notorious Stephen Burroughs of New Hampshire* (New York: The Dial Press, 1924), p. 67. This edition includes the Frost preface.

39 Richard Peters, ed., *United States Statutes at Large,* 98 vols. (Boston: Little, Brown, 1845), I, 115; *The Statutes at Large from the Magna Carta to the End of the Eleventh Parliament,* 107 vols. (London, 1794), vol. 36, p. 606.

40 Darnton, *Mesmerism,* p. 89.

41 *The Annual Register . . . for the Year 1783* (London, 1800), p. 137.

42 Wieland's essay quoted in John A. McCarthy, "Shaftesbury and Wieland: The Question of Enthusiasm," in *Studies in Eighteenth-Century Culture,* vol. 6, ed. Ronald C. Rosbottom (Madison: University of Wisconsin Press, 1977), p. 88.

43 Miller, "The Moral and Psychological Roots," p. 273.

44 Quoted in Bernard Fay, *The Revolutionary Spirit,* p. 174.

45 *Treaties and Conventions between the United States and Other Powers,* p. 296.

46 Fay, *The Revolutionary Spirit,* p. 220. Washington himself used the phrase "great and good ally." See Washington as quoted in Samuel Stillman, *Thoughts on the French Revolution* (Boston, 1795), p. 12.

47 Fay, *Revolutionary Spirit,* p. 104.

48 Daniel Defoe, *The True Born Englishman* (Philadelphia, 1778).

49 Howard Mumford Jones, *America and French Culture* (Chapel Hill: University of North Carolina Press, 1927), pp. 233–4.

50 Ibid., p. 191. More than Francophilia contributed to this decision. Following Locke, many educational reformers agreed with James Beattie's objection to having youth spend their best days "embittered by confinement . . . under the scourge of tyranny; and all for no purpose, but that the memory may be loaded with words of two languages that have been dead upwards of a thousand years," or with Benjamin Rush's contention that "Shakespeare owes his fame, as a sublime and original poet, to his having never read . . . a Latin or Greek author." Both writers are quoted in Linda Kerber's excellent account of the debate over the classical tradition in *Federalists in Dissent,* pp. 106, 117.

51 Joseph Galloway, *Candid Examination of the Mutual Claims* (New York, 1775), p. 3.

52 Sherwood, *The Church's Flight,* p. 21. Sherwood is, of course, referring here to the parable of the ten virgins.

53 Dulany, *A Discourse of the Times* (Norwich, 1776), p. 15.

54 Quoted in Beveridge, *John Marshall,* II, 9.

55 Charles A. Beard, ed., *The Journal of William Maclay* (New York: Fredrick Ungar, 1965), pp. 50–51.

56 Hugh Henry Brackenridge, *Modern Chivalry,* ed. Claude M. Newlin (New York: Hafner, 1937), p. 431.

57 John Lathrop, *An Oration* (Boston, 1796), p. 7.

58 John McKnight, *The Divine Goodness* (New York, 1795), pp. 12–13.

59 John Lowell, *An Oration* (Boston, 1799), p. 18.

60 Dunlap, *André,* p. 46.

61 Harold C. Syrett, ed., *The Papers of Alexander Hamilton* (New York: Columbia University Press, 1969), XV, 102. All future references to the *Pacificus Papers* from this edition.

62 Ibid., XV, 84–5.

63 Quoted in Prescott, ed., *Hamilton and Jefferson,* p. xxxvi.

64 Oliver Goldsmith, *The Citizen of the World* (1762; Albany, 1794), p. 37.

65 Fitzpatrick, ed., *The Writings of Washington,* vol. 35, p. 234.

66 Paine, *An Oration,* pp. 6–8.

67 Ibid., p. 9.

68 Julius W. Pratt, "James Madison," in *The Concise Dictionary of American Biography* (New York: Scribner, 1964), p. 629.

69 Quoted in ibid., p. 630.

70 Henry Adams, *The History of the United States of America during the Administrations of Jefferson and Madison,* abridged ed. (University of Chicago Press, 1967), p. 217.

71 William K. Bettorf and Arthur L. Ford, eds., *The Works of Joel Barlow*, 2
   Vols. (Gainesville, Fla.: Scholar's Facsimiles and Reprints, 1970), II, 311.
   As late as the middle of the nineteenth century, political exegetes of the
   Farewell Address, such as Lincoln's Secretary of State Seward, still continued to rebut the time-honored isolationist reading:
   > It may well be said that Washington did not enjoin us [to follow a
   > program of nonintervention] as a perpetual policy. On the contrary,
   > he inculcated [noninvolvement] as the policy to be pursued until the
   > Union of the States, which is only another form of expressing the
   > integrity of the nation, should be established, its resources should be
   > developed and its strength adequate to the chances of national life,
   > should be matured and perfected.

   Seward quoted in the Introduction to Burton Ira Kaufman, ed., *Washington's Farewell Address: The View from the 20th Century* (Chicago: Quadrangle
   Books, 1969), p. 31. This concern with adolescence may partially explain
   what Leslie Fiedler has described as the adolescent character and preoccupations of American fiction. *Love and Death in the American Novel*, pp. xviii–
   xix.
72 James Fenimore Cooper, *The Prairie* (New York: New American Library/
   Signet, 1964), p. 286.
73 Herman Melville, *Billy Budd, Sailor,* ed. Milton R. Stern (Indianapolis:
   Bobbs-Merrill, 1975), p. 124.
74 John Tyler, *An Eulogy* (Norwich, 1800), p. 6.
75 Plumb's comment appears in his prefatory essay to Ryskamp, ed., *Early
   Children's Books and Their Illustration*, p. xxi.
76 *The Happy Family, or Memoirs of Mr. and Mrs. Norton* (Philadelphia, 1799)
   p. 28.
77 Susanna Rowson, *Charlotte Temple*, ed. Clara M. and Rudolf Kirk (New
   Haven: College and University Press, 1964), p. 77.
78 Mark Twain, *The Adventures of Tom Sawyer* (New York: Bantam Books,
   1966), p. 73.
79 Hannah Foster, *The Coquette* (Boston, 1797), p. 248.
80 Ariès, *Centuries of Childhood*, p. 413. See also on this point Bailyn, *Education in the Forming of American Society*, p. 25.
81 Ierley, *The Year that Tried Men's Souls*, p. 72.
82 See Hitchcock, *Music in the United States*, pp. 84 ff.
83 Quoted in Doyle, "Sentimentalism in American Periodicals," p. 50.
84 Crèvecoeur's antirevolutionary tale, "The American Belisarius," opens with
   a symbolic and prophetic account of the effects of a storm, reminiscent of the
   one in *Lear:* "After a violent storm of northwest wind I never see even a
   single oak overset, once majestic and lofty, without feeling some regret at
   the accident. I observe the knotty roots wrenched from the ground, the
   broken limbs, the scattered leaves. I revolve in my mind the amazing ele-
   mental force that must have occasioned so great an overthrow." *Sketches of
   Eighteenth-Century America*, pp. 228–9. The familial oak in "Amelia," like
   the liberty tree before it, replaces the great patriarchal oak now fallen. Prior
   to the Revolution the letter "O" was represented in the rhymed alphabet of
   The New England Primer by a verse that alluded to King Charles II, "The

Royal Oak / It was the Tree / That sav'd his / Royal Majesty." After the war it is replaced by "The Charter Oak / It was the tree / That saved to us / Our Liberty." See Ford, *Primer*, p. 62 of the Introduction.

85 Both quoted in Herbert Brown, *The Sentimental Novel in America* (Durham, N.C.: Duke University Press, 1940), pp. 36–7.

86 Voltaire, *Candide* (New York: Random House/Modern Library, 1930), p. 149.

87 At one level, argues James Rieger in his introduction to *Frankenstein or the Modern Prometheus* (1818; Indianapolis: Bobbs-Merrill, 1974), Mary Shelley's novel concerns "the role of education in the liberation or enslavement of the personality." Fundamentally the book is an examination of the moral responsibilities of the tutor/parent/creator. See p. xxx of Rieger's introduction. For the degree to which her treatment of the moral accountability issue may derive from her reading of Brown's *Wieland* (itself influenced by the writing of Shelley's father, William Godwin), see F. C. Prescott, "*Wieland* and *Frankenstein*," *American Literature*, 2 (1930), 172–3. Hawthorne's tale (1844) also deals with the consequences of "tampering with ordinary nature" and offers a critique of post-Lockean perfectionism. *Selected Tales and Sketches* (New York: Holt, Rinehart & Winston, 1970), p. 352.

88 William Richardson, *An Oration Pronounced at Groton* (Amherst, 1801), pp. 6–7. Sensabaugh briefly discusses Richardson's analogy in *Milton in Early America*, p. 242.

89 These oppositions have as one point of origin the tension in post-Lockean educational theory as to whether the primary role of a parent was to provide a model for filial imitation or to nurture and to cultivate the innate character of the child. This second Rousseauistic position stands in marked contrast to what Weems had stated to be the intention of his book – to provide his adolescent readers with a model of greatness. In a Swiftian pamphlet entitled *Sunbeams May Be Extracted from Cucumbers, But the Process is Tedious . . .* (1799), David Daggett, very much a Federalist, satirized what he saw to be the dangerous "Republican" tendency in childrearing. The passage appears in Gordon S. Wood, ed., *The Rising Glory of America*, (New York: Braziller, 1971):

> It has lately been discovered that the maxim, "Train up a child in the way he should go, and when he is old he will not depart from it," is an erroneous translation, and should read thus: "let a child walk in his own way, and when he is old he will be perfect." Volumes have been written, and much time and labor expended to shew that all reproof, restraint, and correction, tend directly to extinguish the fire of genius, to cripple the faculties and enslave the understanding (p. 179).

Daggett defended the inculcating of "habit" as against what he saw to be the specious cultivation of "genius."

Timothy Dwight, perhaps the last great Federalist/Congregationalist, preaching in the following year a century sermon entitled *A Discussion of Some Events of the Last Century*, developed Daggett's point. Its scriptural text from Deuteronomy 32:7 may be said to be the Federalist motto of the

period: "Remember the days of old, consider the years of many generations: ask thy father, and he will shew thee; thy elders, and they will tell
thee." Though the Protestant child of seventeenth- and eighteenth-century
America was urged to follow the model of his parents, he was also warned,
in the words of Michael Wigglesworth's bestseller *The Day of Doom,* not to
"men's example / your Director make." Christ and Scripture were the
only true guides. Protestantism itself provided the terms by which the
reign of exempla would be overthrown, and the experience of the son
eclipse the wisdom of the father.

90 On the psychology of the nineteenth-century revolt against the legacy of
the founding fathers see Rogin, *Fathers and Children,* which argues the
centrality of infantile rage in the character of Jackson: "Had the post-revolutionary generation to choose, as loyalists insisted to their revolutionary
fathers, either to fan the fatal flames of discord, or else to remain 'children'
forever? Andrew Jackson, westward expansion, and Indian removal offered
another alternative" (p. 37). The process by which a territory achieved
statehood may be said to recapitulate the adolescent rite-of-passage into
adulthood. For an interesting treatment of the psychological issues of the
following period see Forgie, *Patricide in the House Divided;* also Gilmore,
"Eulogy as Symbolic Biography," p. 157.

INDEX

accountability, moral: of Adam and Eve, 32; in *Death of Abel*, 164; in *Frankenstein*, 314 n87; and French Revolution, 243; of parents for children, 2, 22, 33; in sentimental novel, 88; and taxation, 102; theological debate over, 164–8; in *Vicar of Wakefield*, 56–7; in *Wieland*, 239; *see also* gratitude, debate on; honor, debt of; will, freedom of

Adam and Eve, 32, 83–4, 128–30, 162, 168

Adams, Abigail, 134, 286, n29

Adams, Henry, 257, 258

Adams, John, 41, 105, 243; on Britain as unnatural parent, 99; on *Clarissa*, 89, 236–7; on Jehovah, 156; on marriage, 133–4; on *New Eloisa*, 133; on power of birth, 230; on George Washington, 223

Adams, John (of Philadelphia), 153

Adams, Nabby, 134–5

Adams, Samuel, 97, 157

Addison, Joseph, 86; *Cato*, 60, 152–3; *Spectator Papers*, 16, 31

adolescence, 3, 15, 19, 291 n43; and abridgements of fiction, 80; of colonies, thwarted, 96–9, 185–6; and conversion, 186; national, 258; as new birth, 187–9; Watts on, 19–20; *see also* rite of passage

adoption: in Crèvecoeur, 182; in Marmontel, 51; as stage of grace, 173, 180, 197–8; and George Washington, 197–8; in Wyss, 81; *see also* fathers

affections: alienated from England, 101, 103–5, 132, 248, 252–3; and

Common Sense philosophy, 24; Edwards on, 104; between parents and children, 18, 57, 114–6, 160–1; in politics, debated, 104, 234–5, 251–2, 255–6; transferred to France, 248–9; *see also* sentimentality, sympathy

Alien and Sedition Acts, 235, 256

Alleine, John, 12

Allen, Joseph, 214

"Amelia," 264–5

American Revolution: and adolescent rite of passage, 4, 66, 99, 185–6, 186–7; and consensus between evangelicals and rationalists, 174, 183–4; and cyclical history, 42; and death of Major André, 217–8; and deliverance from sinfulness, 77, 176; familial rhetoric of, 3–4, 93–105, 116–8, 132, 276 n5; and fear of corruption, 28; and Franklin's *Autobiography*, 107; and idea of fiction, 77–8; Jane McCrea as *cause celèbre* of, 140–4; and literary transmission of antipatriarchal ideology of, 4–5, 38–9, 51, 66, 67, 82, 277 n7; medallion commemorating conclusion of, 120; motto of, 113; political cartoons of, 49, 100, 281 n34, 294 n8; psychological legacy of, 240; as quest for union, 126; relation to new family, 1; and right to suicide, 151; and Treaty of Paris, 177–8; and two views of the Fall, 84, 266–7; and virtue, 178; voluntaristic marriage and, 123–31; *see also* George III; Great Britain; liberty; Tories; Whigs